Navigators
Forging a Culture and
Founding a Nation: Volume II

Navigators Founding a Christian Nation in Polynesia

Dedication

THIS BOOK IS DEDICATED TO

THE FIRST FEMALE PRIME MINISTER

OF

THE INDEPENDENT ISLAND NATION

OF SAMOA:

HON. FIAME NAOMI MATA'AFA.

Fata Ariu Levi

Navigators Forging a Culture and Founding a Nation Volume II:
Navigators Founding a Christian Nation in Polynesia
First edition 2022
Published by Ariu Levi

ISBN: 978-1-954076-09-9

Cover image by Faigā Tapusone Asiata and Sheila Deeth

Cover design by Sheila Deeth

Edited by Sheila Deeth

Praise for Previous Volumes in this Series

"Levi's prose is balanced and engaging, as one might expect from a professional orator... He adeptly weaves together various threads of information... Levi is the perfect teller of this tale, and it is a story worth hearing... A captivating trove of ideas about the mysterious settlers of Samoa."

Kirkus Reviews, Nov 9, 2020

"Navigators Quest For A Kingdom In Polynesia" reveals the timeline of the Polynesian Navigators' migration, with waves of voyages following that first migration out of Africa around 60,000 years ago... [a]s well as how the Austronesian-speaking people were an amalgamation of migrants into the Asiatic Archipelago... An eloquent and impressively informative study... will have a very special value for personal, professional, community, college, and university library Cultural Anthropology collections in general, and Polynesian History supplemental curriculum studies lists in particular.

Midwest Book Reviews
Redefining Possible
Ron Alford & Dustin Hillis
Southwestern Publishing Group

Fata Ariu Levi's version of human origins and expansion is rooted in Sāmoa's ways of thinking; he is both our modern Pili and Leatiogie, respectively casting a wide net and wielding the power of the "pen/keyboard" primarily to produce an exegesis of how and where today's Polynesians fit into world history, a group commonly marginalized in diaspora in spite of its critical contribution in world and regional development; secondarily, to mend the hearts and minds of young generations of Samoans and Manuans in diaspora, motivating them to leave behind the insecurities and fears of being different and to stand tall as movers and shakers in the landscaping and peopling of the globe since the beginning of the human race (the homo sapiens sapiens).

M. Luafata Simanu-Klutz

Excerpt from the Foreword to Navigators Quest for a Kingdom in Polynesia

...Orator Fata Ariu Levi's research draws extensively from classical history, recorded history and from the seven fields of science (formal sciences, natural sciences, engineering and technology, medical and health sciences, agricultural sciences, social sciences, and humanities).

That being said, Fata Ariu brings into the process a net that he casts over the historical reefs of conventional science and research. The essence of his net is *I'ike*, which in Samoan means attunement, synonymous with intuition. In Hawaii, 2,500 miles north of the Samoan archipelago, it is called *I'ike* with the same meaning. His I'ike is channeled by traditional practices supported by a heritage of noble orators and a genealogy traditionally linked to Polynesia's primogenitors, Tagaloa Lagi and Papa.

Fata Ariu shares an I'ike, in the first few pages of his book. *"I hear the constant and relentless whisper from the spiritual wind of our ancestors."* An I'ike is a profound experience among a people that believes death does not separate one from the living and that the wind carries the messages between the two dimensions; either as a whisper, a tap upon the shoulder, or cool breeze pleasant to the skin engendering an intuition or attunement.

Nobel Prize winner Albert Einstein was emphatic regarding his belief that *"The only real valuable thing is intuition."* He is also credited with a quote that strengthened my resolve as a young lecturer at the University Business College to hold on to my world with its I'ike and kinship ties to Papa, Earth Mother. *"The intuitive mind is a sacred gift. The rational mind is a faithful servant. We have created a society where we have honored the servant and forgotten the gift."*

Fata Ariu's net is unique in that the bare spaces between the net's strands are as significant as the strands themselves. The net not only harvests the material but also captures the spiritual treasures unmoved by time. The empty space merely makes room for the wind to nest as it carries the whispers of the wind that convey messages from the ancients and the sacredness of the other. I'ike, or attunement, is the gift of discernment...

Fata Ariu reminds me, through the sweeping tapestry of his book that covers the ancient quest of our common ancestors, that I and all traditional leaders have a sacred obligation to promulgate measures to preserve and perpetuate the wisdoms of our Oceania and Samoan heritage. ...

Susuga Papali'i Dr. Failautusi Avegalio.
Director, Pacific Business Center Program
Shidler College of Business
University of Hawaii System, Honolulu, Hawaii

Excerpt from the Foreword to this two-volume work Navigators Forging and Culture and Founding a Nation

Orator Fata's quest to "exercise the responsibility of being an orator chief," as custodian of culture, history, and praxis in diaspora, is evident of his laser-like focus on the settling of the archipelago by navigators who (re)imagined an identity of being Samoan and Manu'an... This volume... is a history about Samoa's and Manu'a's past with Orator Fata's 'Āiga Sā Malietoa' anchor and guiding star illuminating and leading us to and from familial and political constellations and connections...

Forging a Culture is a cartography of crisscrossing gafa (genealogies), tuā'oi (boundaries), and fāiā (relationships). The popular maxim "knowledge is power" is what one will feel after an immersion, if not submersion, in a network of roots and routes which the ancestors planted and stretched respectively beyond the shoreline. This is about a culture that has spiraled from a matrilinearity to being both matrilineal and patriarchal and in which women have remained both anchors and sails alongside their men. It is not about deboning a fish, but a reboning that reflects how and why Fa'asāmoa has survived multiple invasions and colonization...

[T]hose born and raised outside of Samoa, and those leaving Samoa at an early age... have been concerned with not quite knowing who or what they are, either in the singularity of being ethnically Samoan, or as hyphenated ethnic nationals, the Samoan-American. In a way, there is a hint here of a Dr. Jekyll and Mr. Hyde bipolar ethos which... has been perpetuated by the media and research, and by a ritualization of Fa'asāmoa by community organizations, family, and church... [W]hat has been missing, however, in any attempt to model a balancing of competing cultural and social priorities and identities, is a comprehensive grounding of theory and practice *in history*, in what Orator Fata deems the "deep well of the past," which he defines in *Navigators: Quest for a Kingdom in Polynesia*—the first book in a trilogy that traces the origins and migration for thousands of years, of the ancestors of Samoans and Manu'ans out of Africa and later Southeast Asia, and their eventual settling of an archipelago of volcanic islands which Jerome Grey sings about as "green, blue, and lush with beauty..." These islands are the roots of a

Samoan identity, of a culture shaped by knowledge and skills internalized for survival in the long durée of a search for a place to call our own...

Forging a Culture is richly sourced with archival records and Orator Fata's lived experiences. He is both source and teller of oral traditions scented by the tōfā and fa'autaga—knowledge and wisdom—of the ancestors and memorialized and recited in oratory each time there is an obligatory event, or fa'alavelave, such as a funeral (maliu), wedding (fa'aipoipoga), or title investiture (sāofa'i)... For the diasporic, the struggle to feel Samoan is mitigated by this narrative, it is presented in accessible prose and with rich examples of how and why certain traditions such as the sua (gifting of food), ava ceremony, tattooing, gender relations, boundaries, and respect system, were forged and sustained. To a large extent, Orator Fata's text is not about a single past or one history, but many, where the weavings are not so much about accuracy of where and when an event happened (the "stuff" of an academically driven history), but about the teller's and reader's mosaic of interpretations or meaning making—simply, their truths.

Tuiloma Loau Luafata Simanu-Klutz, Ph.D.
Retired Associate Professor,
University of Hawai'i at Mānoa

Acknowledgements

To my late brothers Faigā Asiata and Taliaoa Fa'alepo Vaotu'ua who both passed away this past May 2021, due to complications in their diabetic illnesses. They are dearly missed.

To my late cousin High Chief Lealaifuaneva Peter Reid Jr. and his wife Julie Reid. His guidance and wisdom allowed me to build a network of relationships across the American Samoan leadership community.

To my sisters Selaina Miller Levi and Avasā Kitty Levi for their unwavering support of my work and our family.

Orator Chief Moemai Joseph and Shirley Kleis have been my reliable sources of encouragement and support. Chief Moemai has and will always be a mentor to me. His has been a reliable source of ancient cultural legends and references throughout my Orator career and I thank them both.

To Le Sūsūga Fa'amatuainu Jones Iakopo Tu'ufuli for his much-needed assistance in our Dialogue seminar.

To Reverend Henry and Katie Yandall for sponsoring the Church Youth Dialog seminar.

To my friends out in Newport Beach California, Guy and Trish Johnson; I can always count on their support. And to James Edwards for his wisdom and guidance in business and in the cultural diversity of Southern California and the country of Mexico.

My many thanks and gratitude to my friend and business partner Tony Wong for his support and assistance for the last twenty years.

To Tuiloma Loau Luafata Simanu-Klutz, Ph.D. Retired Associate Professor, University of Hawai'i at Mānoa, Hawai'i. Fa'afetai lava mo lau faivamanaia i le Foreword.

And a special thanks to Sheila Deeth for wisdom and expertise in guiding this effort to fulfillment.

Navigators
Forging a Culture and
Founding a Nation: Volume II

Navigators Founding a Christian Nation in Polynesia

By Fata Ariu Levi

This book is also dedicated to my daughter,

Manaia Launoa (Iliganoa) Levi

as a reminder
of her mother's undying love and care for her
and as a token of her father's love.

Disclaimer

As I wrote in Volume I of this work, Samoan and Manu'an history belongs to the people. So everyone has their own version of it. It's based on personal experience and knowledge of local events in history, as chronicled by local and island historians and by the chieftain system.

There are Samoan and Manu'an writers who have recorded events in the history of the archipelago, in the vernacular of the islands. I have aggressively collected and acquired many written works, in both the English and the Samoan languages, as foundations to my research efforts. Many of these works are included in the reference section of this book. I'm not able to list them all, due to limited space, but I am indebted to them all nevertheless.

I have relied on several writings because of their comprehensive coverage of history, and the independence of their sources.

- *O le Mavaega i le Tai* by Lafai Sauoāiga Apemoemanatunatu, of Apia, Samoa, 1988, is an effort that resulted from the collaboration of in excess of thirty chiefs across the Samoan and Manu'an Archipelago. It was reviewed and approved by the Congregational Church of Samoa, E.F.K.S. (Old LMS Mission Church). Their collaborative effort is not diminished by the fragmentation of tales of events in the history of the archipelago.
- *Palefuiono* by S. P. Mailo of Tutuila, American Samoa, likewise represents the collaboration of in excess of fifteen chiefs across the archipelago.
- Fuimaono Na'oia Tupua's *O le Suaga a le Va'atele* was the result of his research done under the Department of Tourism of the Government of Samoa, of which he was one of the directors and manager. This effort required Fuimaono Na'oia Tupua to visit every village in Upolu, Savai'i, Apolima, and Manono Islands, gathering his research data.
- Ali'i Felela Fred Henry's (Marist Brothers) *Talafa'asolopito o Samoa* was reviewed by K.R. Lambie, the Director of the

Department of Education of the Western Samoa Government, in 1958.

- *Lagaga: A Short History of Western Samoa* by Malama Meleisa was a collaborative effort with over thirteen co-authors at the Institute of Pacific Studies, University of the South Pacific, Apia, Samoa. Again, this effort was sanctioned by the University of the South Pacific at Apia, Samoa.
- *Samoa Ne'i Galo* is a collective effort by the Ministry for Youth, Sports, and Cultural Affairs, Youth of the Government of Samoa, 1994. Hon. Pule Lameko was the final editor, and approval is under his signature. The taskforce collectively performed research and documented the myths, and also translated the results into English. The English language translation was invaluable in my effort. And the important issue is the wide range of collective opinions that were incorporated into the work, that gives measure to the writing.

Referencing these works allowed me to rely on the vetting process these authors had already gone through.

Moreover, there is Dr. Augustin Krämer's monograph which stands erect and uncontested. This is an heirloom of the archipelago. While some Samoans and Manu'ans might have complaints about specific details of Dr. Krämer's *The Samoa Islands*, their complaints are usually at a local or village level and cannot minimize the impact and value of the work to Samoan culture, history, and people.

A Word on the Genealogies

The genealogy charts shown on the timeline periods of this book are not meant to be complete for the families being highlighted in this phase. Rather, they are there to show the interrelationships of families' connections across Samoa and Manu'a. I have listed in the Notes Section (at the end) the respective references, so the reader can satisfy their need to know the extent of the references' completeness in the particular family genealogy. This is particularly true with information taken from Dr. Krämer's *Samoa Islands Volume I*. My purpose is to show relationships that were not clearly evident or correctly stated in Dr. Krämer's exhaustive monograph, but that are critical to illuminating the intricacies of the Island Nation family organization structure. Also, note my focus on the ancient ancestry genealogy in order to revitalize and spotlight the foundational families, so that current and future generations can easily trace their particular genealogical identity to their mythological beginning.

Introduction

by Fata Ariu Levi and Sheila Deeth

This book, being Volume II of *Navigators Forging a Culture and Founding a Nation*, completes the second of three works in the *Navigators* series:

- Navigators: Quest for a Kingdom in Polynesia (released in 2020)
- Navigators Forging a Culture and Founding a Nation
    - Volume I: Navigators Forging a Matriarchal Culture in Polynesia (released in 2021)
    - Volume II: Navigators Founding a Christian Nation in Polynesia
- Navigators Return: God's "Charge of the Light Brigade" Missionaries

The first book, *Navigators Quest for a Kingdom in Polynesia*, looked at where we came from and how the many sciences of the modern world help us trace our migration path to this place.

In the second book, the author is looking at who we became as a people when we arrived here, and how we became who we are. Space considerations compelled him to release the book in two volumes, so this volume, *Founding a Christian Nation in Polynesia,* focusses on the history of the Island Nations and how that history was affected by and affects our culture and cultural identity. Volume I, *Forging a Matriarchal Culture in Polynesia,* focused more on the culture of Manu'a and Samoa, how that culture was formed, both in isolation and on the arrival of Western influences, and how it continues to be formed

The third book in the series, *God's "Charge of the Light Brigade" Missionaries*, will explore what we have done with God's great gift to us and where we have taken it.

History

The arrival of European missionaries and social scientists in the 1800s shed a whole new light on Samoan experience and understanding. Those missionaries and scientists began their first documented history of the archipelago, but this took place as recently as 1830, and that early documentary narrative stayed frozen for over 191 years (1830-2021), hence the urgent need for an update.

Previous efforts to move the narrative of Samoa and Manu'a forward, using the methodology of current technology, have not shaken off the old bias of the missionaries' view, giving Christianity's imagined history of Samoa and Manu'a. It's this author's purpose to move the narrative forward and illuminate it better for the future generations.

In these two volumes of his second book, the author hopes to show also how the Samoan history, philosophy, and cultural development is different from Western views. For example, despite appearances, history and cultural developments are not linear functions. They are better imagined as spatial images of networks of events, much like the view of the heavenly bodies in the darkness of night, observed from the middle of the large body of water. And, while Western culture developed from linear (goal-oriented) land-migrations, Samoan culture developed from the Navigators' great migration across the vast expanse of the East Pacific Ocean.

The path of the Navigators was measured through the relationships of space and time—the rising and setting of stars, changing ocean currents, winds, and seasons, and the migrations of sea creatures. In this way, their philosophy and culture developed, based on shifting relationships, not on the fixed points of mountain passes and forests. So Samoan and Manu'an culture and history cannot be chronicled in the standard Western way, with standard historical methodology, because the history does not fit into that linear "blueprint" map. Thus the authors's motivation and reasoning for taking a different approach in writing this narrative. It is time for a new, more modern narrative of Samoan and Manu'an history. And the dominant event in the life of the Polynesian Navigators is their seafaring movement.

Cognitive Development

Unlike land-based homesteads, an ocean-based homestead moves and breathes in waves, currents, and swells, which were intuitively observed by travelers on a canoe. Viewed through the lens of philosophy, this shows the universe of Samoan cognitive development, based on the ocean's water rather than on unchanging land. They came to understand their Pacific Ocean and universe as a continuous wave of a single system, not as separate parts which make a whole.

The relationships of celestial movements and directions (of the stars and planets, moon, and sun) appeared to the Navigators to correspond with changes in the tides and swells, directions and strength of ocean currents, winds directions, force, and speed, and the temperature. They saw this also related to the behavioral patterns of fish and birds, their feeding and resting patterns. These multiple variables had to be correlated and regressed to hone their predictability for the Navigators, so determining the path and direction, as well as timing and resources, required for their journey.

This required, effectively, a mathematical function: In order to predict the when, where, what, and how of their seafaring trip, they had to define it as a function of weather (meteorological data points), oceanography (physical and chemical data points, and data points derived from biological behavioral patterns), geophysics (data points describing the earth and its environment in spatial patterns), and navigational intelligence (location derived from other data points). Added to this, they had to develop the necessary skills—tools and techniques, and characteristics and features—as well as creating technical descriptions, cultural references and data points, and many more that would have to be correlated to find specific relationships that were meaningful to the planning and management of their seafaring journey.

We now have a much greater appreciation of the scenes mentioned above, as we have more fully developed the math and equations. But for the ancient Polynesians, these things had to be learned through experiences in "on-the-job-training," so to speak.

So we see, their cognitive development processes had to be honed through regression—i.e. through deliberate repetition (observation and memory)—for a considerable period of time. Today, we have considerable knowledge of the basic functions of different parts of the brain, and we know that the brain's two hemispheres have several areas dedicated to functions involved in regression of necessary information, human senses, and anatomical functions. So today, we see the task of sorting out the required sciences, as listed above, to predict a journey's compass, is, significantly, a question of mathematical functions and equations that we have to derive, in order to do a decent job in replicating the Navigators' quest across such a large ocean.

Mythology

Just as the Navigators' journey was built on non-linear equations, and their cognitive development was founded on spatial and scientific relationships, so the Samoan and Manu'an mythology is unlike other mythologies. More "linear" mythologies taught good governance and leadership from a basis of cruelty and corruption—the story of a path that aims directly for a goal. But the Navigators' mythology taught emotional depth, gift-giving reciprocity, and love for the family at large, and was founded on the complexities of their journey.

Philosophy

As we look to the future, the Western world is only now coming to recognize the importance of relationships. How the world continues to pollute the Pacific Ocean, how climate changes are exacerbating effects on the ozone layer, how overfishing is depleting the fish population, and the impending exploitation of resources underneath the ocean floor—all these have a global impact on ocean ecosystems and environmental conditions. But the ocean is the breadbasket of the world, and it is the last frontier for economic development in the world. From its surface to the deep-sea floor and below, it has not been explored to its full potential. But the harvesting of its potential must take into account all the interconnected relationships. A linear approach, from investment to personal profit, will no longer work.

3,000 Years

Samoan culture originated with the development of human society through family organization, just as other ancient cultures did—this, according to social scientists who have labored 250 years in the study of humans and this society, since Louis Antoine Bougainville (who named the Island Navigator) landed and traded with the Manu'ans in 1768. (We should note, Jacob Roggeveen, who sighted the island in 1722, by contrast did not land or engage with the people.)

But Samoan history did not begin with the arrival of Christianity in the islands. Nor did it end. It is a history of a people living in isolation for over 3,000 years, their family organization, and the culture they brought with them, which carried them through the planning and management of a perilous sea journey, carried them through the founding of settlements in a new homeland, and carried them again through their meeting with different cultures after the arrival of Western civilization.

And so, in this book, we will look at the (linear) timelines of Samoan and Manu'an history, but we will view them, using an aerial-view approach, through the people of history, their relationships and their stories.

Part I: Forging a Culture

Volume I of this book was released as *Navigators Forging a Matriarchal Culture in Polynesia* and includes Part I of this study, as follows:

1. A summary of the culture and social structure the Navigators brought with them, leading to a matriarchal culture, and the history of matriarchal leaders in Samoan and Manu'an society.
2. The combination of matriarchal and patriarchal culture in tribes or clans, loosely scattered across the island chain, leads to the forging of a family-centric society and a chiefdom culture.
3. The cultural glue, binding history and governance, is seen in its titles and salutations.
4. Orators arise as custodians of history, genealogy, and culture.
5. The culture's mythology, legends, and folklore are preserved in the Mornings (*Taeao*) and retold by the orators.
6. Growth via expanding family genealogies through intermarriage leads to customs, protocols, and rituals for meetings, including the building of meeting houses and assignment of house-post seating protocols.
7. The ava ritual is central to the meeting protocol, and it has a rich history of its own.
8. Modern organizations and laws grew out of the history and culture of the island nation, first in isolation, and then in response to the influence of Western cultures.
9. Meanwhile cultural skills in language, navigation, house-building, mat-weaving, tattooing, and agriculture continue to be maintained.

This volume ends with an analysis of where the culture could or should go in the future.

Part II: Building a Nation

This second volume, *Navigators Founding a Christian Nation in Polynesia,* looks at how mythology and the written records of history combine to give a timeline of Samoan and Manu'an history that led to the culture and modern government of the Island Nation.

The timelines of history will cover several periods, recorded in oral or documented history. These can be viewed as eight overlapping periods:

1. The Navigators' migration to the archipelago, and the legend of Pulotu and PapaAtea.
2. The period of Tagaloalagi, and the decrees to delegate authority to human leaders.
3. The children of Tagaloalagi, and the move from myth to genealogy.
4. The period of TuiManu'a, TuiAtua, and TuiA'ana
5. The beginning of the consolidated ruling authority in Samoa.
    a. Major families
    b. The Warrior Queen Nafanua period
    c. The women of the matriarchal families organizing the consolidated ruling authority.
    d. Decrees delegating authority, responsibility, and salutations
    e. The wars for consolidation of ruling authority with Warrior Queen Nafanua's warrior troops
6. The beginning of the modern history of Samoa.
    a. TuiA'ana Tamālelagi and the first Tafa'ifa Salamasina, ruler of all Samoa.
    b. The growth of major families' authority and prominence.
    c. The first civil war of Samoa—peace and decrees establishing the modern royal houses of Samoa and paramount chiefs to lead the country.
7. The dawn of the arrival of Christianity
    a. Christianizing the Samoans and Manu'ans
    b. Establishing mission stations across Samoa and Manu'a

8. Forging a modern, parliamentary form of government.
    a. The arrival of Europeans and the development of trading enterprises
    b. The introduction of European common laws and parliamentary rules and organizations
    c. Major families dispute the single ruling authority, leading to tribal warfare.
    d. Peace agreements with the Americans, Germans, and British form a path to independence.

This volume will, again, conclude with an analysis of where the Island Nation goes from here, with particular reference to the role of the global community in education, economy, and ecology.

Contents

Navigators Forging a Culture and Founding a Nation

Part II: Founding a Christian Nation in Polynesia

To recap: As we saw in *Navigators Quest for a Kingdom in Polynesia,* archeologists, geneticists, anthropologists, linguists, and ethnologists have concluded, based on evidence in their respective fields, that the Island of Vanuatu had already developed a hierarchical chiefdom society by around 2,000 B.C. It is not clear whether the Samoans acquired the chiefdom system from the Vanuatu'ans. However, Samoans and Manu'ans have a belief that they brought this concept and many other ideas with them and developed them along the migration path. Then they refined the structure when they settled in the Manu'an chain of islands.

It is evident that this form of family structure and hierarchical authority is common throughout Asia, Anatolia, the Fertile Crescent, Arabia, and Africa. But Samoan history contains no reference to copying or learning this family-centric hierarchical chiefdom structure from any other group of people in any island in the Pacific. To Samoans and Manu'ans this is their own invention, as a way of protecting family, culture, environment, and way of life.

Polynesians brought many things with them during their eastern migration—their history, genealogy, language, culture, tool technology, food crops, and livestock. They also brought knowledge acquired along the migration path—navigational skills, environmental skills, oceanic skills, and skills in warfare. Then, when they finally settled, they began to hone these attributes—these treasured tidings from the past.

In Volume I of this book, *Navigators Forging a Matriarchal Culture in Polynesia,* we introduced Samoan and Manu'an culture and how it is shaped by history, particularly how the matriarchal culture can be seen in the lives of its famous women, and how history is recorded in the *Taeao* (or Mornings). In this second volume, *Navigators Founding a Christian Nation in Polynesia,* we will look at the historical process of founding the nation of Samoa, from the time of mythology to the present day. We will look at the dates of history (from written records and from calculations), and the stories (myths, legends, genealogies, and the writings of explorers and historians) that tie the times and people together from ancient times to the present day.

These "timelines" of history are derived from a combination of pre-history (myth and legend), recorded history (including the calculations and records made by Dr. Augustin Krämer), the history uncovered by modern science (as described in the first book of this trilogy, *Navigators Quest for a Kingdom in Polynesia*), and oral history preserved in family genealogies.

Timelines of History

Oral History: Numbering the Generations

Dr. Augustin Krämer, in his ethnological study recorded in his book *The Samoa Islands* in 1902, used a simple method to establish dates for the generations in Samoan genealogy, assessing the average length of a generation to be about 30 years. His method was as follows:

- Starting with interviews with leaders of the various families across Samoa, at the village level, asking about their lineage and genealogy,
- then walking backward, and approximating the ages and dates in time, and
- finally concluding that he was looking at 33 generations of Samoan genealogy, at an average of 30 years per generation.

Using 1890 as a base year (his study started in 1898), and counting back 33 generations with 30 years per generation, we can determine the year in which an ancestor lived by the following:

For example, if we know the "Generation Number," out of 1 to 33 with the first generation being the furthest back in history, we can find approximately what year an ancestor lived in. If the ancestor is from generation #10, we subtract 10 from 33 giving 23; multiplying this by 30 equals 690. Now we subtract this from 1890, the base year, giving the year A.D.1200. The formula is 1890 minus 30 times the difference between 33 and the "Generation Number," (or equivalently, 900 plus 30 times the generation number).

For this purpose, generation numbers are important.

Dating the Legends

The challenge I have is in reconciling Dr Krämer's dates, based on 30-year generations, with the implied age of the legends. The problem arises because of the connection between mythology and the real people descended from that mythology. Dr. Krämer is constrained by his fixed genealogical calculations. But the Samoan Court Administration, ruling over family titles and land disputes, often uses a more elastic (rubber-band) measuring tape to account for generational discrepancies in the timeline.

For example, according to Krämer, the *Nafanua* generation lies between generation 9 and 10, making the stories date to late A.D.1100 or early 1200. The mythology of *Saveasi'uleo* and *Ulufanuasese'e* falls at around generation 5 or 6, which would be around A.D.1050-1070. But the stories would seem to imply that *Nafanua* should be dated much closer to *Saveasi'uleo* and *Ulufanuasese'e* than the date Krämer derives.

Another discrepancy arises in the period of *Salamasina* and the Wars of Pāpā, dated to around A.D.1520-1550, Given the relationship between *Salamasina* and *Nafanua,* we have a discrepancy of over 400 years when we compare this with the dates for *Nafanua*. The explanation in this case is that the *Nafanua* name or title was perpetuated by her offspring and descendants, throughout those intervening generations, as is the case with many names that originate in legend and mythology.

This, then, is the challenge of trying to reconcile purely oral history with what has been documented, in midstream as it were, to get an accurate accounting of history.

Similar generational benchmarking is used in the Scriptures, in the Old Testament, so that dating the real age of the more ancient figures, like Cain and Abel, or Noah and many others, is difficult but not impossible. The ages as documented in the Bible can be reconciled, but when we compare them with the discoveries of modern archeological science, major discrepancies arise and need to be resolved.

Genealogy and Life Expectancy

The length of a generation is not the same as the expected lifespan of a person. In A.D.1500, life expectancy in Europe was 71 years, dropping to 69 in A.D.1600. Life expectancy fell to 39 years of age in Europe in 1700—the same as in the post-bubonic plague years of A.D.1300-1400. So an assumption of life expectancy being 30 years per generation would be pretty conservative. But the 30-year number is intended strictly for calculating the generation, which dates from when a child is born to when the child becomes a parent, rather than to when a parent dies.

As an example of Samoan life expectancy, the elder family members interviewed to determine the ancestors' time periods were much older than average. Many were noted to be of very advanced age, even in their 90s.

It should be noted that, before colonization or the arrival of missionaries, the Samoan diet consisted of simple fish and cooked roots, like taro, yams, bananas, and lots of vegetables, which would be conducive to good health and long life. The various diseases from the outside world did not enter the islands until the late 1700s to A.D.1830.

Written and Oral Transmission

In cultures with more written records—such as the world of Homer's Iliad, the Hebrew or Christian Bible, and the Sanskrit Reg Vedas—we find that the time difference between when an oral narrative begins and when it is finally written down can range from

400 to 800 years. But these documents are accepted, in the established literary world, as foundational to chronicling human evolutionary development and mankind's journey across the globe.

Thus we conclude, for example, that the events of the Iliad took place around 1200 B.C., and Homer wrote about them around 800 B.C., or 400 years later. The Hebrew Bible was finally composed around 800 B.C., chronicling the story that started with Abraham immigrating to Canaan, as per God's instructions, in around 2200 B.C., a difference of 1400 years. Even if we assume that the oral tradition began around the time of the exodus out of Egypt in 1220 B.C., the time difference is still about 420 years. And in the case of the Reg Vedas, the four sacred canonical texts of Hinduism, the oral tradition began around 2200 B.C. (during the Indo-Aryan period) and was finally written down around 1500 B.C. The time difference is about 700 years.

So, we can conclude that the time difference between when an oral narrative (mythology, legend, and tales) begins and when it is finally written down can be very significant. It could be, on average, up 700 years or more—(400 + 1400 + 420 + 700) ÷4 = 2920÷4 = 730.

While there is little archeological evidence to illuminate the ancient existence of Samoans and Manu'ans in the archipelago, some evidence exists, as in the case of the Mulifanua Lapita-style pottery, which is dated using Carbon-14 to around 1100 B.C. This fits in consistently with the reconciliation and extrapolation of the generations and their respective time periods.

Timelines of Samoan and Manu'an History

The events of Samoan and Manu'an history and legend can be organized into separate, overlapping time periods, and combined with history uncovered through the sciences. The search for the earliest times in that history is described in my first book: *Navigators Quest for a Kingdom in Polynesia*.

The Mornings (the *Taeao*) are repeated by orators and record these events. For every excellent orator thrives on the history and mythology of Samoa. The more an orator understands the history of Samoan genealogy and origin, the more effective the orator is, as they are able to connect and protect the ancestry.

Period I: The Navigators' Migration

Events: 1700 – 250 B.C.

1700-400 B.C.

This is the time of the ancient Polynesian Migration to explore the East Pacific Ocean, and the Lapita trading period when Polynesians arrived in Samoa and Manu'a. Evidence is found as below:

- Site and artifacts at Toa'aga, Ofu Island, Manu'a Kingdom reveal human occupation.[i]
- Stone quarries (ten) at Tataga-Matau, Tutuila Island (American Samoa) produced basalt and obsidian for trade across the East Pacific Islands.[ii]
- A set of rich artifacts and ceramics found at 'Aoa village in Tutuila Island reveals human occupations.[iii]

1000 B.C.

- Human occupation sites and artifacts found at Vailele and Luatuanu'u, Upolu Island.[iv]

1000-800 B.C.

- Ceramic pottery with crude Lapita design has been excavated at Mulifanua shore (a ferry vessel dock) in Upolu Island and carbon-dated to this period.[v]

800 B.C.

- The DNA Sequencing project undertaken at Oxford University, UK, Stanford University, US, and Chile University, Chile (September 2021) dates the Samoan settlement of the Archipelago to around 800 B.C.[vi]

500 B.C.

- The migration from 'Atea and Pulotu
- The war between PapaAtea and Pulotu
- The original settlement of Manu'a, Savai'i, Manono, and Tutuila
- The victory of the Warrior *Elo*
- The defeat of the Warriors *Utuma* and *Utumau'u*

250 B.C.

The reign of the Warrior *Fitiaumua* (half Manu'an and half Fijian) over Samoa, Fiji, and all of Polynesia. Legend has it that *Fitiaumua* conquered all of Polynesia. Other Polynesian Islands refer to him with different names, but the description is of a Manu'an Warrior.

Stories

At this time:

- The story of the PapaAtea and Pulotu war tells how the people came to Samoa (see Stories of PapaAtea and Pulotu, page 75).
- The *manuali'i* (the sultana bird, porphyrio) and the *panea* (the shell trumpet, cassis cornuta) make an appearance in the form of gifts.
- *Tuli* (the golden plover) makes a first appearance as the servant of *Tagaloalagi*, also known as *Tuli-a-leTagaloalagi* (ambassador of the Tagaloalagi—see The Manu'an Creation Poem, page 79, given in Period II as the periods overlap and the poem refers to *Tagaloalagi*).
- Dating from somewhat later, around 100 B.C., we have a parallel legend to the PapaAtea and Pulotu war, describing the populating of the Manu'a Archipelago—the story of *Lua* and his sister *Ui* (see Luama'a and LuaUi, page 77). This story marks the first appearance of *Lā* as the Sun (or light or *Ao*). *Lā* is also a reference to *Tagaloalagi.*

Period II: The Legendary Tagaloalagi

Events: 300 – 50 B.C.

The reign of the Warrior *Fitiaumua* over all of Polynesia continues during this time period. And the Manu'an Creation poem describes the creation of the islands.

Stories

As mentioned earlier, these periods are not strictly separate from each other, and will frequently overlap.

300 B.C.
This is the first time period where the beginning of the heavens and celestial bodies such as the Sun, *La*, appear in legend. The implications in mythology are that *Tagaloalagi* is the creator, but the heavenly bodies begin with *Po* (night or dark) and *Ao* (light or day). So the parents of *TagaloaLā* are *Po* and *Ao,* while, in the pre-migration period before the arrival in Polynesia, *Tagaloalagi* resides in the tenth of the Ten Heavens.

Legends referring to this time include:

- Union of *Po* and *Ao* (Night and Day) giving birth to *TagaloaLā.*
- Union of *O* and *Lua* which begets *Sega* (the parrot). In Manu'an legend, *O* and *Lua* are celestial bodies, princes of the TuiAtua family—they are members of the *Tagaloalagi* family, residing in Heavens 1 through 9.[vii]
- Union of *Malamagaga'e* (light of the East) and *Malamagaga'ifo* (light from the West) which begets *Lupe* (pigeon).
- Union of *Lupe* (pigeon) and *Ma'ata'anoa* (solid rock) which begets *Palapala* (female).
- Union of *Palapala* and *Nu'u* (village) which begets *Tagata* and *Tupufua* (the first man originating out of nothing).

The story of Lu begins here, with the union of *Tupufua* and *Suluimauga* which begets *Lu* with his House of 100 Pillars. The House of 100 Pillars signifies *Lu's* power and authority—*Lu* was a cruel half-human, half-spirit warrior (possibly practicing cannibalism, so the pillars could refer to 100 human beings). And *Suluimauga*'s name means "stumble and lay down to form a mountain," according to the *Lu* genealogy. Alternatively, it means "torch-light on the mountain," or "for fishing," in the *Pili* and *Lu* genealogies of Manu'a.

We should also note the Atua version of this legend, where TuiAtua *Moso* is a demonic half-man, half-spirit who lives in Savai'i and Upolu simultaneously, who marries a lady from Uafato, in Atua district, Upolu, and begets *Lu*. The first *Lu* is *Lufasiāitu*, with his flock of chickens (see The Story of the Demigod *Lufasiāitu*, page 96 in Period III).

Another legend of *Lu's* birth gives his parents as *Tuasivi* (mountain ridge) and *Palapala* (mud), who give birth, in the village of Uafato, Atua, to two children, *Lufasiāitu* and his sister *Fatukoama*.[viii] *Fatukoama* marries *Galu* and gives birth to three boys, *Niumea*, *Niuui* and *Niualava*. In this version of the story, a later *Lufasiāitu* is the son of TuiAtua *Moso*, and becomes TuiAtua *Lufasiāitu*.

Tagaloalagi is also associated with the village of Uafato (see The Rock at Uafato, page 85). His wife *Ila*, grand-daughter of TuiAtua *Moso* and *Sinalesopoalemalama,* brings him to Uafato and to his residence Malata, in Atua. So we should note the genealogy of *Ila* which is:

- TuiAtua *Moso* and *Sinalesopoalemalama* give birth to
  - *Puana*, who marries *Leao*, giving birth to two girls, *Ila* and *Tualafalafa.*
    - *Ila* marries *Tagaloalagi*, giving birth to a son (name not known).

When *Tagaloalagi* comes into being, we find The Manu'an Creation Poem and stories of *Tagaloalagi's* family clan residing in the first through ninth heavens (similar to the places where different angels live). This is the period of *Tagaloalagi's* reign over all of Samoa and Manu'a. *Tagaloalagi* continues with several marriages and begets many children, a genealogy that eventually leads to the TuiManu'a genealogy.

250 B.C.

The entrance to the underworld—to Pulotu and Salefe'e—appears in legend around this time. The guardians of Pulotu—*Fe'e* (the octopus) and the sea eel (or moray)—have their counterparts in Greek mythology's stories of Elysium and Tartarus.[ix] In the legends, the demon *Fe'e* possesses fire, and *Ti'eti'eitalaga* will wrestle with him to obtain it for cooking (see The Story of Fire, page 86).

Fe'e comes to live in Manu'a with *Tagaloalagi* and becomes the father of the demonic beings *Sinasa'umani* and *Sasa'umani* (see How *Fe'e* came to Manu'a, page 85). *Sinasa'umani* marries *TagaloaUi*, and *Sasa'umani* marries *Togia,* as we shall see in Period III: *Tagaloalagi's* Offspring and Descendants, page 15.

This is also the time of the discovery of fishing hook by *Luagia*, the master fisherman.

50 B.C.

The story of Sauā (where *LuaUi* and her son built their first house at the Faleniu property) continues at this time with the birth of *Galea'i* (see The Story of the First TuiManu'a, page 81), who becomes the first human paramount royal chief of Manu'a. *Galea'i's* son is the first TuiManu'a.

People

TuiAtua

300 B.C.

The TuiAtua Lineage begins here with the Atua version of the pedigree of *Lu* and *Pili*:

- A lady from Uafato, Atua district, Upolu, and the Warrior TuiAtua *Moso* beget *Lu.*
  - The union of TuiAtua *Lu* and *Lagituaiva* (also called *LeAmoa,* of the Ninth Heaven, daughter of *Tagaloalagi*) begets:
    - *Lupoto,*
    - *Lunofo,*
    - *Luta'oto,* and
    - *Lutausili i nu'u*

Lutausili i nu'u succeeds his father *Lufasiāitu* and grandfather TuiAtua *Moso* to rule over the Atua district, and some believe *Lutausili i nu'u* is the first TuiAtua.

- Union of TuiAtua *Lutausili i nu'u* and *Lagiaunoa* (open firmament, or emptiness of heaven) begets *Lagimafola* (a daughter, flat firmament or flat sky).
    - Union of *Lagimafola* and *Tagaloalagi* (her great-grandfather, and god of the Tenth Heaven) begets *Pilipa'ū* (the first *Pili*, the lizard that fell from Heaven).

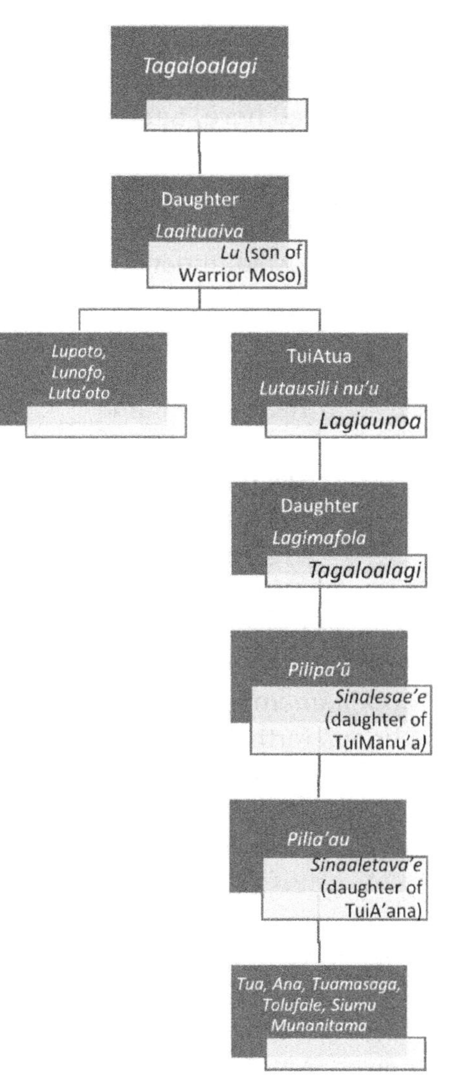

Then we come to the children of *Pili*:

- Union of *Pilipa'ū* (the lizard that fell from Heaven) and *Sinalesae'e* (daughter of TuiManu'a) begets *Pilia'au* (the swimming lizard).
    - Union of *Pilia'au* and *Sina-a-le-tava'e* (*Sinaaletava'e,* daughter of TuiA'ana) around **A.D.1** begets:
        - *Tua* (gifted with the digging pole for planting),
        - *Ana* (gifted with the spear/club, war warrior),
        - *Tuamasaga* (stands between the twin brothers. Decreed with the orator's staff and flail as the Mediator),
        - *Tolufale* (the supplier of the war troops), and
        - *Siumu Munanitama* (assistant of war).

TuiA’ana

The TuiA’ana lineage should also be noted here, beginning with:

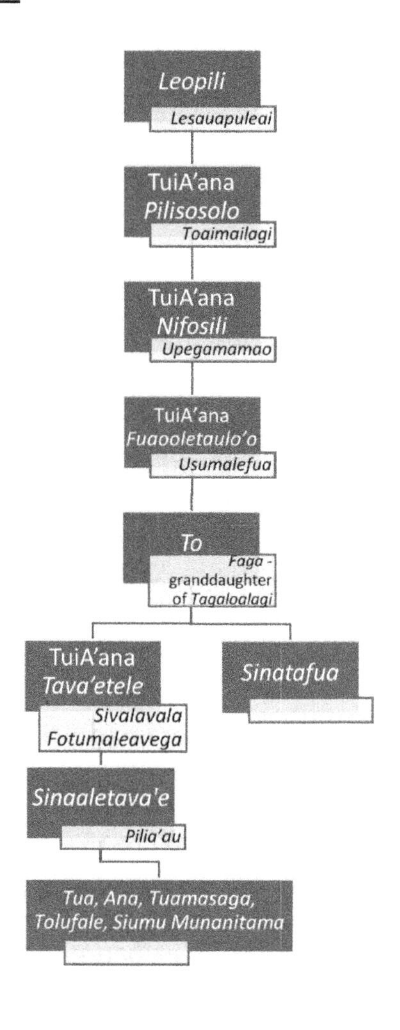

- *Leopili,* whose union with *Lesauapuleai* births *Leopilisosolo*, meaning crawling lizard.
  - *Leopilisosolo* becomes TuiA’ana, hence the name TuiA’ana *Pilisosolo*. His union (one of his marriages) with *Toaimailagi* gives birth to *Nifosili*, meaning buck teeth.
- TuiA’ana *Nifosili*’s union with *Upegamamao,* from Nofoali’i, brings forth *Fuaooletaulo’o*,
  - whose union with *Usumalefua* (also from Nofoali’i) begets *To*.
- *To’s* union with *Faga*, daughter of *Leatumailagi* (the son of *Tagaloalagi* and his wife *Funanuanuatele*) gives birth to:
  - A daughter *Sinatafua* and
  - a son TuiA’ana *Tava’etele,* whose union with *Sivalavala Fotumaleavega* (she carried the load on her shoulder) begets *Sinaaletava’e*
    - who marries *Pilia’au* (TuiAtua lineage, previous section) around **A.D.1**, giving birth to the boys listed there.

The lineage from *Sinaaletava’e* (i.e. the female genealogy) then branches off to their children, while the male genealogy continues to TuiA'ana *Sagaate,* who is defeated by the famous TuiA'ana *Tamālelagi,* beginning the line from TuiA'ana *Tamālelagi* down to Tafa'ifa *Salamasina* in the 1500s.

Tagaloa

250 B.C.

During this first time period, *Tagaloamatua*, *Tagaloanimoimo*, *Tagaloasu'enu'u* and *TagaloaLā* are all referred to with the same name, *Tagaloalagi*, making it hard to give a consistent timeline.

The lineage of *Tagaloalagi* is combined with the lineage of TuiAtua here, as we have just seen, when *Tagaloalagi* marries *Lagimafola*, daughter of *Lutausili i nu'u*, the son of *Lu* and *Lagituaiva,* who is *Tagaloalagi's daughter*. (*Tagaloalagi*—or his descendant—is marrying the great-granddaughter of *Tagaloalagi* at this point). His lineage also combines with that of the TuiFiti, the TuiManu'a, and with *Fe'e* (the octopus).

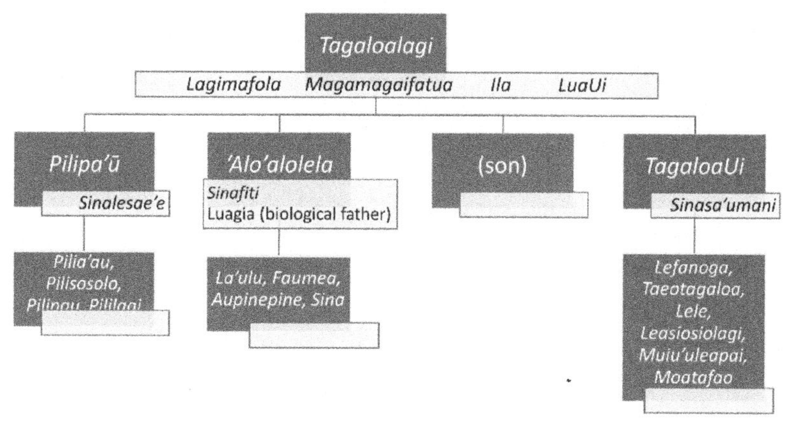

- As we saw above, *Tagaloalagi's* union with *Lagimafola* begets *Pili* (also known as *Pilipa'ū*, Pili-fall from heaven, because he fell from heaven).
    - Union of *Pilipa'ū* and *Sinalesae'e,* daughter of TuiManu'a, begets
        - *Pilia'au* (Pili that swam),
        - *Pilisosolo* (Pili that crawls),
        - *Pilipau,* and
        - *Pililagi.*

- *Tagaloalagi's* union with *Magamagaifatua* begets *'Alo'alolelā* who uses the fishing hook.
  - Union of *'Alo'alolelā* and *Sinafiti* (daughter of TuiFiti) around **50 B.C.** produces four children (their biological father is Luagia—see The Story of the Master Fisherman, page 82):
    - *La'ulu* (from whom the La'ulu title comes),
    - *Faumea,*
    - *Aupinepine,* and
    - *Sina* (their sister).
- *Tagaloalagi's* union with *Ila,* granddaughter of TuiAtua *Moso,* gives birth to a son whose name is not known.
- Union of *TagaloaLā* (same as *Tagaloalagi*) and *LuaUi* (who fled the sun and brought up her son at *Sauā*—see Luama'a and LuaUi, page 77) begets *TagaloaUi*. At this time *Ti'eti'eitalaga* wrestles with *Fe'e,* the octopus who lives in Pulotu and Salefe'e—see The Story of Fire, page 86—to bring up fire for cooking.
  - Union of *TagaloaUi* and *Sinasa'umani* (daughter of *Fe'e*) begets (also around **50 B.C.**):
    - *Lefanoga* who brings the *sega* to the Malietoafaigā,
    - *Taeotagaloa* famous for the first ava ceremony,
    - *Lele,*
    - *Leasiosiolagi,*
    - *Muiu'uleapai* (a daughter), and
    - *Moatafao* (a daughter).

TuiManu'a

A.D.1

The genealogy of TuiManu'a begins when *Aga'euta* and his wife *Aga'etai* give birth to *Galea'i, who* is appointed the first king of Manu'a by *Tagaloalagi.* His son is the first TuiManu'a.

There is an alternative version of the story, in which *Galea'i* is a son of *Tagaloalagi's* union with *Aga'euta* (or *Aga'etai*) up in the tenth heaven; or, according to Lafai Sauoāiga Ape in *Mavaega i Le Tai, Galea'i* is a son of *TagaloaLā* and a daughter (possibly *LuaUi*) of *TagaloaUi* up in the ninth heaven.

- *Galea'i* marries *Valooleto'elau* from Sauā, Fitiuta, who gives birth to a girl *Alavatualua* and a boy.
    - *Alavatualua* marries one of the Warrior Chief brothers *Pago* in Tutuila, birthing the boy from the mountain, who would be called
        - *Mauga,* beginning the SaMauga lineage.

Period III: *Tagaloalagi's* Offspring and Descendants

Events: 50 B.C. – A.D.500

50 B.C.

This period covers the time of *Taeotagaloa,* son of *TagaloaUi* and *Sinasa'umani* (daughter of *Fe'e*). The lineage of *Tagaloalagi* continues with the union of *Muiu'uleapai* (sister to *Taeotagaloa*) and TuiFiti (the king of Fiji) which gives birth to a son *Leataataofiti*.

A.D.250

In the later part of this period we find *Tagaloalagi's* proclamation of paramount authority to:

- *Fiamē* of Samatau, Upolu (due to *Losi's* warring human warriors who defeated *Tagaloalagi's* demigod children),
- *Taimalelagi* of Mulifanua, Upolu,
- *Tuifa'asisina* of Satapuala, Upolu ,
- *Lavasi'i* of Lefaga, Upolu,
- *Setafune* in Safune, Savai'i, and
- *Folasā* of Fitiuta, Manu'a.

A.D.500

- This is the time when TuiToga begins his cruel treatment of Samoans at various small villages where he sojourns for provisions.

Stories

At this time, legends tell how:

- *Sasa'umani* (sister of *Sinasa'umani*—these are the half-demon half-human daughters of *Fe'e*) marries *Togia*, a chief of the west coast of Savai'i, in the Gaga'emalae district. *Sasa'umani*

is known as the great fisherwoman, and she gives birth to a boy named *Sa'umani,* later given the name *Pulelei'ite.*
- *Sinasa'umani* marries *TagaloaUi.*
- The *sega* (most revered parrot) is brought back to Manu'a from Fiji Island by *Lefanoga* (brother to *Taeotagaloa,* though some say *Taeotagaloa* brought the parrot). The sega was originally stolen from Manu'a by *Olo* and *Fana.* (See Stories of the Sons of *TagaloaUi*, page 106).

The story of Sauā continues with:
- The mythology of *Maui* the explorer, and
- the mythology of the explorer *Lata* (see *Lata's* Double-hulled Canoe, page 112).
- The famous seafarers, *Gaiuli* and *Gaisina*, travel with *Taeotagaloa* to the aid of his sister *Muiu'uleapai*, when the TuiFiti blames her for a famine (see The Story of *TagaloaUi's* Daughter, page 108).
- The story of *Saveasi'uleo* with a tail like a sea eel appears at this time (though its historical connotations in the history of Tonumaipe'a genealogy give a later date—see Period III, Transition to Mythological Figures, page 118).
- The story of the conjoined twins, *Taemā* and *Tilafaigā* appears here too (see The Story of Tattooing and the Conjoined Twins, page 115).
- The mythology of Chief *Vaea* and *Apaula* appears here, after which the **Apaula** family genealogy begins (see *Apaula*: the Early People of Savai'i, page 130).

This period also includes the stories of:
- *Pili* (sometimes called *Pilia'au*—Pili that swam in the ocean) the explorer, famous across Polynesia mythology. There are tales from various islands of Polynesia (Hawaii, Tahiti, Maori...) about *Pilia'au's* excursions. He is the son of *Pilipa'ū* (the first *Pili*) and *Sinalesae'e* (daughter of the TuiManu'a)—see The story of *Pili*, page 98.
- *Lefanoga* (brother of *Taeotagaloa)* is also renowned for his exploration throughout the archipelago and is mentioned (together with *Taeotagaloa)* in tales of Malietoa Faigā *Uilamatūtū's* cruelty, dating from this period.

- The mythology of *Losi* the fisherman dates to here—see The Story of *Losi*, page 93—
- as does the story of *Lu* and his flock of chickens—see The Story of the Demigod *Lufasiāitu,* page 96—
- and the story of *Ti'eti'eitalaga* being given fire from Salefe'e, after wrestling with *Fe'e* (this appears in Period II among the stories of *Fe'e*—see The Story of Fire, page 86).
- Also the story of *Pava* attending the first Ava ceremony with *Taeotagaloa* dates back to this time (see *Taeotagaloa* and the First Ava Ceremony, page 107).

Some very important genealogies begin in this period also, including the genealogies of TuiManu'a, TuiA'ana, and TuiAtua. While these have been listed at earlier dates in mythology, the genealogies themselves can be dated to begin historically around A.D.250.

People

A.D.1

The story of *Saveasi'uleo* who has a tail like a sea eel begins with:

- *Papa* and *Maluapapa*, the parents of the girl *Popoto.*
    - *Popoto* marries *Masa* and bears a girl *Taufa* (or *Taufa-le-matagi*).
        - *Taufa* marries *'Alao* of Falealupo, Savai'i, bearing
            - a boy *Saveasi'uleo* who has a tail like a sea eel,
            - a boy named *Sālevao*, and
            - a younger son *Ulufanuasese'e*
                - whose daughters are the conjoined twins *Taemā* and *Tilafaigā.*

A.D.500

This is the time of *Fa'alualuatele* and *Aveautetele*, half-brothers to the Siamese twins *Taemā* and *Tilafaigā* (daughters of *Ulufanuasese'e,* above). Their genealogies will appear in Period V, in the Tonumaipe'a lineage, page 44.

Period IV: TuiManu'a, TuiAtua, and TuiA'ana

Events: A.D.500 - 1200

- Throughout this period, TuiToga increases in cruelty across all Samoa.
- *Lealali* decrees that his sons, *Salevaogogo* and *Sausi,* will live in the Leulumoega seat of government of TuiA'ana, and they become the authority of the TuiA'ana title.
- *Lealali's* other sons, *Tupa'imatuna*, *Tupa'ilelei*, and *Tupa'isiva* are decreed to remain in Savai'i and be paramount chiefs over all of Savai'i.
- The **Matai'a**, **Mata'afa** and **Faumuinā** titles form the tripod ruling authority of the Faleata district.
- At the end of this period, TuiA'ana *Sagaate* is defeated by TuiA'ana *Tamālelagi,* beginning the line from TuiA'ana *Tamālelagi* down to Tafa'ifa *Salamasina* in the 1500s.
- The **LeTelesā** lineage is found at the end of this period
- as is the **Tonumaipe'a** lineage.

Stories

A.D.500

While the legends tell of times much earlier than this, their original appearance can be dated to this time:

- The union of *Malama mai Aga'e* (the light from the East) with *Malama mai Aga'ifo* (the light from West), giving birth to
- *Lupe* (pigeon) whose union with *Papatū* (upright cliff) gives birth to
- *A'alua* (tree root) whose union with *Papamau* (solid cliff) gives birth to
- *Papafoagia* (split cliff) whose union with *Ma'ata'anoa* (scattered rocks) gives birth to
- *Papa'ele* (cliff soil) whose union with *Palapala* (mud or swamp or fertile ground) gives birth to (*Papamavae* and/or)

- *Papalaulau* (flat rock or volcanic rock) whose union with *Papalega* (soft clay) births
- *Papasuatia* whose union with her husband *Ma'ata'anoa* gives birth to *Si'imoa*, a daughter.

This list is not the same as the one given in Period II, as it represents the continuing evolution of the legend.

At this juncture, as we consolidate different versions, the TuiA'ana, TuiAtua, Tagaloa, and Malietoa mythologies begin to combine with each other. For example, in the diagram we now have *Tagaloa* as an ancestor of *Tupufua* (the first man) and *Lu*, as follows:

Malamagaga'e
Malamagaga'ifo
Lupe
Papatū
A'alua
Papamau
Papafoagia
Ma'ata'anoa
Papa'ele
Palapala
Papamavae
Imoa
Salasala
Tagaloanimonimo
Tupufua
Leletaimalia *Tamaotufaiga*
Leopili
Lu

- *Papamavae* (fissuring cliff), the first female (a name symbolic of female anatomy), is the daughter of *Papa'ele* and *Palapala*. Her union with *Imoa* the rat gives birth to:
  - A girl, *Salasala*, who marries *Tagaloanimonimo* (the immeasurable Tagaloa), giving birth to:
    - *Tupufua*, the first man originating out of nothing, who marries *Leletaimalie* begetting *Lu*, beginning the TuiAtua genealogy.

In another story, dating to this time, *Lea'auta,* daughter of the blind man *Oleāifale'ava* seeks out the long-haired warrior *Taemanutava'e* and marries him. The story of their journey is given in the first book of this series—*Navigators Quest for a Kingdom in Polynesia.* That story gives names to many places.

A.D.750

- The sisters *Lulai* and *Lulago* bid farewell to *Tupa'isafe'e* when they depart to marry *Si'utaulalovasa.* One sister is carrying the child of *Tupa'isafe'e.* Their story is given in Volume I of this narrative, *Navigators Forging a Matriarchal Culture in Polynesia*.
- The grandson, *Tafa'igata*, of *Lulai* and *Lulago* marries *Sauopualai* who bears *'Ai'i* (also known as *Tafa'i* of *Mata'afa*), *Vaitagutu* (also known as *Tafa'i* of *Mata'afa*), *Mata*, *'Afa*, and *Mata'afa*.

A.D.1000

- *Leatiogie,* son of *Fe'epo* and *Leipaleatele*, defeats *Salevaogogo* in a club match in Momoa (see Story of Leatiogie and Salevaogogo, page 155).

People

<u>TuiAtua</u>

A.D.750

According to Atua legends, the TuiAtua genealogy begins with the legendary warrior *Moso*:[x]

- TuiAtua *Moso* is the father of
  - TuiAtua *Lu,* who marries *Lagituaiva* (daughter of Tagaloalagi) and begets:
    - *Tuapu'u* (hunchback or short back),
    - *Tuaumi* (long back or normal back), and
    - TuiAtua *Tuafaigā* (the cruel), who marries *Lemaluitogapapa* and begets:
      - TuiAtua *Tuaefu,* who marries *Sinataufafa* and begets:
        - TuiAtua *Uitua.*

A.D. 900

The TuiAtua genealogy continues in this period with:

- TuiAtua *Uitua,* who marries *Sinalei* or *Paepaetele* and begets:
  - TuiAtua *Leilua* who marries *Sinafetuga* and begets:

- *Pulutua* who marries *Laualae* and begets:
    - TuiAtua *Sagapolutele* who marries *Luafaletele* and begets:
        - TuiAtua *Tualemoso* who marries *Feiliva'a* and begets:
            - TuiAtua *Tuanu'u.*

We should note, according to Pratt's *Genealogy of the Kings and Princes of Samoa* these are forerunners of the TuiAtua kings. Thus, not all were given the TuiAtua title salutation but in legends, for example, *Pulutua* was TuiAtua.

The line continues through further generations:

- TuiAtua *Tuanu'u* marries *Sautale* and begets:
    - TuiAtua *Teneila* who marries *Senilafaga* of Moamoa and begets:
        - TuiAtua *Tuloutele* who marries *Sina* of Lotoma'a and begets:
            - *Malaetele* who marries *Samalaulu*, daughter of the TuiManu'a, who begets:
                - TuiAtua *Maileitele* who marries *Utufau* of Satoi and begets:
                    - TuiAtua *Maileilealea.*

A.D.1000

In this period, the TuiAtua genealogy continues:

- TuiAtua *Maileilealea* marries *Siliomaga* and begets:
    - TuiAtua *Taemo'otele* who marries *Ulufa'ana* of Manono Island and begets:
        - TuiAtua *Taemo'omanaia* who marries *Fetutafeilo* and begets:
            - TuiAtua *Leutelelei'ite,* whose descendant, Paramount Chief *Leutelelei'ite*, marries the second child of the *Fe'e* and *Sinatualalafā*, the girl *Samalaulu,* in around A.D.1213. TuiAtua *Leutelelei'ite* marries Lefe'eialali, giving birth to *Sinalegogo,*
                - who marries *Lealali*, giving birth to *Salevaogogo* and *Sausi.*

TuiA'ana

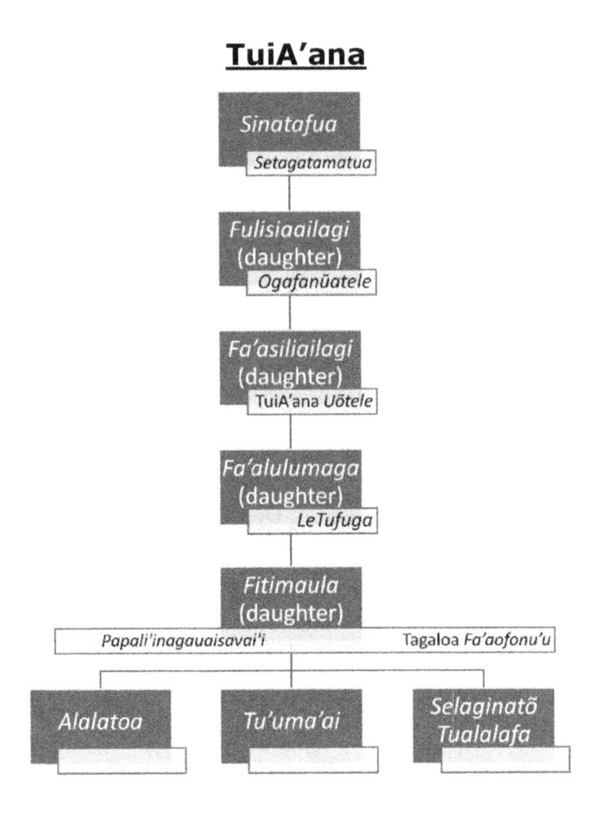

A.D.1300

The TuiA'ana lineage (as begun in Period II, TuiA'ana , page 12) now continues along two lines—the female line and the male line.

The female line continues from *Sinatafua,* daughter of TuiA'ana *Nifosili* and sister to TuiA'ana *Tava'etele*:

- *Sinatafua* marries *Setagatamatua* of Taula (around A.D.1350) bearing a daughter,
  - *Fulisiaailagi,* who now carries the genealogy. *Fulisiaailagi* marries *Ogafanūatele* of Leulumoega, bearing a daughter,
    - *Fa'asiliailagi* who marries TuiA'ana *Uōtele* and bears a daughter,
      - *Fa'alulumaga* who marries *LeTufuga* of SaFotulafai, bearing a daughter,
        - *Fitimaula* who marries Tagaloa *Fa'aofonu'u*

(around A.D.1470) bearing the boy, *Selaginatõ (Selaginatõ Tualalafa). Fitimaula's* other sons (from her marriage to *Papali'inagauaisavai'i*), are *Alalatoa* and *Tu'uma'ai, Selaginatõ's* half-brothers.

Following the male line from TuiA'ana *Tava'etele,* (see Period II, TuiA'ana, page 12) we have:

- TuiA'ana *Tava'etele's* union with *Sivalavala Fotumaleavega* begets a daughter, *Sinaaletava'e.*
    - *Sinaaletava'e* marries *Pili* (*Pilia'au,* who is also TuiA'ana *Leopili*). They are the progenitors of the brothers who began the district organization of Samoa:
        - *Tua* (gifted with the digging pole for planting)
        - *Ana* (gifted with the spear/club, war warrior)
        - *Tuamasaga* (He stands between the twin brothers. Decreed with the orator's staff and flail as the Mediator)
        - *Tolufale* (the supplier of the war troops) and
        - *Siumu Munanitama* (assistant of war).

The TuiA'ana line continues from the original TuiA'ana *Pilisosolo* as follows:

- TuiA'ana *Pilisosolo* is followed by
- TuiA'ana *Lelaolao*
- TuiA'ana *Olomaene*
- TuiA'ana *Fa'atupunu'u*
- TuiA'ana *Gagaifoolepou*
- TuiA'ana *Gaga'eolepou*
- TuiA'ana *Fa'apilipili*
- TuiA'ana *Fuaoletauloa*
- TuiA'ana *Lealaolõ*
- TuiA'ana *Salevao*
- TuiA'ana *Alevale*
- TuiA'ana *Letopelu*

- TuiA'ana *Fiamē* who marries *Titilimulimu*, giving birth to *Aiteleai, Niuapai,* and *Samatau*
- TuiA'ana *Lelauvi*
- TuiA'ana *Vaemā*
- TuiA'ana *Sagaate* or *Sanaate.*

Then in **A.D.1470**, *Selaginatõ* (from the female line) marries *Vaetamasoāali'i,* who gives birth to *Tamālelagi,* who defeats TuiA'ana *Sagaate* (or *Sanaate,* the TuiA'ana from the male line) to become TuiA'ana *Tamālelagi*, father of *Salamasina.*

LeTelesā Lineage and the Mata'afa, Matai'a, and Faumuinā Titles

The **LeTelesā** genealogy (see *LeTelesā:* Early Matriarchy in Samoan History, page 133) begins with TuiA'ana *Leopili* (not *Pilia'au*, who was known by the same name):

- TuiA'ana *Leopili* and *LeSauopualai mai Gaga'e* give birth to *Pilisosolo.*
  - TuiA'ana *Pilisosolo* marries *Toaimailagi* who gives birth to *Nifosili*, meaning buck teeth.
    - TuiA'ana *Nifosili*'s union with *Upegamamao,* from Nofoali'i, brings forth *Fuaooletaulo'o*,
      - whose union with *Usumalefua* (also from Nofoali'i) begets *To* (see TuiA'ana in Period II, page 12).
  - TuiA'ana *Pilisosolo* marries *Manavafea'a*, a woman from Faleata, who bears *'Ata'atanoa* and his sister *LeTelesā* (around **A.D. 1070**).
    - *LeTelesā's* brother *'Ata'atanoa* marries *Tofili* (the first *Matai'a's* sister) who bears:
      - *Fa'auli* and *Umi,*
      - and a daughter *Fa'aulimaumi,* who marries *Ata,* son of *Lulai* or *Lulago.*
    - *LeTelesā* adopts *Umi* and he is given the name *Faumuinā*, beginning the Faumuinā title, which is the third leg—with Matai'a and Mata'afa—of the tripod ruling authority of the Faleata district.

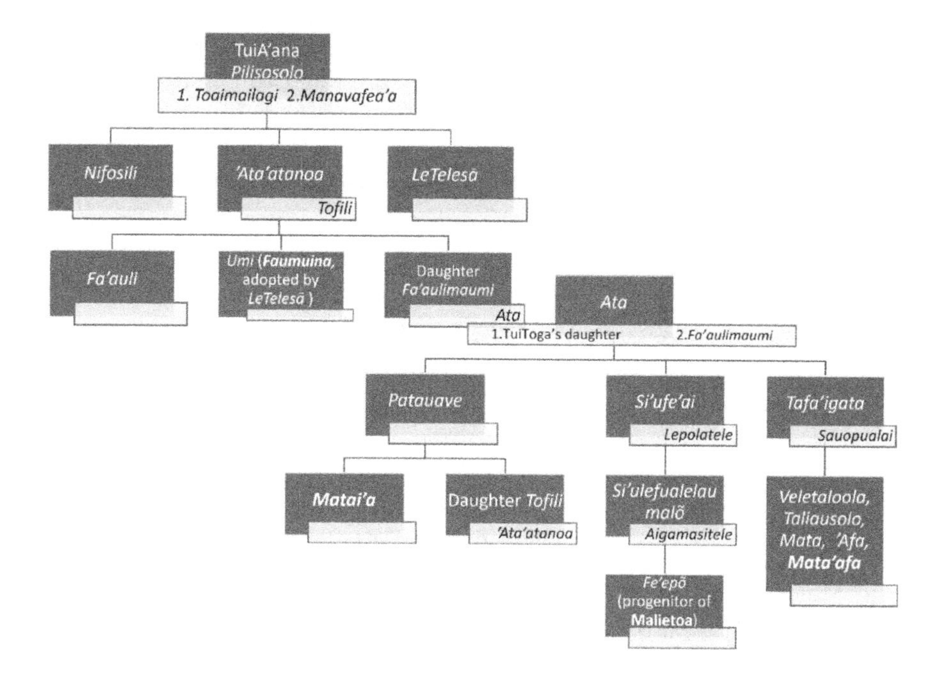

A.D.750

Ata enters the story when *Lulai* and *Lulago* marry *Si'utaulalovasa.* One of them is carrying a child by *Tupa'isafe'e*, as told in the Morning of the Farewell of the Sisters Lulai and Lulago—this story is given in Volume I of this work. So...

- *Lulai* and *Lulago* bear sons *To'o* and *Ata.*
  - *Ata* marries a daughter of TuiToga, bearing *Patauave.*
    - *Patauave* marries a woman from Vaitele, who bears the first **Matai'a,** and his sister *Tofili.*
      - *Tofili* marries *'Ata'atanoa* (brother to *LeTelesā,* above) and bears:
        - A daughter *Fa'aulimaumi* who marries her great-grandfather *Ata,*
        - a son *Fa'auli*, and
        - a son *Umi* (who is adopted by *LeTelesā* and called ***Faumuinā***).
  - *Ata* marries his great-granddaughter *Fa'aulimaumi* (above) who bears *Si'ufe'ai* and *Tafa'igata.*
    - *Si'ufe'ai* marries *Lepolatele* of Pola village giving birth to:

- *Si'ulefualelaumalõ* whose marriage to *Aigamasitele* of Faleata district, gives birth to:
  - *Fe'epõ* the progenitor of the **Malietoa** clan.

- *Tafa'igata* marries *Sauopualai* (or *LeSauopualai*) who bears:
  - *Veletaloola* (originally named *'Ai'i*) or *Vele,* Tafa'i of Mata'afa,
  - *Taliausolo* (originally named *Vaitagutu*), Tafa'i of Mata'afa,
  - *Mata,*
  - *'Afa*, and
  - *Mata'afa* of the **Mata'afa** title, the *Ao* or crown of the Faleata district.

The Matai'a, Mata'afa, and Faumuinā titles form the tripod ruling authority of the Faleata district.

Malietoa

Fe'epõ
Leipaleatele
Malalatele
Sinalagilagi
Leatiogie
Tauaiupolu
Daughter Sina
TuiManu'a
Daughter Lelāpueisalele
Blind man Oleāifale'ava
Malietoa Savea
Tuna, Fata, Lealali, Ve'ataui a, Leimuli
Leatiatigieleala iaolõ
Daughter Lea'auta
Taemanutava'e
Va'afuti, Fata, Maulolo and Luafatasaga

A.D.1000
Fe'epõ, as mentioned above, is the progenitor of the Malietoa clan:

- *Fe'epõ's* marriage to *Leipaleatele,* daughter of *Niu* of Afolau village, A'ana district, gives birth to *Malālatea, Sina,* and *Leatiogie*:

- *Malalatele* or *Malālatea* (ancestor of *Va'afuti*, ***Fata***, ***Maulolo***, and their sister *Luafatasaga*) marries *Sinalagilagi* (daughter of *Tagaloalagi*) giving birth to:
    - *Lelāpueisalele*, and her blind brother, *Oleāifale'ava* (or *Leāifale'ava*). We shall see them again in the Period V Tagaloa lineage—see Tagaloa in Period V, page 31).
- *Sina* marries the TuiManu'a, who finds her walking on the shore.
- *Leatiogie* marries *Tauaiupolu*, daughter of *Ale* of the Toamua hamlet of Faleata, giving birth to the following children, in order (around A.D.1100):
    - *Lealali* (or *LeAlali*),
    - *Sāvea* (the first **Malietoa**),
    - *Tuna,*
    - *Fata,*
    - *Ve'atauia,*
    - *Leimuli,*
    - and a daughter, *Leatiatigielealaiaolõ* (her full name, sometimes shortened to *LeAtiatigie*)[xi]

Lealali and TuiA'ana Lineage to *Funefe'ai* and *Lafai*

A.D.1000

The Lealali family begins around the year A.D.1000.

- TuiA'ana *Pili le So'opili's* union with *Tuamanuleleilemimo* gives birth to *Apa'auula.* (Note, TuiA'ana *Leopili* and *Pilisosolo* are also known as So'opili.)
    - *Apa'auula's* union with *Ufiufi* gives birth to *Lealali.*
        - *Lealali's* union with *Sinalegogo* (daughter of *Leutelelei'ite* of Falefā, Atua, Upolu) gives birth to sons:
            - *Salevaogogo* (who was defeated in a club match by *Leatiogie*, father of the first Malietoa) and
            - *Sausi*
        - *Lealali's* second union, with *Malelegaaleto'elau* (daughter of *Tuisafua* of Iva, Savai'i) gives birth to three sons:
            - *Tupa'imatuna, Tupa'ilelei,* and *Tupa'isiva.*

This is when *Lealali* decrees that *Salevaogogo* and *Sausi* will live in the Leulumoega seat of government of TuiA'ana, becoming the authority of the TuiA'ana title, while *Tupa'imatuna*, *Tupa'ilelei*, and *Tupa'isiva* will remain in Savai'i and become paramount chiefs over all of Savai'i.

A Togan lady called *Laufafaetoga* comes into the story now (see The Sacred Forest of the TuiFiti at Matautu, Savai'i, page 119). She visits and marries *Tupa'imatuna*, and gives birth to:

- *Va'asiliifiti.*

The Lady *Laufafaetoga* also marries a Fijian Chief (not TuiFiti) and bears three sons:

- *Ututauofiti* (of Matautu village/district),
- *Tauaofiti* (of Sataua village/district), and
- *Legaotuitoga* (of Salega village/district).

Then she remarries *Tupa'imatuna* and bears a daughter:

- *Fotuosamoa* (of Safotu village/district)

In the next generation (Period V):

- *Va'asiliifiti* (first son of *Tupa'imatuna* and *Laufafaetoga*) marries *Malelegasavai'i,* giving birth to:
  - *Va'asiliuli.*
- *Va'asiliifiti's* second marriage, to two women from Sagaga and Sale'imoa, Tuamasaga, Upolu, gives birth to:
  - *Funefe'ai* (a son by Lady *Fe'egaga*), and
  - *Laifai* (a son by Lady *Fe'easoa*).

Va'asiliifiti's son *Laifai* is the same *Laifai* (also spelled *Lafai*) who has seven sons to further populate Savai'i (as we will see in Period V). *Lafai's* brother *Funefe'ai* is that same *Funefe'ai* who accepts a crown from *Tagaloalagi* in exchange for the lady *Sinaalāua* who loves him.

Period V: Forging A Nation. Defeating Toga

Events: A.D.1050 - 1500

A.D.1050

This period starts in the time of *Fe'epõ's* children:

- *Fe'epõ's* sons are *Malalatele* (or *Malālatea*) and *Leatiogie* (who is the father of the first Malietoa, thus connecting the Malietoa with *Fe'epõ*); his daughter is *Sina.*
- *Salevaogogo* (who was defeated in a club match by *Leatiogie*, father of the first Malietoa) is decreed to rule over Savai'i ma Sausi, to organize the Leulumoega district.

A.D.1200

- At this time, Samoa defeats Toga in all of Samoa.
- *Tupa'imatuna's* union with *Laufafaetoga* (see previous section) leads to Savai'i Island being populated by people with both Samoan and Fijian genealogy.
- Manu'a's organizational structure is created and decreed.
- *Tagaloalagi* gives his crown to *Funefe'ai* in exchange for *Sinaalāua,* who has fallen in love with *Funefe'ai* in Savai'i Island. This is a pivotal event that begins *Funefe'ai's* inheritance of the Tagaloa title and clan. It also marks the modern human history of the deity *Tagaloalagi*, through his daughter *Sinalagilagi*.
- The brothers *Funefe'ai* and *Laifai* (or *Lafai*), progenitors of the founding families, appear at this time.
- The first Malietoa, Malietoa *Sāvea,* marries the sister of *Fata* and *Maulolo.*

A.D.1300

Now comes the reign of the Malietoafaigā (or Malietoa Faigā *Uilamatūtū*, son of Malietoa *Sāvea*), known as: "He to whom all Samoa listened," *Na Faalogo iai Samoa*.

- This represents a period of resurgence of the Paramount families in Samoa (TuiAtua, TuiA'ana, Malietoa, Laifai, SaMuliaga, Tagaloa-Funefe'ai and others).
- During this period, the acquisition of PāPā (*Ao*) crowns follows wars fought to secure them.
- Warrior Queen *Nafanua* sends war warriors to assist in the war for the TuiAtua, TuiA'ana, Gatoa'itele and Vaetamasoāali'i PāPās.
- Upon her triumph, *Nafanua* keeps the PāPā crowns in her custody for over 30 years.

A.D.1500

Then we come to the landmark period of Samoa's modern history, with the TuiA'ana *Tamālelagi* reign. His last child is *Salamasina*, whose reign marks the founding of the first Tafa'ifa, combining the TuiA'ana, TuiAtua, Gatoa'itele, and Vaetamasoāali'i crowns.

Stories

- *Tagaloa* gives his crown to *Funefe'ai* in order to marry *Sinaalāua* (see The Story of Funefe'ai and Tagaloalagi, page 179).
- The story of *Tagaloa-A'opo* and his house of 100 (see The story of Tagaloa-*A'opo* and the 100 posts, page 182) occurs around this time.
- Tagaloa *Funefe'ai's* great-great-grandson, *Tagaloa-SeFa'atautele* is given the name *Savai'inaea* after swimming to Atua, following a turtle (The legend of *Savai'inaea*, page 182).
- According to legend, *Sina,* daughter of *Fe'epō* and *Leipaleatele*, is taken by TuiManu'a to be his wife when he is on his way back to Manu'a from Savai'i, while she is out fishing on the reef at low tide at Faleata. This marks the first connection of the Malietoa family with TuiManu'a.
- Malietoa *Uitualagi,* son of the Malietoafaigā, falls in love with a princess called *Gasoloaiolelagi,* whose brother, *Manaia,* is a very handsome and popular prince (see The Story of Malietoa *Uitualagi*, page 151).
- The grandsons of La'ulu *Nofovaleane* are raised by giving them exercise in the early morning on flat rocks on the seashore (see The Story of La'ulu *Nofovaleane*, page 191).

People

We will see the beginning of several important family genealogies in this time period:

- Beginning of **Tolufale** genealogy
- Beginning of **Tagaloa-Funefe'ai** genealogy
- Beginning of **Tonumaipe'a**
- Beginning of the **Laifai** genealogy

Tagaloa

A.D.1320

Tagaloalagi's union with *Sinaalāua* (daughter of *Lafaisaotele*), who was in love with *Funefe'ai*, leads to the birth of *Tagaloalagi's* daughter, *Sinalagilagi*:

- *Sinalagilagi's* union with *Malālatea* gives birth to *Lelāpueisalele*, and her blind brother, *Oleāifale'ava* (or *Leāifale'ava*).
    - The blind man *Oleāifale'ava* has three children:
        - *Lea'auta,* his daughter, marries the longhaired warrior *Taemanutava'e* and births:
            - *Va'afuti* (also known as *Va'afa'i*)
            - *Fata*,
            - *Maulolo*, and their sister
            - *Luafatasaga* who marries the first Malietoa *Sāvea.*
        - *Tāoa*, *Oleāifale'ava's* son, becomes the founder of the large district named after him, the district of Tāoa. He is also known as Tagaloa Tāoa and is one of Tagaloa *Funefe'ai's* Eight Orator Chiefs.
        - Another son is *Fāese.*

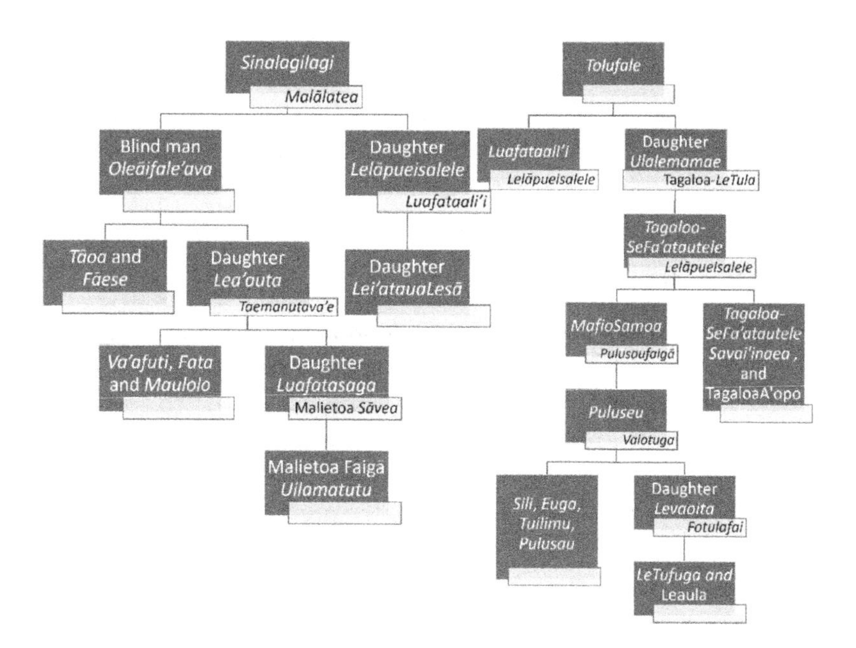

- *Lelāpueisalele* (sister of the blind man) marries *Luafataali'i* (son of *Tolufale*) and bears *Lei'atauaLesā* (who is therefore granddaughter of *Tolufale* and half-sister to *Tolufale's* daughter *Ulalemamae*—see The story of *Lei'atauaLesā*, page 180).
    - *Lei'atauaLesā's* half-sister *Ulalemamae* marries *Tagaloa-LeTula* (grandson of Tagaloa *Funefe'ai*), giving birth to:
        - *Tagaloa-SeFa'atautele,* who marries *Lei'atauaLesā's* mother *Lelāpueisalele*, giving birth to:
            - *Tagaloa-SeFa'atautele Savai'inaea,* and
            - *MafioSamoa,* and:
            - adopting *Tagaloa-A'opo* (known, as we have seen, for his house of 100 posts).
- So... as above, we find *Lelāpueisalele's* second marriage is to *Tagaloa-SeFa'atautele* (son of her daughter's half-sister *Ulalemamae*) giving birth to *Tagaloa-SeFa'atautele Savai'inaea* and his sister *MafioSamoa.* So *MafioSamoa* is *Lei'atauaLesā's* half-sister and the granddaughter of *Lei'atauaLesā's* other half-sister.
    - *MafioSamoa* marries *Pulusaufaigā* of Salelologa, giving birth to:
        - *Puluseu,* who is now the son of the half-sister of the first *Lei'atauaLesā* of Manono. *Puluseu* marries a lady from Salelologa, who bears *Pulusau*.
            - *Pulusau* marries *Vaiotuga*, daughter of TuiAtua *To'otuna,* who gives birth to *Sili*, *Euga*, *Tuilimu*, and a daughter *Levaoita.*
                - *Levaoita* marries *Fotulafai,* giving birth to *LeTufuga* and *Leaula*, who become the authorities of Savai'i Island.

- *Sinalagilagi's* second marriage, to *Avaletaua,* bears:
  - *Vinileo'o* who marries *Maugafa'asala*, giving birth to a daughter, *Sa'amõ* who marries *Peseito'elau,* and bears a daughter *Mimisapu'a* and a son *Folasāle'i'ite.*
    - *Folasāle'i'ite* (*Folasā* the Prophet), is named after *Folasā* of Fitiuta, Manu'a, the Peacemaker and head of the TuiManu'a ava ceremony, who, according to Manu'an legend, came from heaven with the ava from *Tagaloalagi's* council. *Folasāle'i'ite's* daughter is:
      - *Leutogitui*, who marries to *Fa'asega*, the son of TuiUēa (the king of Uēa, Wallis Island, west of Savai'i) and the prodigious *Leutogitupa'itea* (see the Tonumaipe'a lineage, page 44). Through this marriage, Orator Chief *Folasāle'i'ite* of Falelima, Savai'i, is decreed to be the first holder and authority of the office confirming the title Tonumaipe'a for the Tonumaipe'a family clan.
    - *Folasāle'i'ite's* sister, *Mimisapu'a*, marries Prince *Latuivai*, the son of *Nafanua* (*Suaifanua*) and TuiToga *Manaia* (see Tonumaipe'a, page 44) bearing:
      - *Faletapa'au* and
      - a daughter *Taigalugalu* who marries Lilomaiava *Seve* of Safotu, Savai'i, becoming the ancestor of the Tonumaipe'a family clan.
- *Sinalagilagi's* third marriage is to *So'oialo* (or *So'oalo* according to Dr. Krämer), the son of Lady *Fotuosamoa*—the founder of Safotu village in Savai'i—and *To'alepai* of Matautu, Savai'i. They produce a daughter *Fetui*.
  - Lady *Fetui* will be the ancestor of *Taupõimasina,* who marries TuiToga *Fa'aulufanua*. They give birth to:
    - *Vaetoifaga* who marries TuiA'ana *Tamālelagi*, giving birth to:
      - Tafa'ifa *Salamasina*.

Since *Tagaloalagi* gave his crown to *Funefe'ai* in order to marry *Sinaalāua*, the Tagaloa lineage properly continues from *Funefe'ai:*

A.D.1320

The union of *Va'asiliifiti* and *Lefe'egaga* of Sagaga, Upolu, begets:

- *Funefe'ai* whose first marriage (**A.D.1350**) to *Tetoafaigā* (from Vaisa'ulu and Vaiafai villages, in Iva, Savai'i) begets:
    - *Tagaloa-Ega* whose union (**A.D.1380**) with *Lanuopouli* of Sili, Savai'i, begets *Tagaloa-LeTula* and *Tagaloa-A'opo* (with his house of 100 in A'opo, Savai'i, adopted by *Tagaloa-SeFa'atautele*).
        - **A.D.1410** *Tagaloa-LeTula*'s marriage to *Ulalemamae* (daughter of *Luafataali'i* of Manono Island, and half-sister, as we have just seen, to *Lei'atauaLesā*, granddaughter of *Tolufale*) begets:
            - *Tagaloa-SeFa'atautele* who, as we have seen, marries *Lelāpueisalele* (mother of his mother's half-sister, *Lei'atauaLesā*—we should remember, *Lelāpueisalele* is the daughter of *Malalatele—Malālatea*—and *Sinalagilagi*, the daughter of *Tagaloalagi* and *Sinaalāua*). Their union gives birth to:
                - *Tagaloa-SeFa'atautele Savai'inaea*
                - and *MafioSamoa,*
                - and they adopt *Tagaloa-A'opo* (brother of *Tagaloa-SeFa'atautele's* grandfather).
- *Funefe'ai's* second marriage, to *Tauanu'ufaigā* (daughter of *Tuliaupupu* of Letogo) begets a daughter:
    - *Utufa'asili*

A.D.1440

The first marriage of *Tagaloa-SeFa'atautele* (or *Fa'atautele*), to *Lelāpueisalele* (sister of the blind man, and daughter of *Malālatea* and *Sinalagilagi* of Tagaloalagi) begets, as we have seen:

- A son called *Tagaloa-SeFa'atautele Savai'inaea,* and
- a daughter, *MafioSamoa*, who is the grandmother of:

- *Leaula*,
- *LeTufuga*, (*LeTufuga* and *Leaula* will be seen again in the family of *Lafai*)
- *Saleaula*, and
- *Safotulafai*

Tagaloa-SeFa'atautele's second marriage, to *Tu'umoega* from Sili, Savai'i begets:

- *Fa'aolatane* and
- Tagaloa *Fa'aofonu'u*

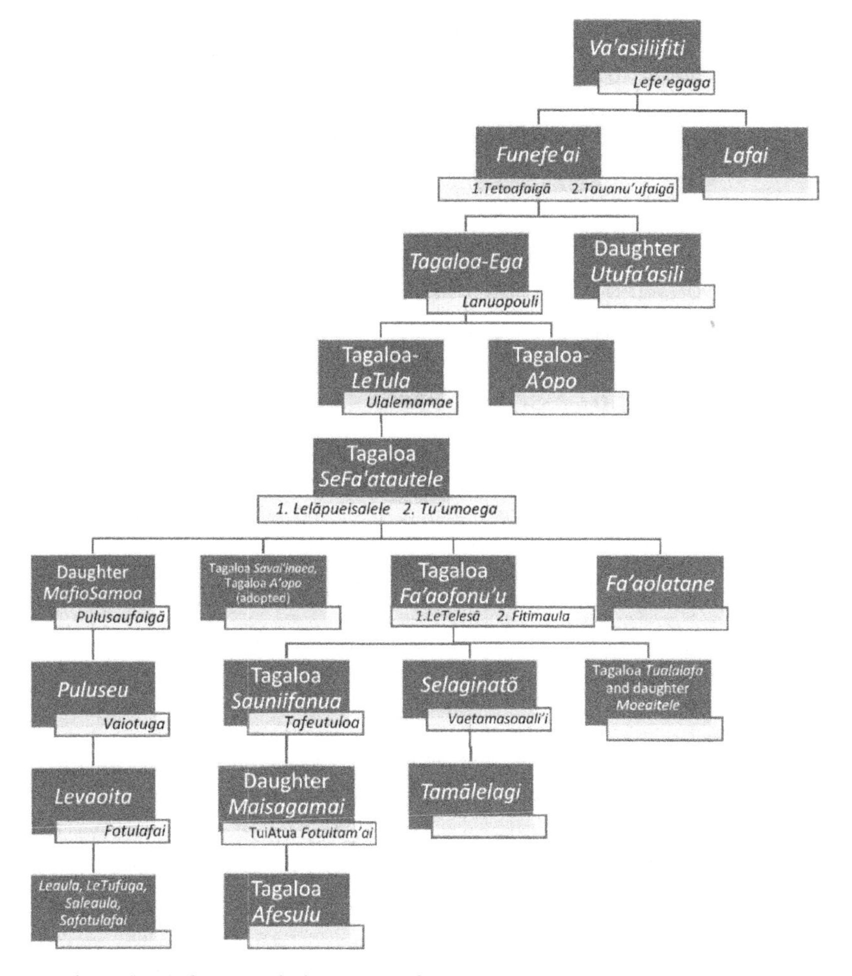

Tagaloa-SeFa'atautele's son (Tagaloa *Funefe'ai's* great-great-grandson), *Tagaloa-SeFa'atautele* (called *Savai'inaea* after swimming to Atua, following a turtle—see The legend of

Savai'inae, page 182), marries a lady in Falefa village, giving rise to the family there Alai'asā (the Path of the Turtle). Then he marries a lady in Lotofaga, Atua, of SaLeValasi clan. And then he marries the daughter of Chief *Leota* in Solosolo village. Thus he has children in the TuiAtua genealogy at Atua, Upolu.

A.D.1470

Tagaloa *Fa'aofonu'u*'s first marriage to *LeTelesā* of Faleata (this is also the name of *Faumuinā's* daughter) begets:

- Tagaloa *Sauniifanua,* whose marriage (**A.D.1500**) to *Tafeutuloa* begets a daughter:
    - *Maisagamai*, whose marriage (**A.D.1530**) to TuiAtua *Fotuitam'ai* begets:
        - Tagaloa *Afesulu* whose union (**A.D.1560**) with *Oloitoa* (daughter of TuiToga) begets the daughters:
            - *Fatumiti* and *Tala'i*

Tagaloa *Fa'aofonu'u*'s second marriage, to *Fitimaula* (daughter of *LeTufuga* of SaFotulafai—see Period IV TuiA'ana, page 22—many of these dates are approximate) begets:

- *Selaginatõ* (who marries *Vaetamasoāali'i* giving birth to TuiA'ana *Tamālelagi),*
- Tagaloa *Tualalafa*,
- and a daughter *Moeaitele.*

A.D.1590

The first marriage of *Fatumiti* (above, great-granddaughter of Tagaloa *Sauniifanua* and daughter of Tagaloa *Afesulu* and *Oloitoa*), to *Tanuvasavasamanaia* of Mulifanua, begets:

- *Taito*, and
- *Tumanuvao.*

Fatumiti's second marriage, to Malietoa *Taulapapa* of Solosolo, Atua begets a daughter *Iliganoa Taulalo'ese* and a son *To'omata*:

- *Iliganoa Taulalo'ese* is the Sa'o aualuma (*Sa'o* of the aualuma or the Tagaloa family of Savai'i, also referred to as the Sa'o Tama'ita'i). She marries *Tupuivao*, *Taufau's* son who is disinherited from the TuiAtua and TuiA'ana titles.
- *To'omata's* union (**A.D.1620**) with *Tofoipupū* (daughter of *Ta'uo* of Gautavai) begets *Amituana'i.*

- *Amituana'i* marries *Tinaitaala,* daughter of *Tuigona*, and bears:
    - *Leotatoga* who marries *Oilau,* daughter of *Fanene* giving birth to:
        - *Lealamanu'a Aumoegalogo*, who marries *Lagi* giving birth to *Lealamanu'a*, ancestor of current Tagaloa clan, which means his genealogy carries the Tagaloa lineage to today.
- *Amituana'i's* marriage to *Fa'aautatanu*, daughter of *Tago* of Amaile, Atua district, begets a daughter:
    - *Poto,* who marries *Letamaaleāitumaletagata* begetting:
        - *Leleisi'uao* of Palauli,
        - And his sister Samalaulu *Taneilemasina.*

Malietoa

A.D.1000

The Malietoa version of the clan's history starts with *Pilia'au's* union with *Sinaaletava'e*, leading to connections with the founders of TuiA'ana, TuiAtua, Tuamasaga and Tolufale families. As we saw in the early Period II TuiAtua, page 10:

- Around A.D.1, the union of *Pilia'au* and *Sinaaletava'e* (daughter of TuiA'ana) begets:
    - *Tua* (gifted with the digging pole for planting),
    - *Ana* (gifted with the spear/club, war warrior),
    - *Tuamasaga* (He stands between the twin brothers. Decreed with the orator's staff and flail as the Mediator)
    - *Tolufale* (the supplier of the war troops), and
    - *Siumu Munanitama* (assistant of war).
- *Ana's* union with *Sinalemana* gives birth to:
    - *Matofaoa'ana* and
    - *Moaoa'ana.*
- *Matofaoa'ana's* union with *Sinaletula* gives birth to:
    - *Veta*, whose marriage to *Afulilo* gives birth to:
        - *Tuiveta*, whose union with *Toelauo'o* births:
            - *Toso*, whose union with *Titilagipupula* daughter of TuiManu'a gives birth to:
                - *Si'usei'a.*

In this version:

- *Si'usei'a* marries *Tapalemalama* (*Tapa-le-malama*, meaning reach for the light) of Faleata who births *Si'utaulalovasa* (*Si'u-tau-lalo-vasa*, meaning tail-hit-bottom-ocean or a tail that hits the bottom of the ocean).
    - *Si'utaulalovasa* marries *Lulai* and *Lulago*, though one is carrying the child of *Tupa'isafe'e*. They give birth to *To'o* and *Ata.*
        - *Ata* marries *Fa'auliUmi* who bears *Si'ufe'ai* and *Tafa'igata,* and *Si'ufe'ai* is the grandfather of *Fe'epõ*, progenitor of **Malietoa** clan.
            - *Fe'epõ* marries *Leipaleatele,* daughter of *Niu* of Afolau village, A'ana, giving birth to:
                - *Malālatea or Malalatele,*
                - *Leatiogie*, and
                - *Sina,* who marries TuiManu'a—This marks the first connection of the Malietoa family with TuiManu'a.
        - *Ata* marries a Togan princess who bears *Patauave*, who becomes a Senior Chief in Faleata.
            - *Patauave* marries a lady from *Vaitele who* births **Matai'a** and his sister *Tofili.*

A.D.1100

Leatiogie, son of *Fe'epõ*, fathers six sons, *Sāvea, Fata, Tuna, Lealali, Leimuli, Ve'atauia,* and a daughter *Leatiatigielealaiaolõ* (or *LeAtiatigie*), with his wife *Tauaiupolu.* The first Malietoa is Malietoa *Sāveatuvaelua* (or Malietoa *Sāvea*, son of *Leatiogie*).

A.D.1200

- Malietoa *Sāvea's* first marriage produces a son:
    - Malietoa *Gagasāvea,* who marries Princess *Pate* of the TuiToga, residing in Vaimauga district, Tuamasaga, Upolu. They have six sons: *Seupule*, *Toagana* and *Nu'uiali'i*, *Luatua*, *Sāveatama* and *Fuataogana*. These are jointly called the *Leatigaga* or *Sagaga*.
- Malietoa *Sāvea's* second marriage, to *Luafatasaga*—the daughter of the long-haired warrior *Taemanutava'e,* and the

sister of *Fata, Maulolo* and *Va'afuti* (*Va'afa'i*)—produces a son *Uilamatūtū* (lightning without rain) who becomes the Malietoafaigā *Uilamatūtū.*

At this time, *Fata* and *Maulolo*, brothers of *Luafatasaga*, are appointed by decree to be the leaders (known as *Faleta'ita'i* or the House of Authority) of the Malietoa Vanguard Warrior clan of Afega and Tuana'i villages (see The Importance of *Fata* and *Maulolo*, page 148).

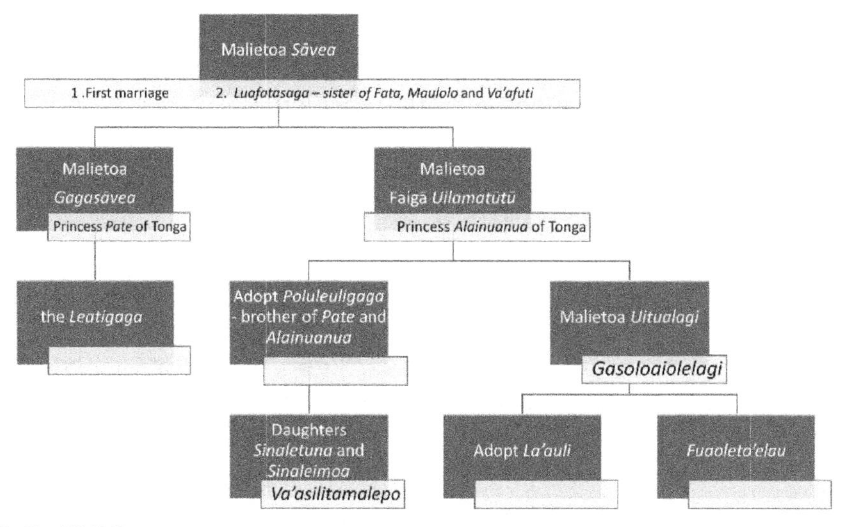

A.D.1300

- Malietoafaigā *Uilamatūtū,* marries Princess *Alainuanua*, sister to Princess *Pate* (above) who is married to his half-brother Malietoa *Gagasāvea.* They have a son, Malietoa *Uitualagi*, and adopt *Poluleuligaga*, the son of TuiToga *'Ulufanuatele* (the brother of *Pate* and *Alainuanua*).
    - *Poluleuligaga* (also called the original *Luatua*, while the second *Luatua,* listed above, is the son of Malietoa *Gagasāvea*) has daughters:
        - *Sinaletuna* and *Sinaleimoa*, who marry *Va'asilitamalepo*, the son of *Laifai.*
    - Malietoa *Uitualagi* marries *Gasoloaiolelagi* giving birth to:
        - *Fuaoleto'elau*
        - and adopting *La'auli.*

- Malietoa *Sāvea's* sister *LeAtiatigie* marries Tagaloa *i Pata* of Pata hamlet, Falelatai village, A'ana, Upolu.

La'auli, the adopted son of Malietoa *Uitualagi,* becomes Malietoa *La'auli.*

- *La'auli* marries *Gauifaleai* and her sister *Totogatā*, giving birth to the two sisters *Gatoa'itele* and *Gasolo-ai-ao-o-le-lagi.*
    - *Gatoa'itele* marries *LeSanalāla,* giving birth to:
        - A son, *Lalovimāmā*, who marries TuiAtua *Togiai Sefa'ataulemauga*, the daughter of TuiAtua, and begets:
            - TuiAtua *Mata'utia* (or *Fa'atulou*),
        - a daughter, *Vaetamasoāali'i*,
        - and a daughter, *LeAtougaugaatuitoga,* who marries Tonumaipe'a *Sauoāiga* (**A.D.1440**), giving birth to:
            - *Tauiliili,*
            - *Tupa'ivaililigi* (War messenger of the goddess *Nafanua*), and
            - a daughter *LeValasi* who marries her first cousin (her uncle *Lalovimāmā's* son) TuiAtua *Mata'utia Fa'atulou,* and cares for her niece *Salamasina.*

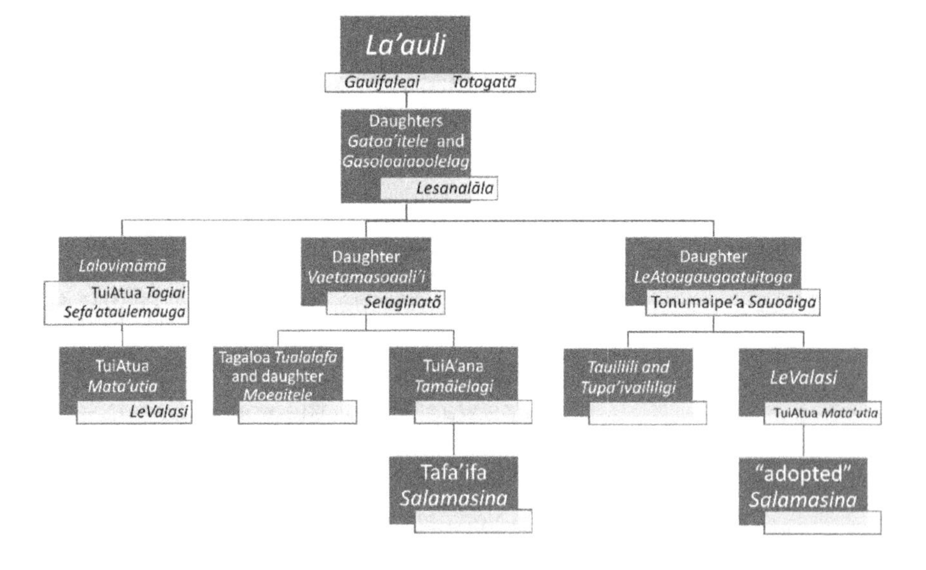

Thus, reading these lineages, we see how *Tagaloalagi*, the demigod (half human half spirit), continues his genealogy across Samoa and Manu'a, and how the Malietoa clan connects their genealogy to Pilia'au and TuiManu'a.

Laifai

Laifai and *Funefe'ai* are the sons of *Va'asiliifiti's* second marriage, to two women from Sagaga and Sale'imoa, Tuamasaga, Upolu—see Lealali and TuiA'ana Lineage to *Funefe'ai* and *Lafai*, page 27.

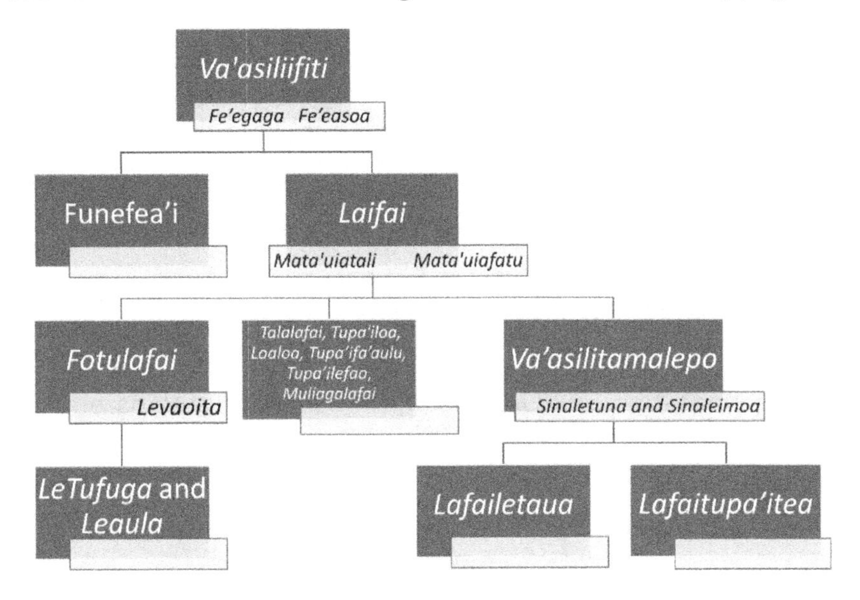

A.D.1320

Laifai marries *Mata'uiatali* and has seven sons.

1. *Fotulafai* who was the founder of the eponymous village or District of **SaFotulafai** (*Sa* means family or clan of),
2. *Talalafai* who founded **Iva**,
3. *Tupa'iloa* who founded **Falealupo**,
4. *Loaloa* who founded **Safe'e**,
5. *Tupa'ifa'aulu* who founded **Neiafu**,
6. *Tupa'ilefao* who founded **Asau**,
7. and *Muliagalafai* founded **SaMuliaga**.

Laifai's second marriage, to his sister-in-law, *Mata'uiafatu*, begets:

- *Va'asilitamalepo*, "a boy born in the dark," who marries two sisters, *Sinaletuna* and *Sinaleimoa*, daughters of *Poluleuligaga* (son of the king of Toga, adopted—see previous section—by the Malietoafaigā) from Saleimoa. They give birth to:

- *Lafailetaua*, the founder of Palauli, and
- *Lafaitupa'itea*, the founder of **Tupa'itea**, who marries a young lady from Upolu, giving birth to:
    - *Tevalefua*, who marries (around **A.D.1440**) *Pipilimatualimausaga* from Falealili, birthing:
        - *Muliagalapaitagata* and
        - *Muliagalapaiaitu.*

A.D.1440

Laifai's oldest son, *Fotulafai*, the founder of SaFotulafai, marries *Levaoita*, who is the daughter of *Pulusau* (who is descended from *Lelāpueisalele,* while the Malietoa family is descended from *Lelāpueisalele's* brother, the blind man *Oleāifale'ava*), and they beget:

- *LeTufuga* and
- *Leaula*, the founder of **SaLeaula**.

LeTufuga and *Leaula* are later decreed to be the authority of Savai'i, Island. We saw them earlier the Tagaloa lineage.

Laifai's youngest son is *Muliagalafai*, the founder of the paramount family **SaMuliaga**.

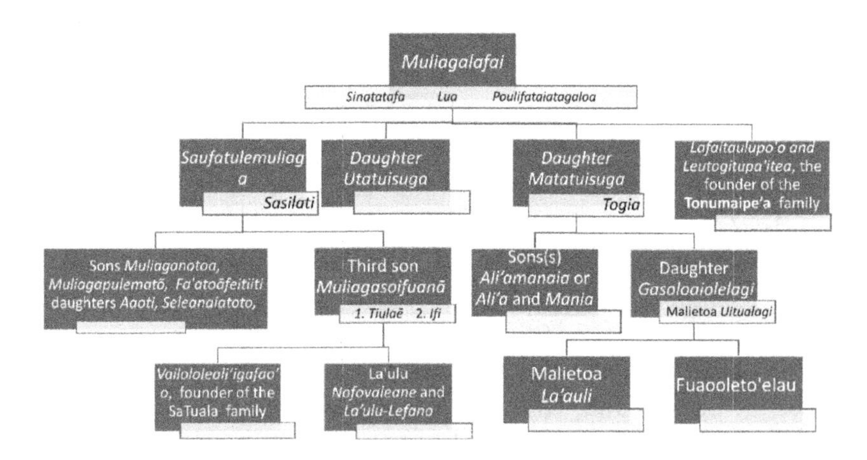

- *Muliagalafai* marries *Sinatatafa* of Iva, giving birth to:
    - *Saufatu-le-Muliaga,* whose union with *Sasilati* of the village Tufu Gataivai begets children:
        - *Muliaganotoa*,

  - *Muliagapulematõ*,
  - *Muliagasoifuanā*,
  - two daughters, *Aaoti* and *Seleanaiatoto,*
  - and *Muliagafa'atoāfe-iti-iti* (or *Muliagafa'atoāfeitiiti*), also known as *Fa'atoāfeitiiti*.

- Later *Muliagalafai* marries *Lua* of from Vaimauga, Upolu (Krämer has this as his third marriage), and begets:
  - daughters, *Uta-tui-suga* and
  - *Mata-tui-suga*, who marries *Togia* of Tifitifi in the Faleata district, Upolu. They give birth to:
    - sons *Ali'a* and *Manaia* (or one son, *Ali'amanaia*—see Stories of SaMuliagalafai, page 189),
    - and a daughter, *Gasolo-ai-o-le-lagi*, who marries Malietoa *Uitualagi*, bearing:
      - Malietoa *La'auli* and
      - *Fuaoleto'elau* (or *Fuao-le-to'elau*). The union of *Gasolo-ai-o-le-lagi* and Malietoa *Uitualagi* connects the SaMuliaga and the Malietoa clan.
- *Muliagalafai* later marries his third wife (or second according to Krämer), *Poulifataiatagaloa*, daughter of *TuiAsau* (or *LeTuiAsau—Funefe'ai's* descendant). They beget:
  - *Lafaitaupo'o* and
  - a daughter, *Leutogitupa'itea*, who is the progenitor of **Tonumaipe'a** dynasty. It is at this point that the royal constellation of the Lafai family history moves toward the first consolidated queen of Samoa, *Salamasina*.

Laifai's great-grandson *Muliagasoifuanā*, *Saufatulemuliaga's* third son, marries *Tiulaē* of Savai'i and begets:

- *Vailololeali'igafao'o*, the founder of the **SaTuala** family.

Muliagasoifuanā later marries *Ifi*, the daughter of *LuaAtua*, and begets *La'ulu-Nofovaleane* and *La'ulu-Lefano*.

- *La'ulu-Nofovaleane's* first marriage, to *Fuli-sia-i-lagi-tele* (*Fulisiailagitele*), daughter of *Tu'uma'ai* from SaFotulafai, begets a daughter:
    - *Tuaetali* who begets a son,
        - *Tapumanaia*.
- *La'ulu-Nofovaleane's* second marriage, with *Lefa'aanāpulu*, daughter of *Pulusau* of Saleloga begets a daughter:
    - *Fa'atupuigati* who begets a son,
        - *Pesefeamanaia*.
- *La'ulu-Nofovaleane's* third marriage, to *Pouliotaua*, daughter of *Tu'u* of Safune, begets a daughter:
    - *Maupenei* who begets a son,
        - *Aumoana, whose* genealogy becomes the origin of the **Tupuivao**, **Mata'afa**, and **SaLeValasi** families.

Tonumaipe'a

A.D.1200

The genealogy of the two warrior brothers *Funefe'ai* and *Laifai* is reunited in the marriage of *Poulifataiatagaloa* (daughter of Tagaloa *Funefe'ai's* orator chief) and *LeMuliaga* (*Laifai's* youngest son *Muliagalafai*) as we shall see here:

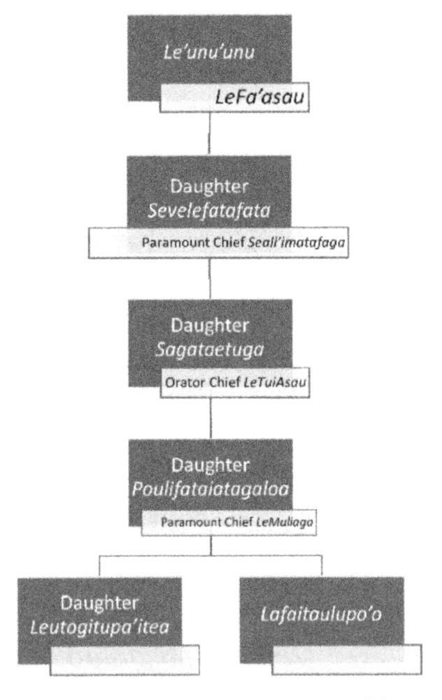

LeFa'asau marries *Le'unu'unu* and births a girl:

- *Sevelefatafata* who marries Paramount Chief *Seali'imatafaga* and bears a girl:
    - *Sagataetuga* who marries *LeTuiAsau* (Orator Chief of LeTagaloa *Funefe'ai* in Asau village, Savai'i) and bears a daughter:

- *Poulifataiatagaloa* whose union with Paramount Chief *LeMuliaga* (*Muliagalafai*, progenitor of the SaMuliaga or SaLeMuliaga clan) births:
  - A daughter *Leutogitupa'itea* and
  - her brother *Lafaitaulupo'o* who is the great-grandfather of the first Tonumaipe'a *Sauoāiga*

Then *Leutogitupa'itea's* union with the TuiUēa births a son:

- *Fa'asega,* who marries *Leutogitui*, daughter of Paramount Chief *LeFolasā* of Falelima, Savai'i, giving birth to a daughter:
  - *Finetele* who is an ancestor of Princess *Tuaetali*, daughter of La'ulu *Nofovaleane*.

At this point we should note the genealogy of *Saveasi'uleo* and his brother *Ulufanuasese'e*, as they combine with the Tonumaipe'a lineage.

A.D.1200

The union of *Ulufanuasese'e* and Tagaloa *i Pata* of Falelatai village births the boys:

- *Aveautetele* and *Fa'alualuatele.*

The union of *Ulufanuasese'e* and *Sinalalofutu-i-Fagaiofu* births the conjoined twin girls:

- *Taemā* and *Tilafaigā* (or *Taematilafaigā*).

The union of *Ulufanuasese'e's* brother *Saveasi'uleo* and his niece, *Tilafaigā* (also called *Pi'ilua,* daughter of *Ulufanuasese'e*) begets the daughter:

- *Nafanua* (the warrior queen), also called *Suaifanua,* whose union (**A.D.1230**) with TuiToga *Manaia* begets:
  - *Latuivai* whose union (**A.D.1260**) with *Mimisapu'a* of Fai'a'ai begets:
    - *Faletapa'au* and his sister
    - *Taigalugalu,* whose union (**A.D.1290**) with *Lilomaiava Seve* of Safotu begets a daughter:
      - *Foalo* whose union (**A.D.1320**) with *Lologavivao* of Samata, Savai'i begets a daughter:

- *Maisina* whose union with *LeFouafa'asani* of Tuamasaga (**A.D.1350**) begets the sisters *Masu* and *Leanui.*

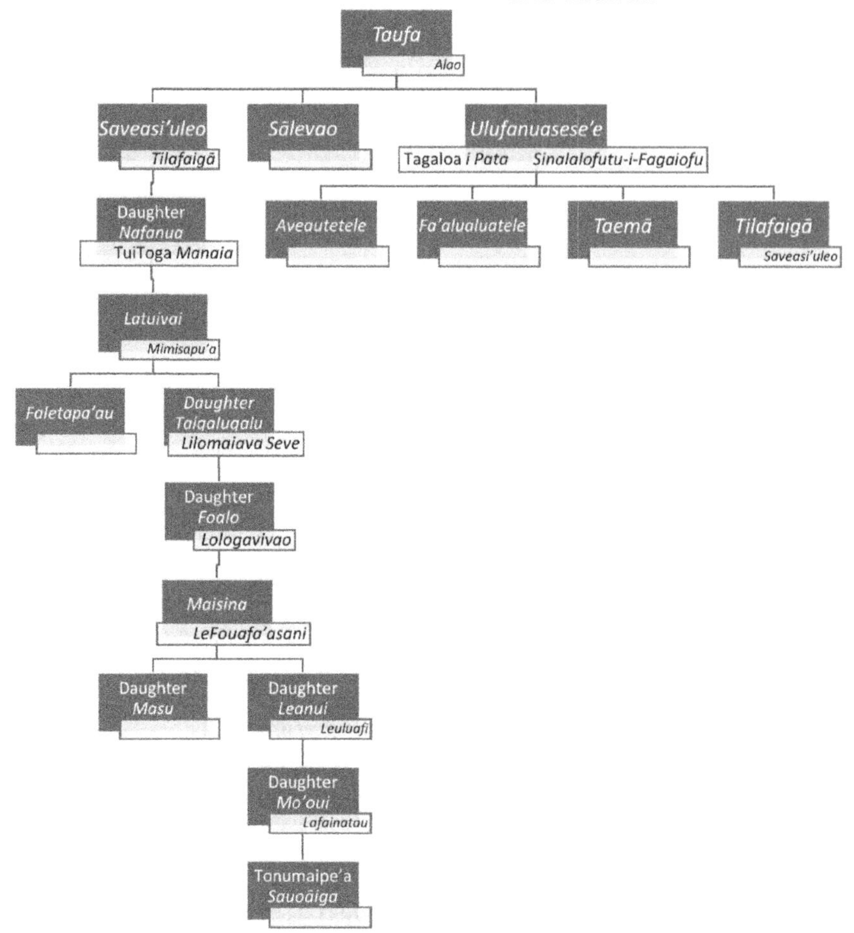

A.D.1380

Leanui (above) marries *Leuluafi* of Fogasavai'i and begets a daughter:

- *Mo'oui* whose union (**A.D.1410**) with *Lafainatau* from Palauli (grandson of *Lafaitaulupo'o* of SaMuliaga) begets:
    - *Le Sauoāiga* (Tonumaipe'a *Sauoāiga*).

A.D.1440

The union of Tonumaipe'a *Sauoāiga* and *LeAtougaugaatuitoga* (daughter of *LeSanalāla* and *Gatoa'itele* of Malietoa) begets:

- *Tauiliili* (also known as *Ali'i o Aiga*),
- *Tupa'ivaililigi* (War messenger of the goddess Nafanua,) and
- a daughter *LeValasi* (also known as So'oa'emalelagi *i Vaitapu i Leulumoega*).

A.D.1470

Tauiliili's first marriage, to *Liutogitui* (daughter of *Tuifa'asisina* of Satapuala, Upolu), begets:

- *Saumaipe'a* (LeTonumaipe'a *Saumaipe'a*)
- and a daughter, *Valasi i Ologa.*

His second marriage, to So'oa'emalelagi (daughter of TuiA'ana *Vaemā*), begets a daughter:

- So'oa'emalelagi.

His third marriage, to *Moeleoi* (daughter of *TuiSamoa* of Falealili), begets:

- *Ali'imalemanu*,
- and a daughter *Tu'ua'uatō.*

A.D.1500

LeTonumaipe'a *Saumaipe'a*'s first marriage, to *Tuaetali* (daughter of La'ulu *Nofovaleane* of SaMuliaga), begets:

- *Tapumanaia,* whose marriage (**A.D.1530**) with *Salamasina* Queen of Samoa begets:
  - a son, who is kidnapped at birth (named *LeSatele*), and
  - a daughter *Fofoaivao'ese.*

His second marriage, to *Sivalavala* (daughter of *Anafili* of Salailua, Savai'i), begets:

- A daughter *Uati,* and
- a son Tagaloa *Tō.*

Period VI: TuiA'ana *Tamālelagi* and the Tafa'ifa

Events: A.D.1530 – 1830

A.D.1530

- This is the time of TuiA'ana *Tamālelagi's* Children.
- TuiAtua *Mata'utia Fa'atulou* marries his cousin *LeValasi* (a story told in Morning of the Edict of the Forest, proclaimed between TuiSamoa *Nonumaifele* and *Li'amanaia*—this story is given in Volume I of this work: *Navigators Forging a Matriarchal Culture in Polynesia*).
- *Salamasina* enters the story, daughter of *Tamālelagi,* adopted by *LeValasi.*
- *Asomua* and *Tapusalaia Tauaituatasolo* appear here (their story is told in the Morning of The Decree in the period of Tiumalumalilomaiava *Tumailagi*, also told in Volume I of this work).
- Malietoa *Taulapapa* is too late to receive a title gift from Warrior Queen *Nafanua.*
- Tauiliili *i Papa* appears around this time,
- as does Malietoa *Tuilaepa* (remembered in the Morning of the parting decree at Falepunaoa),
- and the famous ladies *Taetelelēmā, Taeteleligivale* and *Taetelelagolasi*, ancestors of many famous families.

A.D.1600

This is the period of the Samoan Civil War caused by the TuiA'ana TuiAtua *Faumuinā*:

- TuiAtua TuiA'ana *Faumuinā* takes the place of
- *Tupuivao,* only son of TuiA'ana TuiAtua *Taufau,* who is disinherited.
- Tafa'ifa *Fonotī, Faumuinā's* son, is victorious in the Samoan Civil War.
- Another son, *Va'afusuaga,* and his son *Toleafoa,* are defeated.
- *Samalaulu,* daughter of *Faumuinā* is also defeated.

A.D.1680

Now we have the birth of Tafa'ifa *Muagututi'a* (son of Tafa'ifa *Fonotī*), who is followed (around **A.D.1710**) by Tafa'ifa *Tupua*

Fuiavailili (fulfilling *Salamasina's* deathbed pronouncement to remember the stolen child—see Salamasina's Children, page 203) and sons (from **A.D.1740**). He is followed by:

- *Afoafouvale*
- Tafa'ifa *Galumalemana* (son of *Tupua*)
- *Luafalemana*
- *Tautisusua*
- *Tufugatasi*

A.D.1700

This royal reign is defined by the first Tafa'ifa Tupua *Fuiavailili* of the male line of the Tafa'ifa *Salamasina* genealogy, the emergence of the **SaTupua** Dynasty, and the fulfillment of Tafa'ifa *Salamasina's* wishes and parting words of farewell to the **SaLevalasi** family and her children's children (remembered in the Morning of Tafa'ifa *Salamasina's* Deathbed Pronouncement).

- Tafa'ifa *Muagututi'a* marries *Fenunuivao*, daughter of Paramount Chief *Leutelelei'ite* of Falefā, Atua, and younger (much younger) sister to Princess *Fenunuivao Sailau*, of the **SaFenunuivao** family.
- Tafa'ifa *Muagututi'a* and Lady *Fenunuivao* are not able to have children. So *Muagututi'a* asks his wife about the possibility of adoption. They go to her sister's family, to Paramount Chief *Fuimaono*, to ask about adopting his son, his only child Tupua *Fuiavailili*, because *Fuimaono* is the only son of *Sifuiva*, the only son of *Tapumanaia*-III and Lady *Fenunuivao Sailau*—see *Muagututi'a*, page 216.
- So the female line of the Tafa'ifa is handed to the (male) *Tapumanaia*-II line.

A.D.1710

Tafa'ifa Tupua *Fuiavailili* reigns. His reign is smooth with no major conflict.

A.D.1740

Tafa'ifa *Galumalemana*, second son of Tafa'ifa Tupua *Fuiavailili*. wins the Tafa'ifa from his older brother *Afoafouvale*. *Afoafouvale* is elevated to the Tafa'ifa, but jealousy of his younger brother *Galumalemana*, leading to having to go to war with *Galumalemana*, means he unfortunately he loses his kingdom. Simply put, the women rave over *Galumalemana* and not over

Tafa'ifa *Afoafouvale*, and for that he loses the war and thus loses the kingdom. *Galumalemana* has five marriages and about 14 children.

A.D.1800
Tafa'ifa *I'amafana* is the young son of Tafa'ifa *Galumalemana*, and *Galumalemana* decrees *I'amafana* to succeed him. After *Galumalemana* dies, his older son, *Nofoasāefā* (ancestor of *Tamasese*), immediately goes to claim the TuiA'ana title, followed by claiming the TuiAtua title, defeating his cousin Mata'afa *Fa'asuamaleui*. He is on his way to Savai'i to claim the Tonumaipe'a title when he is assassinated at Asau village in Savai'i for his cruelty and practice of cannibalism. Thus, *I'amafana*, the son that *Galumalemana* decreed to succeed him, becomes Tafa'ifa. His is a relatively peaceful Tafa'ifa and, on his visit with family in Sapapali'i, with Malietoa *Fitisemanū*, he ends up decreeing the Tafa'ifa to Malietoa *Vaiinupō*, son of Malietoa *Fitisemanū*.

A.D.1830
Tafa'ifa Malietoa *Vaiinupō* is fighting a war with A'ana district, wrestling for the TuiA'ana title to add to the Gatoa'itele and Vaetamasoāali'i titles (TuiAtua was secured in 1835), thus legitimizing his Tafa'ifa. The ship carrying the "Message of Peace," with the missionaries led by John Williams and company, drops anchor in Sapapali'i, Savai'i. *Taimalelagi*, brother of *Vaiinupō*, sends word to Malietoa *Vaiinupō* in A'ana to come, as he has guests from the outside world to meet with him.

People

Children of *Tamālelagi*

A.D.1530
TuiA'ana *Tamālelagi* (father of Tafa'ifa *Salamasina*) has many wives and children.

1. TuiA'ana *Tamālelagi's* first marriage is to *Namoaa'itele,* daughter of *Folasāitu* from Faleata, who bears a son *Tuala*, the founder of the eponymous **Tuala** family, known as Āiga **SaTuala**, which is one of the largest families in Samoa.
2. His second marriage is to *Gese*, the daughter of *Malufau* of Lauli'i, Upolu, and results in a son *Malufau*.

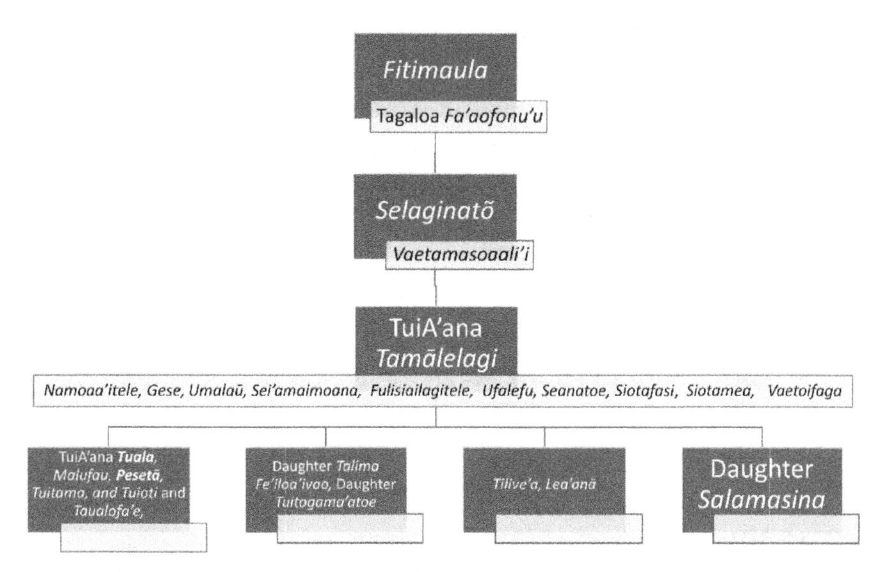

3. His third marriage, to *Umalaū*, daughter of Lilomaiava *Seve* of Safotu, Savai'i, also gives rise to a son, ***Pesetā***. According to Bülow,[xii] *Umalaū's* mother, Lady *Se-ana-toe* is a daughter of Lilomaiava *Seve* and *Fa'atupuigati*, daughter of *La'ulu-Nofovaleane. Seanae* is adopted by her uncle *La'ululolopõ* (her mother's brother) and becomes TuiA'ana *Tamālelagi's* seventh wife.
4. His fourth marriage, to *Sei'amaimoana* (also called *Seiomana*, *Vaovasa's* daughter from Faleasi'u, or *Si'usei'a*) gives birth to another son *Tuitama*.
5. His fifth marriage is to *Fulisiailagitele*, daughter of *Tu'uma'ai* of SaFotulafai, Savai'i. They have two sons, *Tuioti* and *Taualofa'e.*
6. His sixth marriage is to *Ufalefu,* daughter of *Talima* of Faleatiu, Upolu, and gives birth to a daughter, *Talima Fe'iloa'ivao*.
7. His seventh marriage, to *Seanatoe* (or *Seanae*) daughter of *La'ululolopõ* of Gaga'emalae, Savai'i, gives birth to the first daughter, *Tuitogama'atoe*. *Tuitogama'atoe* carries the Gatoa'itele and Malietoa genealogy to modern times, beginning with Malietoa *Taulapapa* and his sister *Sinalemanaui*, down to and through Tafa'ifa *Vaiinupõ*. The Gatoa'itele genealogy is carried down by *Sinalemanaui*, the female lineage, down to the Saena clan and Fata and Maulolo and Tuisamau. *Taulapapa* inherited the Malietoa title, and *Sinalemanaui* inherited the Gatoa'itele Pāpā, the Saena, Fata and Maulolo, and Tuisamau

genealogy. Tafa'ifa Malietoa *Vaiinupõ* receives Christianity in 1830, and the genealogy continues through subsequent title-holders until the late Malietoa who reigns from 1938 to 2008.

8. TuiA'ana *Tamālelagi's* eighth marriage, to *Siotafasi*, daughter of *Puni* of Samatau, Upolu, begets a son, *Tilive'a*.
9. His ninth marriage, to *Puni's* other daughter, *Siotamea*, brings forth another son, *Lea'anā*.
10. And his tenth marriage, to *Vaetoifaga,* daughter of the King of Toga, brings forth *Salamasina.*

So the **Tuala** and **SaTuala** family genealogies begin here, as do the **Pesetā** and **SaPesetā** families.

Salamasina

A.D.1530

Salamasina's marriage to *Tapumanaia*-I gives birth to a son, *Le Satele* (stolen at birth), and a daughter, *Fofoaivao'ese*:

- In Falealili, *LeSatele* marries *Gasegaseivao,* daughter of *Tapusoa* of Saluafata, and has two children, *Alaifea* and *LeSatele*-II:
    - Their daughter *Alaifea* marries *Mata'utiamoelala* of Falealili village, a descendant of the Tolufale lineage. She has sons:
        - The Warrior High Chiefs, *Lutu* and *Solosolo* (see The Story of the Warriors *Lutu* and *Unutoa*, page 223),
        - And a daughter *Alapataume* who marries *Alaimoana*, a high Chief from Toga Island. They have a daughter:
            - *Tofono* who marries *Tafilipepe* and bears *Fanene*.
                - High Chief *Fanene's* daughter *Oilau* is the mother of Tafa'ifa Tupua *Fuiavailili.*
    - Their son, *LeSatele*-II, and their descendant T*apumanaia*-III belong to different generations (#21 and #22)—see next page.

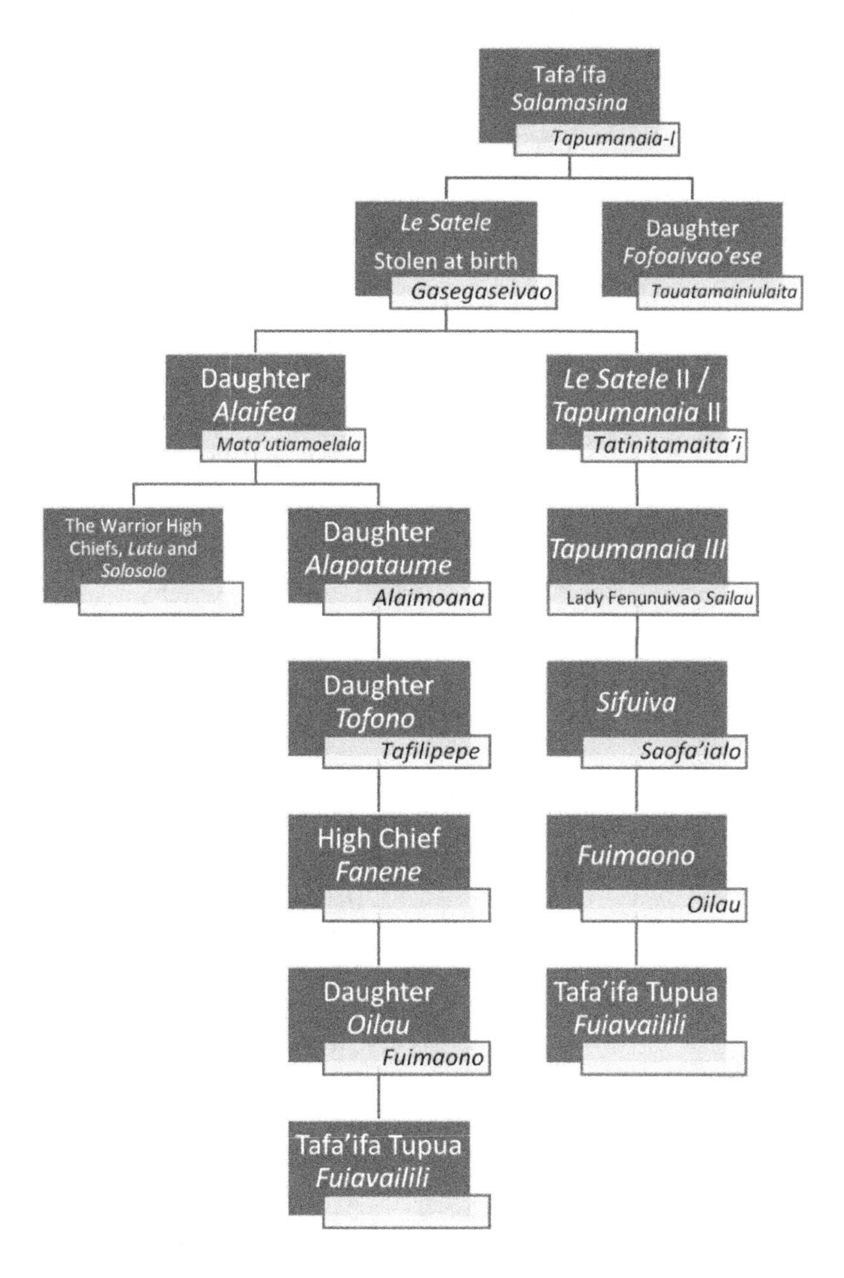

- The identities of *Tapumanaia*-II (generation #22) and *LeSatele*-II (generation #21) are complicated by name changes. *Tapumanaia*-II follows *LeSatele* and marries *Tatinitamaita'i* or *Tatini-tama'i-ta'i*.

They have a son, *Tapumanaia*-III, who marries Lady *Fenunuivao Sailau* and has a son *Sifuiva.*

- *Sifuiva* marries *Saofa'ialo* and has a son
    - ❖ *Fuimaono*, who marries *Oilau* (daughter of High Chief *Fanene,* above) who bears a son:
        - Tupua *Fuiavailili,* who has three sons, including *Galumalemana* and *Afoa.*
            - ▪ *Galumalemana* has sons, the oldest being *Nofoasāefā,* and the youngest *I'amafana.*

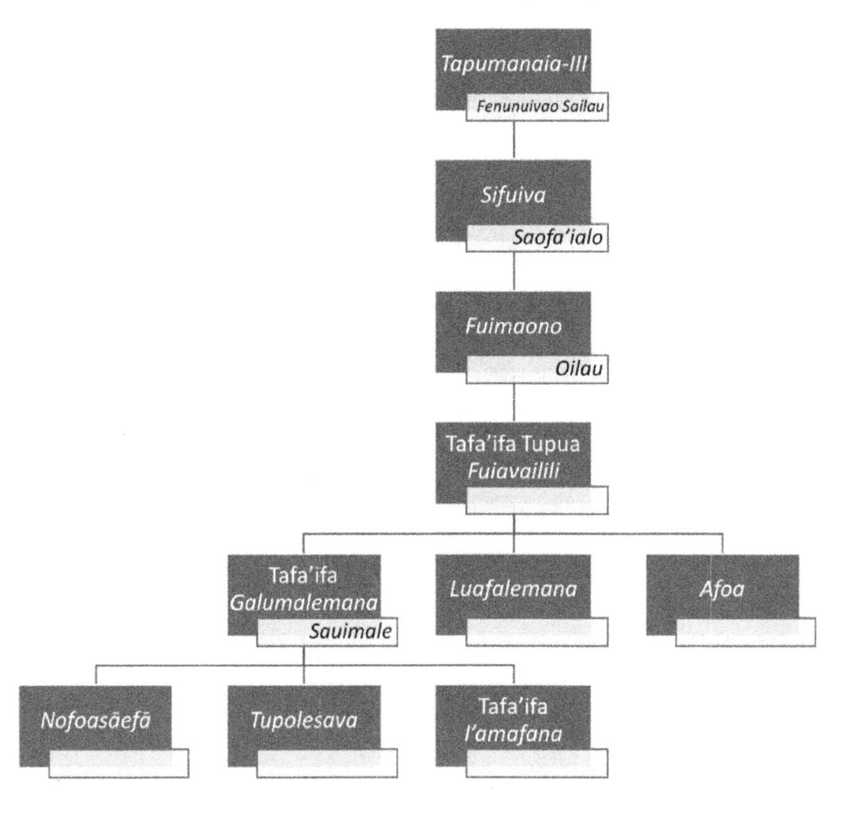

I'amafana later becomes Tafa'ifa, and *Nofoasāefā's* grandson *Moegagogo* challenges *I'amafana.*

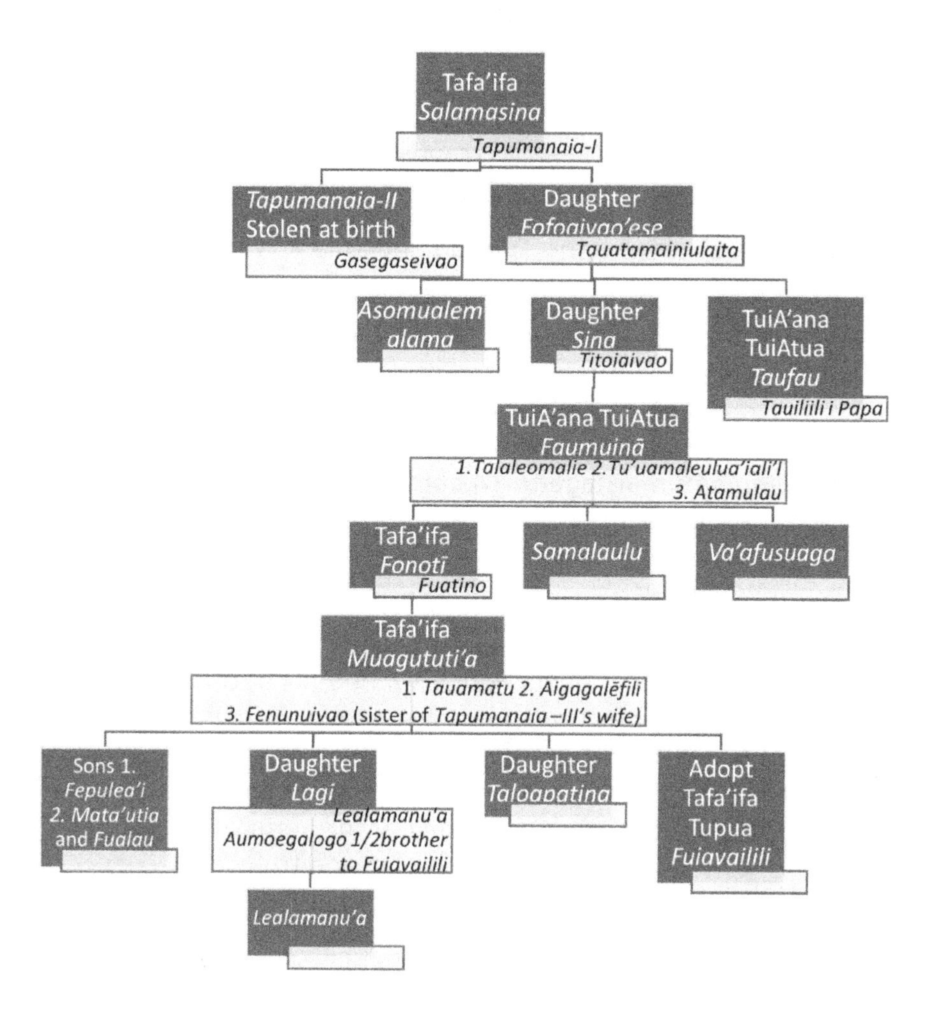

- *Salamasina's* daughter *Fofoaivao'ese* (which means "heal in the bush") marries *Tauatamainiulaita* (**A.D.1560**) from the Palauli and Tonumaipe'a clan, giving birth to:
  - A son *Asomualemalama*
  - A daughter *Sina,* who marries *Titoiaivao* and bears a son and a daughter, *Faumuinā* and *Asou,*
  - and another daughter TuiA'ana TuiAtua *Taufau.* TuiA'ana TuiAtua *Taufau's* union with *Tauiliili i Papa* of the SaMuliaga clan (A.D.1590) gives birth to:
    - *Tupuivao,* the cruel cannibal who is disinherited from the crown, due to his

disobedience in not going to see his mother to receive the decree (see *Taufau*, page 208). The crown is given to *Taufau's* nephew, *Faumuinā,* and the TuiA'ana TuiAtua *Faumuinā* reign begins.

Thus *Faumuinā* obtains the TuiAtua and TuiA'ana titles.

Faumuinā's marriage to *Talaleomalie* (a daughter of *Alolenei* and *Vaovasa,* son of *Tauiliili i Papa*) begets:

- *Fonotī,* who becomes the second Tafa'ifa. *Fonotī's* marriage to *Fuatino* (sister of *Su'afaigā*) produces a son
  - *Muagututi'a* who inherits his throne.

Then Faumuinā's marriage to *Tu'uamaleulua'iali'i* begets:

- *Samalaulu.*

And his third marriage, to *Atamulau,* begets:

- *Va'afusuaga.*

Muagututi'a's first marriage is to *Tauamatu*, daughter of *Toa* of SaLuafata, Upolu, who bears *Fepulea'i,* and his sister *Lagi.*

- *Lagi* marries *Lealamanu'a Aumoegalogo,* half-brother of Tupua *Fuiavailili,* giving birth to:
  - *Lealamanu'a*, whose genealogy (as we saw earlier—see Tagaloa in Period V, page 31) carries the Tagaloa lineage to today.

Muagututi'a's second marriage is to *Aigagalēfili*, daughter of Lilomaiava *Nailevaiiliili* of Palauli, Savai'i, who bears:

- *Mata'utia,*
- *Fualau,*
- and a daughter *Taloapatina.*

His third marriage is to *Fenunuivao* of the SaFenunuivao family. She is the younger sister of Lady *Fenunuivao Sailau* who is married to *Sifuiva*, the son of *Tapumanaia*-III, above. They adopt her sister's great-grandson:

- Tupua *Fuiavailili* who inherits the title. Then Tupua's son
  - Tafa'ifa *Galumalemana* inherits the title, which eventually goes to his youngest son:
    - Tafa'ifa *I'amafana,* who decreed it to:
      - Malietoa *Vaiinupō.*

Fiamēumulefolau's daughters

Taetelelēmā, Taeteleligivale and *Taetelelagolasi,* daughters of *Fiamēumulefolau,* are the famous ladies whose genealogies produce many famous families and connections:

- *Taetelelēmā* marries Paramount Chief TuiSamoa and bears two daughters, *Moeleoi* and *Tavatele*:
  - *Tavatele* or *Letavatele* marries *Matu'u*, son of *Seiulimalolo Leota,* and bears:
    - *Lemafaitu'uga* who marries his cousin *Salimagalemai's* wife, *Tuitogama'atoe*, the daughter of TuiA'ana *Tamālelagi.* They will be the ancestors in the modern genealogy of the current **Malietoa** clan, beginning with Malietoa *Taulapapa* and his sister *Sinailemanaui*. Thus the lineage of the modern Malietoa clan is carried over through *Gatoa'itele*, through *Vaetamasoāali'i*, through *Tamālelagi*, and through his daughter *Tuitogama'atoe* to her two children: *Taulapapa* and his sister *Sinailemanaui*.
      - *Taulapapa* is decreed to inherit the Malietoa title and
      - *Sinailemanaui* carries the Gatoa'itele through her genealogy, through the Saena or LeSaena family clan and the Fata and Maulolo and Tuisamau clan. Thus there is a balancing act between the brother and sister, with the Malietoa title and the Gatoa'itele and Vaetamasoāali'i PāPās.
  - *Moeleoi* marries her first husband, Chief *Tauiliili Saumaipe'a*, brother of *Levalasi* and *Tupa'i*, the ambassador of *Nafanua*. A major family is named after her, **SaMoeleoi**. They give birth to:
    - *Ali'imalemanu* and
    - a daughter *Tu'ua'uatõ* who is the progenitor of the **Aiga o Mavaega**.
  - *Tauiliili* dies and *Moeleoi* marries his brother *Tupa'ivailiiligi*, *Nafanua's* high priest. They produce two boys:
    - *Loli* and
    - *Asiata*, founder of **SaAsiata** family clan.
  - *Moeleoi's* genealogical siblings are decreed custodians of the Tonumaipe'a royal family crown.

- The famous lady *Taeteleligivale* is the ancestor of the **Fanene** family, which is why Fanene's children decree the **Fiamē** title to their grandfather *Samatauā* or *Samatauānu'u* of Lotofaga.

Fanene is the father of:

- *Oilau* who marries the first Chief *Fuimaono* (great-grandson of *Tapumanaia LeSatele*, that son of Tafa'ifa *Salamasina* who was stolen at birth by Orators *Talo* and *Ofoia* of their district, Falealili).
  - This marriage gives birth to Tupua *Fuiavailili* who becomes Tafa'ifa after Tafa'ifa *Muagututi'a* (the son of Tafa'ifa *Fonotī*).
- *Oilau's* marriage to *Leotatoga* gives birth to:
  - *Lealamanu'a Aumoegalogo* who marries *Lagi,* giving birth to *Lealamanu'a* who is, as we noted above, the ancestor of current Tagaloa clan.

Lilomaiava

The genealogy of the Lilomaiava clan starts back in Period V and continues forward with many important connections:

A.D.1470
The union of *LeAli'ifanovalevale* of Palauli, Savai'i and *Fililesalue*, daughter of **TuiAtua** *Fa'aso'utele* begets two daughters:

- *Popoai* and *Taufaitoa* who both marry **TuiToga** (A.D.1500) begetting:
  - *Togialelei,*
  - *Puipuiifatu,* and
  - *Tuiavi'i.*

Tuiavi'i's first marriage, to *Siaposuisui* (daughter of *Pei* of Sagafili) begets:

- *Tuifa'asisina* (founder of the **Lilomaiava** clan).

His second marriage, to *Letele* (daughter of the **Mata'afa** of Faleata), begets:

- *Taua'aleto'a*—who marries into the Tauiliili clan in Amalie, Atua district and becomes an ancestor of the TuiAtua clan that produces Mata'afa *Fa'asuamaleu*—

- and a daughter *Unusialeto'a*—whose genealogy will connect to *Vaovasa,* the son of *Tauiliili i Papa* of **SaLeMuliaga**.
    - *Vaovasa's* daughter *Talaleomalie* marries *Faumuinā* and produces a son, the Tafa'ifa *Fonotī.*

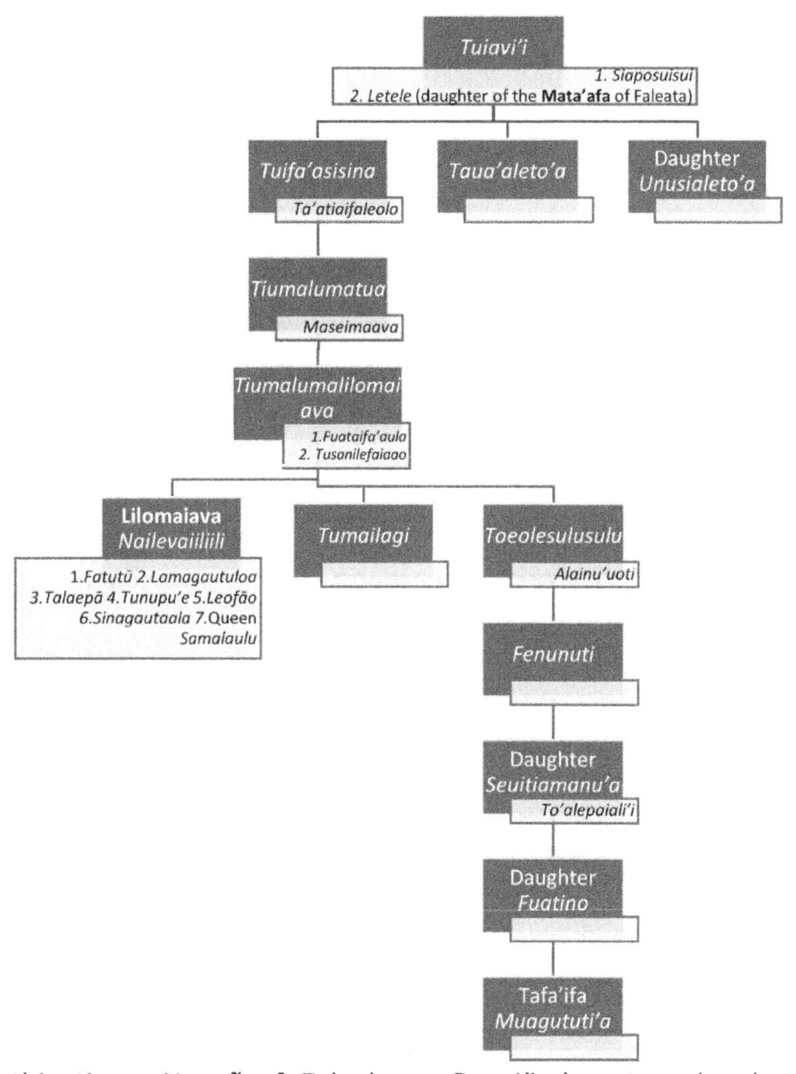

At this time, *Ugapō* of Falealupo, Savai'i, has two daughters, *Alolenei* and *Maseimaava. Alolenei* marries *Vaovasa* (above, son of *Tauiliili i Papa)* and begets *Talaleomalie* who marries **King** *Faumuinā.* And *Maseimaava* marries *Tiumalumatua* (son of

Tuifa'asisina) and begets *Tiumaluma**lilomaiava**,* which means "A tuna fish gift from the old man Lilo that was caught outside the reef." So:

A.D.1530

The first marriage of *Tuifa'asisina* (son of *Tuiavi'i,* above, and founder of the **Lilomaiava** clan), is to *Ta'atiaifaleolo* (daughter of *Taito* of the **Tagaloa** clan, residing in Satapuala, Upolu), and begets:

- *Tiumalumatua* whose union with *Maseimaava*, daughter of *Ugapõ* (above) bears:
  - *Tiumaluma**lilomaiava**,* whose first marriage, to *Fuataifa'aula* daughter of *Silofau* of Papa village, bears two sons:
    - **Lilomaiava** *Nailevaiiliili* and
    - *Tumailagi,* progenitor of the **Su'a** family clan.

Tuifa'asisina's second marriage, to *Lomialagi* from Falelatai, begets:

- *LeTagaloatele* (or Letagaloatele).

A.D.1620

So, *Tiumalumalilomaiava's* first marriage gives birth to:

- **Lilomaiava** *Nailevaiiliili,* whose marriages are listed below,
- and *Tumailagi.*

His second marriage, to *Tusanilefaiaao* (or *Tusanitama*, meaning *Tusani* with no buttocks, as her body ended at her abdomen—for which reason *Tusanilefaiaao,* daughter of LeManu'a *Lesanalāla* of Safata, is brought in as substitute[xiii]) begets:

- *Toeolesulusulu*, grandfather of the famous *Su'afaigā. Toeolesulusulu* marries *Alainu'uoti* (daughter of *Safuta* of Satapuala, Upolu) who bears:
  - *Fenunuti* of SaTuala of Falease'elā, whose daughter:
    - *Seuitiamanu'a* marries *To'alepaiali'i* and bears *Fuatino*, mother of Tafa'ifa *Muagututi'a.*

The famous *Su'afaigā's* genealogy begins with Tagaloa *Funefea'i,* then becomes part of Tiumalumalilomaiava, progenitor of the Lilomaiava family clan, then splits into its own Su'a family clan (see The Story of Tattooing and the Conjoined Twins, page 115). His princess sister *Fuatino* (above) marries Tafa'ifa *Fonotī* and is also the Taupou or Sa'oTama'ita'i of SaTuala clan in Upolu (*Tuala* is *Tamālelagi's* older son). *Su'afaigā's* other sister, *Melegalenu'u*, is the ancestor of *Pototaumulimalei'a*, a daughter who married TuiA'ana *Afoafouvale*, defeated by his brother *Galumalemana.*

A.D.1650

Here we find the marriages and children of Lilomaiava *Nailevaiiliili.*

His first marriage, to *Fatutū* (daughter of Orator Chief *Mataafā* of Palauli village, Savai'i), begets:

- *Salū*, orator at large of the **Lilomaiava** family.

His second marriage, to *Lamagautuloa* (from Asau, Savai'i) begets:

- *Leilua* of Sagone,
- *Faliuga,*
- *Tauavāmea,*
- and a daughter *Lomialagi.*

His third marriage, to *Talaepā* (from Siumu, bringing a connection to the **Asomua** clan of Siumu), begets three children:

- *Tilafono*,
- *Fa'avaoga*,
- and a daughter *Ufagapiu* (also known as *Mati of Luatuanu'u*, Upolu).

His fourth marriage is to *Tunupu'e* of Samata (though others in Satupa'itea say she is *Tumupu'e*, daughter of Chief *Valomua* of Satupa'itea (see "This is Laloifi", page 123), who was married to Tupuivao son of TuiA'ana TuiAtua *Taufau*. Others say they are one and the same lady). This marriage begets two boys, *Seve* and *Tilimafana*:

- *Seve* (Lilomaiava *Seve* or Lilomaiava *Seveailaoamanu*) of Samata, Savai'i, marries *Seanae*, daughter of *Tuifa'asisina* of Satapuala and Sagafili, Upolu, giving birth to:
    - *Umalaū* who marries TuiA'ana *Tamālelagi*—see Children of *Tamālelagi*, page 50).

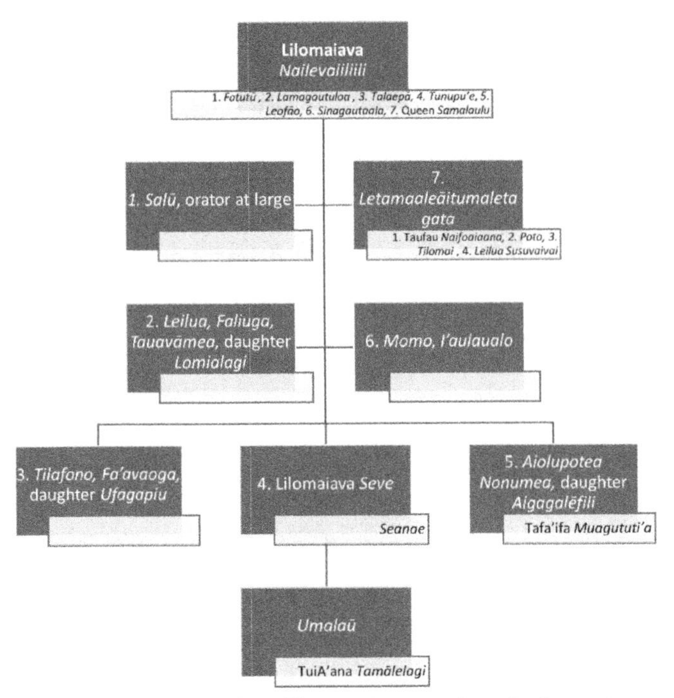

His fifth marriage, to *Leofão* (from Satupa'itea), begets:

- *Aiolupotea Nonumea*, and
- a daughter, *Aigagalēfili,* who marries King Tafa'ifa *Muagututi'a*, son of *Fonotī.*

His sixth marriage, to *Sinagautaala* (daughter of Tuitele of Leone, Tutuila Island), begets two sons, *Momo* and *I'aulaualo.* Both names are titles in Palauli, Savai'i and Amaluia, Tutuila.

- *I'aulaualo*'s name means "Samoan Jonah." He is an actor in the Samoan version of Jonah and the Whale and died on the shore of Fausaga village, a hamlet of Safata district village.

His seventh marriage, to Queen *Samalaulu* (daughter of King TuiAtua TuiA'ana *Faumuinā*), begets:

- *Letamaaleāitumaletagata*, whose first marriage, to his second cousin Taufau *Naifoaiaana,* daughter of *Laumatiamanu* (*Laumatiamanu* is the son of *Toleafoaiolō,* the son of *Va'afusuaga-Toleafoa* who is the brother of Queen *Samalaulu*) bears:
    - Tuimaleali'ifano *Tuitalili.*

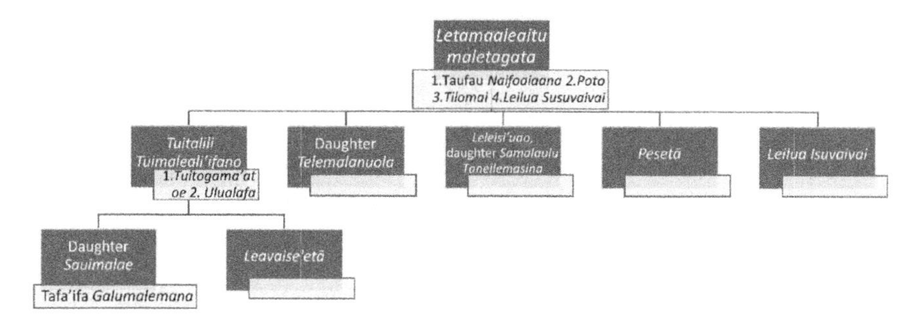

Legend has it that Lady *Seanae,* wife of Lilomaiava *Seveailaoamanu* (Lilomaiava *Seve*), and mother of TuiA'ana *Tamālelagi's* fourth wife, was a daughter of Lilomaiava *Seveailaoamanu* and *Fa'atupuigati*, daughter of *La'ulu Nofovaleane.* She was adopted by her uncle *La'ululolopō* and became TuiA'ana *Tamālelagi's* seventh wife. *Seanae* later married TuiToga, living in Toamua, a hamlet of Faleata district, where *Tuiavi'i* married Letele *Talaeia*, daughter of Mata'afa of Faleata, producing, as we have just seen, *Taua'aleto'a* and his sister *Unusialeto'a*. *Tuiavi'i* also married *Siaposuisui*, daughter of *Pei* of Sagafili, producing *Tuifa'asisina*. TuiToga *Puipuiifatu,* brother of *Tuiavi'i* also married *Timuipaepaetele,* daughter of Elder Orator *Ale* (or *Ulu*) of Toamua, Faleata, Upolu, giving birth to *Seiuliali'i,* the father of *Tunumafono* (*Satunumafono*—see The Vaetamasoāali'i Crown, page 176) and his sisters *Taulapuitaua* (who married TuiAtua *Letauā*) and *Lefe'eonu'u* (who married *Va'afusuaga-Toleafoa*).

A.D.1680

The first marriage of *Letamaaleāitumaletagata*, to his second cousin, Taufau *Naifoaiaana* begets:

- Tuimaleali'ifano *Tuitalili,* whose marriages are listed below (A.D.1710),
- and a daughter, *Telemalanuola,* Sa'o Tama'ita'i of Tuimaleali'ifano.

His second marriage, to *Poto*, daughter of *Amituana'i* of Solosolo, Atua, Upolu (son of *To'omata* and *Tofoipupū*) and *Fa'aautatanu* (daughter of *Tago* of Amaile, of Solosolo, Upolu) begets:

- *Leleisi'uao* of Palauli,
- and a daughter *Samalaulu Taneilemasina.*

His third marriage, to *Tilomai* (Sa'o Tama'ita'i of the Tonumaipe'a clan and his second cousin, daughter of his first cousin *Toleafoaiolõ,* son of *Va'afusuaga-Toleafoa*) begets:

- *Pesetā.*

His fourth marriage, to *Leilua Susuvaivai* (daughter of TuiManu'a and *Leilua*, *Fanene's* daughter, of Falealili) begets:

- *Leilua Isuvaivai.*

Leilua and *Meleiseā* are half-sisters of *Fanene's* daughter *Oilau*. *Tuatagaloa* and *Te'onapõailenu'u* are *Oilau's* half-brothers.

A.D.1710

The first marriage of Tuimaleali'ifano *Tuitalili*, to *Tuitogama'atoe* (daughter of *Tauiliili* of Amaile, of the Atua and SaLeValasi family), begets:

- A daughter, *Sauimalae*, who marries King Tafa'ifa *Galumalemana*, son of King *Tupua*.

His second marriage, to *Ulualafā* (daughter of *Pula* from Saleimoa, Upolu), begets

- *Leavaise'etā*, who is decreed to prepare the ava ceremony of Tuimaleali'ifano clan.

Period VII: The Arrival of Christianity

The arrival of Christianity in Samoa and Manu'a should be viewed against the events of the western world, as the invasion of the western world brought change to the Islands.

Events: A.D.1400 - 1900

A.D.1400 - 1600

The Europeans are coming—and have been coming for some time:

- The Colonial Era begins with:
- Prince Henry of Portugal prepares for Navigation (1400s).
- Christopher Columbus enters the New World (1493).
- Ferdinand Magellan of Portugal discovers the Pacific Ocean (1520).
- The Spanish Voyages take place at this time.
- Sir Francis Drake of England circumnavigates the globe (1577).
- The Italian Jesuit Missionary, Matteo Ricci, establishes a mission in China (1582).

- The Dutch Colonial Establishment begins (from 1599).
- The conversion of Asia to Christianity takes place.

A.D.1500 – 1800

Meanwhile, Christianity has been changing, with the beginning of Protestantism and famous leaders:

- The monk, priest, and teacher, Martin Luther of Germany (1517)
- King Henry VIII of England who receives Protestantism for England (1534)
- The Protestant leader John Calvin (1509-1564)
- The reign of Queen Elizabeth I of England (1558-1603)
- The reign of King James I of England (1603-1625)
- John and Charles Wesley, founders of the Methodist Church (1740)
- Christian Missionaries reach Tahiti and Toga (late 1700s, early 1800s)

A.D.1700 – 1800

Early contact with Europeans starts here:

- The arrival of Admiral Jacob Roggeveen and Company (1722)
- The observation of the natives
- The arrival of Louis Antoine Bougainville (1768)
- The massacre at Asu Bay, Tutuila (1787)
- The arrival of George Bass Bowden

A.D.1750 – 1900

The political environment at the arrival of Christianity in Samoa and Manu'a is complicated:

- Malietoa *Vaiinupõ* (1765-1841)
- The war between TuiA'ana *Nofoasāefā* and TuiAtua *Mata'afa*
- The tyrant Lei'ataua *Tamafaigā* (late 1700s early 1800s)
- Malietoa *Vaiinupõ* receives the Tafa'ifa title (1879)

A.D.1800 – 1900

Then comes the Wind of Christianity into the South Pacific:

- King *Põmare*-II of Tahiti converts to Christianity (1815).
- The first Protestant missionaries arrive in New Zealand (1814).
- Christianity arrives in Hawai'i from Boston, USA (1820).
- Queen *Ka'ahumanu* of Hawai'i converts to Christianity (1825).
- King George *Tupou*-I of Toga converts to Christianity (1831).
- The Messenger of Peace arrives in Samoa (1830).

People

Mauga

There is fragmentary information (oral and written) about Paramount Ma'oupū Chief *Mauga's* genealogy. One story tells of his origin from his mother, *Alavatualua*, daughter of *Galea'i* and her brother TuiManu'a *Li'a*. Also, his honorific title and salutation Ma'oupūTasi, meaning the Most Senior Ma'oupū Chief of all the Ma'oupū, is decreed by *Tapusalaia*, sister of Paramount Chief *Asomua* of the Malietoa dynasty. However, Dr. Krämer's account of Tutuila Island history lists Mauga's lineage, and I feel it's important to include it here.

The sequence of Mauga title holders is not quite clear, but what is clear is that those who carried the title are clearly noted in the annals of the family and village of Pago Pago:

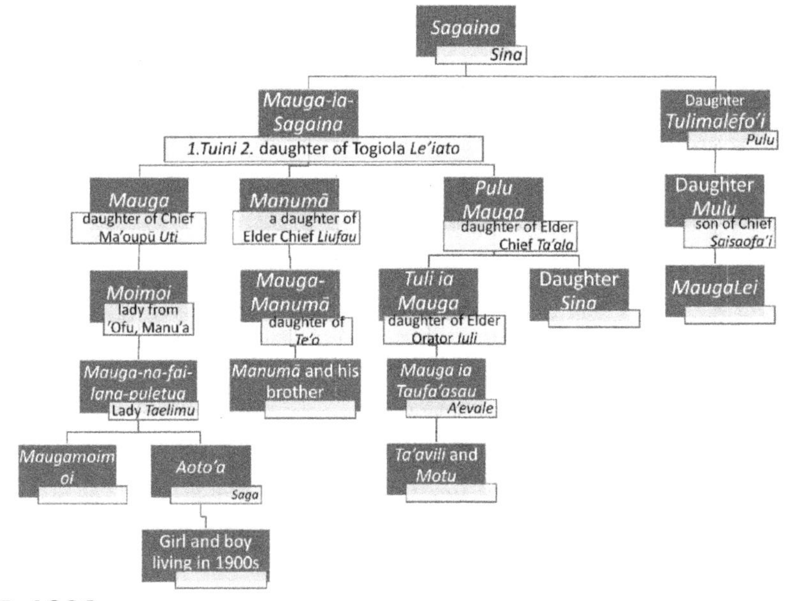

A.D.1800s

- *Sagaina's* union with *Sina,* daughter of the famous Warrior Chief *Fua'au* (meaning "ancestor of warrior who freed Tutuila from the Togan yoke") in Pago Pago bears *Mauga-ia-Sagaina's* and a daughter *Tulima* (or *Tulimalēfo'i*, Sa'o Tama'ita'i of Mauga).

- *Tulima* marries Elder (Mātua) High Chief *Pulu* of Pago Pago and bears a girl *Mulu*.
  - *Mulu* marries a son of Chief *Saisaofa'i* giving birth to *MaugaLei*. (The Paramount Chief *Talamaivao* in Fagaloa, Upolu is also called *MaugaLei*.) *MaugaLei* would contest the Mauga title against *Mauga-Manumā* in 1883.
- *Tulima's* brother, *Mauga-ia-Sagaina*, marries *Tuini*, daughter of *Asuega* of Pago Pago village, giving birth to sons *Mauga* and *Manumā*:
  - *Mauga* receives the title Mauga. He marries a daughter of Chief Ma'oupū *Uti* of Aūa village in the district of Fagaloa, Tutuila, giving birth to *Moimoi*.
    - *Moimoi's* union with a lady from 'Ofu, Manu'a, births *Mauga-na-fai-lana-puletua*, meaning "Mauga who had his paramount authority" or "a party opposed to the government," hence "Mauga that organized a party opposed to the government."
      - *Mauganafailanapuletua* marries Lady *Taelimu* of Nu'uuli village, who bears a son *Maugamoimoi* and a daughter *Aoto'a*.
        - *Aoto'a* marries *Saga* of Fasito'otai giving birth to a boy and a girl still living in the 1900s.
  - *Mauga's* brother *Manumā* marries a daughter of Paramount Mātua (Elder) Chief *Liufau* of Aūa village, bearing a son *Mauga-Manumā* (who is exiled by the Germans to Jaluit with Malietoa *Laupepa* in 1887).
    - *Mauga-Manumā* marries a daughter of *Te'o* of Pago Pago village, giving birth to (another) *Manumā* and his brother (whose name is not known).

- It's not known if this *Manumā* was the contestant for the Mauga title against *MaugaLei* in 1883, or if it was his father *Maugamanumā*. This author believes that, when Paramount Chief *Ma'oupū Maugamanumā* went with Malietoa *Laupepa* to Jaluit, he was struck with an illness, succumbing shortly after they were brought back to Samoa in the same time period 1883-90.

- *Mauga-ia-Sagaina's* second marriage, to a daughter of Togiola *Le'iato* of Aoa village (a translator for Dr. Krämer), gives birth to *PuluMauga.*
  - *PuluMauga's* union with a daughter of Elder (Mātua) High Chief *Ta'ala* of Pago Pago (*Pulu—Tulima's* husband—and *Ta'ala* are now Mātua of Pago Pago) bears *Tuli ia Mauga* and a daughter named *Sina.*
    - *Tuli ia Mauga* marries a daughter of Elder Orator *Iuli* of Leone (there is also a *Iuli* of Tula) giving birth to *Mauga ia Taufa'asau.*
      - *Mauga ia Taufa'asau* marries *A'evale*, daughter of *Aumoegalogo* (also known as Lealamanu'a *Aumoegalogo*, son of Princess *Oilau*—the daughter of *Fanene*—and *Leotatoga,* making him half-brother to Tupua *Fuiavailili*—see *Fiamēumulefolau's* daughters in Period VI, page 57. *Leotatoga* is the son of *Amituana'i* and grandson of *To'omata*, and great-grandson of Malietoa *Taulapapa* who married *Fatumiti* of the Tagaloa clan). The marriage of *Mauga ia Taufa'asau* and

A'evale produces *Ta'avili* and *Motu.*

After the death of *MaugaLei's* great-uncle *Mauga* (*Mauga-ia-Sagaina* son of *Sagaina*, above) in 1883, *Mauga-Manumā* and *MaugaLei* fight for sovereignty in 1889.

Vaiinupõ

Malietoa *Vaiinupõ's* grandfather is Malietoa *Ti'a.*

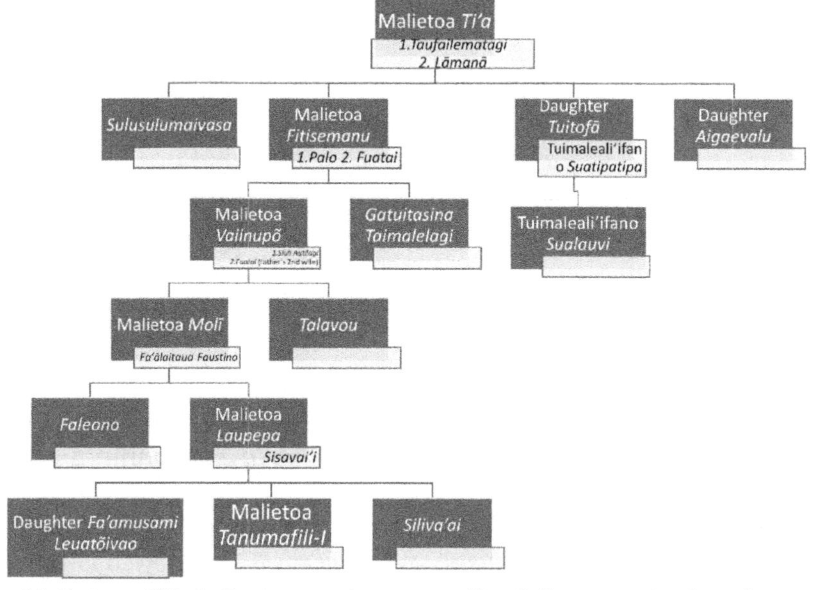

- Malietoa *Ti'a's* first marriage, to *Taufailematagi*, daughter of *Li'o* of Sapapali'i village in SaFotulafai district, Savai'i gives birth to two sons:
  - *Sulusulumaivasa* and
  - Malietoa *Fitisemanū*, whose marriage to *Palo*, daughter of *Memea* of Sapapali'i, Savai'i gives birth to:
    - Malietoa *Vaiinupõ*, who marries *Siulī Autilagi*, daughter of *Gatoloai* of Iva, giving birth to:
      - Malietoa *Molī*, who marries *Fa'ālaitaua Faustino*, daughter of *Su'apa'ai* of Iva, Savai'i, giving birth to:
        - *Faleono* and
        - Malietoa *Laupepa,* the first ordained minister of Afega

village). Malietoa *Laupepa* marries *Sisavai'i*, daughter of *Niuva'ai* of Palauli (his grandmother, *Sailiemanu* is the sister of *Lāmanā* who also marries Malietoa *Ti'a*), giving birth to:
- A daughter, *Fa'amusami Leuatõivao,*
- Malietoa *Tanumafili-I* (1890), and
- *Siliva'ai.*

▪ Malietoa *Vaiinupõ's* second marriage, to *Fuatai* (his father's second wife), bears:
• *Talavou.*

➢ Malietoa *Fitisemanū's* second marriage, to *Fuatai* daughter of *Gaugau* of Sapapali'i, Savai'i, gives birth to a son:
▪ *Gatuitasina Taimalelagi* (*Vaiinupõ's* half-brother).

o Malietoa *Ti'a's* second marriage, to *Lāmanā*, daughter of *Taisi* (the son of Tafa'ifa *Galumalemana* and the brother of *Nofoasāefā*) from Asau, Savai'i, gives birth to daughters *Tuitofā* and *Aigaevalu*.

➢ *Tuitofā* marries Tuimaleali'ifano *Suatipatipa* (grandson of Tuimaleali'ifano *Tuitalili*, the son of Lilomaiava *Letamaaleāitumaletagata*, son of TuiA'ana *Samalaulu* and Lilomaiava *Nailevaiiliili*—see below). *Tuitofā* bears
▪ Tuimaleali'ifano *Sualauvi*.

Tuimaleali'ifano

Tui-ma-le-ali'i-fano (*Tui* stand erected, *ma* and, *le* the, *ali'i* high chief, *fano* died wastefully) is named after the high chief from Palauli, *Ali'ifanovalevale* (*LeAli'ifanovalevale* see Lilomaiava above, page 58).

The royal Tuimaleali'ifano genealogy begins with TuiA'ana *Samalaulu*, one of the three Paramount Royal Chief children of Paramount TuiAtua TuiA'ana *Faumuinā*. Her mother, *Tu'uamaleulua'iali'i*, is daughter of High Chief *Manua'ifua* (*manu*—bird, *a'i*—eat, *fua*—fruit or flowers), a descendant of the Malietoa and the Gatoa'itele royal house, of Afega village, Tuamasaga district, Upolu.

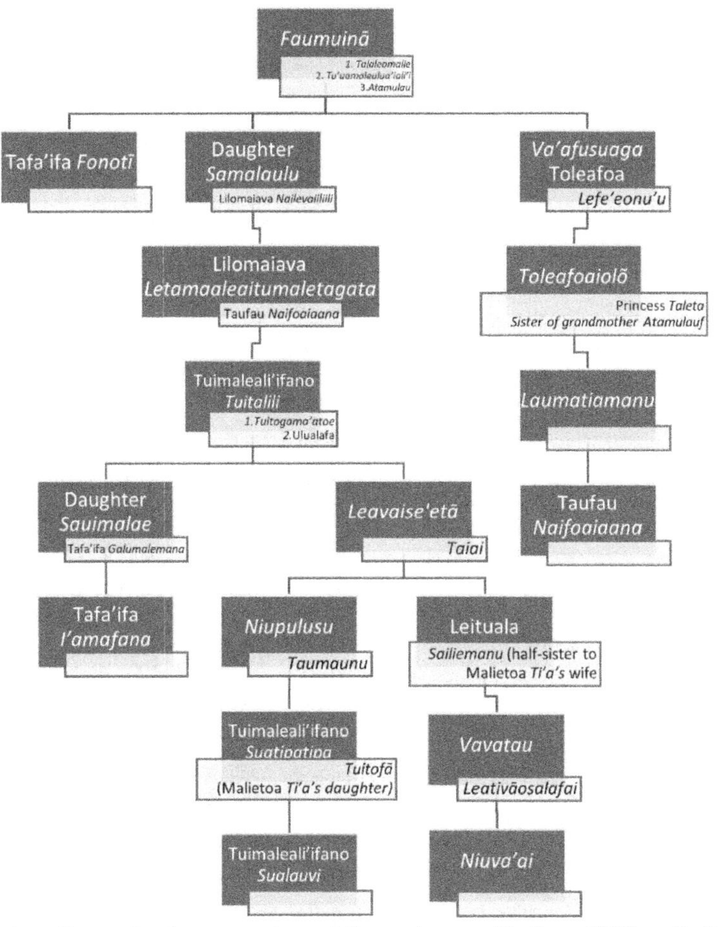

- Lady *Samalaulu* marries Lilomaiava *Nailevaiiliili* of Palauli village (see *Lilomaiava* in Period VI, page 58—he is of great age at the time) and gives birth to:
  - ➢ *Letamaaleāitumaletagata* ("the son of the demon and a human"), who inherits his father's Lilomaiava title and his mother's TuiA'ana title and salutation. Lilomaiava *Letamaaleāitumaletagata* marries Taufau *Naifoaiaana*, daughter of *Laumatiamanu* (grandson of *Samalaulu's* brother, *Va'afusuaga*), giving birth to:

- Tuimaleali'ifano *Tuitalili* who marries *Tuitogama'atoe*, daughter of *Tauiliili* of Amile, giving birth to a daughter:
    - *Sauimalae,* who marries Tafa'ifa *Galumalemana* and bears:
        - Tafa'ifa *I'amafana,* who decrees the Tafa'ifa title to Malietoa *Vaiinupõ*.
- Tuimaleali'ifano *Tuitalili's* second marriage, to *Ulualafā,* daughter of Paramount Chief *Pula* of Saleimoa village bears:
    - *Leavaise'etā*, who marries *Taiai,* daughter of *Faolotoi* of Lepa, Atua, giving birth to two sons:
        - *Niupulusu* (*Lilopogi*, not a titleholder of Tuimaleali'ifano), who marries *Taumaunu*, daughter of *Taefu* of Falelatai, who bears:
            - Tuimaleali'ifano *Suatipatipa,* who marries *Tuitofā* (daughter of Malietoa *Ti'a,* and granddaughter of Tafa'ifa *Galumalemana*) bearing: Tuimaleali'ifano *Sualauvi;*
        - and *Leituala* (not a titleholder of Tuimaleali'ifano), who marries *Sailiemanu* (half-sister to Malietoa *Ti'a's* wife *Lāmanā*), giving birth to:
            - *Vavatau,* who marries *Leativāosalafai*, giving birth to *Niuva'ai,* whose daughter is *Sisavai'i,* who marries Malietoa *Laupepa,* giving birth to Malietoa *Tanumafili*-I (as we have just seen).

This connection to Malietoa and to the genealogy of Tafa'ifa *Galumalemana* makes Tuimaleali'ifano a Ma'oupū title to the modern Malietoa monarch. He can claim the Sa'o Tama'ita'i title, To'oa Malietoa. The connection with *Taisi Galumalemana* that produced *Niuva'ai* and his daughter *Sisavai'i* is another reason for Malietoa *Tanumafili*-I and *Tanumafili*-II having the salutation *Aloali'i*, an address that is reserved exclusively for *Galumalemana* descendants.

As a footnote: while the SaTupua clan has laid claims to the Tafa'ifa Salamasina genealogy, from the TuiAtua and TuiA'ana PāPās, the Malietoa monarch has its claims tied up with Gatoa'itele, Vaetamasoāali'i, TuiA'ana Tamālelagi and, of course, the Malietoa title. The Tuimaleali'ifano title is clearly the mediator between the two monarchs.

Period VIII: Forging a Modern Government

Events

Finally, modern government begins to change with the arrival of Christianity:

- Christianizing the Samoans and Manu'ans,
- establishing mission stations across Samoa and Manu'a,
- bringing the Europeans and development of trading enterprises,
- and the introduction of European common laws and parliamentary rules and organization

We will look at these events in detail later—they are the events recorded by Western historians. But first, with all these timelines in mind, we will look at the people of Samoa and Manu'a and their stories, and how the whole of this history affected Samoan and Manu'an people, culture, traditions, and government.

People

Tafa'ifa *Galumalemana* married 5 times and had 11 sons. However, history only chronicles events concerning the following:

Galumalemana's sons are:

- *Taisi,*
- *Nofoasāefā,* who becomes TuiA'ana *Nofoasāefā,*
- *Tua-lau-lelei,*
- *Tupolesava*, who challenges his brother Tafa'ifa *I'amafana* and loses—he is banished to Tutuila—
- *Tuala-ma-salā* (name of two sons, descendants of *Tuala* at SaMuliaga, Savai'i, the SaTuala of Savai'i branch),
- *I'amafana,* who becomes Tafa'ifa *I'amafana,*
- and *Tae-o-ali'i.*

Galumalemana's daughters are:

- *Letele-ma-lanu-ola*, Sa'oTama'ita'i of Tuimaleali'ifano,
- *Taloapatina,*
- and *Fua-memea.*

TuiA'ana *Nofoasāefā* marries *Tusoloimalie*, daughter of the Matai'a of Faleata district, Upolu—this is how *Nofoasāefā*, *Galumalemana*, and *Tamasese* come to be in Faleata. The marriages produces a child:

- *Lea-sio-lagi* or *Leasiolagi,* who marries *Usipua,* daughter of *Nonu-ma-sesē* of Faleasi'u (this how the *Aiga o Mavaega* comes to Faleasi'u), who bears a son:
  - *Moe-ga-gogo*, who marries *Tae-leu-mete*, daughter of Leilua *Fau-olo* of SaFotulafai, bearing a son:
    - Tamasese *Titi-a-maea* (the first *Tamasese*). He marries *Fuatino*, daughter of *Taimalie-utu* of Nofoali'i, A'ana district. (An earlier *Fuatino* was the wife of Tafa'ifa *Fonotī* and mother of Tafa'ifa *Muagututi'a*). This marriage gives birth to:
      - Tamasese *Lealofi* (who is 40 years old in 1898).[xiv]

Period I: The Navigators' Migration

Creation Mythology

Classic mythology begins with the birth of cliffs and rocks, then marshes, then mountains, and, finally, a female human who finds a male human who deflowers her (he slashes her with the shark's tooth to create her female organs, thus the first woman) and begets a girl named *Taufa* (water, or water in the wind, or strong wind).[xv]

Stories of PapaAtea and Pulotu

Arrival in Samoa

Then comes the story of *PapaAtea* and Pulotu. This tells of the war which caused the original migration journey to escape and thus discover the new homeland, Manu'a and Samoa. It can be considered as overlaying the genealogical chronology of Dr. Augustin Krämer's pedigrees, accounting for the period when the earth is full of darkness, and the union of Dark with Light begets Night and Day. At this juncture in Krämer's chronology, we see the beginning of creation being rationalized and manufactured into folklore and mythology.

The legend of *PapaAtea* and Pulotu begins when King *Elo* (the warrior *Elo*) rules over Pulotu. A married couple, *Si'usi'uao* (meaning tail end of day) and *Uluao* (meaning beginning of day), have four children: *Lagi* (heaven), *Ua* (neck), *Tala* (side of the meeting house) and *Fali* (the grass). In this story, the children are sent to *PapaAtea* to bring water and, instead, are badly mistreated, mocked and laughed at by *PapaAtea's* people. A war ensues, and *PapaAtea* and his people suffer a "great slaughter" (*fa'apapateaina*). The result is that only four couples survive the war and escape, and they populate Samoa: *Ma* and *Nu'a* become Manu'a, *Tutu* and *Ila* become Tutuila, *U* and *Polu* become Upolu, *Sa* and *Va'ai'i* become Savai'i.[xvi]

The Story of the Warrior *Elo*

Pulotu is the Samoan equivalent of the lands of Hades and Elysium in Greek mythology, and PapaAtea is the "rock island gifted from the firmament." According to Samoan legend, the battle between Pulotu and PapaAtea represents the first war in remembered history.

In another version of the story, the daughters of TuiPulotu, the King of Pulotu, were sent to fetch water and were mocked and humiliated by the PapaAtean people, and this caused a war.

The paramount chief of Pulotu was angry and ordered his warrior chiefs to launch an all-out war, organizing a war party with the wise Pulotu warrior *Elo*, against Tui PapaAtea and his people. Upon hearing this, Tui PapaAtea responded aggressively and quickly launched an attack on Tui Pulotu's people.

Seeing Tui PapaAtea's massive war fleet approaching, Tui Pulotu instructed his warrior *Elo* "not to engage the warring party at sea but to wait until they come on land"—*'Aua le taia i le tai a'e fa'aa'e i fanua*. This advice became a proverb frequently used by orators, meaning both to be patient, and that your strength is on the land. In peaceful times, this proverb means one should welcome the arrival of guests on land and into one's house, as opposed to on the shores and the docks.

Warrior *Elo* paid heed to the paramount chief's advice. When the ships landed on shore, *Elo* and his war party launched their attack. The battle was fearsome, and casualties were plenty on both sides; blood ran like a river on Pulotu, land and sea.

The two warriors of Tui PapaAtea, *Utuma* and *Utumau'u*, saw that they were outnumbered, with no means of resupplying their forces. They began to retreat back to the fleet for an orderly escape.

The PapaAteans were soundly defeated by the Pulotu, and the two PapaAtean warriors were pursued by the Pulotu warrior *Elo*. They landed on the east coast of the Island of Upolu, Samoa, where, instead of being killed by *Elo*, they chose to be transformed into tiny island rocks, the islands of Utumau'u and Utuma, rising up on the coast between the villages of Solosolo and Luatuanu'u.

Luama'a and LuaUi

Dating from somewhat later, around 100 B.C., a parallel legend to the PapaAtea and Pulotu war describes the first population of the islands. This is the story of *Lua* and his sister *Ui* (also known as *Luama'a* and his sister *LuaUi*—where *Ui* means the same as dark or *Po*). They are the children of *Fiso* and *Ufi.* Brother and sister escape the wrath of the Sun (or *Lā*), going toward the East Pacific, through Tokelau Island, and on to their landing on Manu'a. Their journey lands them in a place they name *Sauā* (meaning cruel) referring to the Sun's cruelty. Sauā produces plenty of coconut trees, and *LuaUi* and her son build their first house and call the land the Faleniu property in Sauā.

This story marks the first appearance of *Lā* as the Sun (or light or *Ao*). *Lā* is also a reference to *Tagaloalagi.*

Period II: The Legendary *Tagaloalagi*

Stories of Creation

The Manu'an Creation Poem

Ancient history, as told in the language of mythology, begins with one god, *Tagaloalagi*, for Samoans and Manu'ans have always practiced monotheism, believing in one god, *Tagaloalagi*, that resides in the tenth heaven.

The god *Tagaloalagi* is also known by several other names: *Tagaloanimonimo* (invisible heaven), *Tagaloafa'atupunu'u* (creator of islands), *Tagaloa*, and *TagaloaLā* (sun). His presence is ubiquitous in the legends of origin of almost all of Polynesia.

The Manu'an Creation Poem starts where the heavens open up and the god, *Tagaloalagi*, looks down:

Tagaloalagi summons the winds and the waves; then he commands them to be still and calm, for he wants to rest. Now he calls out to the heavens for a few small pebbles which he organizes into islands, naming them: first Manu'atele, then Upolu, Tutuila, and Savai'i. He creates the various sacred meeting and resting grounds for himself and his chiefs. Then he pulls up the thousands other islands from the abyss of the ocean and distributes them throughout Polynesia—these include the Togan archipelago, the Fiji Islands, and the rest of the little islands, but Manu'a is first.

Tagaloalagi flies over these islands and surveys the landscape. He weighs and measures their spacing, and he see that it is good.

At this point *Tagaloalagi* sends down creepers to populate Tutuila, Upolu, and Savai'i, but he sees, there, maggots that do not have soul, feet, hands, head, or heart. So he dispatches his messenger, *Tuli* (the Golden Plover), to see what is wrong with the maggots, and *Le Tuli o le Tagaloa* says they do not have a soul. So *Tagaloalagi* pulls out limbs and appendages on the maggots, and brings down the soul and, behold, humans are born.

You can see my translation of the poem in my first book, *Navigators Quest for a Kingdom in Polynesia.*

Creation of the Islands

The Manu'an Creation Poem describes the creation, by *Tagaloalagi*, of the many islands, Manu'a first, then Savai'i, followed by Malae Alamisi, the Togan Archipelago, the Fiji Islands, and the little islands around the East Pacific archipelago.

Alamisi, in Samataiuta, Savai'i, is the dwelling and resting place of *Tagaloalagi* and of his retinue. Upolu is only a small rock and Tutuila is a small pebble, but *Tagaloalagi* enlarges the islands by lifting them up as resting places for chiefs, all of whom look toward *Tagaloalagi*.

Tagaloalagi creates the cliffs and counts 110 islands. Fititele is in the islands of the East, and everywhere mountains are scattered. Manu'atele is the land away from the wind, the Matāsaua, on Manu'atele, and the lee land is in Ofu and Tufoa'i. Fiji and Toga have smooth cliffs and stark plants which spread out leaves which support the falling sky.

Savai'i is as broad as a tethered leaf; in vain its mountains surpass the biggest mountains in height, but they are nothing special. They are shoots of Fatulaii in Manu'a and Fatueleele.

Stories of Places, Warriors and Heroes

Sons of "Great Heaven"

This period in history and legend is described by Dr. Krämer as being marked by the genealogies of the half-human deities and sons of "Great Heaven" (*Lagiatoatoa*): *Tagaloalagi* (Tagaloa residing in heaven), *Tagaloasu'enu'u* (Tagaloa searching for a village) and *Tagaloanofonu'u* (Tagaloa residing in the village).

The legends of *Tagaloalagi* and his many marriages show evidence of his growing genealogy, foundational to all Manu'a and Samoa. His children are the source of folktales and of key events in the annals of the prehistoric time period of Samoa and Manu'a. The introduction of the Tagaloalagi and his siblings leads to the continuum of mythologies that define Samoan and Manu'an beginnings and existence.

Almost all ancient legends and mythologies have a thread that leads to the "heavenly god" *Tagaloalagi*. We will show how his genealogy gives rise to real human figures whose genealogies will give birth to the major families that eventually settle the whole of the island chains. These legends include:

- the source of the invention of tools—the acquisition of fire leading to cooked meals, the construction of the first Samoan thatch house, the invention of scaffolding, etc.
- the beginning of customs and formalities—a funeral's ten heavens, the fetching of the ava from heaven, ceremonial protocols, etc.
- many cultural apparatuses—the orator staff and scepter (both from a coconut tree)
- the names of people, objects, and things
- and the procedures and protocols (ways of doing things)

The birth of the "sun god" *TagaloaLā* (*Tagaloa* the Sun) and *Tagaloa*—the two sons of *Tagaloalagi*—is followed by *Tagaloa* marrying *Lagimafola* (wide-open heaven) giving birth to *Pili* (lizard). *Pili,* grandson of *Pili*, will become a famous adventurer, mentioned in folklore in Tahiti and Hawaii. He is the ancestor of families that will become paramount chiefs of the Samoa island chains.

TagaloaLā's union with *Magamagaifatua* begets *'Alo'alolelā* (sunbeam) who marries *Sinafiti* (daughter of the Fijian King) and bears *TagaloaUi*.[xvii]

The interweaving of half-human warriors and reptile and sea creatures into the genealogical ancestry of Manu'a and Samoa is also evident in this stage of the islands' evolution.

The Story of the First TuiManu'a

At this time *Aga'euta* (land toward the mountains) marries his wife *Aga'etai* (land toward the sea) in the hamlet of Sauā (where *LuaUi* and her son built their first house at the Faleniu property—see Luama'a and LuaUi, page77). *Aga'etai* gives birth to a boy who is given the name *Galea'i* by the SaTagaloa (the Tagaloalagi family, which, as we have seen, occupies the first through ninth heavens). The myth says that *Galea'i* was brought down by the SaTagaloa before the birth of *Aga'euta* and *Aga'etai's* son, and SaTagaloa instructed the couple to name him *Galea'i*. A crown was bestowed from heaven by *Tagaloalagi* on this *Galea'i*. Thus he became the first (human) paramount royal chief of Manu'a. The *Galea'i* royal crown, given to him by *Tagaloalagi,* was transferred to his son, the TuiManu'a.

The Story of the Master Fisherman

The guardian demonic spirits of *Ao* and *Po's* sacred "House of Spears" (*Tulutuluitao*) gave *'Alo'alolelā* (son of *TagaloaLā* and *Magamagaifatua*) a choice of two fishhooks (*pa*). The first one was well-polished and shiny, and appeared to be a "real winner" and a successful fishhook, hence called the "the blessed one." The second was the one that looked not too pretty; it was unimpressive and was called the "disaster one." *'Alo'alolelā* was instructed by his father to choose the "disaster one" (*au o mala*), for the nature of this fishhook (*pa*) is that it begins with disaster and more disaster, and then finally gives success. The "blessed one" (*au o manū*) starts out with blessings and more blessings then turns to disaster. Hence the Samoan saying: *Au o manū, au o manū, au o mala. Au o mala, au o mala, au o manū,* which is an introduction to the nature of chances—that the more you try and fail, the higher the chance is that success is near; as the saying goes, rain is always followed by dryness. For likewise, the more initial successes you have, the higher the chance that failure is near. And so, *'Alo'alolelā* obeyed the command of his father and selected the *pa o mala*.

And now, in his search for a master fisherman to tie the whale-tooth fish-hook that he had received from *Ao* and *Po*, *'Alo'alolelā* met *Luagia* who was unloading his abundant catch at the nearby beach. *'Alo'alolelā* asked *Luagia* if he could help teach how to tie and use the fishing hook. Otherwise *'Alo'alolelā* was going to be killed by his father-in-law, the TuiFiti. *Luagia* said, "I cannot go with you, but I will have my children go with you. They are also master fishermen." And *'Alo'alolelā* was so happy that he thanked *Luagia* many times over.

While *Luagia's* sons were on the vessel, ready for departure, their sister *Sina* insisted that they take her with them on their journey. And they could not decline her request.

Upon meeting the TuiFiti on their arrival in Fiji, *'Alo'alolelā* introduced the boys and their sister to the king of Fiji as his adopted children from Savai'i, Samoa. They were successful with the fish-hook, but *Sina's* brothers disapproved of the TuiFiti living together with *Sina,* so they wanted to escape back home to Savai'i. Each of the brothers, individually, sacrificed themselves by jumping into the ocean, where they transformed into a reef to derail the TuiFiti and his warrior vessels, to ensure safe swimming and a safe arrival for their sister *Sina*. Thus, they all died in the ocean in their escape to ensure *Sina's* safe arrival.

Sina continued the legend and her lineage in Savai'i.

The Cove of Spirits

The Cove of Spirits, according to legend, is the place where the spirits of the dead, in the whole of Samoa and Manu'a, would enter the deep blue sea and swim toward Fafa-o-Sauali'i. There are two paths: one for the chiefs and one for the general population. This is, effectively, Samoa's version of Hades (Greek) or Pluto (Roman) in classical mythology. Samoans would also refer to it as the land of Pulotu (as in The Story of the Warrior *Elo*), where Pulotu always conjures up a land somewhere far, far away. It's somewhere in the distant past, like referring to a place where the ancestors came from.

This is where Samoan culture differs from Christianity's view of resurrection. In Samoan culture, the belief about spiritual resurrection is that the living can still communicate with their loved ones who have passed on. They exist, to Samoans, in a spiritual form.

Unlike Hades in Greek mythology, there is no god of the Samoan underworld. The Greek gods and deities judge you and determine which part of Hades you will go to, but the Samoan view is simple; all go to Pulotu. Samoan legends include stories of the octopus (the demon *Fe'e*—see Stories of the Legendary Octopus *Fe'e*, page 85) and the moray eel who live in Pulotu and Salefe'e, and this is where fire comes from in legend.

In the words often recited by the orators: "the language, and all of its cultural appointments have already been determined and settled in Pulotu." *'O upu o Samoa ua uma ona malepe i Pulotu*.

Resurrection, for Samoans, is evidenced by the belief that their ancestors speak to them on a daily basis. Samoans call on their ancestors when in need. The spirit of their dead ancestors watches them and knows what they are doing. Sometimes they speak their mind when they are not happy. In this, the missionaries found parallels with Christianity—the practice of believing in God and of constant communication with God through prayer. You will find out more about this in my next book, *Navigators Return: God's "Charge of the Light Brigade" Missionaries.*

The Pandemonium

The Filled Ocean Water Pit and The Dry Water Pit in Lotofaga, Upolu, are said to be further resting places for spirits, or perhaps places where they bathe. The water-pool is located 50 yards from the rocky shoreline, up on a cliff. It is deep, 30 feet down to the waterline, and about 20 feet wide. The round radius opening is like a water-well; the seawater comes in and fills it during high tide and disappears during low tide. The wind, when it's blowing, finds a path where the water flows down the cliffs settling in the pool, and it makes a pandemonium sound. Thus the legend that the spirits travel from the underworld into the pool for convocation.

The Young Man's River

Tagaloalagi and his wife, who was already several months pregnant, went night fishing, and she had a miscarriage at the beach rocks, abandoning the fetus. *Tagaloalagi*, not much concerned, went on home.

In the early morning, birds pecked on the fetus and it began to move and grow; the birds started to hover over the discarded fetus, and it took on a human form—the form of a boy who grew up—and the spirits named him *Tuutogiagogo*. *Tagaloalagi* began to recognize that the young man was the aborted fetus that had been abandoned on the rocks at the shore.

The small spring under the cave that nurtured boy to life is called the Young Man's River—a place that is life-saving for all those who travel by and seek fresh water to drink and a place to bathe for refreshment.

Moso's Footprint

The famous demigod Warrior *Moso* (TuiAtua *Moso,* father of *Lu,* in some versions) is said to have left a giant footprint when he stepped from Fiji to Samoa. One footprint is in Samoa. The other is on Viti Levu in Fiji.

The Rock at Uafato

In the village of Uafato, Upolu, there is a rock with sacred water that villagers believe nurtured all the demigods canvassing there.

Tagaloalagi is associated with the village of Uafato. The Warrior *Moso* lived in Uafato, and *Tagaloalagi's* wife *Ila*, grand-daughter of TuiAtua *Moso* and *Sinalesopoalemalama,* brought *Tagaloalagi* to Uafato and to his residence Malata, in Atua. Also, the story of *Lu's* stolen chickens is said to take place at Uafato. For according to Fuimaono Na'oia, *Lufasiāitu* (*Lu*) and his sister *Fatukoama's* parents were *Tuasivi* (mountain ridge) and *Palapala* (mud) in the village of Uafato, Atua—this is the story of first *Lufasiāitu*, the one with a flock of chickens (see The Story of the Demigod *Lufasiāitu,* page 96)[xviii]—a later *Lufasiāitu* was the son of TuiAtua *Moso,* also in Uafato, and became TuiAtua *Lufasiāitu*.[xix]

Also in Uafato, *TaeoiAtua* and his sister *Talalaufala* were born from their father *Tanu* and mother *Fili*. *TaeoiAtua* is the one who discovered, when his parents were summoned to Tuana'i village to work farm the Malietoa's plantation, that only the Malietoa salted his food. In spite of the Malietoa's tapu against going to the sea, *TaeoiAtua* went to fetch salt water to dry food and thus salted the food. Then the Malietoa decided to allow all of Samoa to use salt for their food.

Stories of the Legendary Octopus *Fe'e*

How *Fe'e* came to Manu'a

According to the Manu'an legend, recorded by Dr. Krämer, *Tagaloalagi* journeyed to Savai'i to examine his creation and stopped to rest at his residence in Malae Alamisi in Samata-uta and Samata-tai, the village close to Falealupo, in Alataua district. Falealupo is the location of *Fafa-o-Sauali'i*, the entrance to Pulotu and Salefe'e.

Pulotu is the Samoan counterpart to Hades, Elysium, or Tartarus. And Pulotu and Salefe'e are the residence of the demon *Fe'e* (the octopus) along with the sea eel or the moray. The octopus turned human by night and was an octopus by day. He was feared by the villagers and was worshiped as the god of war by the people of Vaimauga district.

As *Tagaloalagi* was strolling on the shoreline, he came upon the *Fe'e* (the octopus) swimming on the coral. *Tagaloalagi* asked *Fe'e*, "Who are you?"

Fe'e answered, "I am *Fe'e*, the ruler of Pulotu and Salefe'e, together with the moray."

Tagaloalagi was curious and followed up with another question, "Who are your parents?"

The *Fe'e* said, "I don't have any parents."

And so *Tagaloalagi* invited *Fe'e* to go with him to Manu'a.

At this point, when *Fe'e* departed with *Tagaloalagi* to Manu'a, the eel (or moray) became the guardian of Pulotu, until the time of *Saveasi'uleo*, the human with the tail like an eel.

Fe'e, now in Manu'a, became the father of the demonic beings *Sinasa'umani* and *Sasa'umani*. *Sinasa'umani* married *TagaloaUi*, and *Sasa'umani* married *Togia*, a chief of the west coast of Savai'i, in the Gaga'emalae district. *Sasa'umani* was known as the great fisher woman, and she gave birth to a boy named *Sa'umani,* later given the name *Pulelei'ite*.

The next mention of *Fe'e* is in the legend of *Ti'eti'eitalaga* (below) who wrestled fire away from *Fe'e* in Salefe'e.

But another legend involving *Fe'e* gives a different origin for *Fe'e* in the tale of *Taputoa,* whose wife's miscarried placenta was thrown into the sea and became the *Fe'e* (octopus). This is the story in my grandmother's family genealogy, going back to *Mualeoā,* the daughter of *Fe'e* (see The Girl who married the Octopus, page 88). This is where *Fe'e* successfully joins his blood with a human to produce two girls, *Mualeoā* and *Samalaulu*, and a boy *Momoemaāitu* who is given the title So'oialo (the joint child).

The Story of Fire

The octopus, *Fe'e*, was known as a demonic god and he lived in the underworld, in Salefe'e, together with the guardian of fire, *Mafui'e* (which means earthquake). According to legend,

Ti'eti'etalaga (the son of *Mafui'e's* sister) acquired fire for cooking from *Fe'e.*

Ti'eti'etalaga was the son of *Ulu* (short for *Uluelepapa,* sister of *Mafui'e*) and a man called *Talaga* from the village of Fagali'i, Upolu. But *Ulu* was childless. One day, on her way to get salt water, she saw a maiden (a Taupou) named *Ve'a*, taking a bath at the place named Saletua. *Ulu* took the young maiden, *Ve'a*, to *Talaga* so they could produce a child. *Ve'a* did produce a boy, and later he was given a name *Ti'eti'eitalaga* (for he was always carried or sitting—*ti'eti'e*—on his father's shoulders).

Ulu was extremely fond of *Ti'eti'eitalaga* and cared for him very well. She cracked the rocks to catch water from the rain, both for drinking and to bathe the boy. And while all other people did not have cooked food, they ate meals cooked and prepared by *Talaga* in the underworld, in Salefe'e, where *Mafui'e* and the *Fe'e* lived.

When *Ti'eti'eitalaga* inquired about why other people didn't have cooked food, Uluelepapa told her son that there was a magic spirit down in the underworld that was used by *Mafui'e* and by his father *Talaga* to cook his meals. And so *Ti'eti'eitalaga* decided he would go down to Salefe'e to bring the spirit up to cook everyone's food. *Mafui'e* lived in Fue'aloa, and the land leading to the underworld cave of Salefe'e was Tauaifu'efu'e.

When *Ti'eti'eitalaga* got to Salefe'e, he discovered that he had to fight *Mafui'e* through various wrestling matches. Upon defeating *Mafui'e*, he was given fire—and he saved the girl *Si'isi'imane'e*. He took her and the firebrand up to his two mothers and *Talaga*.

Mafui'e instructed *Ti'eti'eitalaga* to use dry wood to keep the firebrand lit. But the tale does not mention where the fire originated from. The name *Mafui'e* (meaning earthquake) implies a deep crack in the earth's surface though, where the *Fe'e* lives. This seems to imply a volcanic or lightning origin for fire.

In another version of this legend, according to author Ali'i Felela Fred Henry,[xx] *Ti'eti'eitalaga's* original name is *Maui*, the child who was born a blood clot, implying a miscarriage, and was left at sea by the mother, *Maeatutala*. But the high tide's waves washed the clot to shore, and the father found it and raised the child to life. Thus his complete name is *Maui Ti'eti'eitalaga*, the fire fetcher. The name *Maui* is known across all Polynesia, including Hawaii and

Maori. This title appears in this writer's family genealogy in Taū and Olosega Islands.

The myth is set in the Period where *TagaloaLā* and *TagaloaUi* are contemporaries, for *Tagaloalagi* begat *TagaloaLā* who bore *TagaloaUi*, father of *Taeotagaloa*. *Fe'e* (the octopus) is a war deity, the war god of A'ana and Vaimauga districts—Vaimauga district is where Fagali'i village is located, the birthplace of *Talaga*, father of *Ti'eti'etalaga* who obtained fire.

According to Vaimauga legend, the *Fe'e* is the father of two girls, *Mualeoā* (progenitor of this author's ancestry) and *Samalaulu*, and a boy with the title So'oialo (*so'o* means connected or conjoined, and *alo* means son). So'oialo is the child that unifies the marriage of a human girl *Sinatualalafā* (daughter of *Fa'asavalu* of Falelatai) and *Fe'e* (the animal, the octopus). So'oialo became a paramount chief of the district of Vaimauga, Upolu.

There is a relationship by marriage between So'oialo and TuiManu'a, for So'oialo *Momoemaāitu* married TuiManu'a's daughter *Taupaū*, who gave birth to a son, *Tiaseuga*.

The *Fe'e So'oialo* legend indicates that the girl *Samalaulu* is the origin of the Samalaulu name in Samoa. The marriage of *So'oialo* to *Taupaū,* daughter of the TuiManu'a, is then how the Samalaulu name came to Manu'a, for the TuiManu'a later named his daughter *Samalaulu*, and this is the *Samalaulu* who married TuiAtua *Malaetele*, from which marriage issued *Taepipitele*. Thus Samalaulu is the princess title of TuiManu'a.

The Girl who married the Octopus

On my mother's side, her family are descendants of the legendary octopus in the district of Vaimauga, Upolu. The octopus *Fe'e* married a beautiful girl, named *Sinatualalafā*. They gave birth to a child given the title So'oialo, which means "the joint child" (*so'o* means connected or conjoined, and *alo* means son) so the blood genealogies were enjoined in this child. Thus So'oialo is a paramount title in Vaimauga, a sub-district of the Fale Tuamasaga District, Upolu.

In this legend, *Fe'e* (the octopus) and his brother *To'oa'au* and sister *Si'u* were descendants of a couple named *Taputoa* and *Polulalelei*. *Polulalelei* was a daughter of Chief *Moso* of Aleipata village, and *Taputoa* was a son of the King of Fiji, TuiFiti *Ta-poo* (or *Ca* in Fijian), and *Paula*, a Rarotogan woman. *Taputoa*, also known by his other name *Vaovasa*, came from Fiji to escape the cruelty of his father, and landed in the village of Aleipata.

Fe'e, *To'oa'au,* and their sister *Si'u* were floating on the ocean one day on their makeshift canoe, made out of a few logs. They drifted westward of Upolu Island toward the district of A'ana. They noticed, from beyond the reef, much smoke coming up from Leulumoega, the village capital of the district of A'ana. They decided to investigate and turned toward the Leulumoega lagoon. The brothers instructed their sister *Si'u* to stay on board while they went to find out what the ruckus, coming from the village, was all about.

When they reached the village, the brothers discovered a battle raging between the paramount chiefs TuiA'ana *Sagaate* and TuiA'ana *Vaemā*; they were at war to decide who would inherit the paramount title TuiA'ana for the district of A'ana—i.e. which one would become king.

Paramount Chief *Sagaate* asked the brothers for assistance. The brothers accepted the challenge and so, with the aid of their strengths that were half-human and half-spirit, warrior-like, and ferocious, TuiA'ana *Sagaate* emerged victorious.

During this episode, *Fe'e* (the octopus) fell in love with *Sinatualalafā*, the daughter of High Chief *Fa'asavalu* of Falelatai. He proceeded to ask the high chief for his daughter's hand in marriage. Although High Chief *Fa'asavalu* was in agreement, the daughter was totally appalled with this ugly "animal creature." However, in accordance with the will of her father, she reluctantly went with *Fe'e* as his bride.

The octopus said to *Sinatualalafā*, "Come, get on my back and let us go and see my brother *To'oa'au* and sister *Si'u*," as written by Lafai Sauoaiga Ape in *O le Mavaega i le Tai*.[xxi] Their journey ended in the village of Apia, the capital town of Samoa, in the district of Vaimauga. So now the octopus told *Sinatualalafā* to get off and make this place her home, and said, "I will go up the river Vaisigago, and I will live up the hill so I can keep an eye on you from up there."

And so the couple lived, separately, until one day the *Fe'e* came down and expressed his desire to consummate their union with a child of this marriage between a beautiful woman and an octopus.

It didn't take long, and she got pregnant and gave birth to a daughter, called *Mualeoā*, which means pandemonium—for the people down the beach village were told by the octopus to make an uproar so he could hear and know she was giving birth to their child.

This first-born girl, *Mualeoā,* was also given the salutation of the "child that consummated the marriage between a human female and an animal creature," Soso'oialo—the joint child. The second child was also a girl, and she was named *Samalaulu*, and the third and last-born was a boy who was given the name *Momoemaāitu*—"sleeping with the spirit;" the name was given because he slept with the demonic spirit in a cave in Vailima village. He was also given the high chief title So'oialo (or Soso'oialo), which is a paramount title in Vaimauga District, which includes Apia town proper.

Momoemaāitu's descendants are the paramount chiefs *Seumanutafa* and *To'omalatai*, and *Tofaeono* and *LeNiu* (*Momoemaāitu's* sons-in-law). *Tofaeono* and his younger brother *LeNiu* were descendants of *Asomua* of the Malietoa clan. When *Tofaeono* died, *LeNiu* became Tofaeono *LeNiu*, so this is how Tofaeono chief title came from the Siumu district to the Vaimauga district of the Tuamasaga in Upolu. Tofaeono *LeNiu* married *Mualeoā*-II, daughter of So'oialo *Momoemaāitu*, and they produced *Tofaeono's* daughter *Samalaulu*. *Samalaulu* married Malietoa *Taulapapa*—he who received *Nafanua's* prophesied "Kingdom from Heaven" decree (see *Nafanua* and the Kingdom of God, page 176)—and produced a son *Leulua'iali'i*. *Leulua'iali'i* married *Monolaui'e*, daughter of Paramount Orator Chief *Alipia*, who bore a girl, *Ta'ulesulu*. She married Paramount Chief *Manua'ifua*, son of Chief *Saena*, who was a descendant of Malietoa *Taulapapa's* sister *Sinalemanaui*, of Afega village, and produced *Savea*, *Ututa'aloga* and a girl, *Tu'uamaleulua'iali'i*, who married TuiA'ana TuiAtua *Faumuinā,* giving birth to *Samalaulu*. All of this gives us another convenient way to roll up all the mats securely within the Malietoa family clan.

My mother is descended from the first-born girl, *Mualeoā,* in Vaimauga District, who wed *Saena Faigā*, son of Malietoa *Sagagaimuli* and *Sinalemanaui* (sister to Malietoa *Taulapapa* who succeeded his brother-in-law, Malietoa *Sagagaimuli*.)

On December 18, 1995, the Supreme Court of Samoa's Land and Titles Court System issued a final decision Number L.C.454P1-P11, that confirmed that the ruling authority of the title So'oialo and others, as well as land properties, is vested in the descendants of the first-born girl *Mualeoā* and the last-born boy *Momoemaāitu*, who was given the paramount title. It took us four years to argue our case, and that is considered a short time to elapse. It is not unusual to take some 20 to 30 years to battle out these family heirloom cases.

The Ubiquitous *Samalaulu* Princess Name

According to our family history, the legend as told and now recorded in our supreme court decision of 1995, the second child of the *Fe'e* and *Sinatualalafā* was the girl *Samalaulu*. She married Paramount Chief *Leutelelei'ite*, descendant of TuiAtua *Leutelelei'ite*, in around A.D.1213. Her genealogy (that of her actual descendants) has died out. However, the name has been carried forward by family relatives. Her brother So'oialo *Momoemaāitu* married *LeTelesā*, paramount chief and ruler of the adjacent district of Faleata, giving birth to two girls (named *Mualeoā*-II and *Samalaulu*-II, for his sisters), and a son *Pua'asegisegi* (which means "undomesticated pig").

As we saw above, Paramount Chief *Tofaeono*, grandson of the illustrious Chief *Asomua* of the Malietoa clan, married *Mualeoā* who bore a girl named *Samalaulu* in memory of her sister. Then Malietoa *Taulapapa* (in the Tafa'ifa *Salamasina* time period) married *Samalaulu,* who bore a son *Leulua'iali'i*. *Leulua'iali'i* married the daughter, *Monolaui'e*, of *Alipia,* the senior ruling orator authority of A'ana. She gave birth to a girl named *Ta'ulesulu*. She married a paramount chief of Afega village named *Manua'ifua* with the issue of two sons (*Savea* and *Ututa'aloga*) and a girl named *Tu'uamaleulua'iali'i*.

Paramount TuiAtua TuiA'ana *Faumuinā* came calling for *Tu'uamaleulua'iali'i's* hand in marriage and was accepted. *Faumuinā* and *Tu'uamaleulua'iali'i* produced a girl that was named *Samalaulu* in memory of her great-great-grandmother. This *Samalaulu* was also called TuiA'ana *Samalaulu*, sister to TuiA'ana *Fonotī* and TuiA'ana *Va'afusuaga-Toleafoa*. This is the tripod of royal children that caused the only civil war in all of Samoa. The war ended with *Fonotī* victorious, and he claimed the Tafa'ifa title for himself. Thus he became the second Tafa'ifa after *Salamasina*.

In this way, the name *Samalaulu* originated with *Fe'e* in Vaimauga, traveled to Manu'a, then traversed to Atua and A'ana and the rest of Samoa. There are many princess titles, prince titles, and other titles that are likewise memorialized by family in the form of namesakes. This is an example of how names are perpetuated in living memories and in family kinship. There are fragmented family tales of how they derived a name but, if one would look deeper into the origin of a name, one should find the source of the river in a tiny stream, metaphorically speaking.

Period III: *Tagaloalagi's* Offspring

Designation of Tasks

As the Manu'an Creation Poem continues, chiefs are named, and tasks are assigned to them. The first chief is *Alele*, *Tagaloalagi's* son, who "slides down (from heaven) to the *Malae* of the *Vesi*" (the meeting ground for war). And in the quiet peace of the *Malae* of the *Toto'a* (the meeting ground for peace), *Tagaloalagi's* circle of chiefs watch to see who will receive the first cup of ava.

Losi is decreed to fish in the sea and take the best fish up to heaven. And the first carpenter receives the first ava of his title; happy voyage for his boat for which he lays the keel. The first ship heads to Manu'a, and the title is carried to the *Faletufuna*, which is the circle of chiefs and carpenters.

Samoans have always believed that the *matai*'s titles came from *Tagaloalagi*. They use their authority to designate the *matai* title. In ancient days they really didn't have first names. Instead, very much like the American Indians, their names were given by something that you did, or that your ancestors did.

And so, mythology, legend, and folklore continue the story of Manu'an and Samoan ancient history.

The Story of *Losi*

The Legends of *Losi*

Losi is referred to as Chief *Losi* with his two servants. It appears he is part of that early, or even the first, generation of heavenly celestial gods that broke away from the SaTagaloa (the family of Tagaloa in the heavens) to be human.

Manu'an legend refers to *Losi*, *Folasā*, *Taeotagaloa*, *Lefanoga,* and in some cases also *TagaloaUi* and *TagaloaLā* as being in the same generation. The legends cryptically say they were all descendants of *Tagaloalagi* or the heavenly celestials and were members of the SaTagaloa in the first through ninth heavens. In legend, *Losi, LeFolasā*, *Lefanoga* and others orchestrated a war with *Tagaloalagi* in which they were victorious. They brought taro, fish, and many other foods, and the ava down to earth.

In the Samoan legend, *Losi* went up to heaven on his second trip and came back down with the ava plant. Manu'an legend says *Folasā* and *Losi* brought down the ava plant together. But what we do know is that *LeFolasā* was in charge of the ava and the aumaga (the men) of the TuiManu'a. Also, the Pa'u name and title (the title of Pa'u Young Jr., son of the missionary Young—see Orator Chief Pa'u, page 259) originates from the legend of *Losi*.

According to legend, *Losi* (the spirit) took fish to heaven for *Tagaloalagi's* meal and ended up fighting a war with *Tagaloalagi's* children. *Losi, LeFolasā, Lefanoga*, and others organized the battle that defeated the SaTagaloa clan, and thus they brought to earth different foods, including the ava plant, brought by *Folasā*. They also brought to earth the authorities for the chiefs—*Fiamē, Taimalelagi, Tuifa'asisina, Lavasi'i* and others, including the title Telea'ai (or Telei'ai). Hence, the origin of the Telei'ai in Samatau village, with the Fiamē family clan, and the Telea'ai in Fitiuta, Manu'a, with the Leasaū family clan.

The Origin of *Losi*

Chief *Losi* does not have a human pedigree: The acid test for a human pedigree is whether the character in the story has an origin in the human or the celestial, and whether there a continuing lineage from the character. This is like with the *Fe'e* or the eel, who might be born from a blood clot from a miscarriage that is often thrown into the sea, and in his case later survives.

The story of *Leutogitupa'itea* (see *Leutogitupa'itea*: Progenitor of the Tonumaipe'a Dynasty, page 131) tells how she was marooned on a desert island which had only *Losi*, the demonic spirit, living there. But *Losi* was enterprising in organizing the war with the celestials, whereby they were defeated and *Tagaloalagi* had to surrender the *Ao*, or crown-like titles, to the various families. The implication is that, before *Tagaloalagi* surrendered those sacred *Ao* or crown titles, they were just ordinary names—that's my interpretation.

So *Losi* is a descendant of *Tagaloalagi*, and, like *Folasā,* he came down to earth, but his pedigree did not survive.

The Story of the War between Human and Heavenly Beings

Losi was decreed to fish in the sea and take the best fish up to heaven. But, when he brought the fish, he was asked, "Is this a meal for *Tagaloalagi's* whole circle of chiefs? No, take all the fish, with the exception of the *poitoa*; that is for *Tagaloalagi*." *Poitoa*, the snail fish, is a delicacy—Samoa's equivalent of French escargot. It was left for *Tagaloalagi*, as Chief *Losi* instructed his servant, *Vaeau*.

Later the present of a fish from *Losi*, which *Vaeau* took to heaven to *Tagaloalagi* and his people, resulted in a combination of misunderstandings, which led to a comedy of errors, causing a war between the heavenly beings and humans.

The legend of Chief *Losi* describes an early attempt of humans to acquire material gifts from the god *Tagaloalagi*—gifts such as food, tools and knowledge, and, of course, wisdom. On his first visit to the god *Tagaloalagi* in Heaven, *Losi* stole a taro shoot and hid it in a secret recess of his body. The celestials (*Tagaloalagi's* children) searched him but, not finding the plant, gave him a thrashing and chased him down to earth. *Losi* swore to have his revenge and prepared with some demon spirits. He sent his speedy servant *Vaeau* to spy on the celestials up in heaven, and in one day *Vaeau* he returned with a favorable report for his chief.

In the meantime Chief *Losi* had just fished out some stingrays that he immediately earmarked as gifts for the god *Tagaloalagi*. And so *Losi* and his companions went to heaven, to take the stingrays for *Tagaloalagi*. They arrived before daybreak, and so they laid the stingray fish between the door posts. When the celestials came into the house they stepped on the slippery backsides of the flat stingrays, and they slipped and hurt their heads!

The celestials were not happy campers, so they planned to avenge themselves on the humans. They invited *Losi* and his men to float down the river, which tumbled over a waterfall. This was without any danger to the Immortals, but it was supposed to bring the humans to grief. But *Losi's* demonic spirit, *Fulufuluitolo*, posted himself near the waterfall, caught the terrestrials one by one, and saved them all—hence the saying: *O le lave a Fulufuluitolo* (saved by *Fulufuluitolo*).

Losi then stole the *ava* plant, breadfruit, and coconuts. The tale ends with a war in which the celestials were defeated and *Tagaloalagi* had to surrender six titles (six *Ao*) which were divided among the warrior companions of *Losi* as follows:

1. *Tagaloa i Pata* of Falelatai
2. *Fetafune* of SaMauga
3. *Lavasi'i* of Lefaga
4. *Tuifa'asisina* of Satuimalufilufi
5. *Taimalelagi* of Mulifanua
6. *Fiamē* of Samatau[xxii]

The Story of the Warrior *Moso*

TuiAtua *Moso* is the Spirit Warrior, well-known throughout the whole of Polynesia, also known for his meanest temper. His human descendant became one of the earliest holders of the TuiAtua title. In mythology, *Moso* is a demonic half-man, half-spirit that lives in Savai'i and Upolu simultaneously. He is omnipotent and all-powerful. He marries a woman, *Sulu-i-mauga* from Uafato, in Atua district, who gives birth to *Lu* (see below), the thrasher of the Spirits—*Lufasiāitu*. (In the story of the origin of humankind, below, *Lu's* parents are given, instead, as *Tupufua,* the first human, and *Suluimauga.)*

The Story of the Demigod *Lufasiāitu*

The legend of *Lu* is the Samoan legend of the rooster—or *moa*, a general word for chicken—and is often referred to as the source of the name *Sa* (sacred) *Moa* (chicken), making Samoa.

Following another genealogical line, *Lupe's* (pigeon or chicken's) union with *Ma'ata'anoa* (loose rocks) produced *Palapala* (swamp, a fertile place conducive to producing and sustaining life). She united with *Nu'u* (a village) to produce *Tagata*, a human being born out of nothing, also known as *Tupufua*, the first human born out of nothing.

Tupufua married *Sulu-i-mauga* (the light shone over the mountains) and begat *Lu*. At this juncture, the Samoan and

Manu'an genealogical pedigrees unite, for Tagaloalagi's children are said to have occupied the first through the ninth heavens, while Tagaloalagi resides in tenth heaven.

The demigod warrior, *Lu*—later known as *Lufasiāitu* from *Lu* (his name), *fasi* (thrashing or beating), *āitu* (spirit)—lived in Uafato village in the District of Fagaloa, Atua. He is also the ancestor of the legendary, ubiquitous *Pili* in Polynesia.

Lu gathered up the chickens from across the island and built himself a chicken enclosure or farm. He made his chickens *tapu*; no one was permitted to eat the consecrated (*sa*) chicken. But then the people of *Tagaloalagi*, on their return home to heaven from a fishing expedition, discovered *Lu's* sacred chicken farm and decided to help themselves to the chickens. Upon *Lu's* discovery that his chicken had been stolen, his wrath descended on Tagaloalagi's people, starting with those residing in the first heaven. He waged war on them.

As *Lu* thrashed and whipped the people, they retreated upward to the next heavenly tier until they reached the ninth heaven, where Tagaloalagi's princess *Lagituaiva* resided—*Lagi* meaning sky, *tua* meaning circle, *iva* meaning ninth.

At this point, the omnipotent *Tagaloalagi* saw that *Lu* was approaching the tenth heaven, the location of his sacred throne. Thereupon *Tagaloalagi* said to *Lu*, "I beg your forgiveness. I offer you my princess *Lagituaiva* as a ransom for my people and my kingdom." At which point, the beautiful princess threw herself down, lying across *Lu's* warpath as an obstacle to gain his attention, with the hope of stopping him and his rage. And *Lu* now inherited that additional part of his name—*Lu-fasi-āitu* (Lu the destroyer of spirits).

Upon looking at the beautiful princess lying in front of him, *Lu* was mesmerized and touched by her bravery and her honorable sacrifice, made for her father and their people. While *Lu* was temporarily stunned by this act of "human sacrifice" made by this beautiful princess, *Tagaloalagi* spoke out saying, "*Lu*, may the burden be lifted. Take my daughter as atonement for the sins of SaTagaloalagi." (SaTagaloalagi means the household of *Tagaloalagi*.) Almost immediately *Lufasiāitu* replied, "*Tagaloalagi*, your people will live, their sin forgiven, because of Princess *Lagituaiva's* brave sacrifice."

In this version, *Lagituaiva* is also known as *Moa* (chicken or rooster). After this event princess Lagituaiva is also known as *Fa'alavaleAmoaileala* (the chicken lying on the sacrificial path).

The story of *Pili*

Pili, or *Pilipa'ū* (the Lizard that fell from Heaven) was the son of *Tagaloalagi* and *Lagimafola (Lu's* granddaughter). *Pilipa'ū* married *Sinalesae'e*, the TuiManu'a's daughter, who bore *Pilia'au* (the swimming lizard, also known as *Piliopo* or *Pilisosolo*, or *Pilipau*—these other names are given in the various versions of legends about *Pili*).

At this time, the paramount chiefs began giving birth to "demigods" including, for example, TuiManu'a, TuiAtua, TuiA'ana, TuiToga, TuiFiti, and, much later, after the Samoan/Togan war, the Malietoa *Sāvea*.[xxiii]

All this leads up to the era (A.D.180–A.D.300) of the major families and clans, headed by paramount chiefs decreed by the "god" or "deity," *Tagaloalagi,* and his demigod children:

- TuiManu'a (the name comes from *Tu*, to stand erect, *i*, here in, *Manu'a*)
- TuiToga, TuiA'ana, TuiAtua, TuiFiti
- other demigods and warriors such as *Lufasiāitu*,
- *Lata*, the boat-builder and adventurer,
- the warrior *Fitiaumua*, of whom legend has it that he was the first to conquer the whole of Polynesia.

And thus *Pili's* family genealogy and others grow longer, as we'll see in the lineages below.

The many names of *Pili*

Pili of Manu'a is known in Samoa by so many names that it often confuses the reader—for example, *Pilitavave*, *Piliuli*, *Pilipaū*, *Pilitaimalelagi*, *Piliopo*, etc. There are several legends that are worth summarizing here to get clarity on his story. The first is from Manu'a and the second is from Samoa.

The Manu'an Legend of *Pili*

Pega and *Pega* of Lefaga, in Taū, Manu'a, had three children, a girl named *Sina*, the firstborn boy named *Pilimoelagi* (which means *Pili* sleeps in heaven), and the second brother named *Pilimoevai* (*Pili* sleeps in the water-pool at Lefaga). The water-pool is named *Punafofoa* (which means, the water-spring that gave life).

The parents, *Pega* and *Pega*, forbade *Sina* from bathing in the water-pool, because of *Pilimoevai*. But *Sina's* desire to bathe and swim in the water-pool was tempting, and so she decided to go for a bathe and swim. And *Pilimoevai* swam by. He touched *Sina's* lower body, and she was shocked by it.

Sina jumped out of the water-pool but realized she had just met her brother *Pilimoevai*. Thus, *Sina* fled Lefaga to go to the Aualuma promontory, in Fitiuta. She met and married *Pulelei'ite*, who is also known as *Sa'umani* (son of *Fe'e's* granddaughter, the great fisher woman—see How *Fe'e* came to Manu'a, page 85). And she found a water-pool nearby, so she frequently liked to go for a bath there, where she applied the pollen of a Samoan flower, turmeric powder, to her skin. Thus the name of the pool is Vailega (water-pool for applying the turmeric powder—*my translation*).

Sina did not know that her brother *Pilimoevai* had followed her to Fitiuta and lived by *Sina's* house, by the water-pool *Vailega*. But when *Sina* went for a bath, and *Pilimoevai* swam by, and his tail touched *Sina*, she realized it was her brother again.

This became immediately known to *Pulelei'ite* because he had demonic spirit power. And so *Pulelei'ite* summoned *Pilimoevai* up to the house, so the two could have serious talk. It's at this point *Pilimoevai* gave his parting words of farewell to *Sina* and *Pulelei'ite*, that he would go away; however, if *Sina* should have a successful childbirth and it should be a boy, he decreed that *Pulelei'ite* would name him *Pili*; if it were a girl, *Sina* would choose her name.

And it came to pass that *Sina* had a baby boy, and he was named *Pili*. The boy *Pili* grew up to be a proficient fisherman and loved to travel, to chase his catches across the archipelago. He left for Fa'alava, where *Tuitau* lived, and they became good friends until, one day, they had problems, and so *Pili* moved to Fagasāmeme. Shortly after, he left for Mulinu'u Faleasao, in

Manu'a, and he went into the ocean there. He swam (*a'au*) to the village of Vatia, in Tutuila, and he was called *Pilia'au*.

Pilia'au swam to Savai'i Island and landed on A'opo, so he was named *PiliA'opo* or *Piliopo*. His descendants were *Leopili* and *Pilisosolo*, as recorded in the *Manu'a Poem of Pili*.[xxiv]

The Samoan Legend of *Pili*

The second legend is from Samoa. A half-human, half- demonic man named *Loa* (some say *Lea*) married a girl named *Sina*. *Loa* and *Sina* had four children—the boys *Pili*, *Fuialaeo*, and *Ma'oma'o*, and the girl *Sina*.

The prophetic wind carried word of *Sina's* beauty. And the TuiFiti picked up the news and rushed right over to Fagaloa, in Atua, Upolu, where *Loa* and *Sina* and the family lived. TuiFiti was successful in winning permission for *Sina* to marry him and travel with him to Fiti Island.

Sina's brother *Pili* begged *Sina* to please take him with her to Fiti Island. At first she declined, but later she decided to take him with her in the side pocket of her lavalava, made from the leaves of the ti plant.

The ocean journey ran into a bad storm, and the Fijians blamed *Sina* for bad omens for the storm. And *Pili* whispered to Sina. He said how to guide the fleet of vessels through the storm, and they were saved. Not long after, a Fijian sailor saw *Pili's* head showing up on *Sina's* ti leaf lavalava, and was scared about *Sina* being a demon, not human. They were about to kill her or throw her off the vessel, but *Pili* whispered to *Sina*. He told her how to talk to the TuiFiti about her skills in navigating the vessel to safety, and TuiFiti agreed. But instead of *Sina* being thrown overboard, they threw *Pili* into the ocean.

Loa saw what was happening to his son, and so he sent the two brothers *Fuia* (black bird) and *Ma'oma'o* (a ground bird) to save *Pili*. They were able to get there in time to help *Pili* to a nearby island called Puagagana, which means a talking hibiscus tree. It's here that the two sons of *Tagaloalagi* named *I'uao* and *Uluao* lived. And *Pili* (who was a handsome man) begged them profusely to please help him get to Fiti (Fiji) Island, so he could be with his sister *Sina*.

In the meantime, *Sina's* journey finally arrived at Fiti Island. However, there was a bad famine, and the people were starving, and the TuiFiti blamed *Sina's* bad omen. *Pili* had already established his ufi (yam) plant on the island, but *Sina* was not aware of it. And so *Pili* planted the ufi vine, so it would grow toward where *Sina* was living. As *Sina* slowly discovered the ufi (yam) vine and realized it was a root for cooking and eating, she began to harvest the vine of the plant, and she followed the plant until she arrived at *Pili's* hut, by the kitchen hut of the TuiFiti. *Sina* informed the TuiFiti that there was a yam plant (like sweet potatoes) growing by the kitchen hut at the back by the forest, and again, *Pili* saved the Fijians, this time from starvation.

Pili told his sister that the ufi plantation had plenty for the rest of the bad weather season, and there was enough for the people for a good period of time. And so *Pili* said farewell to his precious sister *Sina*, and he left to go to heaven. This is how *Pili* left for heaven, and how, later, he fell back down onto Manu'a and thus was called *Pilipaū* (Pili fell from heaven).[xxv]

Gods and Houses

***Pili* and the Golden House**

In Manu'an mythology, the origin of the house is that it comes from heaven, gifted from the god *Tagaloalagi* as a home for his son TuiManu'a. Somehow the gift, the *Fale Ula* or Golden House, was placed originally on top of the mountain between Tau and Fitiuta in Manu'a. Nobody could reach up into the sky to get it down, until the boatmen urged *Pili*, son of TuiManu'a, to go up and bring the house down. (*Pili*, according to the original genealogy, is the son of *Tagaloalagi*, but he's also known as the son of TuiManu'a, son of *Tagaloalagi*.)

Manu'an folklore tells how *Pili* woke up from his rest and used the mast of the vessel as a ladder which he climbed up to bring down the Golden house, the *Fale Ula*, for TuiManu'a, who was Paramount High Chief of all Samoa and Manu'a.[xxvi]

The mythology continues to express the half-human, half-spirit strength of *Pili*, as a descendant of the god *Tagaloalagi*. Additionally the myth serves to indicate the original source of the first house, as being a gift from the god to the Manu'ans, as a sacred residence of TuiManu'a and of later the chiefs. Hence the name of the TuiManu'a's residence title: *Fale'ula*.

House of One Hundred Posts

It is said that the original Golden House (*Fale'ula*) had posts made from human beings to hold and support the house. This house is populated with the spirits, to assist in governing the affairs of TuiManu'a. So other half-human and half-spirit paramount chiefs or warriors showed off their power and authority by emulating TuiManu'a's house, using posts made from humans. For example, TuiAtua *Lu* had his "house of a hundred posts" (*Faleselau*), Tagaloa *A'opo* also had his house of one hundred posts. And, of course, *Tagaloalagi* also had a house with one hundred posts of human beings, at Le Faga, Fitiuta, Manu'a.

Grand Architects

Further legend has it that Tagaloalagi gave his decree to the first carpenter, *Manufili*, at the same time that scaffolding (*fatamanu*) was first created.

Samoan and Manu'an culture is not the only culture to include their god in the design of houses. There are many examples of architects being revered in Western culture, including, for example, the iconic Imhotep, the ancient Egyptian architect who designed the step pyramid at Saqqara for King Djoser around 2,667 to 2,600 B.C.[xxvii] In H.W. Wallis's work on the creation myths of the Rigveda of ancient India, we read that "the building of the world was done very much like the building of a house by architects and artificers."[xxviii] He was, of course, referring to Tvashtar, the clever-handed carpenter-god who, in particular, manufactured, with his hatchet, the thunderbolt of Indra. And there is the Grand Architect: In the Old Testament of the Bible—Proverbs 8:27—it is said that "When he established the heavens... he drew a circle on the face of the deep," yielding an image of a creator God using the tools of architecture (a compass) to establish a divine measure upon the world.

Likewise Samoans and Manu'ans give reverence to the designated Chief Carpenters of a house, as well as to the carpenters of a boat, canoe or vessel. *Lata*, for example, is a well-known character in Polynesia—the first builder of a sailing vessel, and the first Polynesian to immigrate to New Zealand. His name is *Rata* in Maori, son of *Wahieroa* of Tregear.[xxix]The same status of revered honor is given to the *Tatau* (tattooing) architect, Chief *Su'a*, and clan.

The House of *Sina*

There is a legend that tells of how women defeated the men in a house-thatching contest. The famous Chief *Tigilau* from Falelatai, Upolu, came calling on the maiden, *Sina*, in Falealupo, Savai'i. As was customary, *Tigilau* brought his entourage of young men to help in serving the chief and to make a good impression on *Sina* and her parents and village folk. On this occasion, a contest ensued, between *Tigilau's* entourage and *Sina's* maiden entourage, as to who could finish the thatching of the house first. That evening, *Tigilau's* entourage were all so tired from the evening's festivities that they overslept; when they awoke in the late morning, they found the women had already thatched the house. The women had shown the men that they were capable of doing the work, and that they depended little on the men. Chief *Tigilau* and his entourage, in shame, made a hasty departure. Not only had they lost in winning *Sina's* love, but also they brought disgrace to the men of Samoa.

Other Stories of *Pili*

Pili and the Ava Plant

Another story is quoted by Krämer and Ali'i Felela Fred Henry and other writers of Mr. Stuebel.[xxx] *Faleaseu*, in the village of Vailele, in Vaimauga, Upolu, had two daughters, *Tinopoula* and *Sinaafalua* or *Sina*. The two girls were on their way home from their search for their father's hunting expedition and they saw a large fleet of vessels at the lagoon in front of Mulifanua, in A'ana, Upolu. And, out of curiosity, they went to the vessels and inquired if they could maybe catch a ride to the shore of Vailele village.

They found that the TuiFiti was on board, looking for a treatment for his stomach illnesses. And so the girls said they could help. And so the TuiFiti took the girls with him to Fiti Island, to find a treatment for his stomach disease. *Sina* came up with a concoction of the sweet coconut juice; she added salt seawater and fermented it for a few days, and then it made a drink. This helped cleanse the intestines.

The TuiFiti was happily recovered and became fond of *Sina*. They were married, and *Sina* gave birth to two boys and a girl. The boys were called *Suasamiavaava* (juice of sea water and ava juice) and *Soalateteleupegaofiti* (*Soa* is of the TuiManu'a genealogy, known for his extraordinarily large Fijian fishing net). The girl was *Muliovailele*.

Suasamiavaava died at a young age and decreed that his brother and sister should take the plant, which would grow up on his grave, to Samoa in his honor. The plant is the ava plant. It grew up in the form of a human hand, with fingers represented by the roots of the ava plant.

Muliovailele brought the ava plant to her father's home in Vailele, and her brother *Soalateteleupegaofiti* brought the ava to Palauli, Savai'i. Then *Muliovailele* married *Tagaloalagi* and gave birth to a firstborn son named *Pili*. *Pili* was quite "ornery," and his parents threw him down to earth, where he landed on Manu'a. Thus, again, *Pili* that fell from heaven, or *Pilipaū*.

Pili and the Taro Roots

Pilipaū married the daughter of the TuiManu'a. But *Pili* didn't like the way the Manu'an cared for his tools and fishing apparatus, and so he left for Vatia, on Tutuila. From Vatia village, *Pili* went on to Aleipata village, in Atua district, Upolu, but didn't stay long. He left for Savai'i Island and landed in A'opo village, where he planted a very, very large plantation of taro and was the envy of all Samoa. A'opo bestowed him the title Tagaloa A'opo, or *Piliopo*.

Piliopo moved from A'opo to Palapala, at the back boundary of Amoa village, in Savai'i. One day *Pili* received Paramount Chief TuiA'ana *Tava'etele* from A'ana, Upolu, and delegates looking for taro shoots for his proposed plantation. And so *Pili* said to TuiA'ana *Tava'etele* to go help himself to the taro shoots. TuiA'ana instructed his aumaga (young men) to prepare the taro shoots. The problem was, they picked too much, and thus they couldn't carry it to the vessel. So *Pili* stood up and carried the load on his shoulder with a carrying stick, and the TuiA'ana *Tava'etele* was amazed by his superhuman strength.

When TuiA'ana Tava'etele left *Pili*, he invited him to come visit him in A'ana. Shortly thereafter, *Pili* left Satupa'itea for Fasito'o and later Lefaga, in A'ana, where he helped build TuiA'ana *Tava'etele's* taro plantation. *Pili* met and married TuiA'ana *Tava'etele's* daughter, *Sinaaletava'e*, and begat *Tua*, *A'ana*, *Saga*, *Tolufale*, and *Siumu Munanitama*.

Pili and the Nine-Headed Pigeon

In another story, a descendant of *Piliopo* slew the nine-headed pigeon, the *Lupe uluiva*, that flew from Falealili, Upolu. And thus the warriors from Upolu came and found him and slew him, and he was transformed into a pigeon and into stone in A'opo village.

Stories of *Tagaloa*

The Tagaloa lineage begins in the time of mythology and is quickly tied to the TuiManu'a lineage (with *Pilipa'ū's* marriage to *Sinalesae'e,* the daughter of TuiManu'a—*see* The story of *Pili*, page 98), the TuiFiti lineage (with *'Alo'alolelā's* marriage to *Sinafiti,* the daughter of the king of Fiji—see *TagaloaLā's* union with *Magamagaifatua* in the Sons of "Great Heaven" page 80), the TuiAtua lineage (with the Tagaloa's marriage to *Ila,* daughter of TuiAtua *Moso*—see The Rock at Uafato, page 85), and to the octopus *Fe'e* (with *TagaloaUi's* marriage to *Sinasa'umani,* giving birth to *Lefanoga* and *Taeotagaloa*—see Stories of the Sons of *TagaloaUi*, page 106).

The Story of *TagaloaUi* and the Ava Plant

Manu'ans tell a story of how the ava plant came from heaven to Manu'a, but, unlike the Golden House (see *Pili* and the Golden House, page 101), the plant was not a gift. *Tagaloalagi's* grandson, *TagaloaUi*, sneaked up and stole the ava, despite its being *tapu* (forbidden) because of its sacred nature. Then *TagaloaUi* brought the ava down onto earth for the first TuiManu'a.

In another legend, *Tagaloalagi* had two sons from one of his many wives, one called *Avaavaali'i* and the other *So'oso'oali'i*. This legend follows the same storyline as with Samoan story of the King of Fiji and the two Samoan sisters from Vailele (see *Pili* and the Ava Plant, page 103). In this case *Avaavaali'i* dies and the ava plant grows on his grave, with five branches that resemble the fingers of a man's hand. The people of Tagaloalagi call this plant ava, in memory of *Avaavaali'i*, the son of their god *Tagaloalagi*.

Then there's the Samoan legend of *Futi* and *Sao* which tells of a couple who came from Fiji to have their daughter, *Sinalalotava*, wed a smart Samoan called *Tagatapopoto*. Instead, she ended up marrying his brother *Lauifia*, begetting *Mausautele* who became the progenitor of one of the royal houses of *Gatoa'itele* and *Vaetamasoāali'i*. The legend says this couple brought the ava plant with them and gifted it to the village of Safotu, Savai'i.

Stories of the Sons of *TagaloaUi*

Lefanoga and *Taeotagaloa* were sons of *TagaloaUi* (son of *TagaloaLā* and *LuaUi*) and his wife *Sinasa'umani* (daughter of *Fe'e*). The legend below concerns the Malietoa Faigā *Uilamatūtū,* whose reign is dated to around A.D.1300. Matching the dates between legendary characters and historical events helps us see how history and mythology intertwine.

***Lefanoga, Taeotagaloa* and the Malietoa Faigā**

Lefanoga was known for his exploration throughout the archipelago. He had heard the tales of Malietoa Faigā *Uilamatūtū's* cruelty. Malietoa Faigā *Uilamatūtū* was the second son of the first Malietoa *Sāveatuvaelua*, and he practiced cannibalism and slavery on his people. *Lefanoga* wanted to see this for himself. His expedition culminated in a visit with Malietoa Faigā *Uilamatūtū* at Malie village.

The legend of *Lefanoga* also refers to his brother *Taeotagaloa* who tamed and domesticated the tropical parrot bird (the *sega*) that Malietoa Faigā *Uilamatūtū* so much desired. Either *Taeotagaloa* or *Lefanoga* brought the parrot bird down and gifted it to Malietoa Faigā *Uilamatūtū*.

Legend has it that when *Lefanoga* entered Malietoa Faigā *Uilamatūtū's* sacred residence, he sat for a while without being recognized by Malietoa Faigā *Uilamatūtū*, without any customary salutation and greeting. And so *Lefanoga* decided it was time for him to leave and return to Manu'a, given the inhospitable reception he was getting from this cruel chief.

Just before *Lefanoga* stood up to depart, Malietoa Faigā *Uilamatūtū* (the Malietoafaigā) said, "*Lefanoga*, I didn't know you were there. Please stay so we can have a conversation."

Lefanoga answered back, "If you want to know something, ask a Manu'an"—*Fesili i le Manu'a e malamalama ai—my translation*.

This is a frequently used proverb. This Manu'an version emphasizes that the Manu'an has all knowledge, thus he doesn't need to ask for clarification—he already knows. The Samoan interpretation is slightly different, saying *e fesili le Manu'a pe fia malamalama,* meaning the Manu'an will ask if he wants to know.

In the meantime, the Malietoafaigā was impressed with this young man. Then he asked for the parrot bird he'd heard *Taeotagaloa* had brought with him from Fiji, when he visited his sister *Muiu'uleapai* (who married the TuiFiti—see below in The Story of *TagaloaUi's* Daughter, page 108). The legend concludes with the Malietoafaigā giving up his cruelty and his enslavement of his people. It should be noted that Malietoafaigā's cruelty and ruling authority extended to all of Savai'i and the Tuamasaga district of Upolu, based on Tuamasaga legends.

***Taeotagaloa* and the First Ava Ceremony**

The first ava ceremony took place at Sauā, between *Taeotagaloa* (grandson of *Tagaloalagi*) and *Pava* the farmer. This story can also be found in the legends of *Lefanoga*.

The first and only two attendees at the ava ceremony were *Taeotagaloa* and *Pava*.[xxxi] It was at this event that *Taeotagaloa* lost his patience and disclosed his spiritual power (*mana*) when he became angry at *Pava's* son for constant disruption of the ava ceremony. *Taeotagaloa* grabbed the boy and tore him into two pieces, straight down the middle from head to toe.

Pava was terrified and full of grief. He begged *Taeotagaloa* for mercy, for he now realized *Taeotagaloa* had the *mana* also to restore his son's life. And so *Taeotagaloa*, feeling sympathy and empathy for *Pava*, put back together the boy's two halves, and, lo and behold, the boy came back to life. Then *Pava* continued, completing the ava ceremony.[xxxii]

The Story of *TagaloaUi's* Daughter

Muiu'uleapai, sister of *Taeotagaloa* and *Lefanoga,* married the TuiFiti and was later blamed for a famine in the Island of Fiji. The TuiFiti banished her to the mountainous region of the island, while the TuiFiti resided by the seashore.

Taeotagaloa went to Fiji to save his sister *Muiu'uleapai* by planting the *ufi* plant, which is similar to sweet potatoes but grows like vines, with its roots so abundant they can feed a whole village. This *ufi* plant grows wild in the forests in Samoa. Its abundant roots (potatoes) are the reason why they call the Malietoa family clan the genealogy of *Ufi*.

Taeotagaloa's generosity with the *ufi* plant saved *Muiu'uleapai* and quenched the hunger of the Fijian people. Then *Taeotagaloa* returned home to Manu'a with the *sega* (the parrot). Among a few other heirlooms, he also took *Muiu'uleapai's* son from the TuiFiti. The son was named after the phrase whereby *Muiu'uleapai* told her husband to "move the village inland" toward the mountains, because the soil was fertile for farming and especially for the *ufi* plant. This translates as *Liu* (turn toward) *uta* (the inland) of *Fiti* (Fiji) village, or *Liu-Fiti-uta*—in short, *Fitiuta*.

When *Taeotagaloa* arrived in Manu'a, the young boy, named *Liufitiuta*, was directed to make his home in the area close to the hamlet of Sauā (see The Story of the First TuiManu'a, page 81), and he called it Fitiuta. This whole area is considered the ancient, historical place where Tagaloalagi resides, and where he pronounced *Galea'i* as the paramount chief with the Tagaloalagi PāPā which he then, later, bestowed on the first TuiManu'a.

The Story of *Fitiaumua*

There were Fijian servants who came on *Taeotagaloa's* journey, assigned to take care the TuiFiti's son, *Liufitiuta*.

A boatbuilder, by the name of *Tufulemata'afa* (*tufuga,* which means carpenter or builder, and *mata'afa*, which means three threads of coconut sennit woven to produce a twine rope, also called *'afa*) came to build his boat in Fitiuta. And, in the course of working with the people helping him, he found there was a food shortage, a shortage of large taro roots, also known as *ape* or *ta'amu* of the taro family.

It turned out that *Veu* and *Veu,* a couple believed to be either Fijian or Samoan-Fijian, had harvested all the *ape*. This made *Tufulemata'afa* angry, so he chased the couple away to be marooned on some island in the archipelago.

Veu and *Veu* landed in Muliava, the Rose Atoll east of Manu'a. *Veu* was pregnant when they left Fitiuta, Manu'a, and, shortly after settling down, she gave birth to a boy who they named *Fitiaumua*. This name *Fitiaumua* comes from *Fitiuta au* (a unit or team of warriors) and *mua* (the vanguard or first to do something, like fighting a war).

Every so often the couple would talk, reminiscing about their home in Fitiuta, Manu'a. And so, one day, *Fitiaumua* asked his parents, "Where is our home?" And *Veu* and *Veu* told the story of how and why they were exiled to Muliava.

So, *Fitiaumua* kept the story in his mind and slowly began to prepare and organize himself, to avenge his parents' exile from Fitiuta. He found a *koa*-like tree and cut it down, to make his war-club, and it was magnificent, but it needed testing. So *Fitiaumua* used it on his nursemaid, named *Fe'esinasina*, and, sadly, he killed her.

A common thread in legends of warrior heroes of this period is the initial discovery of a war-club, because it represents a new technology paradigm. Finding the right, straight, and robust tree to carve a Samoan war-club was very important. Carpentry and weaver-skills would be exclusive to the appointed ones. Thus, owning a war-club was a sign of a prominent warrior. And drawing blood with the club made for a successful, heroic warrior. So, with this generation, the first descendants of the demigods or deities—such as *Taeotagaloa*, *Lefanoga*, *TagaloaLā*, *Alo'alolela*, *Ti'eti'eitalaga*, *Lefolasā*—were the recipients of warrior fighting skills and weaponry paradigms. Thus *Fitiaumua* was one such (human) Manu'an to take up the warring behavior and career.

After *Fitiaumua* tested out his war-club on *Fe'esinasina*, it was time to avenge his parents' exile, their ostracization from Fitiuta. And no one could counter or defend Fitiuta from the wrath of the warrior *Fitiaumua,* and he single-handedly trashed all of Fitiuta.

Word of Fitiuta's defeat spread quickly to Taū, Manu'a, and no one dared to confront *Fitiaumua*. The Manu'ans were in constant trepidation, whenever *Fitiaumua* was present in the area. The Manu'an poem about *Fitiaumua* gives some indication that he traveled across the archipelago to Savai'i and then to the A'ana and Atua tribes in Upolu. This was before there was a serious tribal group in the Tuamasaga district. And so he conquered Upolu and Savai'i.

Fitiaumua now traveled across the archipelago to Fiji, for his parents had told him about their ancestors in Fiji with the TuiFiti, king of Fiji. *Fitiaumua* had heard about the cruelty of the TuiFiti, and so he wanted to challenge the warriors of the TuiFiti. It took *Fitiaumua's* defeating several warriors to make the TuiFiti surrender.

The poem makes brief mention of *Fitiaumua's* battles on Toga and the Rarotoga Islands also. And there are fragments of tales in other kingdoms of Polynesia—Maori legends and Hawaiian ones from the Big Island—mentioning *Fitiaumua*.

Although it cannot be confirmed, the Manu'an legend tells clearly of *Fitiaumua* conquering many of the kingdoms, if not all, of Polynesia. Reverend Turner, based on his source in Tutuila, noted that the name *Fitiaumua* came from Fiji, after *Fitiaumua* successfully defeated the warriors of the TuiFiti. Also, Turner and several local Manu'an Orators believe that *Fitiaumua* may be the first king of Samoa and Manu'a, preceding the TuiManu'a. And *Fitiaumua* is credited with the naming of Manu'atele. (It should be noted that all the kingdoms in Polynesia, and many of the Island Nations of eastern Melanesia, are well aware of TuiManu'a and his kingdom of Manu'atele in ancient times.)

Fitiaumua eventually died in Matautu, Manu'a.

The Story of *Lata*, the Warrior Explorer

Another famous warrior is *Lata. Lata* has become one of the most important characters in the history of Polynesia. His legend spans not only the Manu'a and Samoa Archipelago but all of Polynesia, and his origin story covers Tutuila and Manu'a.

As noted by Dr. Krämer, the Tutuila version of this legend starts with Chief *Tago—Tagoilelagi*, son of *Tagoilelagi Gaoteote,* and a daughter of *Ma'ilo* of Fagatogo village; Fagatogo is the sister village to Pago Pago where *Tavai* resided. *Tagoilelagi* married a daughter of *Aumua* who bore the first *Lata*. *Lata*-I married a lady from Lauli'i village of Tutuila, who bore:

- *Tago,*
- a daughter *Omeli,*
- and *Lata*-II,

while the Gaoteote genealogy continued through the *Tavai* lineage and authority. This is where the genealogical connection between *Lata* and *Tavai* (Chief *Tavai* of Pago Pago village, Tutuila) occurs.[xxxiii] Krämer further comments that this is the same *Lata* mentioned by Tregear in the New Zealand legend that lists *Tawhaki* (*Tafa'i* in Samoan) as *Lata's* ancestor, referencing Stuebel's comment that the original *Lata* came from Tutuila.

Tavai's ancestors on his mother's side are the Togiola *Le'iato* family clan at Sa'ilele village in Tutuila. *Tavai* was driven from Pago Pago village due to his cruelty, and he came to live, temporarily, with the Tagoilelagi clan. That is why he had a bonding (genealogical) relationship with the Tago Gaoteote family of Vatia village, Tutuila, for the Tavai and Tago Gaoteote families intermarried at this period. In a much later generation, *Tavai* married *Olomua's* daughter in Aoa, giving birth to *Uilai'a* who became Tavai *Uilai'a Talauega*. This Tavai *Uilai'a Talauega* married *Lā*, the daughter of *Aumoegalogo* who bore:

- *Gaoteote,*
- *Tausuai,*
- and *Talauega*.

According to the Manu'an version of the *Lata's* legend, *Tafa'i* is father of *Lata*, while, as we have seen, the Tutuila version says the father is *Tagoilelagi* (*Gaoteote*), thus giving a close genealogical connection with *Tavai*. It is understood that the Maori, *Rata*, of New Zealand claimed he migrated there from Samoa and the same story is told in the Manu'an legend.

In another version, *Lata* was a son of *Fafieloa* and *Tula* of Tafagafaga on the east coast side of Taū, in Manu'a. *Fafieloa* was a descendant of *Tafa'i* and *Henpiripiri*, a Maori or Rarotogan lady, while *Tafa'i's* first marriage was with *Sinataeolelagi* (daughter of

Tagaloalagi, hence the connection with the Tagaloa lineage) giving birth to four children:

- *Lā* (sun),
- *Matiu* (a daughter),
- *Logaloga* (a daughter),
- and *Sa'asa'a* (a daughter).

This part of the legend, with *Tagaloalagi's* daughter *Sinataeolelagi*, would eventually merge with legend of *TagaloaLā*.[xxxiv]

This time period, of *Lata's* brief and cryptic lineage, is the same time as the various *Pili* stories, and those of *Taeotagaloa*, and maybe of *TagaloaLā* and *TagaloaUi*.

***Lata's* Double-hulled Canoe**

Lata was the builder of a famous canoe. The main reason *Lata* built his double-hulled canoe with sails was to search the Pacific to find the warrior *Matu'uta'ota'o* who killed his father *Fafieloa*. The story has it the warrior was hiding in the village of Fogatuli, in Savai'i.

Lata's first vessel ran into the reef at the harbor near Fogatuli, Savai'i, and it turned into stone at the reef; the place is called Lata, even today.

Upon inquiring about *Matu'uta'ota'o*, *Lata* found out that the warrior had fled to the island of Toga. And so *Lata* built another vessel, this time with the assistance of female demigods, authorities of the forest, and so the vessel is known as the "vessel-of-spirits" or *va'aāitu*. *Lata* also named it after his progenitor, *Pua*, and the Samoan word for speed like the wind, *lele*, hence *Pualele*.

Lata found *Matu'uta'ota'o* in Toga and invited him to have a fight. The two warriors were fearless, but *Lata* was much stronger, like a half-spirit half-man; it didn't take long before *Matu'uta'ota'o* fell down, and *Lata*, with one powerful swing with his Uatogi war-club, severed *Matu'uta'ota'o's* head from his powerful warrior body. Then *Lata*, as was customary for a warrior with a demonic spirit, took out *Matu'uta'ota'o's* heart and ate it. The Togans were frightened to see this typically Samoan, warrior-like practice.

Before *Matu'uta'ota'o* died, he cursed *Lata's* vessel, and thus the vessel was debilitated. Then *Lata* found the necessary trees, for wood that was perfect for shipbuilding, for his next vessel.

According to the Manu'an legend, *Lata* went on to Rarotoga, Hawaii, and other islands, and finally to the Maori of New Zealand. This would be around A.D.550-775. Both the Manu'an and the Maori legends note that *Lata* lived and died in the South Island of New Zealand.

Legends throughout Polynesia, especially Maori legends, view *Lata* as an explorer and discoverer of many places in New Zealand.

The Story of *Tigilaumaolo*

The legend of *Tigi*—his name before acquiring the latter part, *lau*—is also well-known across Polynesia. Almost all indigenous populations of Polynesia have their own version of the *Tigi-lau* or *Tinilau*. But Samoans claim the ethnic nationality of *Tigilau* as being a Samoan chief in Amoa, Savai'i.

Tigi was quite a handsome man, and the story of women across the archipelago desiring him for a husband is told with minimal embellishments.

Chiefs *Olo* of Falelatai, Upolu, and *Tigi* of Amoa, Savai'i, were courting Lady *Lau* of Falelatai, Upolu. She preferred *Tigi*, but the village Chiefs Council and the orator chiefs organization, the Faleupolu, disapproved of her decision. In accordance with customs and protocols, the Chiefs Council and Faleupolu often make a compelling argument for whomever they best approve for the family and village. So *Lau*, unfortunately, had to marry Chief *Olo*. And so, the wedding went according to plan, and *Tigi* went sadly home to Amoa, Savai'i.

A short period passed and, before *Lau's* memory of *Tigi* disappeared permanently, *Tigi* came visiting the couple's home. And *Lau's* desire for *Tigi* recurred in her every thought and, of course, gained him her favor.

When *Lau* became pregnant, *Tigi* decided to return to Amoa, Savai'i. *Lau* gave birth to a healthy young son, but they had not yet given him a name. The boy grew to help his father in chores. And one day they went fishing, and he was quite disobedient and annoying to *Olo*. And so, out a quick emotional outburst, *Olo* scolded the boy by saying, "You are not my son."

After they arrived home, the boy immediately went to his mother and asked if he was not *Olo's* son. *Lau* confessed that his father was *Tigi* of Amoa village in Savai'i. The boy was very sad and upset, and so he ran away to his father *Tigi* in Amoa village. And *Lau* was suspicious that this might happen, so she followed her son to Amoa, Savai'i.

When they arrived at *Tigi's* place they, *Tigi* and *Lau*, were talking about a name for their son, and they came up with the name that combined their names, *Tigi* and *Lau*, or *Tigilau*. But while they were talking in that evening, unbeknownst to them Chief *Olo*, who had followed *Lau* and the boy to Amoa to see *Tigi*, was sitting outside. He heard the whole deliberation about a name for the boy. And so *Olo* said, "If he is to be called after *Tigi* and *Lau*, why not add the name of *Olo*"—*A ua Tigi ma Lau, ta'u ane ai ma Olo*. Hence, the boy's name was *Tigilaumaolo*. *Tigi*-*lau*-and-*olo*.[xxxv]

Stories of *Saveasi'uleo* and *Ulufanuasese'e*

The legend of the brothers *Saveasi'uleo* (with a tail like a sea eel), *Sālevao,* and *Ulufanuasese'e* is dated around A.D.800-900.[xxxvi] In this story, *Saveasi'uleo* had several brothers who loved to surf. But *Saveasi'uleo* was filled with anger, from jealousy because his parents "threw" him—after a "blood clot" miscarriage during the second trimester—into the ocean. The blood clot was swallowed by an eel, and the eel transformed into a half-eel, half-man who was *Saveasi'uleo*. He always felt his parents cast him into the ocean because they didn't love him, hence his cruelty and cannibal appetite.

Saveasi'uleo, in his anger, devised a plan to murder his brothers. He turned himself into an eel. As his brothers surfed, one by one *Saveasi'uleo* dragged them down into the depths of the ocean to feast on their bodies.

One of his brothers scolded *Saveasi'uleo* for murdering their brothers. It was then that a famous decree was pronounced at sea (as told in The Morning of the Farewell at Sea in Alataua, Savai'i—see below): *Saveasi'uleo* ordered his brother to stay in Savai'i to take care of the rest of the family, while *Saveasi'uleo* would leave and go to Manu'a, and carry on the genealogy there. The rest of

Saveasi'uleo's surviving brothers became paramount warriors called the Alataua.

The Morning (*Taeao*) of the Farewell at Sea in Alataua, Savai'i

There is a National Morning, given the recognition of the Malae and Maota, commemorating this decree. *Saveasi'uleo* was decreed to travel east, toward Manu'a, to initiate the planning and development of a kingdom, and his brother *Ulufanuasese'e* would travel west toward Upolu to marry and so grow the family genealogy.[xxxvii] At that time there were very few known inhabitants of Manu'a.

The farewell is a decree to settle their violent differences. Thus the brothers covenanted that they would live separately, forbidden to meet in person, to avoid conflicts, so they could only meet through their offspring. They decreed: "We will meet again though our future genealogies," as promulgated by their parent's decree. *Ta toe feiloa'i i i'u o gafa ae le o ulu o gafa* is the proverb that was coined during this milestone historical event.

Many versions of this legend have been told and written down, originally by several missionaries in their books, including *Samoa: Lest we Forget* by Pule Lameko.[xxxviii] And it is commonly believed that these two brothers stand at the beginning of the foundational genealogies of the major ancient families of Samoa and Manu'a. They are the progenitors the venerable Tonumaipe'a family clan.

The Story of Tattooing and the Conjoined Twins

The story of these brothers continues with the conjoined twins, *Taematilafaigā* (or *Taemā* and *Tilafaigā*), daughters of *Ulufanuasese'e* and *Sinalalofutu-i-Fagaiofu*. *Tilafaigā* and *Taemā* were known to have once shared a body—as conjoined twins—until an unknown man scared the two girls so much they tried to run opposite directions, and their bodies separated. The twins were said to be "demigods" with exceptional, supernatural strength that they showed on many occasions in their journeys across the archipelago.

The twins' journeys took them to Solosolo village in Upolu, and on to Manu'a and Tutuila, where *Taemā* married Chief *Togiola* and bore *Le'iatotogiolatu'itu'iotoga* (ancestor of *Le'iato Togiola*), after which they continued travelling on to Fiji Island. After some period of time, the twins desired to return to Samoa. In their farewell parting with the TuiFiti—the Fijian king—they were given a gift of a little box containing the tools and apparatus for tattooing the body. As the twins journeyed to Samoa, they sang their song: "Tattoo the women and not the men."

The twins arrived at the seaside village of Falealupo in Savai'i, and one of them looked down into the ocean and saw a trident shell. She dived down after it and brought it up into the boat. In the process she forgot the song. Then the sister said, "It goes like this: 'Tattoo the men and not the women.'"

The twins arrived in Safotu, Savai'i, where Paramount Orator Chief *Lavea* resided. The twins called out to Chief *Lavea*: "Hey there! We have a skill we brought with us on our journey from Fiji." But Chief *Lavea* did not pay any mind, and so their journey continued on to the village of Salelavalu, Savai'i, to the residence of High Chief *Mafua*, who also wanted nothing to do with women's gift box. Then the twins went to the village of Safata, Upolu, where they were kindly received by Chief *Su'a's* daughters. The twins were very impressed with the generosity of the Su'a family and, desiring to express their thanks for the Su'a family's kindness and generosity, they gifted the skill box to Chief *Su'a*.

After this the village ladies presented the twins with gifts of barkcloth and curcuma yellow, and the twins were elated.

The Decree at the Sea of Alataua

The well-known "Decree at the Sea of Alataua" district in Savai'i was proclaimed by these twins in Tutuila, decreeing the chief of Alataua, the *Ali'i o le Alataua Tulu'itanu* (son of *Tilafaigā* and *Moaifelo* of Faga'itua) to hold the Vanguard and Rearguard of War. This decree was given on their own authority. And so there is only one paramount chief of Alataua, and one paramount voice of Alataua, in all Samoa, all proclaimed by the same family.

The Connection to History and *Nafanua*

The legends of the surfing brothers at Vaoto and the conjoined twins give an alternative perspective on the legend (and history) of the Warrior Queen *Nafanua* (which will be told later in The Story of the Warrior Queen *Nafanua*, page 172). For in Manu'a, *Saveasi'uleo* married his niece, *Tilafaigā*, often referred to as *Pi'ilua*. (*Saveasi'uleo* was *Tilafaigā's* uncle). *Tilafaigā* and *Saveasi'uleo* begat *Nafanua*, the warrior queen who can be considered to be the Samoan version of the British Boudicca, also called *Suaifanua,* or *Suaifanuanafanua*.

Suaifanua married the TuiToga and begat *Latuivai*. *Latuivai's* union with *Mimisapu'a*, sister of *LeFolasāle'i'ite*—both of them descendants of *Sinalagilagi*, *Tagaloalagi's* daughter (from the village Fai'a'ai—*Sinalagilagi* bore *Mimisapu'a* and *Folasāle'i'ite* in a much earlier generation)—brought forth *Faletapa'au* and *Taigalugalu*. (Note: there is a part of the traditional house where the roof drains the rain. If you sit close to the drain, the rain will drip on you. This is called *tapaau*. *Faletapa'au* is a term that refers to the paramount chief, for in ceremonial practices, the chief is the one to sit next to *tapaaufasisina*. Also, *Taigalugalu* means the ocean tide is rising—*tai* means ocean tide, and *galugalu* means rising or waves.)

Taigalugalu's union with *Lilomaiavaseve* of Safotu produced a girl named *Foalo*, which means to make peace. *Foalo* married *Lologavivao* of Samata, Savaii, and begat *Maisina*.

Brothers of the Conjoined Twins

These legends are dated to A.D.800-900, and also to Period V in the time just before the Tafa'ifa *Salamasina.* For we know that *Salamasina* received the four crowns from Queen *Nafanua,* who was the daughter of *Saveasi'uleo* and his niece, *Tilafaigā* (daughter of *Ulufanuasese'e* and *Sinalalofutu-i-Fagaiofu*).

Aveautetele and *Fa'alualuatele* were half-brothers of *Taemā* and *Tilafaigā*, by their mother's first marriage to Tagaloa-*i-Pata* of Falelatai village—Pata is a hamlet of Falelatai village, in the A'ana district, and his name is often written *Tagaloaipata*. They were designated to go to the Vaimauga district of Tuamasaga and settle there. There is no mention of their mother's name. However, there is mention of Tagaloa-*i-Pata's* marriage to *Leatiatigielealaiaolõ*, the sister of the first Malietoa *Sāveatuvaelua* (see The Founding of the Malietoa Dynasty, page 146), with the issue of *Ulumasui* who assisted in the war against Toga. Dr. Krämer has *Saveasi'uleo* marrying *Tilafaigā* in the 10th generation and *Leatiatigielealaiaolō* in the 13th generation; thus I believe she was Tagaloa-*i-Pata's* third wife. As we can see, the legends and the history sometimes lead to very different dates for the stories.

Aveautetele was to settle in Alaoa, toward the mountains in what is now Apia proper. *Fa'alualuatele* was to settle in the valley of Vailele, Vaimauga, adjacent to the *Fe'e* residence.

The Story of *Leatiatigielealaiaolō*

There is a short story about this *Leatiatigielealaiaolō*. Malietoa *Sāveatuvaelua* (Malietoa *Sāvea*) came down with an illness and, as was customary for a brother, called on to his sister for nursing care and assistance. Since his only sister, *Leatiatigielealaiaolō,* was married to *Tagaloaipata* of Falelatai, quite a distance from Faleata on the west end of Upolu Island, he sent two servants with a message to asking her to come to care for him in his illness. When the servants arrived at her residence, she said she could not come because of her own severe illness. And so the servants went back to Malietoa *Sāveatuvaelua* and told him what she had said.

Malietoa *Sāvea* said to the servants that they should go to *Leatiatigielealaiaolō* and "get it done." The Samoan word used by the Malietoa is *fa'auma loa*. Unfortunately, the servants misinterpreted Malietoa *Sāvea* to mean "finish her," and they killed her!

There are a few tales of this nature, of misinterpreted messages by servants, implying the developmental level of the language at the time, in terms of words with multiple meanings and the difficulty of discerning the sounds of particles (*au*, *aua*, *lau*, *la'u*, *laū*, etc.) to clearly understand the message.

Transition to Mythological Figures

This stage in the prehistoric period of Samoa-Manu'an genealogical evolution is transitional between mythological figures and those that are believed to have really existed in its history. An example would be *TagaloaLā's* grandson *TagaloaUi* who marries *Sinasa'umani*, sister to *Sasa'umani* daughter of *Fe'e*. *TagaloaUi* and *Sinasa'umani* would produce four boys and two girls: *Taeotagaloa*, *Lefanoga*, *Lele*, *Leasiosiolagi* and their sisters

Muiu'uleapai and *Moatafao*. These names appear in stories of the history of the islands.

At the same time, the people of legends become memorialized in places of legend in the islands.

The Sacred Forest of the TuiFiti at Matautu, Savai'i

A spirit called TuiFiti is said to reside in Fagamalo, a village on the coast of Savai'i that was initially settled by Fijians. His home lies in a grove of large trees—the sacred forest, or *vao sa*—and this part of the forest is *tapu* (taboo) in Fagamalo. Legend says the TuiFiti spirit walks as a man, but only strangers can see him.

The TuiFiti, or Paramount Fijian Chief, periodically visited Savai'i and would often stay here for longer period of time. But the origin of the district's political organization goes back to the Togan Lady *Laufafaetoga* who came, wanting to marry a Samoan called *Tupa'ilelei*, son of *Lealali* (a descendant of *Apa'auula* the daughter of *Pili le So'opili*) and *Malelegaaleto'elau*. But *Tupa'ilelei* was not good enough for *Laufafa*, and so she chose his brother *Tupa'imatuna*.

Laufafa went to Toga to have her new baby there, in the custody of her mother, as it is customary in Polynesia to always have the first child at the parents' place. However, the ship lost its course and landed in the Fiji Archipelago. So the baby boy was named *Va'asiliifiti* (*va'a*—the boat, *sili*—went off course, *i Fiti*—toward Fiji islands).

Laufafa left her Samoan husband and married the Fijian Chief *Lautala*. This marriage produced four warrior sons from the Fijian chief. Then, later, *Laufafa* went back to her Samoan husband *Tupa'imatuna,* and they produced the girl *Fotuosamoa*, named after the fact that she was conceived on their journey back to Samoa (*Fotu*—turn the vessel toward, Samoa, hence *Fotuosamoa*, and the name of SaFotu or Safotu district, not to be confused with the SaFotulafai district of Savai'i).

The half-Fijian, half-Togan warrior children (*Ututauofiti*, *Tauaofiti*, *Legaotuitoga*, and *Liliolelagi* who was founder of Falealili, Upolu), organized Matautu as a local residence of the Fijian paramount chief when he visited Savai'i. Also, practices and rituals and taboos, or *tapu,* in the district showed reverence to the Paramount Fijian chief. This, then, is the Fijian foundation of Savai'i's indigenous population, giving evidence of the influence of the Fijians in Savai'i, which led to inter-marriages and the growing population of Savai'i.

This is also the reason the Upolu people referred to Savai'i's indigenous warriors as half-spirit, half-man, feared by the Upolu people (see The Story of *To'o* and *Ata*, page 159, and The Story of *Va'afuti* (or *Va'afa'i*), page 157).

The Reflecting Pool and the House in Amoa, Savai'i

There is a legend of a famous house that is thatched with garlands. Its posts are made of *toa* wood (Hawaiian *koa*), and its beams are made from the breadfruit tree and tied with vines from ficus trees. The landmark of this legend is the "SiuoAmoa," or the most western villages within the district of Fa'asaleleaga in Savai'i Island. It includes the villages of Lano, Pu'apu'a, and Asaga, which lay claim to many legends such as *Le Tama o Alo* and his sister *Metotagivale* (*Meto-tagi,* crying, *vale,* without reason), and *Le Ali'i o Tigilaumaolo* and the red-mouthed herring tales.

<u>The River of Reflection</u>

The legend begins with two sisters who journeyed from the Fiji Archipelago to Savai'i, at a period when there are stories about many Fijians with Samoan genealogical ties. The sisters, *Sinafatuimoa* and *Talai*, arrived at the east coast of the Fa'asaleleaga district. And so they trekked across the Lano and Asaga villages toward the west. As they traveled on, people stared; some even giggled and laughed out loud toward the sisters.

When they finally reached Pu'apu'a village, *Talai* urged her sister *Sinafatuimoa* to rest awhile and drink some fresh water from the river. The two sisters decided to rest by the bank of a small river, more like a stream, and *Sinafatuimoa* asked *Talai* to please fetch her some water from the stream. *Talai* immediately went out to the stream to get water. Shortly after she arrived at the stream, she let out a heart-rending wail and quickly climbed back to find her sister. She held on to her sister, crying profusely and looked terrified. For *Talai* was terrified. When she saw the image of her face reflected in the water, it was terribly disfigured, and it looked like a rat, and so ugly that it scared her no end. She realized that was why people had been staring; they were staring at her ugly face.

Another version has it that *Sinafatuimoa* saw the image of her face and, out of despair, decided to stay in the river forever. She said farewell to her sister *Talai,* and she lived on the river and in a cave nearby. Hence the river is named *O le vaitilofia*, or the "River of Reflection." This place is therefore where Samoans discovered that "still water" can be used as a mirror, almost two thousand years before they had actually seen a real glass mirror.

The House of *Meto*

The legend continues to the time when *Sinafatuimoa*, who lived in the river caves, met and married Chief *Naisaafa* of the promontory piece of land named Punaoa. He was the chief of Punaoa or Imoa (the "rat"), later referred to as the village of Amoa. They produced a boy named *Alo* and a daughter named *Sina*. Other Savai'i historians say there was a third child who was a miscarriage, a blood clot; this child was a girl and the rats of the cave cared for her and nursed her to life in the cave. That's why she remained hidden in her cave, as she was sickly and ridden with sores. The cave was the *Meto's* cave.

Sina and *Alo* were cared for by *Sinafatuimoa's* sister *Talai*. *Alo* became known for his good looks, strength, and exceptional prowess in sport. He was especially skilled in the ancient sport of throwing sharpened wooden spears to hit a specified target—*Taga ti'a* in Samoan. On one day's contest, *Alo* threw his spear, and it landed in the *Meto's* cave. And then *Metotagivale*—*Meto* the crybaby or whiner—found and confiscated it. So when *Alo* came to retrieve his spear, his *ti'a*, he had to beg *Meto* for it. In fact, she ensnared *Alo* in the cave and blackmailed him into building a house for her.

Meto knew *Alo* was the son of the paramount chief of the rats, or *Sa-Imoa*, and that they could build to detailed specifications. Thus, the house *Alo* built for *Metotagivale* in Amoa is thatched with garlands, with posts of toa wood and beams of the breadfruit tree, and tied with vines of the ficus trees.

The legend ends with *Meto* disclosing she was the miscarried child, and in fact she and *Sina* and *Alo* were brother and sisters. And so *Alo* always cared for his sisters, especially for *Metotagivale* because of her physical condition.

The Village of Dwarves

Another legend tell how one day *Mauai*, of Paia village in the district of SaMauga on the island of Savai'i, took his dog and went hunting for wild pigs. As he moved further into the forest, the dog began to get excited and anxious to get his master to follow him into a cave. *Mauai* obediently followed his dog. Suddenly, behold, a bearded, small man appeared in front of the cave. *Mauai* thought he was seeing a spirit, for the bearded man stood no more than two to three feet tall. Likewise, the small man could not believe what he was seeing—a man that stood like a giant.

The bearded, small man told *Mauai* that he was the chief of his little-people clan. As chief, he was very concerned about having the people's village cave become known by everyone in Paia village, let alone by everyone in the district of SaMauga. So the little-people's chief and *Mauai* made a pact to keep the place secret, in return for which Mauai would get anything he yearned for. But the villagers of Paia began to question *Mauai* as to the source of his prosperity. While showing off to them, he revealed the identity and whereabouts of his benefactors. So the little-people packed up their village and vanished from sight, never to be heard from or seen again.

There is no cave of the dwarves to be found, because the agreement was if the chief violated the agreement, the cave and village would disappear without any evidence or remnants remaining. This is consistent with similar legends throughout Polynesia, and the chief's title, together with the fact that the story is very specific to that title and family, is the only evidence that the legend actually happened. The legend is told in other Polynesia kingdoms and is the Polynesian version of the hobbits of Indonesia. I believe that hobbits immigrated probably before or around the same period when the Navigators made their "Quest" for Polynesia.

"This is Laloifi"

Laloifi is a piece of land in Satupa'itea that is used for practice and training matches in wrestling by Chief *Valomua* and the clan. The phrase "This is Laloifi" originates in a legend that took place at Laloifi. The owner (Chief *Valomua*) of the land was teaching a young man how to fight with a club. The apt pupil threw his master down. The master, fearful lest word of the incident should get out abroad, said to the young student, "This Is Laloifi," meaning it can remain a secret here in *Laloifi*: no one saw it.[xxxix]

Period IV: TuiManu'a, TuiAtua and TuiA'ana

Stories of TuiAtua

Samoans anchor their creation story to their genealogical history, telling it through one of the oldest family genealogies in Samoa. It is a story of parents and children.

At a time when the earth was full of darkness, the union of the ancient lights from the East (*Malamagaga'e*) and the West (*Malamagaga'ifo*) begat a lava rock, of bluish sheen, which transformed into *Lupe* (a pigeon or chicken). *Lupe* united with *Papatū* (upright cliff), giving birth to *A'alua* (meaning a root that has a branch, or two tree roots, as in the roots of family trees). *A'alua* married *Papamau* (a solid cliff), giving birth to *Papafoagia* (a demolished cliff). *Papafoagia's* union with *Ma'ata'anoa* (scattered rocks or small rocks) gave birth to *Papae'ele* (cliff soil). *Papae'ele*'s union with *Palapala* (swamp, the most fertile land) begat a female, *Papamavae* (the fissuring or fusing cliff, being a cliff where life can be conceived).

Papamavae, a female, married *Imoa* (a male rat—this name is common in Samoa) and bore a female, *Salasala* (meaning cut off, referring to that which the rat gnawed off). *Salasala* is the first woman and she married *Tagaloanimonimo* (another name for *Tagaloalagi*) and begat *Tupufua* (a free man—the first man). It is at this point that *Tagaloalagi*, of the Manu'an story, makes his appearance in the Samoan genealogy.

Tupufua married *Leletaimalie*, a lady from TuiAtua ancestry, who gave birth to *Leopili* of Manu'a. Then *Leopili's* union with *Lesauapuleai* birthed *Leopilisosolo,* meaning the crawling lizard. Another union of *Tupufua,* with *Tamaoitufaigā* (daughter of *Tagaloalagi*), gave birth to *Lu*, the founder of TuiAtua (though according to Pratt, *Tupufua* and *Leletaimalie* are *Lu's* parents, and *Pili* and TuiAtua are born of *Tupufua* and *Tamaoitufaigā*, daughter of Tagaloalagi). This all comes under the TuiA'ana genealogy.

We should make note of the pattern of ecological processes in the naming of children here, which creates an imagery of building anew and protecting ancient legends. For we begin, as we saw, with a pigeon and a cliff. Later, a root with a branch will take hold of the broken pieces to build a new creation. The cliff will be soon demolished and eventually turn into dirt and then a swamp. Then cliffs begin to fuse together with the help of a rat and a crawling lizard.

The genealogy of the Malietoa (a much later warrior paramount chief), also includes *Ma'ata'anoa,* scattered rocks, and *Imoa*, the rat. Meanwhile the TuiAtua Lineage continues, naming the first TuiAtua *Moso,* father of TuiAtua *Lu*, and giving a more historical genealogy as was shown in TuiAtua, page 20 in the timelines in Period IV.

Stories of TuiA'ana

As we saw above and in the Timelines (see Period II TuiA'ana page 12, and Period IV TuiA'ana page 22) the TuiA'ana lineage begins with *Leopili,* whose union with *Lesauapuleai* birthed *Leopilisosolo*, meaning the crawling lizard. *Leopilisosolo* became TuiA'ana, hence the name TuiA'ana *Pilisosolo*. His union with *Toaimailagi* gave birth to *Nifosili* meaning buck teeth. TuiA'ana *Nifosili*'s union with *Upegamamao,* from Nofoali'i, brought forth *Fuaooletaulo'o*. TuiA'ana *Fuaooletaulo'o,* in union with *Usumalefua* also from Nofoali'i, begat *To*. *To* together with *Faga*, daughter of *Leatumailagi,* begat TuiA'ana *Tava'etele* and his sister *Sinatafua.* TuiA'ana *Tava'etele* in union with *Sivalavala Fotumaleavega* begat a daughter, *Sinaaletava'e*, who married *Pili* (from the TuiAtua line), connecting the TuiA'ana and TuiAtua genealogies around A.D.1140. She gave birth to the boys who were each given gifts:

- *Tua* (gifted with the digging pole for planting),
- *Ana* (gifted with the spear/club, war warrior),
- *Tuamasaga* (He stands between the twin brothers and is decreed with the orator's staff and flail as the mediator),
- *Tolufale* (the supplier of the war troops), and
- *Siumu Munanitama* (the assistant in war).

Following the female line, *Sinatafua* (sister of TuiA'ana *Tava'etele*) married *Setagatamatua* of Taula and begat a daughter,

Fulisiaailagi, meaning "to turn to heaven." Then *Fulisiaailagi* (the female) carried the genealogy. Her union with *Ogafanūatele*, a high chief in Leulumoega, brought forth *Fa'asiliailagi*, meaning "to go past the heaven." *Fa'asiliailagi*'s union with TuiA'ana *Uōtele* birthed *Fa'alulumaga*. She married the *LeTufuga* from SaFotulafai, bearing a daughter *Fitimaula* who married Tagaloa *Fa'aofonu'u* bearing the boy, *Selaginatō*.

Selaginatō married the famous Lady *Vaetamasoāali'i* who gave birth to TuiA'ana *Tamālelagi*, who defeated TuiA'ana *Sagaate* and was the father of Tafa'ifa *Salamasina*.

It is common, in the modern history of Samoa, for the women to carry on the genealogy, and *Sinaaletava'e* line is an example of this. Thus *Tamālelagi* who was TuiA'ana from the female line fought with TuiA'ana *Sagaate* who was TuiA'ana from the male line.

Stories of TuiManu'a

To preface any TuiManu'a genealogy we must note that Manu'ans have always maintained a *tapu* or prohibition on disclosing their genealogy to any person outside Manu'a. While there is information available from European documents, mainly missionaries' documents, one must always remind readers that the sources of the tales and data about Manu'a are not Manu'an sources.

For example, Dr. Krämer relied on *Le'iato Togiola* of Aoa and Orator Chief *Tautolo* of Aunu'u, both of Tutuila, for translation. This *Le'iato Togiola* was a descendant of Paramount Chief *Savea* of my village of Afega. Paramount Chief *Savea* was one of two princes of Paramount Chief *Manua'ifua*, son of *Saena*. In fact, his brother *Tautalatasi* held the title of High Chief *Savea* in our village family clan at the time. Orator *Tautolo's* mother was a descendant of the Moegu *Moso* and *Tuiolosega* of the Olosega family clan in Manu'a, with which my grandfather shared the same ancestors.

Dr. Krämer presented a two-column list of TuiManu'a genealogy comparisons,[xl] in addition to a detailed listing of the Āiga SaTuiManu'a (the Family of TuiManu'a) genealogy.[xli] The Āiga SaTuiManu'a list is different from the list of TuiManu'a title-holders because the holder can be in different genealogical parts of the family tree. Dr. Krämer's results[xlii] can be reconciled with oral (and cryptic) records of my family, and it is important to note that my great-grandfather *Moliga*, on my grandmother *Selaina's* side, was the son of Chief *Ale* Tauanu'u of the Tauanu'u family clan, and his mother was a daughter of *Tauala*. (Note, the accent and capitalization in the word *aiga* or *Āiga* serve for emphasis in formal writing—*O lo'u aiga*, my family, or *Āiga o SaMauga*.)

Dr. Krämer's source is the Mātua (Elder) of *To'oto'o* Tauanu'u, the title holder at the time, with a close family relationship to my great-grandfather, *Moliga Ale* Tauanu'u. We share the same oral family history. Thus the Powell–Tauanu'u list is as follows:

1. *Taeotagaloa* (demigod) TuiManu'a or TuiManu'a *LeFolasā* (also came from heaven)
2. Tagaloa *Fa'aeanu'u* (son of *Taeotagaloa*) was also referred to as TuiManu'a
3. TuiManu'a *Sao-io-io-manu* (*Saoioiomanu*) son of Tagaloa *Fa'aeanu'u*
4. TuiManu'a *Saoloa* son of Tagaloa *Fa'aeanu'u*
5. TuiManu'a *Lelologa* son of TuiManu'a *Saoioiomanu*
6. TuiManu'a *'Ali'amatua* son of TuiManu'a *Lelologa*
7. TuiManu'a *'Ali'atama* (A.D. 1460-1470) son of TuiManu'a *'Ali'amatua*
8. TuiManu'a *Fa'aeanu'u* son of *'Ali'atama*
9. TuiManu'a *Puipuipo* brother of *Fa'aeanu'u*
10. TuiManu'a *Siliaivao* brother of *Puipuipo* and *Fa'aeanu'u*
11. TuiManu'a *Ti'aligo* son of TuiManu'a *Puipuipo*
12. TuiManu'a *Semanu* son of TuiManu'a *Siliaivao*
13. TuiManu'a *Fa'atoalia* son of *Semanu*
14. TuiManu'a *Taliutafa* son of TuiManu'a *Fa'atoalia*
15. TuiManu'a *Ti'aligo*
16. TuiManu'a *Seuēa* daughter of *Taliutafa*.
17. TuiManu'a *Salofi* son of *Taliutafa* and brother of *Seuēa*
18. TuiManu'a *Taliutafa-II* son of *Salofi*
19. TuiManu'a *Talolomana*
20. TuiManu'a *Moa'atoa*
21. TuiManu'a *Vaomana* son of *Talolomana*
22. TuiManu'a *Talolo* son of *Vaomana*
23. TuiManu'a *Talolofa'aleleinu'u*
24. TuiManu'a *Tuiaaitu*

25. TuiManu'a *Ta'alolofana'ese*
26. TuiManu'a *Levao* (ruled before 1820)
27. TuiManu'a *Mamana* or *Tauveve* (1832 received Christianity)
28. TuiManu'a *Alalamua* (1840)
29. TuiManu'a *Matelita* (1898)
30. TuiManu'a *Elisala* son of *Alalamua* (1900-1923)

TuiManu'a *'Ali'atama* (1460-1470), had a daughter with the famous name, *Samalaulu*. Then the family tree continues (through one of three Pupuaali'i or Aloali'i—*Moliga, Leasaū,* and *Nuanualefeagaiga*) down to TuiManu'a *Salofi* (or *Talofi*).

The Pa'u family branch, in Fasito'o village, goes back to TuiA'ana *Uōtele's* daughter *Fa'alulumaga* who married *LeTufuga* of SaFotulafai, Savai'i. *Pa'u* (son of Young, an American expatriate converted Christian, head of the LMS church in Manu'a) married a woman from Fasito'o village, giving birth to TuiManu'a *Matelita* (A.D.1898).

The First TuiManu'a

According to legend, *Aga'euta* (land toward the mountains) married his wife *Aga'etai* (land toward the sea) in the hamlet of Sauā. *Aga'etai* gave birth to a boy, who was brought down from heaven by the SaTagaloa (the family of *Tagaloa*, in the first through ninth heavens) and given the name *Galea'i.* A crown was bestowed from Heaven on this *Galea'i* by *Tagaloalagi*. Thus *Galea'i* became the first (human) Paramount Royal Chief of Manu'a.

Galea'i's children, and especially the daughters of his children, appear in many other genealogies. For example:

- *Taupaū* (daughter of TuiManu'a) marries *So'oialo,* giving birth to *Samalaulu* (see The Girl who married the Octopus, page 88)
- *Sinalesae'e* (daughter of TuiManu'a) marries *Pilipa'ū* (Period II, TuiAtua, page 10)
- *Samalaulu* (daughter of TuiManu'a) marries TuiAtua *Malaetele*
- And *Titilagipupula* (daughter of TuiManu'a) marries *Toso* in the Malietoa lineage (see Period V, Malietoa, page 37)

The Story of *'Ie'ie*

A story is told of TuiManu'a's daughter *'Ie'ie.* The TuiManu'a brought his daughter, *'Ie'ie*, to wed a chief in Savai'i. And the village of the chief, of the husband-to-be, came with so many gifts of fine mats that the calling out of the individual mats took up the whole day, so that, according to *'Ie'ie's* diary, they were not all called out and given proper words of praise.[xliii]

Stories of Famous Ladies

The stories of many famous ladies were given in Volume I of this book, *Navigators Forging a Matriarchal Culture in Polynesia*, but it is worth revisiting some of those stories here, as they are important in the history of the islands.

Apaula: the Early People of Savai'i

An early legend describes the genealogy of the famous woman *Apaula*, because she is the progenitor of the earlier people of Savai'i: The legend says that she came from Toga, with her brothers, to fight the TuiVaea in the district before it became Tuamasaga. But they were defeated, and the sister, *Apaula*, was given as ransom to Chief *Vaea*. The chief died and left *Apaula* with two sons: one went to Savai'i and the other stayed with *Apaula* and was killed by Fijians who were sojourning in the district of Vaea. So began the journey of *Apaula* to find her husband's brother, *Va'atausili*, to avenge the death of her son; and this came to pass.

Apaula gifted her name, Apaula, to her brother-in-law, *Va'atausili*, and so today her name is a princess title (the Sa'o Tama'ita'i title) in the district of Falealupo and Tufutafoe, the home place of *Va'atausili*. (We should remember, *Sa'o* means "Paramount head of the family" or Chief and is followed by the name of the title.)

Leutogitupa'itea: Progenitor of the Tonumaipe'a Dynasty

One of the major families of Samoa is the Tonumaipe'a. The Tonumaipe'a family began to rise up during the reign of TuiToga *Manaia*, and the genealogy of this family is carried through the women.

Leutogitupa'itea is the pride and progenitor of the Tonumaipe'a dynasty. Her genealogy starts with *LeFa'asau's* union with *Le'unu'unu* around A.D.1200, which produced a girl named *Sevelefatafata*. She married Paramount Chief *Seali'imatafaga* (a name which means "high chief standing on the beach") and bore a girl, *Sagataetuga*. *Sagataetuga* married *LeTuiAsau*, orator chief of LeTagaloa *Funefe'ai* in Asau village, Savai'i, and bore *Poulifataiatagaloa. Poulifataiatagaloa* became the mother, with the ubiquitous Paramount Chief *LeMuliaga* (progenitor of SaMuliaga or SaLeMuliaga clan), of *Leutogitupa'itea* and her brother *Lafaitaulupo'o*

It was this union of *Poulifataiatagaloa* and *LeMuliaga* that reunited the genealogy of the two warrior brothers, *Laifai* (or *Lafai*) and *Funefe'ai* (who was now known as Tagaloa *Funefe'ai*). *Laifai* and *Funefe'ai* are commonly referred to as the modern founders of Savai'i society (see Stories of *Funefe'ai*, page 178, and Stories of *Laifai*, page 184, in Period V).

Leutogitupa'itea's legend is well-known, because of her punishment for a cruel action. She killed a baby boy, son of TuiToga *Manaia* from his second wife, out of envy and jealousy, for the boy was the heir apparent to the Togan Kingdom. One day *Leutogitupa'itea* invited the Togan mother to bathe with her at the pool of a nearby waterfall. When they arrived at the waterfall, the Togan woman wanted to bathe first and asked *Leutogitupa'itea* to hold her baby. *Leutogitupa'itea* agreed, but, while the Togan woman was in the water, *Leutogitupa'itea* took the rib of the coconut leaf (which is like a toothpick) and thrust it into the boy's head, and the boy died.

TuiToga *Manaia* started to investigate what had happened. The mother of the child accused *Leutogitupa'itea* of murdering her son, and TuiToga *Manaia* believed her. He then ordered the execution of *Leutogitupa'itea* by tying her to a branch (*maga*) of the *fetau* tree (a tree of the Calophyllum type) and burning her to death. So the TuiToga's servants built a pyre under *Leutogitupa'itea* and lit it up with fire. But, just as the fire was beginning to burn ferociously, *Leutogitupa'itea* called out to her brother *Lafaitaulupo'o* for help. He commanded (*fa'atonu* or *tonu*) a swarm of white bats or foxes (*pe'a*) to "look over" (*tilotilo mai*) how they might help *Leutogitupa'itea*. They saw (*tilotilo*) what the fire was about to do, and they urinated on the fire to put it out.

TuiToga *Manaia* and the people immediately wondered if *Leutogitupa'itea* might be a demonic, half-human, half-spirit being, as was common with Samoans. With much superstition, TuiToga *Manaia* ordered a servant to maroon *Leutogitupa'itea* on a deserted island in the Toga Archipelago, to let her die there. So the servant took her, as instructed.

The island was a desert, with absolutely no vegetation, just sand and ocean and a population of one—a demonic spirit from Samoa and Manu'a by the name of *Losi* (see The Story of *Losi*, page 93). In the Samoan version of the legend, *Losi* helped *Leutogitupa'itea* by providing and preparing food (breadfruit, taro, bananas, etc.) and finding water. Because there was no vegetation, not even leaves to use as a cover for the *umu* (the Samoan cooking oven), *Leutogitupa'itea* covered her oven with sand pebbles (*iliili* in Samoan).

Some time later, a paramount chief of the island of Uēa or Wallis Island, west of Savai'i, came by on a dugout canoe. He pulled up on shore and he said to *Leutogitupa'itea* that he would like to take her to his island kingdom to be his wife. And so *Leutogitupa'itea* agreed and married the TuiUēa, and gave birth to a son named *Fa'asega*.

Leutogitupa'itea told *Fa'asega* all about her family genealogy in Samoa and about her dear brother *Lafaitaulupo'o*. So *Fa'asega* prepared to travel to Samoa to find the family. The Morning (*Taeao*) of the Edict at the Motu Tu'ufua (told in *Volume I* of this book) records the parting words of farewell between *Leutogitupa'itea* and her son *Fa'asega*: "Come my son; go to Savai'i Island and find my brother *Lafaitaulupo'o* and give the following titles for the family and in memory of me." The titles and proclamations included: *Tonu* (a command) *mai* (from) *pe'a* (flying foxes), which makes Tonumaipe'a; *Tilo* (look on) *mai* (so, look from or on me), which makes *Tilomai,* the name proclaimed as a title for the Sa'o Aualuma, the council of princesses for the Tonumaipe'a title and dynasty; and *Tau* (the covers of the *umu* cooking oven) *ililí* (the sand pebbles that *Leutogitupa'itea* used to cover the umu oven), which makes *Tauiliili,* the name proclaimed to be a title of the firstborn (Ali'ioāiga) of Tonumaipe'a *Sauoāiga*.

Fa'asega went to Savai'i and delivered the proclamations to his uncle *Lafaitaulupo'o* who was the great-grandfather of the first Tonumaipe'a *Sauoāiga*. *Fa'asega* married *Leutogitui*, daughter of Paramount Chief *LeFolasā* of Falelima, Savai'i, who bore a daughter *Finetele* who married the second Tonumaipe'a, named *Saumaipe'a* (Tonumaipe'a *Saumaipe'a*, the son of *Tauiliili*), and begat *Tapumanaia*, thus reuniting *Leutogitupa'itea's* genealogy with that of her brother *Lafaitaulupo'o*.[xliv] *Finetele* became the ancestor of the princess *Tuaetali*, daughter of La'ulu *Nofovaleane*.

LeTelesā: Early Matriarchy in Samoan History

Lady *LeTelesā* was born around A.D.1100, from the union between TuiA'ana *Pilisosolo* of A'ana district and *Manavafea'a* of Faleata. *Manavafea'a* gave birth to a boy named *'Ata'atanoa* and his sister *LeTelesā*.

'Ata'atanoa married *Tofili*, daughter of *Patauave*, who was the son of *Ata* from the daughter of the TuiToga. *'Ata'atanoa* and *Tofili* produced three children: a girl *Fa'aulimaumi* (or just *Ulimaumi*), a son *Fa'auli,* and the boy *Umi* who would later be adopted by *LeTelesā*. Their daughter, *Fa'aulimaumi* married her great-grandfather *Ata* (father of *Patauave,* father of *Tofili*—see the LeTelesā Lineage and the Mata'afa, Matai'a, and Faumuinā Titles, page 24) and bore *Si'ufe'ai* and *Tafa'igata.*

Si'ufe'ai's genealogy is found in the ancestry of the Malietoa dynasty. And *Tafa'igata's* genealogy would eventually produce the Mata'afa royal crown of Faleata district. *Patauave* (grandfather to *Si'ufe'ai* and *Tafa'igata*) was the father of Paramount Chief *Matai'a* and his sister *Tofili* (the mother of *Si'ufe'ai* and *Tafa'igata*).

LeTelesā's authority over a major district, like Faleata, is the only known matriarchal authority in early Samoan history. And while there are very few details known about her life, we do know her Faleata dynasty was real. Her real-estate holdings, that her son *Faumuinā* inherited, form one of the largest in Samoa, giving clear evidence of a matriarchal society.

The name *LeTelesā* is memorialized in the "princess name" LeTelesā of *Faumuinā's* daughter. So people tend to confuse *LeTelesā*, the founder of the matriarchal Faleata dynasty, and *LeTelesā*, princess of the Paramount Chief *Faumuinā*.

The Story of *Faumuinā*

So, the ancient indigenous authority of the village and district of Faleata began with *'Ata'atanoa* and his sister *Telesā* or *LeTelesā*. *LeTelesā* became the paramount high chief authority, and a cruel one, ruling over all of Faleata District. In this epoch, when the Samoan chiefs of supreme paramount authority were practicing cannibalism, *LeTelesā* was both cruel and a cannibal. Her reputation was one of fearsome cruelty to those who crossed the boundaries of her district, and local legend in the district of Faleata describes her as a demonic spirit, one that often transformed into a beautiful lady, and traveled across Tuamasaga district to guard and protect the Malietoa dynasty.

There is no mention of *LeTelesā* ever marrying; fragmented information about her notes that she desired a son, but without a husband this was not possible. One day, according to Faleata folklore, she went to her brother *'Ata'atanoa* and said to him, "I want to have one of your sons to be my son."

'Ata'atanoa replied, "Sure, take that boy that is preparing the Samoan food-oven in the cooking shack." The phrase "preparing the food-oven in the cooking shack," in the Samoan language, is *fai* or *fau* (prepare) *umu* (oven). He added, "And let that be his name—preparing the umu there." So his name was *Fai-umu-i-nā* or *Faumuinā*. So *Faumuinā* inherited *LeTelesā's* paramountcy crown and all her real-estate property in all of Faleata.

This is the origin of the name and chief title, Faumuinā, and of one of two paramount princes and dual authorities in the district of Faleata. The other prince in the district of Faleata is his cousin *Mata'afa,* a descendant of the brother *'Ata'atanoa*.

The Other *Faumuinā*

This name *Faumuinā* should not be confused with King *Faumuinā* (*Tupufia*) in the 17th century. He was the son of *Sina*, granddaughter of Queen *Salamasina*. However, as we shall see, there is a family genealogical connection from that later *Faumuinā* that dates back to the girl named *LeTelesā* (daughter to *Faumuinā* in Faleata). This *LeTelesā* married *Ape* from Fasito'o and bore *Folasāitu. Faumuinā* and *Folasāitu* both inherited land holdings of their mother *LeTelesā. Faumuinā* took the seaward land and *Folasāitu* inherited the land toward the mountains. Hence the namesake, *Faumuinā*, son of *Sina* and *Titoiaivao* of Faleatiu.

So yes, it is always a good rule of thumb to take notice of the names of chiefs in any given village, and to appreciate the potential genealogical family connections when presenting an oration.

The Matai'a, Faumuinā, and Mata'afa Titles

The story of The Matai'a, Faumuinā, and Mata'afa Titles starts with the legend of *Fe'e* and his brother, *To'oa'au* and sister *Si'u* (*Si'u o A'ana* or *Si'uoa'ana*—see The Girl who married the Octopus, page 88). This is the later legend of *Fe'e*, and this is where the name of the village, *Fale o Si'u* or Faleasi'u comes from. For *To'oa'au* told his brother *Fe'e* to stay and take care of their sister *Si'uoa'ana,* living in Faleasi'u village, while he returned home to check on their parents in Aleipata, in Atua district.

On his way to Aleipata, *To'oa'au* sojourned at Faleata village and met and married *LeTelesā*. According to Lafai Sauoaiga Apemoemanatunatu's *O Le Mavaega I Le Tai*, this *LeTelesā* was a daughter of Tui-*Tafa'igata* (son of *Ata* and *Fa'aulimaumi*, and brother of *Si'ufe'ai*, the progenitor of the Malietoa clan in all of Faleata—see the LeTelesā Lineage and the Mata'afa, Matai'a, and Faumuinā Titles, page 24).[xlv]

The connection with the Matai'a, Faumuinā, and Mata'afa titles, as well as with the Malietoa clan (which we will meet in Period V), should be noted here. For *Tafa'igata's* brother *Si'ufe'ai* is the grandfather of *Fe'epō*, progenitor of Malietoa clan. Also Dr. Krämer has *Tafa'igata* married to *Sauopualai*, who bore *Veletaloola, Taliausolo, Mata, 'Afa* and *Mata'afa*, the first Mata'afa. And *Patauave* (grandfather to *Si'ufe'ai* and *Tafa'igata*) was the father of Paramount Chief *Matai'a.* Also it appears that after the passing of the matriarch *LeTelesā*, her son *Faumuinā* inherited her title and real-estate property holdings. And so the whole of the children and grandchildren of *Ata* and *Fa'aulimaumi,* and of *'Ata'atanoa*, brother of *LeTelesā,* became intertwined in this family genealogy at this juncture. Hence, the three paramount royal chiefs of Faleata are: Matai'a, Faumuinā, and Mata'afa. And, of course, the Malietoa became a dynasty and Island Nation monarch.

There are also local legends that allude to *Tafa'igata* having a daughter who was named after the matriarch *LeTelesā*.

Connection with *Tamālelagi*

To'oa'au's *sister Si'uoa'ana* married a man from A'ana and gave birth to a girl named *Si'usei'a* (the name is a combination of *Si'u* and a reference to her brother that turned octopus, *Fe'e*, using a general term *i'a* or fish). And TuiA'ana *Tamālelagi* came calling on *Si'usei'a* to ask her hand in marriage. *Si'usei'a* married TuiA'ana *Tamālelagi*.[xlvi] And the marriage produced a son named *Tuitama. Si'uoa'ana's* name appears in the *To'o, Ata, LeTelesā, Tafa'igata, Si'ufe'ai*, and *Fe'epō* genealogies.

The children of *Tamālelagi*—see Children of *Tamālelagi*, page 50—are listed in Period VI, but there *Si'usei'a* is named *Sei'amaimoana*, daughter of *Vaovasa*. This *Vaovasa* is unlikely to be the same *Vaovasa* as the son of *Tauiliili i Papa*—see Children of *Tauiliili i Papa*, page 205 in Period VI—since the generation is off by 3. But we should note, as we saw earlier, that the father of *Fe'e, To'oa'au* and their sister *Si'u* was the original *Vaovasa* in Samoa, as known at Atua district of Upolu—see The Girl who married the Octopus, page 88—so it makes sense that the name or title of Vaovasa would be found in Faleasi'u village. We should remember, *Fulisiailagitele*, who was originally married TuiA'ana *Tamālelagi,* was abducted by La'ulu *Nofovaleane,* great grandfather of *Tauiliili i Papa*, to be his wife. So it's entirely possible that *Tauiliili i Papa* named his son after the *Vaovasa* who was father in-law of *Tamālelagi* at Faleasi'u village. *Tauiliili's Vaovasa* is a high chief as opposed to the *Vaovasa* in Faleasi'u village, who is Elder Orator Chief, and they are 90 years apart.

It's important to remember here that TuiA'ana *Tamālelagi* was the adopted son of the two paramount orator chiefs,

Apemoemanatunatu (*Ape*) and *Tutuilalematemate* (*Tutuila*). The legend of the two warriors, *Ape* and *Tutuila*, is anchored to this stolen High Chief *Tamālelagi,* who was born around the beginning of A. D. 1500 (see The Story of the Adopted Child, page 165, told in the story of Vaetamasoāali'i). But the story of their genealogical beginnings goes back to three or four generations earlier, which is about 100 years before the *Tamālelagi* legend, which is why we are including it in Period IV.

The LeTele title

The first appearance of the name or title LeTele (short for *LeTelesā*) at the village of Sagafili or Faleatiu (which was all the property of *Fasito'outa* and *Fasito'otai* in the ancient history of the A'ana district), dates back to the #16 generation, around A.D.1380, according to Dr. Krämer's accounting of the SaMoeleoi and Mavaega family lineage.[xlvii] This genealogy begins with ancient Faleata connections, with *Ma'ata'anoa* marrying *Imoa*, the daughter of *Vele* of *Faleata*. *Vele* (or *Veletaloola*) is, of course, the son of *Tafa'igata* and *Sauopualai*, whose generation is consistent with and A.D.1350-1380 time period.

This implies that *To'oa'au's* marriage with *LeTelesā* is the connection that brought the LeTele title to Faleatiu village—the village where *Titoiaivao*, father of *Faumuinā* (A.D.1590) lived, and the Tupufia ("Three Paramount Chiefs") resides today, in the A'ana district.[xlviii]

For *To'oa'au* married *LeTelesā*, daughter of Tui-*Tafa'igata*, giving birth to a boy named *Folasāitu* (meaning "the boy raised by a spirit"). Then *Folasāitu* went to A'ana to search for his uncle *Fe'e* and aunt *Si'uoa'ana*. He met and married *Ape*-II's daughter *Punefulealofi-o-A'ana* (meaning "she is the princess of the Ava ceremony of the A'ana district"). This marriage produced two sons: *Apemoemanatunatu*-III and *Folasāitu*-II. And this genealogical connection of *LeTelesā* is the origin of how the LeTele (short for *LeTelesā*) title came to the A'ana district, and thus also how the name *Faumuinā* name came to A'ana—for later, *Sina's* son, called *Faumuinā,* inherits the crown and titles of his aunt TuiAtua TuiA'ana *Taufau*, granddaughter of Tafa'ifa *Salamasina* (see After Salamasina, page 204).

And now the circle is complete, from *Faumuinā* to *Faumuinā*, from *LeTelesā* to Tafa'ifa *Salamasina*.

Other Famous Ladies

The stories of other famous ladies will be given later: see The Story of *Gatoa'itele*, page 162, The Story of *Vaetamasoāali'i* (*Gatoa'itele's* daughter), page 164, The Story of *LeValasi*, page 169, The Story of the Warrior Queen *Nafanua*, page 172, and The Story of *Salamasina*, page 200.

Period V: Forging a Nation and Defeating Toga

The Togan Yoke

Samoans were under the Togan yoke for 400 years in the period from around A.D.825 until 1225. Prior to this period the Samoan Islands, including Savai'i, were under the rule of the TuiManu'a. And before that, as we have seen, the islands were conquered by the warrior of Manu'a named *Fitiaumua* (see The Story of *Fitiaumua*, page 108). Legend has it that *Fitiaumua* conquered Fiji, Toga, and many islands of the South Pacific. His name is often mentioned in Hawaiian, Tahitian, and Maori legends.

During the 400 years of Togan rule, episodic, long-distance, cruel treatment of Samoa continued until the period of the Samoan and Togan war (A.D1225-1236). The Togan contingent, in Tutuila, was led by TuiToga *Talaaifei'i's* brother *Lautivunia,* who was governor of the Toga territory, and the Samoan warrior responsible for orchestrating the battles and war strategy, almost single-handedly, was *Fua'au*, also known as *Fua'autoa*. *Fua'au* and his brother *Tuisamata* were descendants of *Tele* and *Malae* (also known as *Tõ* and *Ali'i*) of Manu'a.

The Story of TuiManu'a's paramount warriors

The story of the sons and grandsons of *Fe'epõ* and the first Malietoa (see The Founding of the Malietoa Dynasty, page 146) is legendary, and we will look at it soon. But first we will look at earlier wars fought, several generations prior to this, for the liberation of Samoa.

Oral tradition tells a story of the TuiManu'a sending his paramount warriors (his children) to organize strategy for battle against the TuiToga and his military entourage. Thus four brothers—*Alapapa*, *Soalaupule*, *Leago,* and *Toeoso*—came from Manu'a with a group of warriors who were brothers or relatives, to help the Samoans prepare to fight back against the TuiToga's imperialism.

When their ship anchored on the north side of Upolu, the warrior *Tui* and his brother *Mau* were assigned to the north side of Tuamasaga District, while *Laufiso* and his brother *Tapuala* were designated to the northwest A'ana District; *Se'ela* and *Latai* were placed on the southwest side of A'ana; *Fuga* and *Vasa* were assigned to South Tuamasaga; and Atua was given the warrior *Leifi*. The four brothers that captained the ship from Manu'a—*Alapapa*, *Soalaupule*, *Leago,* and *Toeoso*—settled on the south side of Upolu, in the district of Tuamasaga, at their sacred meeting residence Fatufelo.[xlix]

Oral legend implies that these warriors began their respective efforts about four generations before the battle that founded the Malietoa title and dynasty. These earlier generations were foundational to the development of village organization and defenses across the islands of Samoa. For the strength of the TuiToga's regime came from the large size of his warrior group, as compared to the small male population of isolated villages across the islands; the village population was easily overwhelmed by the well-organized TuiToga war machine.

The size of a village, at that time, is estimated to have been 50 to 200 people. Thus the well-organized fleet of anywhere between 200 to 300 ships, each manned by 75 to over 100 warriors, could have easily subdued even the largest villages. Additionally, the authority of the TuiToga over his subjects could not be challenged, for he was "sacred" like a god, for he (and his TuiToga kingdom) had consolidated authority to one single Family since the beginning of its ancient history.

The Story of Tutuila

The Story of *Fua'au* and *Tuisamata*

The Island of Tutuila was also under the subjugation of the TuiToga but gained its freedom in a separate victory in battle, directed by the warrior *Fua'autoa* (*Fua'au*) of the village of Pago Pago, Tutuila.

Legend has it that the brothers *Fua'au* and *Tuisamata* were responsible for preparing the food of the TuiManu'a. And, for some time now, TuiManu'a had not been pleased with their lackadaisical and quarrelsome attitude, so he banished them out of Manu'a, and they floated and landed in Tutuila, at the village of Tula. From there they parted ways. *Fua'au* went toward Fagaloa Bay and landed on Pago Pago shore. *Tuisamata* stayed in Lefutu and built a family there.

Fua'au had long wished for the Togans to be driven out of Samoa and Tutuila. But as *Fua'au* quietly prepared for war, the people of Tutuila were not at all enthusiastic to render support to his initiative. So *Fua'au*, out of frustration, said aloud, "If you are not going to help, I will fight it by myself." And so he planned out the initial battle engagement.

Fua'au knew that the Togan governor, *Lautivunia,* was on a fleet expected to drop anchor shortly at Leone bay. *Fua'au's* plan was to wait until the ships arrived on shore. In the dawn hours, he would attack with his *toa*, his wooden war-club. *Fua'au's* surprise attack was ferocious, and, to his amazement, he saw other people fighting alongside him to destroy the Togans. The war was now taken up by the Tutuila Island population, with individual battles scattered across Tutuila, wherever Togan settlements were located.

The crux of the war took place at the Leone and Alataua district of Tutuila, where the governor *Lautivunia* had just landed. The defeat of the Togans was a slaughter, and many are buried there. *Lautivunia* barely made it back to his fleet of vessels, as he escaped the war wrath of *Fua'au* and the Tutuilans. So *Fua'au* is heralded as Tutuila's warrior hero (hence *Fua'au-toa*) and savior of Tutuilan freedom.

The stories of *Fua'autoa* and *Mauga* (see The Story of the Boy from the Mountain, page 144) can both be mapped to the time period of Malietoa *Uitualagi*, son of Malietoafaigā, who gave *Mauga* his name. That maps to the time of TuiManu'a *'Ali'atama*.

The ultimate defeat of Toga was an initiative undertaken in all Samoa and Tutuila and the Manu'a Archipelago, though Manu'a never suffered under Togan cruelty because no Polynesian kingdom ever subdued the Kingdom of Manu'a—legends have it that all the kingdoms in Polynesia viewed Manu'atele as a sacred Island Kingdom of all of Polynesia, and Dr. Krämer referred to Manu'a as the "Delos" of Polynesia, after the Greek birthplace of their deities, Apollo and Artemis.[l]

Tutuila Island Ruling Princes and the SaMauga family genealogy

The Tutuila Island structure is organized around the founding princes and their paramount families, as noted in the Samoa salutations: "Princes and their families." This is to emphasize the organizational structure and authority of Tutuila. Samoan and Manu'an legends recount that the initial settlers of the island were the couple, *Tutu* and *Ila*, hence the eponymous Tutuila name, as discussed earlier under the mythology of *PapaAtea* or the 'Atea and Pulotu war, and the populating of the archipelago of Samoa and Manu'a (see Stories of PapaAtea and Pulotu, page 75).

The House of Ten

The period of the ruling authority of the "House of Ten," or *Falegafulu* of the Paramount *Mageafaigā*, is benchmarked to the period of *Taeotagaloa* and *Lefanoga* as well as of the Malietoafaigā. At this time there were already other warrior chiefs in other parts of Tutuila who had gained their own authority and paramountcy in their respective district territories. The founding organizational structure of the *Falegafulu*—the "Ten Houses or Seats" under the ruling authority of *Mageafaigā*—evidences the first consolidated organization of Tutuila Island. The real meaning of this is that each "seat" represents a geographical authority of the ten recognized authorities in Tutuila. It's equivalent to the Atua and A'ana *Tuamasaga,* and Savai'i's *Usoga*, or to the brothers, *Laifai* and *Funefe'ai,* defining the original division of Savai'i Island and Upolu and Manono Island.

It should be noted that *Mageafaigā's* Falegafulu Mālõ, or his government, was respected across the East Pacific archipelagos, and it took the Malietoafaigā three attempts, over a period of several years, before *Ape* and *Tutuila*, *To'otai,* and *To'outa* of Fasito'o, in A'ana, defeated this government of the "House of Ten." Thus began the rule of the Malietoa dynasty on Tutuila Island.

As with the challenge of determining the origin of many of the original ancient populations of villages and districts, likewise is the difficulty of determining *Mageafaigā's* ancient genealogy.

Paramount Chief *Le'iato*

On the east side of Tutuila, Paramount Chief *Le'iato*, son of Chief *Togiola Le'iatosā,* was descended from *Taemāmā* (or *Taemā,* one of the well-known conjoined twins—see The Story of Tattooing and the Conjoined Twins, page 115), ruler of the Tonumaipe'a clan in Savai'i.[li] It appears *Mageafaigā* had already organized Tutuila Island into the *Falegafulu* (House of Ten Seats) before the twins arrived in Faga'itua village. *Le'iatotu'itu'iotoga* (his full name) was a first cousin to Warrior Queen *Nafanua*.

Faga'itua is the location of the well-known "Decree at the Sea of Alataua" (see The Decree at the Sea of Alataua, page 116), proclaimed by the twins *Taemā* and *Tilafaigā*, on their own authority, in Tutuila. This decreed the chief of Alataua, the *Ali'i o le Alataua Tulu'itanu* (son of *Tilafaigā* and *Moaifelo* of Faga'itua) to hold the vanguard and rearguard of war. So there is only one paramount chief of Alataua, and one paramount voice of Alataua, in all Samoa, all proclaimed by the same family.

Mata'ena'ena Beach at Vaoto, Savai'i is the location of the edict of *Mavaega i Le Tai,* the decree for *Sālevao* to be the "Voice" or the "Speech" of Alataua. This edict was proclaimed by *Taufailematagi* and *'Alao,* the parents of *Saveasi'uleo*, *Sālevao*, and *Ulufanuasese'e*. *Sālevao* later relocated to Malie, in Upolu.[lii] And *Saveasi'uleo* is the one who had a tail like a sea eel (see Stories of *Saveasi'uleo* and *Ulufanuasese'e*, page 114).

The Landmass across the Ocean

In the middle territory of Tutuila, where the residence of Ma'oupū stands, the Paramount Ma'oupū Chief *Mauga* is the ruling authority, and his ancestry goes back, through the royal genealogy of his mother *Alavatualua,* to the original Paramount Chief *Galea'i* of *Tagaloalagi* and the first TuiManu'a.

According to Manu'an mythology, *Galea'i* was a son of *Tagaloalagi's* union with *Aga'euta* (or *Aga'etai*) up in tenth heaven (see The First TuiManu'a, page 129). But an alternative version of the story, according to Lafai Sauoaiga Ape, says *Mavaega i Le Tai Galea'i* is a son of *TagaloaLā* and a daughter (possibly *LuaUi*) of *TagaloaUi* up in the ninth heaven, implying a departure from godhood, where *Tagaloalagi* is now part of the human race, but still implying *Galea'i's* descent from demigods.

Galea'i then married *Valooleto'elau* from Sauā, Fitiuta, and gave birth to a girl *Alavatualua* and a boy who was without a name at that time. *Alava* was much older than her brother, and we should note that this is the transitional generation between *Galea'i* and the first TuiManu'a. Historians list TuiManu'a *Lelologa's* sons as *'Ali'amatua*, the older, and *'Ali'atama* or *'Ali'a*, the younger one who became TuiManu'a *Lelologa's* successor. The two brothers had a disagreement regarding the crown, and they went to war. Unfortunately *'Ali'amatua* was killed in the Palapala area. We should also note that the reference to *'Ali'a* as *Alava's* brother appears to be a general family term for the brother and sister relationship—remember, there are no terms for cousins, first, second, removed, third removed, etc. And from a genealogical perspective, *Alavatualua* is about three generations ahead before TuiManu'a *Lelologatele*.

Returning to *Alava's* story: *Alavatualua* habitually watched the ocean waves from the cliffs at Fitiuta and wondered about the landmass she saw across the ocean. One day she requested her father to let her go visit the landmass she was seeing every time she looked out from the cliffs of Fitiuta. And so *Galea'i* commanded the servants to prepare a vessel to take his daughter to the island of the couple, *Tutu* and *Ila*.

The legend continues by telling how, when they arrived, *Alavatualua* wanted to live up on the mountain on top of the bay of Pago Pago. According to legend, the village of Pago Pago was founded by two brothers, *Pago* and *Pago,* hence its name. And the mountain ridge is called Alavatualua after the girl, *Alavatualua*.

The Story of the Boy from the Mountain

One of the warrior chief brothers *Pago* married *Alavatualua,* and she gave birth to a boy who later received his name, *Mauga*, meaning the boy from the mountain. The name was given by Malietoa *Uitualagi* at their bird net catching contest with TuiManu'a *Li'a*, who was *Alavatualua's* brother, TuiManu'a *Lia* (*Lelologatele*). Malietoa *Uitualagi* gave the boy this name when the boy brought the chiefs their afternoon supper:

Malietoa asked TuiManu'a *Li'a*, "Who is the boy?"

And TuiManu'a said, "He is my sister's son from up the mountain there."

Then Malietoa replied, "Name him 'the boy from the mountain,'" which is shortened to *Mauga*.

Alavatualua decreed that her son *Mauga* should go to her father's home and give them her message: "My dying wishes are to have my name *Alavatualua* be *Galea'i's* Feagaiga (his Sa'o Tama'ita'i) and his 'ietoga should be named *Alavatualua*." This is also the TuiManu'a 'ietoga or *Auafa* (the high chiefs' formal name of their fine mats). And this is the royal lineage of Paramount Ma'oupū Chief *Mauga* as a descendant of *Galea'i*, *Tagaloalagi*, and TuiManu'a.

The Story of the Banishment of *Tuitele*

Paramount Chief *Tuitele* resided on the western side of Tutuila. Very little is published on the origin of High Chief *Tuitele*. But local legends, based on the genealogy of the paramount chief's descendants, all indicate *Tuitele* was a son of the TuiManu'a (some say of TuiManu'a *Tulagi*) in the period of *Taeotagaloa*, *Lefanoga*, and *Muiu'uleapai*.

According to local legend, *Tuitele* was ostracized and banished to Tutuila by the TuiManu'a for cruelty. There he was to establish and build a kingdom for himself. And he did just that, in this territory of the Island of Tutuila. Hence his salutation, *Fa'atui o le Motu,* which means "stands erected—*fa'a-tu-i-motu*—in the island." This is a Manu'an salutation, the same or equivalent to the Manu'an *Fa'atui* salutation given to paramount chiefs of major territorial districts. *Galea'i* of Fitiuta, *Misaalefua* of Ofu, *Tuiolosega* of Olosega, *Sotoa* or *Soatoa* and *Lefiti* of Taū, and *La'olagi* of Sili district are all also called Tafa'i (meaning custodians and councilors) of the TuiManu'a Pāpā.

It should be noted that Paramount Chief *Tuitele* is an ancestor of *Letutupu*, the mother (with her husband TuiSamoa) of *Gauifaleai* and *Totogatā*. Lady *Gauifaleai* and Malietoa *La'auli* are the parents of the prodigious royal Pāpā *Gatoa'itele* and her sister *Gasolo* (*Gasolo-ai-ao-o-le-lagi)* as we shall see in The Story of Malietoa *La'auli*, page 152.[liii] This genealogy, of course, traces all the way back to TuiManu'a, TuiAtua *Lu*, and TuiToga, to *Fineitalaga Sagapolutele* and TuiSamoa. Thus the strong genealogical relationships between Paramount Chief *Tuitele* and the Malietoa, Gatoa'itele, Āiga SaGauifaleai, and the Tuisamau in Afega and Tuana'i villages.

Family Connections with Tutuila

Many paramount chiefs from across the archipelago came calling in hopes of marriage to a princess of the Tuitele clan. These include *Asomua* who married *Fuotoga-o-laumea*, daughter of Senior Orator Chief *Le Oso*; and Paramount Chief *Sifuiva* who married *Tamaleilua*, daughter of the Tuitele. This is the connection that brought the various family members of *Tapumanaia LeSatele* (connections to *Fuimaono*, *Alo Fanene*, *Te'o* and the Orators) from the Falealili district of Atua to this area of Tutuila. Also, Paramount *Lilomaiava Nailevaiiliili* married *Sinagautaala*, daughter of the Tuitele, and other prominent chiefs extended their family connections to the Tuitele genealogy.

After the fall of Paramount Warrior Chief *Mageafaigā's* government, the "House of Ten Seats" was divided into two: five seats to the west side of Tutuila and five seats to be shared along the eastern side of the island. The divisions of these ten house seats across Tutuila is seen in the salutations of the overall Tutuila Island organizational authority: *O le Falegafulu* or *Tutuila ma le Falegafulu* (Tutuila and its House of Ten).

The Founding of the Malietoa Dynasty

The Samoans finally defeated the Togans with a combination of successive victories in battle, concluding with their final success in A.D.1225. This is marked by the founding of the warrior Paramount Chief Malietoa and his subsequent Monarch Dynasty.

The title, Malietoa, is a word adapted from the King of Toga's proclamation, at the beach of Tulatala, that he and his warriors would retreat in defeat and that they would only return to Samoa in a wind of peace and not in war. The TuiToga shouted to the warrior brothers from the sea: *Malie tau, malie toa*! "Well fought, brave warriors!" and this is how the title Malietoa came into existence.

Sāvea, *Tuna*, and *Fata* were three brothers who led the warriors to battle. They were sons of the brave warrior *Leatiogie*, son of *Fe'epõ*. Of them, *Sāvea*, the eldest, became the first Malietoa.

This tale of ancient Samoan history is a popular legend, ubiquitous with children because their grandparents would recite it in late evenings to put them to sleep. The story of how the Samoans won their freedom from the "yoke," figuratively, or from "servitude" to the TuiToga has many versions, depending on who is speaking and to which district the speaker belongs. For every district has claimed victory in freeing the Samoans from the Togans. But we should remember, the kingdom of Manu'a had never been subdued by any foreign power.

According to legend, a series of battle scrimmages eventually led to the last and final battle, orchestrated by *Leatiogie's* sons, *Alali*, *Sāvea*, *Fata*, *Tuna*, *Leimuli*, *Ve'atauia,* and their sister *Leatiatigielealaiaolõ* (see Period IV Malietoa, page 26 in the Timelines). The battle plan involved several key warriors from all parts of Samoa. For example, the bravery of the sons of TuiAtua *Leutele*, *Taputoa* and *Tapuloa,* helped rally the warriors of the district of Atua to combine with *Ulumasui*, nephew to the *Fata*, *Tuna*, and *Sāvea* brothers, who rallied the warriors of the A'ana District. So the effort was really a collaboration between groups of warriors from all across Samoa.

The Story of Malietoa *Sāvea*

So, *Sāvea* and two unknown warrior men organized the war against Toga, and *Fata* helped fight for independence. Eventually, the TuiToga went out and said, "I will not; I am going home. I will not come with the dark cloud of war, but I will come with a bright day of peace and sunshine; *Malie tau* and *Malie toa*." From this war, *Sāvea* emerged as the first Malietoa.

Malietoa *Sāvea* married and had a son Malietoa *Gagasāvea*. *Gagasāvea* married a princess of Toga and had six sons: *Seupule*, *Toagana, Nu'uiali'i*, *Luatua*, *Sāveatama,* and *Fuataogana*, jointly called *Leatigaga* or *Sagaga*. (Notice their combined salutation forms the foundation of the district of Tuamasaga: *Faleono o Atigaga*, meaning the House of Six of Gagasāvea or Atigaga).

Malietoa *Sāvea's* second marriage was to *Luafatasaga*, the daughter of *Taemanutava'e*. They begat a son who became Malietoa faigā *Uilamatūtū—uila* means lightning without rain, and legends describe *Uilamatūtū's* birth as a day full of lightning yet no rain, weather that was very unusual on the islands. *Uilamatūtū* married Princess *Alainuanua*, sister to Princess *Pate* who was married to his half-brother Malietoa *Gagasāvea* (see in the Timelines, Period V, Malietoa, page 37).

The Story of *Luafatasaga* and her brothers

The legend of *Luafatasaga's* brothers, *Fata* and *Maulolo*, has it that *Luafatasaga* was so frightened of her husband Malietoa *Sāveatuvaelua*, that she thought he would kill her brothers, should he discover them. So it's said that she hid them under the banana leaves that were used for covering the cooking-oven, the *umu*, at the cooking house.

Luafatasaga would excuse herself every mealtime so she could secretly take her leftovers for her brother's food. After a while Malietoa *Sāveatuvaelua* noticed the pattern, and so he asked *Luafatasaga* why she bothered to take her rubbish out, to throw it away at the cooking house, when there were plenty servants to do that for her.

Luafatasaga finally fessed up that she was taking her leftovers out for her brothers who were hiding at the cooking house. And so Malietoa said to her, "How foolish a woman you are. Go and bring your brothers here so we can live together." And this is where Malietoa *Sāveatuvaelua* decreed their House of Authority or *Faleta'ita'i* at Afega village and later to all of the Malietoa dynasty and Tuamasaga district.

The Importance of *Fata* and *Maulolo*

Fata and *Maulolo*, brothers of *Luafatasaga*, were appointed by decree to be the leaders (known as *Faleta'ita'i,* or the House of Authority) of the Malietoa Vanguard Warrior clan of Afega and Tuana'i villages. This led to even more authority once their nephew, Malietoa *Uilamatutu* Faigā or Malietoafaigā, became ruler over the Malietoa dynasty, becoming known as "he to whom all Samoa listened"—*Na Faalogo iai Samoa* in Samoan.

The union of the Malietoa and Tagaloalagi (TuiManu'a) genealogies, through *Malālatea* and *Sinalagilagi* (see Malietoa in Period IV, page 26), gave the Malietoa dynasty and monarch the support of the entire Savai'i Island. *Fata* and *Maulolo's* ability to consolidate all their genealogical connections in Savai'i Island to serving the Malietoa monarch and dynasty became the source of their ruling authority with the Malietoa dynasty.

We should remember that these brothers, *Va'afa'i* (or *Va'afuti*, father of *Li'ava'a*), *Fata*, and *Maulolo* are from Savai'i, the island where the powerful, half-spirit half-man Warriors come from—as we shall see in The Story of *Va'afuti* (or *Va'afa'i*), page 157.

Their influence was further expanded when Malietoa *La'auli* decreed that his daughter *Gatoa'itele* should be cared for by *Fata* and *Maulolo* as their Paramount High Chief (see The Story of *Gatoa'itele*, page 162), and she was the chosen child (chosen by her grandfather Malietoa *Uitualagi*) decreed to be a royal crown equal to the TuiAtua and TuiA'ana PāPā's.

Stories of Malietoa Faigā *Uilamatūtū*

The Warrior *Mageafaigā*

Malietoafaigā (Malietoa Faigā *Uilamatūtū*) was a cannibal and the second son of the original Malietoa. The cannibalistic tradition was practiced in Malie, which is where the Malietoa resided. For Samoans were not accustomed to cannibalism, but it had been acquired, for a while, from the Fijian and Togan warriors.[liv]

It all goes back to a warrior, whose name was *Mageafaigā*. *Mageafaigā*, at one time, ruled a very large part of Tutuila (as we saw in The House of Ten, page 142). He resided up in Fagasā village, the seat of his throne, and the whole of Nu'uuli was his kingdom (which is why Fagasā is referred to as the Nofoali'i of Itu'au district[lv]). He would set up a rope-net contraption that extended from Fagasā hill all the way down to Nu'uuli. Any person who got tangled up in the net would become a victim of the cruel warrior, *Mageafaigā*.

The Story of *Poluleuligaga* and the Malietoafaigā

The cannibal, Malietoafaigā, married a princess of Toga, and the princess' brother—the King of Toga, Tuitoga *'Ulufanuatele*—had a son, *Poluleuligaga,* whom she and Malietoafaigā adopted.

According to legend, Malietoafaigā ruled over Upolu, Savaii, and Tutuila, where he created a schedule for when each village would sacrifice one human being. His army of men would relay the schedule to each village.

A man called *Palaugi* had two boys scheduled for sacrifice. The staging area for such an event to be held was Saleimoa. And early one morning, *Poluleuligaga* was walking along. During his walk he heard a crying voice. Concerned, *Poluleuligaga* asked who was there and, as he searched for the crying voice, he found the two boys. The boys explained they were next to be sacrificed for their villages.

Poluleuligaga told the boys he would return tomorrow with a plan. As the next day arrived, he found the boys still crying. He told them climb up the coconut tree and cut down leaves. The two boys brought the longest leaves and laid *Poluleuligaga* down on the leaves. They wove the leaves to form a basket, just as the Samoans would do to prepare fish. Then they carried *Poluleuligaga* to the boat and paddled to the Malietoa.

Poluleuligaga instructed the boys to lay the basket, face down, in front of the Malietoa. The boys did just as *Poluleuligaga* directed, and the Malietoa was excited to see such a large basket. He asked servants to turn over the gift, woven with coconut leaflets, so he could inspect it. To his amazement, when they opened it up, he saw his son.

Malietoafaigā said, "What is the meaning of this?"

And *Polu* said, "You're about to run out of your citizens if you keep this practice up."

It's at this moment in their father/son/cannibal/king discourse that Malietoafaigā said to *Polu*, "Do you know how many gods Samoans worship? Do you want to be Malietoa?" and "Are there two gods that Samoans worship?" He was referring to being spoken to in this didactical manner. For there is only one "god" that Samoans worshipped and listened to—*Malietoafaigā na Faalogo iai Samoa*. (This is the origin of the Lua Atua or LuaAtua or Luatua, meaning "two gods," family in Saleimoa village in the Tuamasaga district in Upolu).

This provoked the Malietoa to rethink his traditions and his desire to expand his kingdom. From this day forward, the Malietoa stopped the cannibalistic tradition.

The Story of Malietoa *Uitualagi*

Malietoa *Uitualagi* was the son of Malietoafaigā *Uilamatutu*. *Uitualagi* had tried countless times to court a princess called *Gasolo-ai-o-le-lagi.* And *Gasoloaiolelagi* had a brother, *Manaia* (*Ali'amanaia*, commonly referred to as *Li'amanaia* or in short, *Manaia*), who was a handsome and popular prince.

Manaia went out one evening to a social gathering at a nearby village. He returned home later that night, drunk, and saw his sister, *Gasoloaiolelagi*, lying naked on her sleeping mat in the middle of the Samoan open house. He walked to her and covered her with his *lei*, then continued walking away. But she woke up and taunted *Manaia*, saying, "Are you only going to cover me with a lei; why not something more deliberate?"

Then *Manaia* crossed the sacred boundary and violated his sister. *Gasoloaiolelagi* became pregnant, and *Manaia*, ashamed of what he had done, fled the village.

Their father, *Tunavaitele*, was aware of the embarrassing act and began to plan. He was reminded of Malietoa *Uitualagi*, who had tried for many years to court *Gasoloaiolelagi.* He inquired of the Malietoa and said, "*Gasoloaiolelagi* is pregnant. She is willing to marry you to cover up her sinful actions." Without hesitation, Malietoa *Uitualagi* married her, and she bore *La'auli*, which means "stepped over in the night." Malietoa *Uitualagi* and *Gasoloaiolelagi* would later give birth to *Fuaoleto'elau*, half-brother to *La'auli*.

In this genealogy we see a connection between Faleata and Tifitifi. For *Fuaoleto'elau* and *La'auli's* biological mother is the daughter of Chief *Togia* (or *Tuna-vai-tele*) of Tifitifi, a hamlet of Vaimauga, and *Uitualagi's* mother is *Alainuanua*, daughter of the TuiToga residing in Vaimauga and Faleata.

The Story of Malietoa *La'auli*

In the village of Malie, seat of residence of the Malietoa monarch, people were discussing the breathtaking beauty of TuiSamoa and *Letutupu's* daughters, *Gauifaleai* and *Totogatā* (see The Story of the Banishment of *Tuitele*, page 145).

We should note, TuiSamoa was a paramount chief in the district of Falealili and was an ancient family member of the first Malietoa *Sāvea*. His wife *Letutupu* was a daughter of Paramount Chief *Fineitalaga,* the elder of the Sagapolutele family—he was also known as the First Sagapolutele, who married *Fololela*, the daughter (adopted from his son *Tuife'ai*) of the Tuitele of Leone, Tutuila. *Fololela's* mother was *Ualegalu*, daughter of TuiManu'a and sister to *Vainu'ulasi*. And *Vainu'ulasi's* descendants would eventually lead to TuiToga's daughter *Vaetoeifaga,* who would become wife to TuiA'ana *Tamālelagi,* producing a daughter *Salamasina*.

This kind of royal genealogy was quite attractive and compelling to the Malietoa clan, hence their urgency to court the TuiSamoa's daughters. Since *Fuaoleto'elau* was assumed by all to be the one who would take the Malietoa title, because of his being the blood son of Malietoa *Uitualagi*, the talking chiefs and people of the village of Malie took *Fuaoleto'elau* to Falealili to court, and possibly wed, TuiSamoa's daughters.

The girls heard of the festivities to take place and went to freshen up at the river pool. While on their way they spotted a young man hiding in the bushes. It was *La'auli*, engaged in the sport of catching birds. He was covered in mud and wearing camouflage clothing.

The girls teased *La'auli* for being so dirty and ugly. Then *La'auli* replied, "I may be ugly, but I am the best bird-catcher around."

The girls said, "Your hair is disgusting and filthy."

La'auli replied "That's because I'm bird-catching."

Then the girls went on their way and finished washing up.

At the festivities, *Gauifaleai* and *Totogatā* spotted a handsome young man walking by. It was *La'auli*, all washed up. The two girls desired to wed him, instead of *Fuaoleto'elau*.

Fuaoleto'elau, realizing that the girls did not desire him but were falling for his stepbrother *La'auli*, immediately told the orators, who set the young warriors to pack for the journey back to the village of Malie, which was across the other side of the island.

La'auli, however, waited for a while before making the long hike home to Malie that night. To his surprise the girls followed him. *La'auli* told *Gauifaleai* and *Totogatā* he could not marry them, because his brother was going to become Malietoa. However, *Gauifaleai*, *Totogatā*, and *La'auli* ran away to get married and begin a family.

The village realized what happened and decided *La'auli* would be the Malietoa. This marriage to both *Gauifaleai* and *Totogatā* gave birth to *Gatoa'itele* and *Gasoloaiaoolelagi*. The marriage further established the connection between Tuitele and TuiManu'a's daughter.

La'auli and Malietoa Uitualagi

La'auli loved his father, Malietoa *Uitualagi,* so much that he asked *Gauifaleai* and *Totogatā* to periodically visit and massage his father's feet and legs, for Malietoa *Uitualagi* was getting on in age. This really made his father extremely happy and appreciative. He was very touched by *La'auli's* gesture and his wives' kindness in caring for him. Then Malietoa *Uitualagi* decreed that these two women would bear children and they should be given Royal Crowns, equal to the TuiAtua and TuiA'ana.

Malietoa *Uitualagi* decreed that:

- *La'auli* would follow him as heir to the Malietoa title.
- Their firstborn would have a PāPā crown title.
- To proclaim the birth of the royal child, a *usūsū* (a long, extend sound or yell like "chooooo") must be sounded.
- The second-born son (or child) would also have a PāPā title.
- The PāPā titles would be equal to the TuiAtua PāPā title. At this period, TuiAtua was the prominent rival to the Malietoa dynasty. TuiA'ana prominence began with TuiA'ana *Tamālelagi*, father of *Salamasina*.
- Paramount Orator Chiefs *Fata* and *Maulolo* would be the authority and custodians of the PāPā. This decree did not come to fruition until the period of the Warrior Queen *Nafanua*.

So, the Lady *Gatoa'itele* (Royal Queen *Gatoa'itele*) was the child decreed before birth to a royal PāPā (Crown) of the first national matriarchy over all of Samoa, by her grandfather Malietoa *Uitualagi* in A.D.1410. Then *Gatoa'itele* and her husband begat *Vaetamasoāali'i,* and the two names each became Royal Crowns, thus fulfilling the decree of Malietoa *Uitualagi* and setting the stage for the beginning of the modern history of Samoa.

The Malietoa Title

As a footnote to Malietoa *Uitualagi's* decree, we should note that, from the founding of the Malietoa dynasty, the Island Nation had been ruled by successive Malietoa titleholders, but the Malietoa title is a warrior paramount chief title, with no royalty. There is no crown PāPā like there is for TuiAtua, TuiA'ana, TuiManu'a, TuiToga, TuiFiti, TuiUēa and others across Polynesia. Some historians believe this is the reason the Malietoa clan orchestrated this creation of the PāPā titles to be equal to the TuiA'ana and TuiAtua.

Stories of the Malietoa

Many Families, Many Connections

As we have seen, the Malietoa lineage traces back to many families. Around A.D. 1, *Pilia'au* and *Sinaaletava'e* (daughter of the TuiA'ana) gave birth to *Ana.* (*Pilia'au* was from the TuiAtua lineage—see TuiAtua, page 10 in Period II.) *Ana's* union with *Sinalemana* gave birth to *Matofaoa'ana* and *Moaoa'ana*. (*Matofa o A'ana* means *Matofa*—name of the girl—of *A'ana,* hence *Matofaoa'ana*. And *Moa* is a family name, meaning chicken, hence *Moaoa'ana.*) *Matofaoa'ana's* union with *Sinaletula* gave birth to *Veta*. *Veta* together with *Afulilo* begat *Tuiveta*. *Tuiveta*'s union with *Toelauo'o* brought forth *Toso* (see Period V, Malietoa, page 37). And *Toso* united with *Titilagipupula*, daughter of the TuiManu'a.

Toso and *Titilagipupula* begat *Si'usei'a*. *Si'usei'a* united with *Tapalemalama*, from Faleata who begat *Si'utaulalovasa*. He united with a lady from Samata, Savaii, and begat *To'o* and *Ata*. *To'o* died (see The Story of *To'o* and *Ata*, page 159) and *Ata* united with a Togan Princess and begat *Patauave*, a senior chief in Faleata. Elder

Chief *Patauave's* union with a lady from Vaitele resulted in birth of the famous *Matai'a* (third of the *Matai'a*, *Mata'afa,* and *Faumuinā* tripod of descendants of *LeTelesā* and her brother *'Ata'atanoa,* who formed the ruling authority of the Faleata district, the Vanguard of War division of the Malietoa *Tuamasaga* district), and his sister *Tofili*.

Then come the unions of *'Ata'atanoa* (the brother of *LeTelesā*—see LeTelesā Lineage and the Mata'afa, Matai'a, and Faumuinā Titles, page 24) with *Tofili* and *Fa'aulimaumi*. From his marriage with *Fa'aulimaumi*, he begat *Si'ufe'ai and Tafa'igata*. *Tafa'igata* married *Sauopualai,* giving birth to *Vele-talo-ola* ("weeding the taro patch for growth"), *Taliausolo* (with demonic spirit), *Mata*, *'Afa*, and the first *Mata'afa* ("the voracious wild tail"), who was decreed to be the Chief of the Tafa'igata clan.[lvi] *Si'ufe'ai* married *Lepolatele* in Pola village, giving birth to *Si'ulefualelaumalõ*. And *Si'ulefualelaumalõ* married *Aigamasitele* from Faleata, giving birth to the blind *Fe'epõ*. *Fe'epõ* married *Leipaleatele* and begat *Sina*, *Leatiogie*, and *Malālatea* (ancestor of *Va'afuti*, *Fata*, *Maulolo* and their sister *Luafatasaga)*. And *Leatiogie's* son was the first Malietoa *Sāvea*.

Story of Leatiogie and Salevaogogo

Leatiogie was said to be ten feet tall and was believed, among many, to be half human half spirit. He came from a long and powerful line of the warrior clan, Malietoa.

Leatiogie was most notably known for defeating *Salevaogogo* in Momoa. When *Leatiogie's* father, *Fe'epõ*, heard about *Leatiogie's* victory, he began to cheer for his son. *Ua patipati taoto LeFe'epõ* (*Fe'epõ* clapping and cheering, laying down—*my translation*).

And *Leatiogie,* as we have seen, was the father of the first Malietoa.

The story of *Malālatea* (or *Malalatele*) and the *Fale'ula* (or Golden House)

Legends describe how *Sina* (sister of *Leatiogie* and *Malālatea*) was fishing one day, and the TuiManu'a was captured by her beauty from afar. He took her by force and married her. She sent a secret message to her brother to rescue her from the TuiManu'a.

Then *Malālatea* and *Sina* safely returned to Upolu with the TuiManu'a's *Fale'ula*; hence the title of the village of Fale'ula in Upolu.

The "Golden House" or *Fale'ula* was a house gifted to TuiManu'a by *Tagaloalagi*. This is the house that *Tagaloalagi* commanded *Pili* to bring down for the king TuiManu'a (see *Pili* and the Golden House, page 101). It is the house with the "posts" designated or decreed (symbolizing authority) to the various warrior chiefs who went seeking fortune and fame to the king of Manu'a.

The legend of *Malālatea, Sina,* and the Fale'ula (the Golden House) of TuiManu'a is a tale of how *Malālatea* and his sister *Sina* outwitted the TuiManu'a and his Chiefs Council, stopping them from entrapping and killing *Malālatea*. For when *Malālatea* arrived in Manu'a at *Sina's* place, TuiManu'a and his council were in the middle of the sacred ava ceremony.

Sina was filled with joy to see her brother but was also fearful for his life, because he came at an inopportune time, when the king was having his sacred ava ceremony. And so *Sina* said to *Malālatea*, "If they should send for you and give you tasks to do, be sure to come to me first, and I will guide you through them."

And so *Malālatea* was summoned to the presence of TuiManu'a. TuiManu'a gave his first command for *Malālatea*, to go and get some fish for the meal for the ava ceremony. And *Malālatea* went to *Sina* and told her the task—to get fish for the ava ceremony meal. So Sina said, "This task will kill you for sure. You'll be killed by the wild, sacred fish. But here is what you will do. When you get to the pond by the lagoon, take two stones, and throw one to the shallow side of the pond. And the second stone, throw it on the bank of the same side of the pond. When the fish jumps out onto the land of the bank, you must immediately grab it by the gills and drag it on shore, for that's the way to fish out the wild eels."

So *Malālatea* was successful, and he took the fish to the TuiManu'a's ava celebration. And TuiManu'a and his Chiefs Council were surprised to see this. But TuiManu'a was still not convinced that *Malālatea* was a human and not a demonic spirit warrior from Upolu. TuiManu'a said to *Malālatea*, "Go get the ava for the ceremony."

Malālatea went to his sister *Sina* and told her about the next command. And *Sina* said, "Take this short, thick stick with you, to harvest the ava plant. When the first branch hits you, be sure to dodge it and simultaneously hit it with the stick, until it breaks off. And if the second branch rises up to hit you, you must do likewise—dodge and hit, until it breaks off."

Malālatea was again successful, and he brought the ava to TuiManu'a and his entourage at the council meeting. It's at this point that TuiManu'a realized *Malālatea* was really a demonic spirit, not a human being. Meanwhile *Malālatea* went back to *Sina* and said to her, "Let's leave for my vessel, to go home."

TuiManu'a saw *Sina* and *Malālatea* about to board the vessel. He rushed over to convince *Sina* to stay with him, but to no avail. *Sina* was so full of anger and disappointment, quite aside from missing her home and family in Upolu, that she insisted they cast the vessel off from the shore. And this is where and when TuiManu'a said to *Sina*, "Take my Golden House (*Fale'ula*) with you for your family dynasty," prophetically referring to the impending Malietoa dynasty. In addition to the *Fale'ula*, TuiManu'a gifted the reef flat on it, where there were various seashell fishes and lower creatures that were the delicacies of the chiefs.

The legend implies, in a literal sense, that a house was brought over on the double-hulled canoe. With many crews rowing the vessel this is possible, given the TuiManu'a's abundant resources. But another possible interpretation is that TuiManu'a sent along a carpenter, to construct a duplicate copy of the *Fale'ula* for the Malietoa. This coincides with the period when the TuiManu'a was distributing knowledge of carpentry around the archipelago.

Today, the village of Fale'ula is the original residence of the Malietoa dynasty, and its reef and seashore is rich with shellfish (mussels, clams, oysters, etc.), fishes, and lower creatures.

The Story of *Va'afuti* (or *Va'afa'i*)

Va'afuti was a descendant of *Malālatea* together with his brothers *Fata* and *Maulolo* and their sister *Luafatasaga* (see Tagaloa, page 31 in Period V). *Va'afuti,* also known as Tagaloa *Va'afuti*, was another early explorer from Savai'i in around A.D.1320.

Va'afuti's siblings, *Fata*, *Maulolo,* and *Luafatasaga,* were worried about their brother, for they hadn't heard anything from him for a long time, and they were wondering if he was still alive. And so they set out on their makeshift vessel to find *Va'afuti*.

They pulled in and landed in the village of Tuana'i, Upolu, which used to be a resting place for *Tagaloalagi*. It was now where the First Malietoa *Sāveatuvaelua* resided, and they found words from the village people that *Va'afuti* had journeyed on to the village of the Falelatai area. And so the brothers, *Fata* and *Maulolo*, left their sister *Luafatasaga,* who was now married to First Malietoa, *Sāveatuvaelua* (Malietoa *Sāvea,* son of *Leatiogie*), and went on to Falelatai, and found *Va'afuti* married to a local lady *Mataupolu*. *Va'afuti* desired to travel with his brothers, and so he parted with a farewell to a very sad *Mataupolu*.

The makeshift vessel was made up of logs from banana plants (*fa'i*), and thus *Va'afuti* received his newly-found name *Va'afa'i* (meaning "vessel made of banana logs").

The brothers journeyed to Aleipata, Atua, and on to Manu'a to visit their ancestral relatives, the Tagaloalagi clan. On their return trip they sojourned in the village of Saluafata where TuiAtua *To'otuna* reigned. TuiAtua *To'otuna's* son, *To'oia To'otuna,* was a cruel person, and a cannibal, in the district.

Va'afa'i married *Mulilefetai,* the daughter of TuiAtua *To'otuna,* giving birth to a son *Li'ava'a* (which means dreaming, *li'a*, on the boat, *va'a*) and daughter *Tautiugali'a* (*tautiu* means shark-fishing, so, dreamed while on a shark-fishing expedition).

Their son *Li'ava'a* turned out to be cruel and a cannibal himself. When he grew strong and fearsome, he remembered stories of how his uncle, the cannibal *To'oia*, consumed his brothers and sisters until he found out that *Va'afa'i* was from Savai'i, the land of demonic spirit warriors. So *Li'ava'a* decided to avenge his brothers' and sisters' lives by summoning the demonic spirit warriors of Savai'i and instructing them to seek and find *To'oia* and to kill him and bring his liver back to *Li'ava'a*.

The demonic spirit warriors of Savai'i were successful and brought *To'oai's* liver to *Li'ava'a* on a *ti* plant leaf. *Li'ava'a* wrapped it with a woven basket of coconut leaves and placed it on the front part of their vessel. Then their journey continued, and they pulled in to Faleata to visit the family of their ancestors, *Malalatele* or *Malālatea*, the Fe'epō and the Ufi clan.

When they arrived, the brothers *To'o* and *Ata* were having their morning ava at Lepea. The travelers were invited to the ava ceremony. In the course of the ava rituals, *To'o* said to the guests, *Va'afa'i*, *Fata*, *Maulolo,* and *Li'ava'a,* that they had heard a lot of rumors about these demonic spirit warriors of Savai'i, and they would like to fight them. And so *Li'ava'a*, the cruel, immediately responded to *To'o*, *Ata,* and the demonic spirit warriors of Faleata, that they would accommodate their wishes.

The battle was fought, and *To'o* died together many of the Faleata warriors. *Ata's* life was spared, and he was sad about losing his brother *To'o,* and he cried so profusely at his burial ground that his tears turned into a lake, up above the mountains of Faleata district. They called the lake Lanuto'o (tears for *To'o*).

Henceforth, *Ata* married *Tautiugali'a*, daughter of *Va'afa'i* and sister of *Li'ava'a*. She bore *Aoosavai'i—Ao* (head) *o Savai'i,* or *Ulu* (head) *o Savai'i*. *LeAooSavai'i* married a daughter of Orator Chief *Fale* of Fasito'o who bore *Mailo* and *Feana'i*, the founding fathers of Faleasi'u village.[lvii]

The Story of *To'o* and *Ata*

To'o and *Ata* were the sons of *Si'utaulalovasa* (see Malietoa's Many Families, Many Connections, page 154). There are conflicting account about the fates of *To'o* and *Ata* during the war between Faleata's demonic spirit warriors against the demonic spirit warriors of Savai'i, led by *Va'afa'i* and his son *Li'ava'a*. Dr. Krämer has it that *Ata* died in the war. In contrast, according to author Lafai Sauoaiga Ape, *Ata* was wounded and the Savai'ian demonic warriors were about to have *Ata* as the meal of their sacred ava ceremony, but *To'o* intervened and pledged he would fight a Savai'ian spirit-human warrior in exchange for *Ata's* life. And now *To'o* was defeated and was killed.

This story represents the founding of the name Faleata, or House of Ata, and later the name of the district. This supports the continuation of *Ata's* genealogy with his marriage to *Va'afa'i's* daughter *Tautiugali'a* which gave birth to *LeAoosavai'i* (or *Leuluosavai'i*) who married *Sagaia*, a lady from Fasito'o and Faleasi'u villages. *Sagaia* gave birth to *Mailo* and *Feana'i*. On the other hand, *To'o's* genealogy is not found in the latter tales of the village of Faleata.

So the story goes this way: *To'o* died in the war between the demonic spirits of Salafai (Savai'i) against Faleata.

The Story of *Ata's* Head

I was able to solicit a few of the senior orators/historians of Savai'i in the villages where *Va'afuti*, *Fata*, *Maulolo,* and *Luafatasaga* were born, and where the cruel Warrior *Li'ava'a* lived—that is, in Tufu Gautavai and A'opo, place of the legend of *Li'ava'a* and the man, *Tu'ulema'aga,* who lay with a young girl, *Tugatugalei*, when it was tapu, or made taboo, by *Li'ava'a* for her to be his girlfriend. Unfortunately, *Tu'ulema'aga* was killed by *Li'ava'a* for breaking his tapu.

According to orator chiefs from the Salelologa and Tufu Gautavai districts, the local district's legend about the story of *Ata* and *To'o* and the war between the warrior demons of Savai'i—led by *Li'ava'a* and his father *Va'afuti* (also called Tagaloa *Va'afuti*)—and the warrior demons of Faleata—led by *To'o* and *Ata*—goes this way:

To'o was wounded, and *Ata* cried so profusely that his tears gave rise to a lake on top of a mountain (behind Faleata district). The lake is called "Tears for To'o," or Lanuto'o. Then, to save his brother *To'o*, *Ata* declared defeat and gave himself up to the warrior demons of Savai'i. *Li'ava'a* and his victorious warriors took *Ata* with them to Savai'i.

During the protocol procedures to sever *Ata's* head, *Ata* asked for a last wish before he died: he wanted his head to be given as a gift to *Li'ava'a's* sister in her honor. The sister *Tautiugali'a* heard *Ata's* last request and was so moved by it that she said to *Li'ava'a*, "The warrior is a true hero of a warrior. Let him live. I want to marry him." And thus, *Li'ava'a* let *Ata* live because of his sister *Tautiugali'a*.

Ata married *Tautiugali'a* and gave birth to a boy who was named "The head of Savai'i"—*Le-ao-o-Savai'i* or *Le-ulu-o-Savai'i*, which means "*Ata's* head that was earmarked for the warrior demons of Savai'i." This young man, *LeAooSavai'i*, married *Sagaia*, a daughter of Orator Chief *Fale* of Fasito'o, giving birth to two paramount chiefs, *Mailo* and his brother *Feana'i*. These are known as the original settlers of the village Faleasi'u, and their salutation is "Sons of *Āitutagata*," meaning "Sons of a Human and Spirit," again referencing their warrior/spirit ancestors.

The Children of *Va'afa'i*

I should also mention that *Va'afuti,* now called *Va'afa'i,* is the same *Va'afa'i* who is the ancestor of the well-known Paramount Orator Chief *Taloolema'anao* (or *Taloolema'agao*), also known by a shortened name: Orator Chief *Talo*. *Taloolema'anao* (named for the *taro* or *talo* that is planted in a rocky landscape) is the grandson of the Warrior *Manusamoa* of Falealili village, Atua. This is the *Talo* who, with Orator Chief *Ofoia,* stole Tafa'ifa *Salamasina's* son *Tapumanaia*-II to be their Paramount Chief in Falealili district, in Atua, Upolu (see *Salamasina's* Children, page 203).

Talo's father was *Ise,* who was *Manusamoa's* son with *Vai-o-lupe* (meaning *Vai*—water—for pigeons, or *Va-i-o-lupe*—one pigeon after another, for successful pigeon-snaring), a descendant of *Papali'inafetalia'iiaiaiga* (*Papali'i* "for whom the families waited") in around A.D.1380. *Ise* married *Tauanu'ufaigā*, daughter of *Va'afa'i* of Tuna'i village, in Tuamasaga district, Upolu. She gave birth to *Fualau* and *Talooma'anao*. *Talooma'anao* married Lady *Lupemalieifululelei* ("the pigeon that is satisfied with her beautiful feathers") from Lufilufi, in Atua district, Upolu, who gave birth to *Onofia*.

Paramount Chief *Onofia* married Lady *Va-i-lupe-maua* ("a successful pigeon-catching campaign") from Falealili, who bore the "blood brothers," *Fualautoalasi*, *Talauega,* and *Taveuveu*, all in Satalo, in Falealili district, Atua, Upolu, around A.D.1450. They were decreed by Tafa'ifa *Salamasina* to be the authority for the distribution of gifts and food of her son *LeSatele*, also known as *Tapumanaia*-II.

This title, Orator Chief Va'afa'i, together with the titles Fata and Taliaoa (Orator ambassador of the Gauifaleai family) are the core of our family in Afega village, Tuamasaga, Upolu.

More Famous Ladies

At this point we should remember the stories of *Gatoa'itele*, *Vaetamasoāali'i*, *LeValasi*, and the Warrior Queen *Nafanua*.

The Story of *Gatoa'itele*

Origin of *Gatoa'itele's* Name

Malietoa *La'auli* and his daughter, not yet given a name, were seated out in the late afternoon, catching the cool breeze, when *Fata* and *Maulolo* came to visit Malietoa *La'auli*.

Fata and his brother *Maulolo*—brothers of Malietoa *Sāvea's* wife, and so "uncles" to Malietoa *La'auli* (see A.D.1200 in Malietoa, page 37 in Period V)—had been fishing in the freshwater river and caught a huge freshwater fish, commonly known as a *i'gato*. They immediately thought to bring it for the Malietoa.

When they presented the fish, the Malietoa asked, "What kind of fish is this?"

Fata and *Maulolo* replied, "It is a fish caught in the freshwater; it's an *i'gato*."

Malietoa noticed the fish's large size and said, "Well, the *i'gato* must have eaten a lot, for he is so big. Here, you two; come take my daughter and name her *Gatoa'itele* and adopt her as your high chief for your kind service to me." The name *Gatoa'itele* means "fish ate a lot."

Fata and *Maulolo* responded, "Of course we will, Malietoa."

From that day forward, *Fata* and *Maulolo* raised *Gatoa'itele* as their own Princess Chief in a village near the Malietoa, Afega and Tuana'i. This Princess Chief would become one of the Royal Crowns of the Malietoa Monarch. But this did not stop young boys from attempting to court with her. From that day forward, *Gatoa'itele* became *Fata* and *Maulolo's* royal paramount chief. But this title did not become a PāPā title until *Nafanua* proclaimed it to *Salamasina* and thus fulfilled Malietoa *Uitualagi*'s decree.

The Wooing of *Gatoa'itele*

Stories, news, and rumors, about the beauty and royal genealogy of these princesses of the Malietoa dynasty spread across the Archipelago of the Navigators. And so the wooers began to arrive, weekly, at Fale'ula village, the residence of the Malietoa. But none caught the eyes of the sisters *Gatoa'itele* and *Gasoloaiaoolelagi*. Until *LeManu'a-LeSanalāla* (son of a Togan father and Samoan mother) arrived from Lotofagā village, at about the same time as *Folasāitu* or *Folasā-le-āitu* (*Folasā* the demonic spirit) from Faleata.

Gatoa'itele was taken by surprise by the witty nature and handsome looks of *LeSanalāla*. And so she wanted to spend time visiting with him. So the sisters and the young princes were carrying on in the late evening. Then one early dawn, the aualuma of the girls saw that there were more than four feet showing at the bottom of the bedsheets! The ladies of the aualuma said, "At least the feet appear to be those of high chiefs"—*O vae* (feet) *o tama* (young man or warrior) *soā* (servants of the wooing chiefs) *Ali'i* (high chief), hence the origin of the name, *Vae-tama-soā-ali'i* shortened to *Vaetamasoā*, *Tamasoāli'i,* or *Vaetamasoāali'i*. It looked as though the young princes had spent the evening there.

One day *Gatoa'itele* said to her sister *Gasoloaiaoolelagi*, "Come, my dear sister. I am attracted to *LeSanalāla*, and I want to go with him. However, you go and wed *Folasāitu*. But if he mistreats you or is or cruel with you, come and be with me and *LeSanalāla*. Likewise, if *LeSanalāla* mistreats or is cruel to me, I will come and live with you and *Folasāitu*."

Thus *Gatoa'itele* married *LeSanalāla,* and they went to live in Lotofagā, in the Southern Tuamasaga district. *Gasoloaiaoolelagi* married *Folasāitu*, and they went to live in Tuana'i, a village of Tuamasaga.

Before long, *Gasoloaiaoolelagi* was being poorly mistreated by her husband *Folasāitu*. And she remembered the parting words of farewell with her sister *Gatoa'itele*. So *Gasoloaiaoolelagi* left her husband and went to live with *Gatoa'itele* and *LeManu'a-LeSanalāla*. Thus *LeSanalāla,* the grandson of Tuitoga married both the sisters, *Gatoa'itele* and *Gasoloaiaoolelagi* (see Malietoa in the Timelines). They begat two daughters, *Vaetamasoāali'i* and *Atougaugaatuitoga*, and a son, *Lalovimāmā*. These children would be the ancestors of the modern Royal House of the First Tafa'ifa of Samoa, also known as and considered to be the "royal family constellation."[lviii]

The War against Malietoa *Sagagaimuli*

After the children were grown and married, *Gatoa'itele* returned to her residence in Afega village, to better organize her government. This was the period of Malietoa *Sagagaimuli*, son of Malietoa *Falefatu*, son of Malietoa *La'auli*.

Malietoa *Sagagaimuli* was putting a lot of pressure on *Fata* and *Maulolo* to abandon their service and oath to *Gatoa'itele*, as their paramount chief, and come to serve him, the Malietoa, instead. But *Fata* and *Maulolo* refused.

Malietoa *Sagagaimuli* was well aware of Malietoa *Uitualagi's* decree that the PāPā titles should be equal to the TuiAtua and TuiA'ana titles. This became the reason *Gatoa'itele*, *Fata* and *Maulolo*, and the orator group Tuisamau went to war against Malietoa *Sagagaimuli* and the orator group Auimatagi. This is also known as the war of the PāPā of *Gatoa'itele*, where *Nafanua* sent *Tupa'i* with warriors for assistance (see The Gatoa'itele Crown, page 175 in the story of Nafanua, later).

The Story of *Vaetamasoāali'i*

The Wooing of Vaetamasoāali'i

The children of *Gatoa'itele* and *Gasoloaiaoolelagi* (Malietoa's daughters) and Paramount Chief *LeSanalāla* (grandson of TuiToga and the Samoan lady, *Lumapaitogamau* of Safata village) were famous, and many people heard about them. Specifically they had heard about *Vaetamasoāali'i* and desired to marry her for her genealogy. For Royal Queen *Vaetamasoāali'i's* royal PāPā title had been decreed by Malietoa *Uitualagi* before *Vaetamasoāali'i* and her mother *Gatoa'itele* were even born.

Vaetamasoāali'i was the firstborn of *Gatoa'itele* with *LeSanalāla*. Hence, she was the firstborn of the "decree," as her mother *Gatoa'itele* was also the firstborn of *Gauifaleai* and Malietoa *La'auli*. And so *Vaetamasoāali'i* was decreed to be the royal paramount chief of the Safata district of the southern Tuamasaga district. Safata district was the "vanguard" district, working together with the "rearguard" Faleata district in the war of the Tuamasaga district of the Malietoa monarchy.

Word spread rapidly about this beautiful royal princess, descendant of the TuiToga and Malietoa matriarchs, and paramount chiefs came calling for her hand in marriage. But none fit the bill. The TuiFiti came and quickly returned home defeated.

Then TuiA'ana *Vaemā* got a Samoan chief *tatau*, or tattoo, to make a winning impression, but he was in such a hurry and the *tatau* had not completely healed. It turned into sores all over his lower body, so he too was rejected.

The Story of the Adopted Child

Meanwhile, two famous orator brothers (*Ape* and *Tutuila*) from Leulumoega (capital of the A'ana District) realized they were in need of a chief when they didn't receive any gift from a festivity held by the TuiA'ana when *Sagaate*-I visited his family relatives in SaFotulafai, Savai'i. Customarily, during festivities, the guest paramount chief would give gifts or appointments to any person for bravery or generosity extended to the guest high chief. But orator chiefs from a village that does not have a paramount high chief will not receive any gifts.

The two orators went away from SaFotulafai, walking toward the villages of Amoa and Lealatele, of SaMuliaga, Savai'i, and met *Puleoleu'u*, the elder orator chief of Amoa, sitting by the road. Elder Orator Chief *Puleoleu'u* greeted them with a question. "What happened to you two?" So the two orators shared what had happened at the event. And *Pule* explained the reason they did not receive any of the gifts.

Puleoleu'u notified the two orators of the recent birth of a baby boy, born into the Tagaloa and Lafai clans, from SaFotulafai, because the boy's mother was the grand-daughter of *LeTufuga*, paramount chief of the SaFotulafai District, from his marriage to *Fa'alulumaga*, the daughter of TuiA'ana *Uōtele*. This was just two villages over. So *Ape* the Alert (*Moemanatunatu*) and *Tutuila* the Tardy (*Lematemate*) rushed to the residence of Tagaloa *Fa'aofonu'u* to beg of the parents if they could adopt the baby boy.

The orators asked the parents if they could raise the baby boy, *Selaginatō Tualalafa*. The parents, after long and heavy deliberation, granted their request, and the two ambitious orator chiefs took the boy to their villages, Fasito'outa and Fasito'otai, Upolu.

Years went by; the village of Leulumoega heard about the children of *Gatoa'itele* and *Gasoloaiaoolelagi* (Malietoa's daughters) and Paramount Chief *LeSanalāla* (grandson of TuiToga and a Samoan lady, *Lumapaitogamau* of Safata village).

Specifically they heard about *Vaetamasoāali'i.* And the orators, *Ape* and *Tutuila* were now armed with a well-groomed prince with a kingship pedigree to take up to *Vaetamasoāali'i*, to see if she would desire him for a husband. These two brave and ambitious orators were well aware of the competition for *Vaetamasoāali'i* for obvious reasons. But this time, they were ready to present Prince *Selaginatõ, Tagaloa Tualalafa* to *Vaetamasoāali'i.* And miraculously, *Vaetamasoāali'i* accepted Prince *Selaginatõ* as her husband.

The Story of the Stolen Child

The little family of *Vaetamasoāali'i* and Prince *Selaginatõ* resided in Safata at this time. When *Vaetamasoāali'i* was pregnant, the orators of Leulumoega stopped by the nearby family of Elder Chief *TaelegaLeo'o* of the village of Sa'anapu, in Safata District. They asked for an estimate of when *Vaetamasoāali'i* would give birth.

In exactly nine months, word arrived that the lady's pregnancy was well on its way to delivery. The orators, *Ape* and *Tutuila*, immediately set out to hike across the back end of the island, where Lotofaga village is located in the District of Safata, to anticipate her delivery and hope it would a boy. Upon arrival, they discovered that she was within a couple of weeks of having her baby. The orator chiefs immediately begged Elder *TaelegaLeo'o* and his wife, asking if they could hide in the back bush of their property until the exact time of *Vaetamasoāali'i's* delivery. Chief *TaelegaLeo'o* agreed, and in due time the orators were informed that the Lady *Vaetamasoāali'i* was delivering her baby that night.

The conniving orators begged the midwives assisting with delivery to please hand them the baby, so they could see the baby and perhaps they could give the baby a bath at a nearby stream. The midwives at first were ignorant of the orators' intention and complied with their wishes.

Once the baby was handed over to Orator *Ape*, all covered up with fine sheets made of finely woven tree bark, similar to the materials used to weave the tapa cloth, the orators immediately took the baby to the water stream, and *TaelegaLeo'o's* wife assisted in giving the newly born child a bath. And—a moment of euphoria, let alone, eureka! To discover the baby was a boy! The orators owed a lot to *TaelegaLeo'o* for aiding in this rather tricky and involved process, the stealing of the baby, which secured the future foundational beginning of the country's Royal Family child.

Ape and *Tutuila*, after saying all their goodbyes with *TaelegaLeo'o* and his family, immediately began the arduous hike back to Fasito'otai and Fasito'outa. The orators were well aware of the impending violent reaction that the villagers, particularly the orator group, would bring upon them once they discovered what had happened to the baby boy. For, as predicted and advised by *TaelegaLeo'o*, the warrior chiefs of Safata had immediately organized a well-equipped and well-armed chase in pursuit of *Ape* and *Tutuila* for their most heinous crime.

Image 1 tapa cloth, image owned by author

Back in Fasito'otai and Uta, *Ape* and *Tutuila's* uncle, *Lioleanaleavave* (*Lio-e-ana-le-ave-ave*), heard of what his nephews were up to with the stolen child. He began to organize a counter-defense, to give protection for his nephews' escape. Uncle *Lio's* rearguard maneuver came just in time, for *Ape* and *Tutuila* saw how close the Safata warriors were to closing in on them as they were climbing the rather steep mountain ridge separating the two districts.

The two orators' assiduous effort to take care of the fragile baby boy required that they must rest quite frequently, to give the baby rest. The brothers would take turns to provide green, ripe coconut, to feed the baby with the juice and solids with the soft coconut meat, all along keeping a watchful eye on the warring warriors of Safata.

Finally, they arrived in their village and were wondering how to care for boy on a long-term basis. They immediately thought of approaching Elder Orator *Alipia* of A'ana. They right away approached him, and the orator saw, as they entered his residence, that the baby was crying. He immediately asked, with urgency, what was the purpose of their visit. For *Alipia* could not wait when it was clear in his ears that it was a sound of a baby, and he said, "What is it?"

Ape answered, "It is our Paramount High Chief-*Ali'i.*"

"Where did you get this child?" said *Alipia*.

Ape said, "He is from Heaven"—the boy from heaven. It is at this point that the boy got his name, "The boy from heaven," or *Tamālelagi*. And so *Ape* and *Tutuila* began to tell the story of how they planned out the whole orchestration of how they would go about getting a well-pedigreed royal chief.

After hearing this boy's incredible story, *Alipia* moved to care for the boy as his own son. He said, "I will raise this boy from heaven, this *Tamālelagi*. Go make his bed and I will forever be indebted to you." Legend says *Alipia* named the village after the boy's bed, bedding, and pillow, Leulumoega.

As time had passed, the village of Safata had lost hope. And now the orator chiefs of Leulumoega asked Elder Orator *Alipia* to raise the boy to become the high chief of Leulumoega. And *Alipia,* with Leulumoega's Orator Chief Council, raised *Tamālelagi* as their paramount chief. He eventually became TuiA'ana *Tamālelagi* and progenitor of the Tafa'ifa dynasty.

The Birth of *Salamasina*

All this leads, in Period VI, to the birth of the Tafa'ifa *Salamasina.* As we have seen, *Vaetamasoāali'i* married *Tualalafa* or Tagaloa *Selaginatō* (son of Tagaloa *Fa'aofonu'u* of Sili, Savai'i) and begat *Tamālelagi*, which means "boy from heaven or sky," who became TuiA'ana *Tamālelagi*. TuiA'ana *Tamālelagi's* last marriage, his tenth after nine previous marriages, and now getting on in age, was to the Princess of Toga, thirty years younger than he. Her name was *Vaetoifaga* and she begat the beautiful Princess *Salamasina*.[lix]

The Story of *LeValasi*

Gatoa'itele, daughter of Malietoa *La'auli,* and her husband *LeSanalāla* had three children, *Vaetamasoāali'i* (above, who married Tagaloa *Selaginatō* and begat TuiA'ana *Tamālelagi*), *LeAtougaugaatuitoga,* and their brother *Lalovimāmā.*

LeAtougaugaatuitoga, married Tonumaipe'a *Sauoāiga* and begat *Tauiliili, Tupa'ivailiIigi* (who was known as the War messenger of the goddess *Nafanua*—see The Story of the Warrior Queen *Nafanua*, page 172, told next in this volume), and a daughter *LeValasi*. *LeValasi* was also referred to as So'oa'emalelagi, the Sa'o Tama'ita'i of TuiA'ana. She looked after her niece, her cousin TuiA'ana *Tamālelagi's* daughter, the beautiful Princess *Salamasina.*

The Sacred Family of Samoa

The story of *LeValasi* is given in more detail in Volume I of this book, *Navigators Forging a Matriarchal Culture in Polynesia.* The parents of Princess *Valasi* (*SaLeValasi, LeValasi, Levalasi,* or So'oa'emalelagi) were decreed—from the ancient past, from the genealogy and tales of her mother *Vaetamasoāali'i* and her grandmother *Gatoa'itele,* from her husband's genealogy with *Leutogitupa'itea,* and from the decree by *Nafanua's* great-great-grandparents—a decree that big and powerful families of Samoa would be born from them, and that the connections of all these families would lead to great and powerful leadership in Samoa. And history records, orally, that *Valasi's* family would be known as Āiga SaLeValasi. This stands as the only Aiga that has a Salutation of Pa'ia "the Sacred Family" of Samoa, a veneration given to a god or deity, as decreed by Tafa'ifa *Muagututi'a*.

So'oa'emalelagi *LeValasi*

Valasi's cousin, TuiA'ana *Tamālelagi,* had no siblings. And after marriage to nine wives, he now had a young queen wife, *Vaetoeifaga,* from a different Island Nation. He needed help to care for her, especially when she was pregnant. So TuiA'ana *Tamālelagi* sent his messenger to his aunt, Lady *LeAtougaugaatuitoga*, to ask if his cousin *Valasi* could come to help *Vaetoeifaga* in her pregnancy.

Lady *LeAtougaugaatuitoga* and her husband, Tonumaipe'a *Sauoāiga,* were more than ready to give support. Then *LeAtougaugaatuitoga* discussed the trip with her son, who was now Paramount Chief *Tauiliili*, and with his brother, the ambassador *Tupa'ivaililigi* (*Tupa'i*). It was decided that *Tupa'i* would chaperone *LeValasi's* trip to Leulumoega, which was the seat of government of the A'ana district and the residence of *Tamālelagi*.

TuiA'ana *Tamālelagi* conferred with his adopted father, Paramount Orator Chief *Alipia,* and with the House of Nine orator chiefs about *Valasi*'s impending arrival. After quick deliberation, *Alipia* delivered an eloquent message to TuiA'ana *Tamālelagi*, that centered on the need to bestow the princess title So'oa'emalelagi on *Valasi*, in order to appropriately show, to the district of A'ana and the four major families of the TuiA'ana, that a sister of *Tamālelagi* with royal pedigree was here to serve Queen *Vaetoeifaga*. TuiA'ana *Tamālelagi* was extremely pleased with the wisdom of *Alipia* and the House of Nine orator chiefs, and totally accepted their recommendation.

So'oa'emalelagi *LeValasi* immediately took control of domestic affairs. She was also overly protective of *Vaetoeifaga*, because *Vaetoeifaga* was born and raised on her home island of Toga. The So'oa'emalelagi knew *Vaetoeifaga* was not fully accustomed to Samoan culture and language, and thus she needed help as well as needing the friendship of a sister.

Princess Salamasina

The evening of *Vaetoeifaga's* delivery date, So'oa'emalelagi *Valasi* sent a message to *Tamālelagi* that *Vaetoeifaga* was about to give birth. When TuiA'ana *Tamālelagi* received word that it was a baby girl, he said to name her *Salamasina*. Some say the night of her birth there was a bright (*sāsala*) full moon (*masina*), hence *Sāsala le masina* or *Salamasina*.

So'oa'emalelagi acted as "midwife-and-mother" to ensure *Salamasina's* life was secure and one of complete health and wellbeing. *Salamasina* grew up rapidly and with all the training of a royal subject, with good manners and clarity on the cultural norms and practices.

When *Salamasina* was about ten or twelve, Ambassador *Tupa'i,* brother of *LeValasi,* came to speak with *Valasi* about Warrior Queen *Nafanua's* command for the PāPā to be bestowed upon her. It is this meeting that *Salamasina* kept interrupting, so that *Tupa'i* asked *Valasi* several times if she wished to "bestow the titles on the girl playing there," referring to *Salamasina.*

Valasi said, "Why not?"

Tupa'i said, "I have to go back to *Nafanua* and ask."

And the story has it that *Nafanua* said, "If that's *Valasi's* will, then so be it." For Warrior Queen *Nafanua* was well aware that *Salamasina* was, for all practical purposes, *Valasi's* adopted daughter. Certainly, that was how she had been raised—she *was* her daughter.

The Story of *LeValasi's* husband, *Fa'atulou*

At this point the people were well aware that the royal pedigrees—of *Salamasina*, heir apparent to TuiA'ana *Tamālelagi's* throne, and of *Valasi*—would merge into a combined royal family. So then, the two Paramount Orator Chiefs *Leifi* and *Tautoloitua*, later known as *Tafua* and *Fuataga*, came calling on *Alipia* and the House of Nine in Leulumoega, to discuss a courtship campaign for *Mata'utia,* who would later be called *Fa'atulou,* with *Valasi.* For *Lalovimāmā, LeValasi's* uncle, had married TuiAtua *Togiai Sefa'ataulemauga*, the daughter of TuiAtua, and begat TuiAtua *Mata'utia.*

This proposed courtship situation was a major problem, because of the close family connections between So'oa'emalelagi *Valasi* and her first cousin, *Mata'utia Fa'atulou*. So this took time and several iterations. But *Mata'utia* was going to acquire the TuiAtua title and the TuiA'ana title, as their genealogy dated back to the Malietoa clan. So, under pressure from the two talking orators, *LeValasi* married TuiAtua *Mata'utia Fa'atulou*, her first cousin, and he was given the name *Fa'atulou* which means to "lower oneself down as though prostrating oneself" as one would in an apology, asking for forgiveness for the sin of marrying one's first cousin. *LeValasi* was pressured into marrying him in order to combine all four titles.

LeValasi and her husband attempted to have children but unfortunately miscarried. The miscarried baby's name was *Tuimavave*. They buried the remains in Lufilufi. Then *Valasi* and the TuiAtua were presented with five different proposals to adopt certain children because of their genealogy. But they rejected them all. Instead, because of *Valasi's* care for her niece, *Salamasina*, *Salamasina* would become the first Tafa'ifa.

As can be seen from the beginning: when *LeValasi* became the caretaker of *Salamasina,* from birth through to the Tafa'ifa reign, she became a consummately devoted mother to Tafa'ifa *Salamasina*. This was the main reason why Tafa'ifa *Salamasina* moved to Lotofaga, in Atua district, to be with her mother *LeValasi* and her son *Tapumanaia*-II, who was in the nearby village of Falealili. Hence the illustrious name of the Āiga SaLeValasi.

This is also where Tafa'ifa *Salamasina* is buried, at Lotofaga: "What a devoted mother to Tafa'ifa *Salamasina*" the fulfillment of the ancient ancestors' decrees.

The Story of the Warrior Queen *Nafanua*

The Warrior Queen *Nafanua* was born around A.D.1170-1230. This is just about the same period as when the war began between Togans and Samoans, to end the subjugation of Samoa by the king of Toga, the TuiToga—the time of the birth of the Malietoa dynasty. And it is through *Nafanua* that the first Tafa'ifa arises.

Warrior Queen *Nafanua's* parents were *Tilafaigā* (one of the famous conjoined twins) and *Saveasi'uleo* (also known as Savea

Si'uleo). *Saveasi'uleo* was also *Tilafaigā's* uncle, the brother of her father *Ulufanuasese'e*. *Tilafaigā* herself was originally referred to as *Nafanua* by name, before her daughter was named *Nafanua* and *Suaifanua*.

The framing of *Nafanua's* life is the journey across the archipelago by her mother and her mother's sister, *Taemāmā* (or just *Taemā*). The twins were "demigods" with exceptional, supernatural strength that they showed on many occasions in their journey. The twins' genealogy had been decreed by their ancestors, their mother *Taufailematagi* and their father *'Alao*. The well-known legend of the brothers *Saveasi'uleo* (the cruel sea-eel creature) and *Ulufanuasese'e* ended in a decree at the Alataua sea in Savai'i where they parted ways (see The Morning (*Taeao*) of the Farewell at Sea in Alataua, Savai'i, page 115). It was decreed there that *Saveasi'uleo* would go toward the east of the archipelago, to Manu'a Island, and prepare the foundation of the prophesied government; *Ulufanuasese'e* would stay in Upolu to build the family and populate Upolu and Savai'i. It was further decreed that the brothers would not meet again, except in a future generation.

The twins, *Tilafaigā* and *Taemā,* traveled to the land in the east to look for their father's brother, *Saveasi'uleo*. He lived in the place called Sauā, in Fitiuta, Manu'a, where he had gone in fulfilment of the decree. When *Saveasi'uleo* realized these girls were his brother's daughters, he turned human (as opposed to being a sea-eel) and decided to take *Tilafaigā* as a wife. Hence, the promise of the brothers' genealogical connection in a later generation was fulfilled. But the promise to build a kingdom was still a nebulous idea, for their district of Alataua was, for all practical purposes, still subjugated to Paramount Chief *Lilomaiava* and his clan.

When *Nafanua* was a young lady in her teens, TuiToga *Manaia*-I dropped anchor in SaFotulafai, Savai'i, to begin building a Togan village as a basecamp in Savai'i. TuiToga *Manaia*-I wanted to wed *Nafanua Suaifanua,* and her parents gave their approval. But the cry for a warrior leader echoed across Savai'i and Upolu, and *Nafanua* answered the call, for the people's suffering was unbearable. She had the war clubs—*Tafesilafa'i, Ulimasao*, and *Fa'auliulito*—given to her by the spirit warriors, and so she defeated *Lilomaiava* and his clan warriors.

Meanwhile, TuiToga *Manaia*-II married *Leutogitupa'itea* in around A.D.1300-1360, producing one son, *Latuivai*, who married a Samoan lady named *Mimisapu'a* from Fai'a'ai, sister of Paramount Chief *Folasā* (a descendant of *Tagaloalagi* through his daughter *Sinalagilagi*). They had a son, *Faletapa'au*, and a daughter, *Taigalugalu,* who is an ancestor of Lady *Mo'oui* who, with *Lafainatau* (grandson of *Lafaitaulupo'o*, *Leutogitupa'itea's* brother), produced *Le Sauoāiga*, the first Tonumaipe'a *Sauoāiga*. Hence the connection with Tonumaipe'a.

The Warrior Queen

Nafanua was known for the many wars she fought and triumphed in, but the most notable war was the one in which she defeated the formidable opponents *Aeaisisifo* and *Aeaisasae* at Alataua, Savai'i. After conferring with her father *Saveasi'uleo* about fighting the war to free their extended family's district from the harshness of the neighboring district's warring tribes, she was gifted with weaponry in the form of three war-clubs called:

- *Ulimasao* (meaning to guide),
- *Fa'auliulito* (meaning to strike and kill with) and
- *Tafesilafa'i* (meaning to guard the troops with).

These war-clubs had in them the *mana* spirit (power), so that *Nafanua* was literally "thrashing" the enemy.

The enemy began to retreat and, by daylight of the fourth day of continuous battle, the battle had reached the district of Falelima village, and had already crossed the Falealupo and Neiafu villages. As the warrior queen *Nafanua* pressed the troops forward, fighting with the knowledge that victory was near, a wind came up suddenly. *Nafanua* was huddling to her war-club, and the wind blew the warrior queen *Nafanua's* attire off her shoulder, exposing her breasts.

The shocked *Nafanua* was filled with shame and dropped to the ground to cover herself. Then the battle on both sides of the battleground came to a screeching halt. The troops were shocked and filled with disbelief to see that *Nafanua* was a woman warrior!

Nafanua quickly recovered and realized that she had arrived at the boundary in Fai'a'ai village, the *Papaifualaga* that her father *Saveasi'uleo* had decreed she must not cross. This village was the boundary of the Paramount Chief *Tauiliili* of their clan (his sacred residence), and she must not cross it. And so the warrior queen *Nafanua* said the troops and warriors must stop and retreat, because the enemy had already retreated in defeat.

And so began the reign of *Nafanua* in the history of Samoa. She had assembled a large group of warrior fighters and troops to wage war on enemies and protect her extended genealogical family districts. Any monarch of her family, seeking warriors to fight a battle, would send a senior orator chief to ask for assistance from the warrior queen *Nafanua*, to help wage war with their enemy. It was in these wars that Nafanua was able to gather together the four crowns, which would eventually be given to the first Tafa'ifa, *Salamasina.*

***Nafanua* Gathers the Crowns**

The TuiA'ana Crown

Before *Tamālelagi* (*Salamasina's* father) was TuiA'ana, he had an enemy TuiA'ana *Sagaate*. He needed to consolidate his authority over TuiA'ana *Sagaate*. So he sent a servant to *Queen Nafanua* (the famous female warrior) requesting an army be sent over to assist. *Nafanua* would send the army under the condition that the crowns were sent to her to consolidate before bestowing them on one person. *Tamālelagi* complied, and *Nafanua* sent an army of warriors so that *Sagaate* was defeated and pushed to occupy the southwest side of A'ana District, where Falease'elā and Falelatai villages are at today. *Tamālelagi* provided Nafanua with the TuiA'ana crown.

The Gatoa'itele Crown

Malietoa *Sagagaimuli* was upset that *Fata* and *Maulolo*, the paramount orator chiefs of the Malietoa monarch, were treating *Gatoa'itele* as royalty (see The War against Malietoa *Sagagaimuli*, page 163). He went to war with *Fata* and *Maulolo*, *Gatoa'itele* and the Tuisamau. A request was sent to the Warrior Queen *Nafanua* for warriors to help fight the war against Malietoa *Sagagaimuli* and the Auimatagi. Assistants were dispatched, and the war was won.

And the Gatoa'itele title became a crown title, which was sent over to *Nafanua* for custody.

The TuiAtua Crown

The war for the TuiAtua crown was fought between *Foganutea* and *Fogaleula*. *Foganutea* was victorious with *Nafanua's* help and gave the TuiAtua title to *Nafanua*.

The Vaetamasoāali'i Crown

The war between the SaTunumafono and Alauatausuafata resulted in the Alauatausuafata obtaining the *Vaetamasoāali'i* crown, which was also given to *Nafanua*.

So *Nafanua* had gathered all four (crown) titles; TuiA'ana, Gatoa'itele, TuiAtua, and Vaetamasoāali'i. Queen *Nafanua* thus became custodian of the crowns for about 30 years, before bestowing them on Queen *Salamasina.*

The first consolidated Tafa'ifa

In this way, Nafanua obtained all four crowns and the right to deliver them. *Tamālelagi's* decree stated his last born, *Salamasina*, would obtain a royal title and succeed him as the TuiA'ana. But eventually *Salamasina* obtained a title far greater than TuiA'ana, for she became the consolidated Tafa'ifa Queen of all Samoa when *Nafanua* tried to bestow the crowns on *LeValasi* and *LeValasi* chose that *Salamasina* should receive them.

Nafanua and the Kingdom of God

There are many historical events that are attributed to *Nafanua*. But one story that has been immortalized by the Malietoa monarch is this:

Around A.D.1570, Malietoa *Taulapapa* heard that the warrior queen *Nafanua* was sending the high priest and orator messenger *Tupa'i* to bestow all four royal titles on *LeValasi*—and, as we have seen, *LeValasi* wanted to bestow these on her adopted daughter *Salamasina*. When Malietoa *Taulapapa* got wind of this, he immediately dispatched his fleet of canoes to take him to *Nafanua*, on Savai'i Island, to seek a title gift from the warrior queen

Nafanua. But, unfortunately, by the time Malietoa *Taulapapa* arrived at *Nafanua's* residence at Alataua, the high priest had just left for Leulumoega village in Upolu, where *LeValasi* and *Salamasina* were living.

Malietoa *Taulapapa* began with a long salutation and oration to the warrior queen *Nafanua*, asking to be considered for the Malietoa Monarch title. *Nafanua*, after hearing Malietoa *Taulapapa*, felt sad for him, but the decision had already been made. There were no titles left with her, for *Tupa'i*, the high priest, had just left with all the titles. And so *Nafanua* gave Malietoa *Taulapapa* the gift of a prophecy, as follows:

"Malietoa *Taulapapa*, I am sorry that you came too late. *Tupa'i* is on his way to Leulumoega to bestow all four titles onto *LeValasi*. But, come; be patient and wait for your Kingdom from Heaven" (*my translation*).

In A.D.1830 the "Messenger of Peace" vessel, bringing the missionaries and Reverend John William to Samoa, brought a new Kingdom and was received and accepted by Malietoa *Vaiinupõ*, a direct descendant of Malietoa *Taulapapa*. 270 years the Malietoa clan had waited, till they received their Kingdom!

There are others who believe that it was Malietoa *Fitisemanū* that came to *Nafanua* for the titles. But the history is clear that the only time *Nafanua* held all four titles as custodian was at the end of all the wars (the TuiA'ana *Tamālelagi* war, the TuiAtua *Mata'utia Fa'atulou* war, the *Vaetamasoāali'i* war and the *Gatoa'itele* war). In each of these she gave military assistance to achieve victory. This all took place between A.D.1500 and 1580.

After the Togan Yoke

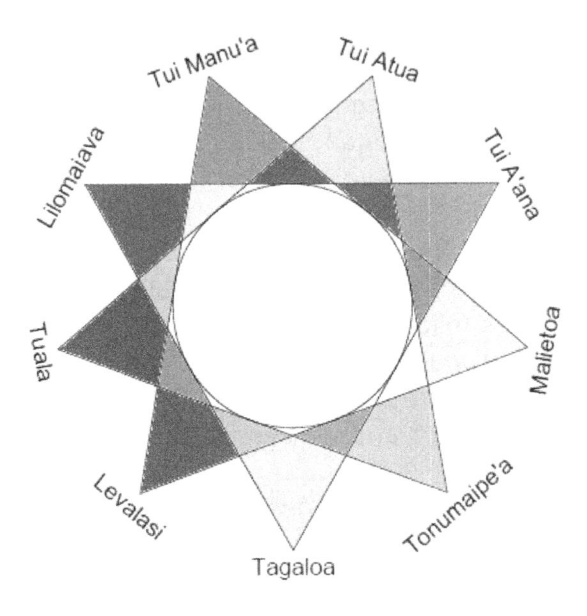

Image 2 image owned by author

The first recording of the history of Savaii begins with the genealogy of *Laifai* and *Funefe'ai,* beginning in around A.D.1310, by which time Samoa was fully populated and had already been liberated from the reign of the Togans.

Stories of *Funefe'ai*

The Birth of *Laifai* and *Funefe'ai*

Around A.D.1310, a Togan Princess visited Samoa and married a son of *Aliali'i*. On her way back to Toga, she gave birth to their son *Va'asiliifiti*, meaning "the boat passed" (it passed Toga). The boat instead settled in Fiji, where the princess would later have an affair with a Fijian man and give birth to their children, before settling with her husband in Samoa.

The princess's son *Va'asiliifiti* married *Fe'egaga* of Sagaga and birthed *Funefe'ai*. Simultaneously, *Va'asiliifiti* married his second wife, *Fe'easoa* from Sale'imoa and begat *Laifai*. The two sons were born around A.D.1320. And *Funefe'ai* inherited the Tagaloa title; this marks the beginning of the Tagaloa family that exists till today.

The Story of Funefe'ai and Tagaloalagi

We should, of course, connect this time with the time of legend, remembering that the household of *Tagaloalagi* filled the first to ninth heavens, and also that the name *Tagaloalagi* was given to his descendants, so it might not always mean the same person.

So, around A.D.1320, one of *Tagaloalagi's* wives was *Sinaalāua* of Savai'i. But when *Tagaloalagi* desired to make *Sinaalāua* his wife, she was attracted instead to *Funefe'ai*. *Tagaloalagi* proposed a trade-off; his Tagaloa title and eight orators, in exchange for relinquishing *Sinaalāua*. *Funefe'ai*, without hesitation, took the title and eight orators!

Tagaloalagi's union with *Sinaalāua* led to the daughter, *Sinalagilagi*, who married *Malālatea*, giving birth to the girl, *Lelāpueisalele*, and her blind brother, *Oleāifale'ava* (or *Leāifale'ava*, the blind man).

In another legend (told in *Navigators Quest for a Kingdom in Polynesia*), the blind brother *Oleāifale'ava* begat a daughter, *Lea'auta*,[lx] and journeyed with her to find the longhaired warrior *Taemanutava'e*, who then wed *Lea'auta*. The couple produced *Va'afuti*, *Fata*, *Maulolo*, and their sister *Luafatasaga*, who married the first Malietoa *Sāveatuvaelua* (see Period V Tagaloa, page 31 in the Timelines). As we saw in *Navigators Quest for a Kingdom in Polynesia*, many place names are derived from the story of *Oleāifale'ava* and his daughter's journey.

Meanwhile the sister, Lady *Lelāpueisalele,* married *Tagaloa-SeFa'atautele* and produced the first (original) *Tagaloa-SeFa'atautele Savai'inaea* and his sister *MafioSamoa*. Tagaloa *SeFa'atautele Savai'inaea* was named *Savai'inaea* because he swam from Savai'i, following his turtle, and landed in Falefa village, Atua, Upolu, while high Chief *Leutele* and his Orators were having their morning Ava (see The legend of *Savai'inaea*, told soon on page 182).

MafioSamoa married *Pulufaigā* of Salelologa (founder of the SaPulu family). Salelologa village is in Savai'i, in the province of SaFotulafai district. The name of the village is derived from TuiManu'a *Lelologatele*. The TuiManu'a and *Laifai* fought a war here in Savai'i and it was here that the TuiManu'a's headquarters for war were based. *Pulufaigā* of the SaPulu clan is the paramount chief in this village. And the Tagaloa clan has a province here called Saletagaloa.

MafioSamoa gave birth to *Puluseu*, half-brother to the first *Lei'atauaLesā* of Manono. *Puluseu* married a lady from Saleloga who bore *Pulusau*. And *Pulusau* married *Vaiotuga*, daughter of TuiAtua *To'otuna*, who gave birth to *Sili*, *Euga*, *Tuilimu*, and a daughter *Levaoita*, all at Salelologa.

Levaoita married *Fotulafai* (son of *Laifai*, the beginning of the slightly changed name *Lafai*), and gave birth to *LeTufuga* and *Leaula* who were later decreed the authority of Savai'i Island.

So we will see the genealogical relationships of these four clans to Malietoa Faigā *Uilamatūtū* and the *Tuisamau* and *Fata* and *Maulolo*:

1. *LeTufuga* of SaFotulafai (see TuiA'ana, page 22 in Period IV)
2. *Leaula* of Saleaula (*LeTufuga* and *Leaula* are both grandsons of *Laifai,* see *Laifai*, page 41 in Period V)
3. *Lei'atauaLesā* of Manono (above, see Tagaloa, page 31 in Period V) and
4. *Tagaloa-SeFa'atautele Savai'inaea* of Gaga'emalae (above, see Tagaloa again, page 31 in Period V)

They are the *feagaiga* of *Fata* and *Maulolo,* because they come from the female side of the family from the *Malietoafaigā*, while *Fata* and *Maulolo* are from the male side of their genealogy.

<u>The story of *Lei'atauaLesā*</u>

Lei'atauaLesā means "the fish of Paramount Chiefs *Taua* and *LeSā*." *Taua* was a descendant of TuiAtua *Letauā*—descendant of Tagaloa *Funefea'i* and his wife *Ulalemamae*—and *LeSā* was a descendant of TuiAtua *Samatauānu'u*, who inherited the Fiame title from *Fanene's* Warrior children: *Te'o*, *Tuatagaloa*, and *Meleiseā*.

Lei'atauaLesā was also known Tamafaigā, the cruel man, and was a descendant of *Lelāpueisalele*, the daughter of *Malālatea* (or *Malalatele*) and *Sinalagilagi*, daughter of Tagaloalagi.

Lei'atauaLesā received his name because of the fish brought over by *Taua* and *LeSā,* Paramount Chiefs from Atua district who heard about the birth of *Luafataali'i's* second son from a descendant of Tagaloalagi—see Tagaloa in Period V of the Timelines.

The Story of *Funefe'ai's* descendants

So, around A.D1320, the union of *Va'asiliifiti* with *Lefe'egaga* of Sagaina, Upolu, begat *Funefe'ai*, who gained the Tagaloa title and eight orators in exchange for relinquishing the woman he loved, *Sinaalāua*.

Funefe'ai's first marriage (around A.D.1350) was to *Tetoafaigā* from the Vaisa'ulu and Vaiafai sub-villages of Iva village, in Savai'i—Vaiafai is one of the four village residences of the LeTagaloa and clan, the FaleSafune clan. *Tetoafaigā* begat *Tagaloaega* (*Tagaloa-Ega).* Then *Funefe'ai's* second marriage, to *Tauanu'ufaigā* (daughter of *Tuliaupupu* of Letogo) begat a daughter, *Utufa'asili.*

Around A.D.1380, the union of *Funefe'ai's* son *Tagaloaega* with *Lanuopouli* of Sili, Savai'i, begat Tagaloa *LeTula* and Tagaloa *A'opo* (with his house of 100 posts in A'opo, Savai'i—see The story of Tagaloa-*A'opo* and the 100 posts, page 182). Then in A.D.1410, the union of Tagaloa *LeTula* and *Ulalemamae* (daughter of *Luafataali'i* of Manono Island and half-sister to *Lei'atauaLesā*) begat *Tagaloa-SeFa'atautele.* His first marriage (A.D.1440), to *Lelāpueisalele* (daughter of *Malālatea* and *Sinalagilagi*, *Tagaloalagi's* daughter) begat a son Tagaloa *Fa'a* (half-brother to *Lelāpueisalele's* son *Lei'atauaLesā*), and a daughter *MafioSamoa.* Their daughter *MafioSamoa* was the grandmother of *Leaula* and *LeTufuga*, (famous grandsons of *Laifai*), *Saleaula*, and *Safotulafai.*

Tagaloa *Fa'a* was also known as Tagaloa *Savai'inaea* (see The legend of *Savai'inaea*, page 182). His second marriage, to *Tu'umoega* from Sili, Savai'i begat Tagaloa *Fa'aofonu'u*, and *Fa'aolatane,* which takes us to around A.D.1470.

The first marriage of Tagaloa *Fa'aofonu'u*, to *LeTelesā* of Faleata begat Tagaloa *Sauniifanua.* And his second marriage, to *Fitimaula* (daughter of *LeTufuga* of SaFotulafai) begat *Selaginatō,* Tagaloa *Tualalafa*, and a daughter *Moeaitele*.

Selaginatõ married *Vaetamasoāali'i* giving birth to TuiA'ana *Tamālelagi*, as told in The Story of *Vaetamasoāali'i*.

Around A.D.1500, the union of Tagaloa *Sauniifanua* and *Tafeutuloa* begat a daughter *Maisagamai*. And in A.D.1530, her union with TuiAtua *Fotuitam'ai* begat Tagaloa *Afesulu.*

Moving onward to A.D.1560, the union of Tagaloa *Afesulu* and *Oloitoa* (daughter of the TuiToga) begat daughters *Fatumiti* and *Tala'i*. Around A.D.1590, *Fatumiti*'s first marriage, to *Tanuvasavasamanaia* of Mulifanua, begat sons *Taito*, and *Tumanuvao.* Her second marriage, to Malietoa *Taulapapa* of Solosolo, Atua begat a son, *To'omata*, and a daughter, *Iliganoa Taulalo'ese*. *Iliganoa Taulalo'ese* is the full name of the SaLeTagaloa's Sa'o Tama'ita'i.

Then in A.D.1620, the union of *To'omata* and *Tofoipupū* (daughter of *Ta'uo* of Gautavai) begat *Amituana'i.*

The story of Tagaloa-*A'opo* and the 100 posts

According to Manu'an legend, *Tagaloalagi* often visited Savai'i and that's why he had a "visiting residence"—*Malae o Alamisi*—in Samata-uta and Samata-tai.

This is the tale of the first Tagaloa-*A'opo* House with 100 posts of human beings and the edict by the cannibal Chief *A'opo* and his village: *A'opo* and the villagers begged *Tagaloalagi* for a gift, and so *Tagaloalagi* granted them their wishes, which, when made known, turned out to be *paepaelei*, the beautiful white seashells used to make a top flooring layer of a house or *Maota*. *Tagaloalagi*, in his amazement, said, "I thought you would be asking for water, due to the aridity of your village land, but instead you asked for seashells, so here are your seashells for your house, and good luck on getting water." *Tagaloalagi* was being facetious in his response to the Chief *A'opo* and to the villagers, for being stupid. Then *Tagaloalagi* gifted the Tagaloa title to Chief *A'opo* and he became the first Tagaloa-*A'opo*.

The legend of *Savai'inaea*

Savai'inaea was the son of *Tagaloa-SeFa'atautele* and *Lelāpueisalele* (who was the mother of the first *Lei'atauaLesā* through her marriage to *Luafataali'i* of Manono).

Savai'inaea was also known as *Tagaloa-SeFa'atautele Savai'inaea.* He had a sister *MafioSamoa* and a brother *TagaloaA'opo* (famous for his house of 100 posts of human beings, above—see Tagaloa, page 31 in the Period V timelines).

Tagaloa-SeFa'atautele Savai'inaea had a pet domestic turtle that he kept in a pool by the lagoon. One day he went out in the morning to feed the turtle, but the turtle had somehow ventured outside the pond and into the lagoon. The young *SeFa'atautele* was worried that his turtle might get outside the lagoon and into the Pacific Ocean. And so he started to look for the turtle in the lagoon. And behold, he could see the tail of the turtle, and he could see that the turtle was rapidly swimming out to the ocean.

The faster *SeFa'atautele* approached the turtle, the faster the turtle swam away from him. When he came up for air and when went back down, he could barely see the tail, and so he continued chasing the turtle, not knowing he was in the middle of the Pacific Ocean until he saw the shadow of a mountain range and the bay the turtle was approaching.

When *SeFa'atautele* and his turtle arrived at the bay of the seashore of Falefa, in Atua district, that is where *Leutelelei'ite* and the orators saw *SeFa'atautele's* head coming up for air periodically, and that is when *Leutelelei'ite* said to his orators, "That must be a Savai'ian's head popping up (*naea*) out in the bay. Go get him out and bring him here."

The orators, *Iuli* and *Moeonoono,* came out to *SeFa'atautele* and brought him to *Leutelelei'ite*. *Leutelelei'ite* asked *SeFa'atautele,* "Who are you, and where do you come from, and why did you swim all this way?" And *SeFa'atautele* said, "I am the son of *Tagaloa-SeFa'atautele* from Sili, Savai'i. I was chasing my turtle (*i'asā* is a formal name for turtle, said in front of high chiefs) and following its path as it got away from the pool in our village lagoon."

The paramount chief and his orator chiefs were astonished to hear this incredible story. But *Leutelelei'ite* recognized *SeFa'atautele's* genealogy, as a great-grandson of Paramount Tagaloa *Funefe'ai* with the fearsome half-man half-spirit reputation. They immediately concluded that this young man was likewise a half-man half-spirit in order to have swum this far.

SeFa'atautele was given the name *Savai'inaea* (*Savai'i-na-ea*). He stayed in the district of Atua for some time and married a lady in Falefa village. The name of the family there is Alai'asā (the Path of the Turtle). *SeFa'atautele* married a lady in Lotofaga, Atua, of SaLeValasi clan. And then he married again, this time with the daughter of Chief *Leota* in Solosolo village, before going back to Sili, Savai'i.

There is a village that is a residence of the original *Savai'inaea* and is called Satuiatua (SaTuiAtua) to remind the people that he had children (from his marriages there) into the TuiAtua genealogy at Atua, Upolu.

It should be noted that *Leutelelei'ite* married *Ulalemamae* (grandmother of *SeFa'atautele Savai'inaea*) in around the same time period.

Stories of *Laifai*

The Seven Sons of *Laifai*

Returning to *Laifai*, brother of *Funefe'ai*, we begin with the seven sons of *Laifai.* In A.D.1350, *Laifai* married *Mata'uiatali* of Falesau in Upolu. *Laifai* and *Mata'uiatali* had seven sons, from whom began the naming the villages of Savaii. These were: *Fotulafai*, the founder of the eponymous village or District of SaFotulafai (Sa means family or clan of—*Fotulafai* is the first with the name *Lafai*); *Talalafai,* founder of Iva; *Tupa'iloa,* founder of Falealupo; *Loaloa,* founder of Safe'e; *Tupa'ifa'aulu,* founder of Neiafu; *Tupa'ilefao,* founder of Asau; and *Muliagalafai* founder of SaMuliaga. The name *Muliagalafai* is a combination of *Muliaga and Lafai.* And Sa indicates the family of Muliaga. Sometimes it will be written SaLeMuliaga, the great family of Muliaga.

Later, *Laifai* married his sister-in-law, *Mata'uiafatu* sister of *Mata'uiatali,* and begat *Va'asilitamalepo*, whose name literally means "a boy born in the dark."

Around A.D.1380, *Va'asilitamalepo*, the son of *Laifai* by his second wife, married two sisters, *Sinaletuna* and *Sinaleimoa*, the daughters of *Poluleuligaga* from Saleimoa. This *Poluleuligaga* was the son of Malietoa *Uilamatūtū Faigā*, adopted from his brother-in-law, the King of Toga, Tuitoga *'Ulufanuatele*. Malietoa Faigā

Uilamatūtū would later be visited by *Laifai's* grandsons, *LeTufuga* and *Leaula,* when he was ill, after which these brother chiefs would become known as the *Pules* of Savai'i (see The Story of *LeTufuga* and *Leaula*, page 186 below).

These two marriages resulted in two sons of *Laifai's* son *Va'asilitamalepo*: *Lafailetaua*, the founder of Palauli, and *Lafaitupa'itea*, the founder of Tupa'itea (or the Satupa'itea district of Savai'i). *Lafaitupa'itea* (founder of Tupa'itea) married a young lady from Upolu, who gave birth to their son, *Tevalefua*. Then (around A.D.1440) *Tevalefua* married *Pipilimatualimausaga* from Falealili village, Atua district, Upolu, and gave birth to sons, *Muliagalapaitagata* and *Muliagalapaiaitu*.

At the same time, *Laifai's* first son, *Fotulafai*, the founder of SaFotulafai, married *Levaoita*, great-granddaughter of *Pulufaigā* and they begat *LeTufuga* and *Leaula*, the founder of Saleaula.

The Founding Villages of *Laifai* and *Fotulafai*

As we have mentioned, the children and grandchildren of *Laifai* became the founders of well-known villages, as seen below.

Name	**Founding Village**
Lafai's Children	
Fotulafai	SaFotulafai
Talalafai	Iva
Tupa'iloa	Falealupo
Loaloa	Safe'e (sub-district in Safune)
Tupa'ifa'aulu	Neiafu
Tupa'ilefao	Asau
Muliagalafai	Samuliaga
Va'asiliifiti's Children	
Lafailetaua	Palauli
Lafaitupa'itea	Tupa'itea
Fotulafai's Children	
Leaula	Saleaula

The Story of *LeTufuga* and *Leaula*

It's important to note that after the liberation of Samoa, the King of Toga did not organize a war to fight the battle again. So, as time has shown, Toga and Samoa became allies. After the defeat, the fathers of Malietoa appointed certain leaders with more authority over Samoa, and so they began to create the Samoan government.

Unlike Upolu, Savai'i had not yet been divided into villages. This is when the chiefs *LeTufuga* and *Leaula* became the two foundational paramount chief authorities of all of Savai'i, as decreed from the authority of the Malietoa Faigā *Uilamatūtū*. They were descendants of the original founding fraternal brothers, *Laifai* and *Funefe'ai* who settled Savai'i. And this is their story:

The Malietoa Faigā, the paramount warrior chief (referred to by many as the king that ruled over all of Samoa around A.D.1375-1335), had been ill for a month with a severe depression which, he later learned, stemmed from a violation of a sacred *tapu*.

As was customary for an angry king or paramount chief, suffering from the illness of depression, treatment would first require diagnosis, usually by a shaman or some other wise person. The person that could make this diagnostic assessment or guess the reason for the king's illness would, of course, be greatly rewarded by the king. Also, every visiting relative would be given some form of token gift, which would be decreed by the king.

Warrior chiefs would often dream of or seek out opportunities like this with other paramount high chiefs and heads of paramount royal families, looking for the potential rewards. The higher the paramount family chief giving the gift, the higher the value of the gift, because it is often decreed as an honor by the whole of that royal family, or across the whole island country. So, many visitors came to the Malietoa, to bring prayers and good wishes and food. And the Malietoa would reciprocate by giving the visitors some form of verbal decree of a permanent title or assignment or designation of some kind.

When the brothers, *LeTufuga* and *Leaula*, heard of the Malietoa Faigā *Uilamatūtū's* illness, they immediately seized the opportunity to gain some valuable gift from the king. They embarked on a journey to Upolu, heading for Malie and Vaitoelau, the village throne of the Malietoa family clan, in order to visit the king.

It goes without saying that the most critical knowledge any visitor to a paramount chief, for whatever purpose, must have, is knowing the genealogy connecting the family, because it is the first thing in the speech that would identify the visiting person and show whether there is family connection or not, related to the purpose of the visit. In this case, *LeTufuga* and *Leaula* knew their ancestral genealogy stemmed from *Tagaloalagi's* daughter *Sinalagilagi* and her husband *Malālatea*, a relationship that produced a girl, *Lelāpueisalele* (*Lela*—a bird that—*pue*—was caught—*i sa*—while in—*ele*—flight—*my translation*), and her blind brother, *Leāifale'ava* (see Tagaloa page 31 in Period V of the Timelines). The brothers, *LeTufuga* and *Leaula*, were descendants of *Lelāpueisalele*, while Malietoa Faigā *Uilamatūtū's* mother, *Luafatasaga*, and her brothers *Va'afuti* (also known as *Va'afa'i*), *Fata,* and *Maulolo* were all descendants of the *Lelāpueisalele's* blind brother, *Leāifale'ava*.

So, when Malietoa Faigā *Uilamatūtū* saw the brothers bowing in reverence to him, he asked who they were, and *LeTufuga* and *Leaula* began to sing out in a chant, like poetry, the genealogy of their family relationships. Of course, the king, Malietoa Faigā *Uilamatūtū,* was impressed and filled with happiness and gratitude. He asked the brothers the reason for their visit, coming from so far away. And the brothers responded with a gift to the king, with two weaponry sticks known as the *Sogā* and *Asage*, and with well-wishes for immediate recovery. *Sogā* and *asage* are the names of plants from which barkcloth comes, with which nets and red shaggy mats are made (Pipturus propinquus).[lxi]

The Malietoafaigā was not clear about the meaning of these gifts, but he was impressed with the brothers' courage and adventurous spirit. So Malietoafaigā sent the gift of the sticks to one of his family clan warriors (half-human and half-spirit "shamans"), a chief named *Li'o*, in Siumu District, to interpret the meaning of the brothers' gifts. *Li'o's* reply to Malietoafaigā was that the brothers came to seek whoever caused Malietoafaigā's illness and destroy them, for the real meaning of the brothers' gifts was that they represented the weaponry needed to seek out and destroy the enemy of the Malietoafaigā—the one that caused his illness.

Malietoa Faigā *Uilamatūtū* asked his paramount orator chiefs, *Fata* and *Maulolo*, if there were any heirloom gifts left for considerations for *LeTufuga* and *Leaula*. The answer was that the only things left were the conch shells (the *pule* in the Samoan language, a word which also means "authority") that helped anchor and balance the canoe. So the Malietoafaigā summoned the brothers and bequeathed and decreed the last two conch shells as gifts to them from Malietoafaigā, King of all Samoa. This was clearly interpreted, by the adventurous brothers, as making them the first two "authorities" over all of Savai'i.

Prior to this period the salutation of Samoa was very simple and straightforward—i.e. *Tulouna Tumua, Aiga ma latou Tama, Tama ma latou Aiga, Faleupolu o tausi va'atele*. Over time the salutation changed to memorialize (witness) the many milestone events in the history of Samoa.[lxii]

It wasn't until 1880, after the war and conflict between *Talavou* and his nephew Malietoa *Laupepa*, that the brothers *LeTufuga* and *Leaula* agreed to distribute this authority to four other districts of the Island of Savai'i, as a reward for fighting and pledging support to Malietoa *Laupepa*, who followed his father Malietoa *Moli*, son of Tafa'ifa Malietoa *Vaiinupõ*, who received the missionary John Williams from England in 1830 (see Samoan government at the Arrival of Christianity, page 246).

The Orator's Rod and Scepter

Returning to the folklore regarding Malietoa Faigā *Uilamatūtū's* illness, let's look at some of his appointments and decrees that exist even to today:

According to the Tuisamau and *Fata* and *Maulolo*, Senior Statesman of the Malietoa Monarch, *Fata* and *Maulolo* (uncles to Malietoafaigā) found out, from a man named *Li'o* (not Paramount Orator Chief *Li'o* of Siumu) of the same village (Tuana'i), that, before his illness, Malietoafaigā went to take an evening bath at his sacred-spring water-pool and, upon arrival, found another man bathing in the sacred pool. This is what angered and annoyed him into a state of depression.

The man was executed, and his head was delivered to Malietoafaigā in a form of a gift. For this act, the Malietoafaigā gifted and decreed the Orator's Rod and Scepter, representing oratory authority of the district and all of Samoa, to the Tuisamau and to the uncles *Fata* and *Maulolo*. The original Orator's Rod and Scepter were gifted and decreed by *Pili*, son of TuiManu'a and progenitor of the original political organizational structure of the islands of Upolu and Savai'i. Atua, A'ana, Saga, and Tolufale are descendants of *Pili,* and their assignments evidence the organizational structure.

Story of LeTufuga Ma'alo'alomailevao

The brother, *LeTufuga—LeTufuga* Ma'alo'alomailevao, which means *LeTufuga,* a human shadow moving like lightning in the thickness of the forest—appears in another well-known story. One day *LeTufuga* was up on the mountaintops catching pigeons. According to legends, TuiA'ana *Uõtele* was visiting his family in SaFotulafai, Savaii. TuiA'ana *Uõtele* was considered a very harsh man. As he was visiting, *LeTufuga* looked down at the village and saw the TuiA'ana people thrashing the people of SaFotulafai. The people were running for cover to the ocean. So *LeTufuga* ran down the mountain to aid his people.

TuiA'ana *Uõtele* saw *LeTufuga* and admired his bravery and skills as he took on TuiA'ana's aumaga. After all was done, TuiA'ana *Uõtele* said to *LeTufuga*, "You are a very angry *LeTufuga* and have all authority, but you are also the *LeTufuga* that loves. Forgive the people."

Hence, Paramount Orator Chief *LeTufuga's* salutations in his village of SaFotulafai: *LeTufuga totama'i, LeTufuga ita, LeTufuga alofa, LeTufuga Pule—* "Your Honorable *LeTufuga*, angry warrior, loving warrior and the supreme authority for SaFotulafai."

Stories of SaMuliagalafai

SaMuliagalafai is the clan of *Muliaga-lafai* (his complete name), the seventh and youngest of *Laifai's* children. He is the founding father of SaMuliagalafai, which is shortened to the SaMuliaga family clan. He carries on the genealogy of his father *La(i)fai's* name, as in *Lafai Taulupo'o* and *Lafai Sauoāiga* or *Tonumaipe'a Sauoāiga*. The Lafai is integrated with the Tonumaipe'a dynasty.

Muliagalafai married *Sinatatafa* of Iva and they birthed *Saufatu-le-Muliaga*.

Muliagalafai later married *Lua* of Tuamasaga and begat *Utatuisuga* and *Matatuisuga*. *Matatuisuga* married *Togia* of Tifitifi in Upolu. They had a son, *Ali'amanaia* (or sons, *Ali'a* and *Manaia*), and a daughter, *Gasoloaiolelagi*, who married Malietoa *Uitualagi* (see The Story of Malietoa *Uitualagi*, page 151). Tuamasaga and Malietoa legends have it that *Ali'a* and *Manaia* are really one person named *Ali'amanaia*. The name *Ali'a* (or *Li'a*) goes back to the first TuiManu'a *Li'a*, and *Manaia* is also a name of one of TuiManu'a's sons, thus the combination is in memory of TuiManu'a's children. But it is only one person, a son named *Ali'amanaia*.

The union of *Gasoloaiolelagi* and Malietoa *Uitualagi* connects SaMuliagalafai and the Malietoa clan.

Muliagalafai later married his third wife, *Poulifataiatagaloa*, daughter of TuiAsau. They begat *Lafaitaulupo'o* and *Leutogitupa'itea*, the founder of the Tonumaipe'a family. It is at this point that the royal constellation of the Lafai family history moves forward, in the history of Samoa, toward the first consolidated queen of Samoa, *Salamasina*. The idea of consolidation, of course, implies combining to produce one single whole, but with the Tonumaipe'a dynastic constellation, one can see unobstructed the thread of illumination from each ancestral family.

Saufatulemuliaga, *Muliaga's* son from his first wife *Sinatatafa*, formed a union with *Sasilati* of Tufu Gataiva. Together they begat four sons; *Muliaganotoa*, *Muliagapulematõ*, *Muliagasoifuanā*, and *Muliagafa'atoāfe-iti-iti* (or *Muliagafa'atoāfeitiiti*) also known as *Fa'atoāfeitiiti*. Their third son, *Muliagasoifuanā*, married *Tiulaē* of Amoa, Savai'i. They begat *Vailololeali'igafao'o*, the founder of the SaTuala family. Then *Muliagasoifuanā* later married *Ifi*, the daughter of *LuaAtua*, and begat *La'ulu-Nofovaleane* and *La'ulu-Lefano*. *LuaAtua* was a descendant of Malietoa *Gagasāvea*, half-brother to Malietoafaigā *Uilamatutu*. The original *LuaAtua* is a second name for *Poluleuligaga*, the adopted son of Malietoafaigā *Uilamatutu* (see The Story of *Poluleuligaga* and the Malietoafaigā, page 150). Thus, there are two LuaAtua titles in Saleimoa village of the Tuamasaga district, Upolu.

The Story of La'ulu *Nofovaleane*

The famous decree of La'ulu *Nofovaleane* is memorialized in the Mornings and known as the Edict of La'ulu Nofovaleane and the three Royal Aualuma of Samoa. This is the story of that decree:

From La'ulu *Nofovaleane's* first marriage, to *Fulisiailagitele*, the daughter of *Tu'uma'ai* from SaFotulafai, he begat a daughter, *Tuaetali*. *Tuaetali* begat her son, *Tapumanaia*.

From La'ulu *Nofovaleane's* second marriage, with *Lefa'aanāpulu*, the daughter of *Pulusau* of Salelologa, he begat *Fa'atupuigati*. *Fa'atupuigati* begat her son, *Pesefeamanaia*. (This *Pulusau* was an ancestor of the orators *Leaula* and *LeTufuga* of SaFotulafai—see The Story of Funefe'ai and Tagaloalagi, page 179—she was a descendant of *MafioSamoa*, who was the daughter of *Lelāpueisalele* and *Tagaloa-SeFa'atautele* and sister to the original *Tagaloa-SeFa'atautele Savai'inaea*.)

From La'ulu *Nofovaleane's* third marriage, to *Pouliotaua*, the daughter of *Tu'u* of Safune, he begat *Maupenei,* and *Maupenei* begat a son, *Aumoana*. *Maupenei's* son, *LeAumoana* (the *Aumoana*), had a much bigger head compared to the other boys.

These are the grandsons who were raised by giving them exercise in the early morning on flat rocks on the seashore at Papa (seashore rocks) i Galagala village in Upolu. The Samoan proverb: *O tama* (sons) *o le fa'atolotologa* (crawling) *i le Papa i Galagala* commemorates this. Another version is: *O le papa o le fa'atolotologa tama*—the seashore rocks of the princes practicing crawling for exercise—*my translation*.

So, to teach their sons to crawl, the three women would take them to these rocks near the ocean. As the waves would hit against the rocks, the infants had to crawl to protect themselves from getting hit. As the boys were on the rocks, *Maupenei's* sisters would ridicule *Aumoana* for having such an unusually big head. The size of his head was out of balance, relative to his body, so much so that it hindered his ability to crawl. *Maupenei* heard her sisters taunting *Aumoana* and began to cry.

La'ulu *Nofovaleane*, *Maupenei's* father, was aware of the mockery taking place. La'ulu favored *Maupenei* and *Aumoana*, and he became very upset, seeing the situation unfold for so long. He commanded his three daughters to meet with him. It was then that

La'ulu revealed his decree over his children and grandchildren. The decree stated:

Tuaetali and *Tapumanaia* will be the Aualuma for Lufilufi and Leulumoega; and *Fa'atupuigati* and *Pesefeamanaia* will be the Aualuma for the "Vae-o-le-nofoa-fia," with the family of *Lilomaiava* in Sagafili village. However for *Maupenei*, her son, *LeAumoana*, will be anointed and appointed to be Aualuma of the mighty SaMuliaga family. He is the boy of decree.

As times passed, *LeAumoana's* genealogy became the origin of the Tupuivao, Mata'afa, and SaLeValasi families.

The Story of *Tu'uma'ai*

Tu'uma'ai was the father of La'ulu *Nofovaleane*'s first wife. As we have seen (see The Story of the Stolen Child, page 166), around A.D.1330, Tagaloa *Tualalafa* (*Selaginatõ*) married *Vaetamasoāali'i*, from the Malietoa clan, giving birth to TuiA'ana *Tamālelagi.* And *Selaginatõ's* half-brothers were *Alalatoa* (father of *Pa'u*) and *Tu'uma'ai* (see Period IV TuiA'ana, page 22 in the Timelines).

Tu'uma'ai's name means *Tu*—stand—*ma*—and—*'ai*—eat, or, in another version, *Tu'u*—leave it—*ma'ai*—foods—or leave the food that you brought with you.

Legend has it that *Tu'uma'ai* had a daughter *Fulisiailagitele.* This daughter was originally married to TuiA'ana *Tamālelagi,* but she was later kidnapped by La'ulu *Nofovaleane*, from SaMuliaga.

Fulisiailagitele's father was embarrassed by what had happened to his daughter, for there were rumors that she didn't resist La'ulu *Nofovaleane* as he kidnapped her. However, there is a genealogical connection that I believe came into play here:

La'ulu *Nofovaleane's* mother, *Ifi*, was a daughter of *Luatua* of Saleimoa village, in Tuamasaga district, Upolu. *Luatua* was the son of Malietoa *Gagasāvea*, elder son of Malietoa *Sāveatuvaelua*. At the same time, *Muliagalafai's* third marriage was with Lady *Lua* of Faleata, Upolu, giving birth to two daughters *Utatuisuga* and *Matatuisuga*. *Matatuisuga* married *Togia* of Tifitifi (or Sagafili), in the A'ana district of Upolu, and bore a son *Ali'a-Manaia* and a daughter *Gasoloaiolelagi*. *Gasoloaiolelagi* married Malietoa *Uitualagi* (Malietoa *Gagasāvea*'s nephew) and bore Malietoa *La'auli* and *Fuaoleto'elau*. And Malietoa *La'auli* was father of *Gatoa'itele*, the grandmother of TuiA'ana *Tamālelagi*.

These paramount chiefs were well aware of their genealogical connection. This is why they didn't go to war at this kidnapping, but instead a peace offering with a *'ifoga* was good enough to mediate the embarrassing situation. The peace offering with *'ifoga* was a prostrated apology whereby the Paramount Chief *Tu'uma'ai* prostrated himself, covered with a fine mat, in front of the victim family's residence—the residence of TuiA'ana *Tamālelagi*—asking for forgiveness, together with a feast.

The answer given by the victim's family chiefs and orator was to "eat your food and don't bother to sit down; leave the rest and leave"—*my translation*. Hence the name *Tu'uma'ai*.

The Story of *Pa'u*

We should note here that *Tu'uma'ai's* brother, *Alalatoa*, married a daughter of *Usu* in SaFotulafai and bore a son *Pa'u*, whose name and title appear again when Christianity is spreading in the region.

But the name *Pa'u* is mentioned in a legend further back in history, in the time of the first Tagaloa *Funefe'ai*. *Pa'u* married Tagaloa *Funefe'ai's* daughter. Her name is unknown, but *Pa'u* was given a name by Tagaloa *Funefe'ai*—*Pa'u-mailei-malo*. *Mailei* means "conspired against the Mālō or Government," and hence the name means "*Pa'u* who conspired against Tagaloa *Funefe'ai's* Mālō." The Funefe'ai time period is the time of Tagaloalagi, whose daughter *Sinalagilagi* is the progenitor of *Va'afuti* (*Va'afa'i*), *Fata, Maulolo,* and *Luafatasaga*, around the *To'o* and *Ata* generation.

Summary of History from the First Malietoa *Sāvea*

- Malietoa *Sāvea* is the father of Malietoafaigā *Uitualagi*.
- Malietoa *Uitualagi* decrees to the wives of his son, *La'auli,* that they will birth a child and a grandchild who will be granted crowns equal to the TuiAtua and TuiA'ana crowns. These are:
    - *Gatoa'itele* (his granddaughter)
    - and *Vaetamasoāali'i* (his great-granddaughter)

- *Gatoa'itele* and her husband, LeManu'a *LeSanalāla,* decree and appoint their children to royal responsibilities. Thus *Vaetamasoāali'i* is decreed to a royal throne or crown (*PāPā*)
- *Tamālelagi*, son of *Vaetamasoāali'i* and *Selaginatō* (Tagaloa *Tualalafa*) is kidnapped at birth by the two warrior orators, *Ape* the Alert (*Moemanatunatu*) and *Tutuila* the Tardy (*Lematemate*) from Fasito'o.

Meanwhile, in the lineage of Tonumaipe'a, the brothers *Ulufanuasese'e* and *Saveasi'uleo* separate.

- *Saveasi'uleo* marries his niece *Tilafaigā* (one of the conjoined twins), giving birth to *Nafanua.*
- *Ulufanuasese'e* decrees to *Nafanua,* to establish and protect the Tonumaipe'a *Sauoaiga* family and heirs, and to liberate *Satupa'itea* from *Lilomaiava's* tyrannical rule.
- The wars to acquire the respective crowns (*PāPās*) lead up to *Nafanua* the Warrior Queen who holds all the crowns until the first **TAFA'IFA**, *Salamasina*. These wars include:
  - The *Tamālelagi* and TuiA'ana *Sagaate* war for TuiA'ana Crown. *Tamālelagi* triumphs and the TuiA'ana crown is given to *Nafanua* as custodian.
  - The war of *Gatoa'itele* and *Fata/Maulolo* against Malietoa *Sagagaimuli* and *Auimatagi*. Malietoa loses and *Gatoa'itele* obtains the crown (PāPā). This is given to *Nafanua,* and *Fata* and *Maulolo* become the Laumua or *Laumua o Tumua*—the Seat or capital of the Tumua; Apia is the capital of Samoa, and Afega or Laumua is capital of the Tumua (Lufilufi and Leulumoega).
  - The War for the TuiAtua crown (PāPā) between *Foga-niu-tea* and *Foga-olo-ula. Foganiutea* is victorious and the TuiAtua crown is given to *Nafanua* as custodian.
  - The SaTunumafono (Vaetamasoāali'i) family go to war against Alataua (in Safata). SaTunumafono is the victor, and the Vaetamasoāali'i title is given to *Nafanua* as custodian.
  - *Tupa'i*, the war general of Nafanua, is installed at each war territory as *Tupa'i* the Pious or the Numinous *Tupa'i*.

Then, as we shall see in Period VI:

- This is followed by the bestowal of all four crowns (PāPās) on *Salamasina*, the daughter of TuiA'ana *Tamālelagi*. This is made possible because of the family constellation of *Gatoa'itele's* children. *Tamālelagi* decrees that his children appoint *Salamasina* to succeed him.
- Queen *Salamasina* decrees that her children remember the (missing) boy, her lost son *Tapumanaia LeSatele*, for he is the male heir.
- And Queen *Salamasina* reigns peacefully over all of Samoa until her passing.

Period VI: TuiA'ana *Tamālelagi* and the Tafa'ifa

It is in the time period of TuiA'ana *Tamālelagi* and the first Tafa'ifa, the 1500s, that people have decided the modern history of Samoa begins, because these stories can be validated. Modern history is no longer talking about mythology.

Using the arrival of Christianity in 1830 as a baseline year—when Reverend John Williams and a young Samoan named *Fauea,* originally from the village of Manono and Apolima, dropped anchor in Sapapaali'i, Savai'i—we can estimate the number of generations back to validate TuiA'ana *Tamālelagi's* generation.

Samoan tradition is that the grandparents or great-great-grandparents are those responsible for teaching family history and genealogies. This means that the baseline generation, in the mid-1800s, had received the stories of family history and genealogy from their great-great-grandparents who lived in the early 1700s. Likewise, they must have been schooled by their great-great-grandparents, who would have heard the stories from their great-great-grandparents, who would have heard from those who had seen or known TuiA'ana *Tamālelagi* in around 1500-1560.[lxiii]

At the time of John Williams and Malietoa *Vaiinupõ*, Samoans were already talking about real people and real families in their ancient history. But the people had additional evidence besides verbal records. They could confirm that these people existed. For history tells how *Salamasina* became the consolidated Tafa'ifa (Queen) of Samoa, and their personal genealogies, with their ancestors, can be confirmed by surviving family members. The Royal Families Constellation, the descendants of *Gatoa'itele's* children that produced the First Tafa'ifa *Salamasina*, is the foundational genealogy from which all Samoan royal families are descended.

Kings and Queens and Tafa'ifa

By the time of TuiA'ana *Tamālelagi,* Samoa was slowly gaining its power back and the population was steadily increasing. Samoan imperialism created an opportunity for the consolidation of power between a King and Queen.

The Samoan word, equivalent to the title King or Queen, is Tafa'ifa. This refers to the acquisition of the four Royal Crowns of the Royal Families of Samoa, not including the Kingdom of Manu'a. The Crowns are:

- TuiAtua (Monarch House of TuiAtua)
- TuiA'ana (Monarch House of TuiA'ana)
- Gatoa'itele and
- Vaetamasoāali'i

(Both these last two, as we have seen, are Monarch Houses of Malietoa).

So, *Tafa'ifa* is the Samoan word for the consolidated, unified "king" or "queen," a person who obtains all four titles. (The current word *Tupu* is from the Samoan translation of the word "King" from the English Bible.) The four titles each have two paramount orator chiefs, who are the titleholders' orators at large and are custodians of the crown, having responsibility to bestow the respective crown title on a person the family at large agrees to be the paramount high chief of the royal family.

The Four Paramount Title Crowns

It is during the reign of *Nafanua* (see The Story of the Warrior Queen *Nafanua*, page 172) that all four paramount title crowns of monarchs—PāPā of TuiAtua, PāPā of TuiA'ana, PāPā of Gatoa'itele, and PāPā of Vaetamasoāali'i—ended up being held in custody by *Nafanua*, until she wanted and agreed to bestow all four titles on *LeValasi*. But *LeValasi* wanted to bestow the title on her adopted daughter *Salamasina*, the biological daughter of TuiA'ana *Tamālelagi* who was first cousin to *LeValasi*—we should remember, TuiA'ana *Tamālelagi's* mother was *Vaetamasoāali'i*, sister to *LeValasi's* mother *LeAtougaugaatuitoga*. *LeValasi's* husband at the time was TuiAtua, and they had adopted their niece, *Salamasina*.

The Gatoa'itele title had been decreed by their mother to the three children—*Vaetamasoāali'i, Atougaugaatuitoga* (mother to *LeValasi*), and their brother *Lalovimāmā* (who was father to TuiAtua *Mata'utia Fa'atulou* who married his first cousin *LeValasi*). Thus they were now all connected together through marriages, as were their titles. They were all cousins, and their grandmother was *Gatoa'itele*. And this is the collective genealogy that brought the island country together under one ruler.

Thus the legend of the Samoan "Warrior Queen" *Nafanua* is foundational to the early development of Samoan "modern" history. This is the phase of Samoa's history which evolved into the beginning of the major families, whose lineages would inter-join, leading to a consolidation through marriages that would allow the eventual production of a consolidated ruler of all Samoa (Tafa'ifa *Salamasina* TuiA'ana Tamālelagi).

The prophetic rise of the "warrior queen" *Nafanua* fulfilled the farewell parting words decreed by her ancestors (the brothers: *Saveasi'uleo* and *Ulufanuasese'e*) at the Pacific Ocean shore, at the LeOne Tai, Alataua and Pulotu at Falealupo, Savai'i, where they said, "We must part in order to keep peace between us. We shall meet again, not at the head or origin of our lineage, but the tail of our lineage." This means that "we," the head and origin of our lineage, will not meet again, but perhaps our respective descendants will cross paths and genealogies. (See The Morning (*Taeao*) of the Farewell at Sea in Alataua, Savai'i, page 115.)

The warrior *Nafanua* is the granddaughter of *Saveasi'uleo*, and her brief genealogical history is as follows:

- *Masa* of Tufutafoe village married *Popoto*; the issue was a girl *Taufa-le-matagi*.
- *'Alao* married *Taufa-le-matagi*; the issue was *Saveasi'uleo* and *Ulufanuasese'e* and others.
- *Ulufanuasese'e* married *Sina* of Falelatai village; the issue was *Taemā* and *Tilafaigā*, the conjoined twin girls. These Siamese twins are quite well-known in the history of Samoa for their journey throughout the Samoan and Manu'an chain of islands producing several paramount families and chiefs in every island where they sojourned.
- *Saveasi'uleo* married *Tilafaigā*; the issue was *Nafanua* or *Suaifanua*.[lxiv]

As we have seen, *Nafanua* gathered the four title crowns, and they were bestowed on *Salamasina*, the adopted daughter of *LeValasi*.

The Story of *Salamasina*, the first Tafa'ifa

The First Tafa'ifa

In A.D.1500, a young princess, *Salamasina* TuiA'ana Tamālelagi, was crowned the first Tafa'ifa of Samoa. Thus Tafa'ifa (Queen) *Salamasina's* acquisition of the TuiA'ana, TuiAtua, Gatoa'itele, and Vaetamasoāali'i titles marks the beginning of the modern history of Samoa.

To address her title and salutation, one would state the following:

> Your Honorable Highness Tafa'ifa *Salamasina*, *Afio le paia maualuga le Afioga TuiA'ana, le Afioga TuiAtua, le Afioga Gatoa'itele, Le paia i le Afioga Vaetamasoāali'i.*
>
> Honorable Highness Tafa'ifa Salamasina, the Honorable TuiAtua, TuiA'ana, Gatoa'itele, and Vaetamasoāali'i.

Salamasina obtained all four titles through her genealogy, beginning, as we have seen, with the third Malietoa, Malietoa *Uitualagi*. He married *Gasoloaiolelagi*, daughter of *Tunavaitele*, also referred to as *Togia*, of Tifitifi village. *Togia's* mother was *Matatuisuga*, the daughter of *Muliagalafai*, a paramount chief of one of the founding families of the island of Savai'i. Thus, in this genealogy, there was now a connection between the villages of Faleata and Tifitifi, and the mighty district of SaMuliaga, Savai'i.

The Story of TuiA'ana *Tamālelagi* and *Vaetoifaga*

As we have seen, *Salamasina's* father, TuiA'ana *Tamālelagi,* had many wives and children (see Children of *Tamālelagi*, page 50 in the timelines).

During *Tamālelagi's* ninth marriage, the King of Toga, his beautiful daughter *Vaetoifaga*, and their party rested in Samatau village, where Paramount Chief *Fiamē* and Orator Chief *Puni* and his daughters (who were wives to TuiA'ana *Tamālelagi*) lived, before going for a visit and festivities to Amoa, Savai'i, where the TuiToga's wife's family lived. TuiToga's wife, *Taupõ-i-masina* (darkness before the dawn of the new moon), the mother of *Vaetoifaga,* was the daughter of *Lefono* of Amoa, Savai'i. On their ship, they had an abundance of Togan fine mats, brought as gifts to *Taupõimasina's* family.

The orators of Leulumoega heard of the beautiful daughter and, more importantly, the fine mats. They devised a plan to convince *Puni* to retrieve the Princess of Toga and the fine mats; in return he would have a piece of the TuiA'ana Royal house in the village of Leulumoega.

Puni told the orators he would discuss this with his daughters, the eighth and ninth wives of TuiA'ana *Tamālelagi*. And the rest of the story is history, told in more detail in Volume I of this book, *Navigators forging a Matriarchal Culture in Polynesia. Tamālelagi,* now advanced in age, married the young Princess *Vaetoifaga,* and their child was *Salamasina. Tamālelagi's* cousin, *LeValasi,* cared for *Vaetoifaga* and *Salamasina,* and was as a mother to *Salamasina* (see The Story of *LeValasi*, page 169).

***Salamasina* Receives the Crowns**

Nafanua sent *LeValasi's* brother to present her with the royal titles. At this time, *LeValasi* and TuiAtua *Mata'utia Fa'atulou* had no children, and they had been caring for their niece, *Salamasina*, for many years.

Valasi's brother presented her with the four titles and proposed she take the titles. During this ceremonial meeting, *Valasi* allowed *Salamasina* to play with her hair and run around. *Tupa'i* asked *Valasi* to tell *Salamasina* to leave the meeting, as she was being highly disrespectful while he was trying to give the titles to become Queen of all of Samoa.

Tupa'i asked, "What is it that you are trying to say, *Valasi*? Do you want to give the titles to *Salamasina*?"

Valasi replied, "If that is the will of *Tupa'i*."

Tupa'i, confused, asked what that meant.

Valasi said, "If you are all in agreement, I will support you. Look at her genealogy. Who else would be perfect for this?"

Tupa'i discussed this with *Nafanua*. Then *Nafanua* stated, "If this is what *Valasi* wants, then so be it."

Valasi and the TuiAtua chose to adopt *Salamasina*, daughter of TuiA'ana *Tamālelagi* and the Princess of Toga. *Valasi* and TuiAtua already had the titles of TuiAtua and Tonumaipe'a. And *Salamasina's* biological parents were from the Malietoa clan and the Tagaloa. Hence, the connection of the Tagaloa clan and TuiA'ana. The four titles were now coming together to establish the Tafa'ifa.

During this ceremonial meeting *Salamasina* was said to be maybe 15 years old. She became queen at around 16-18 years old. The bestowment of the titles on *Salamasina* as queen required about a month to celebrate, as they had to wait for high officials to arrive and witness the first consolidated Queen of Samoa. The bestowment, and the act of providing one person with all authority of Samoa, became the foundation of the Samoan Constitution and government. The government of Samoa desired to keep royalty within a family. One great advantage to this, the Samoans believed, was that it would maintain peace in politics through family.

It should be noted that *Salamasina* had to physically travel to each Royal Crown's sacred meeting place for the ceremony for bestowment of each of the four Royal Crowns; TuiA'ana at Leulumoega, in A'ana District; TuiAtua at Lufilufi, in Atua District; Gatoa'itele at Afega, in Tuamasaga; and Vaetamasoāali'i in Safata, in Tuamasaga.[lxv]

Marriage of *Salamasina*

Salamasina always had a crowd of girls following her. There was a particular young man that accompanied her as well. The two caught birds and fished together. Soon after, they fell in love. However, his genealogy was not of royal ancestry, with the result that their relationship was not blessed.

Relentless orators persuaded Queen *Salamasina* to accept an arranged marriage, as it would be in the best interest of her country. The orators found the perfect genealogical match for *Salamasina*. His name was *Tapumanaia*, son of *Tonumaipe'a*-II.

After some time, *Salamasina* agreed to marry *Tapumanaia* and begat a girl, *Fofoaivao'ese*, and a boy, *Tapumanaia*-II.

Salamasina's Children

Tafa'ifa *Salamasina* had two children, a daughter *Fofoaivao'ese* and a son *Tapumanaia*. The daughter *Fofoaivao'ese* had a different father from *Tapumanaia*, for *Salamasina* was pregnant by her lover when she married the son of Paramount Chief Tonumaipe'a from the village of Satupa'itea, Savai'i. She was pregnant with a girl, appropriately named *Fofoaivao'ese* (which means "grieving farewell in the forest").

Salamasina orchestrated her lover's escape to Toga to be with her mother's family. Otherwise, her newlywed husband would pursue and kill him. Then she gave birth to a son and named him after his father, *Tapumanaia*-II. Well...

The moment that boy came out the womb, and the ladies were preparing him, the two talking chiefs from Falealili (*Talo* and *Ofoia*) came and stole the baby—just as *Salamasina's* father *Tamālelagi* had been kidnapped in the past—and took him to Falealili to be raised as their paramount chief, because of his royal genealogy. When they arrived at Falealili they changed the baby's name to *Tapumanaia*-II *LeSatele*, hence the paramount title Satele in the district of Falealili, Atua.

As the villagers were preparing to search for and kill the people responsible for this kidnapping, *Salamasina* declared that they should not go to war because of this, for her father had been kidnapped as well and became a paramount chief of the TuiA'ana. *Salamasina* decreed that day that the villagers must remember, going forward, where the boy was because he carried the genealogy of the crown.

It took about 150-200 years to bring Paramount High Chief Tafa'ifa (Queen) *Salamasina's* decree (to remember the child) to fulfilment. *Fonotī's* son, Paramount High Chief (King) *Muagututi'a*, remembered this decree and adopted *Tupua Fuiavailili*, the descendent of *Tamālelagi*. When Paramount High Chief (King)

Muagututi'a passed, *Tupua* succeeded him on the throne, inheriting the Tafa'ifa from King *Muagututi'a*.

After Salamasina

After the passing of Tafa'ifa *Salamasina*, the throne was inherited by the female side of the family, by her daughter and eldest child, *Fofoaivao'ese*. *Fofoaivao'ese* was not Tafa'ifa; however, she carried the Royal Crowns of TuiA'ana and TuiAtua. The Gatoa'itele and Vaetamasoāali'i Crowns were returned, back to the Malietoa Royal Family.

After *Fofoaivao'ese* came her daughter, *Taufau*. *Taufau* became TuiA'ana and TuiAtua. She had a son, *Tupuivao,* who was disinherited from the crowns and was banished to the Island of Tutuila. TuiA'ana TuiAtua *Taufau* bestowed the two crowns, TuiA'ana and TuiAtua, on *Faumuinā*, her nephew, the son of her sister *Sina*. Then *Faumuinā* became the TuiA'ana and TuiAtua, while, in parallel, the Malietoa monarch had the other two Crowns—Gatoa'itele and Vaetamasoāali'i.

The First Civil War

Breaking the Tafa'ifa

The Malietoa clan decided to take the Gatoa'itele and Vaetamasoāali'i titles back. This caused the Tafa'ifa to break. However, *Salamasina* remained Queen of Samoa with two titles: TuiA'ana and TuiAtua. This is why only those two titles were inherited by her daughter *Fofoaivao'ese.*

Fofoaivao'ese married *Tauatamainiulaita* from Palauli and the Tonumaipe'a clan. They begat Queen *Taufau* and her sister *Sina*. *Sina* married *Titoiaivao* and begat *Faumuinā*.[lxvi]

We should remember, this is not the first *Faumuinā* (see The Other *Faumuinā*, page 135).

Fofoaivao'ese and *Tauiliili i Papa*

After *Salamasina,* the Royal Crown continued to *Fofoaivao'ese* (daughter of *Salamasina* and her lover). *Fofoaivao'ese* had two daughters, *Taufau* and *Sina*. Her oldest daughter *Taufau* received the titles TuiAtua and TuiA'ana, and she became TuiAtua TuiA'ana *Taufau*. She married *Tauiliili i Papa* of the SaMuliaga clan.

They begat *Tupuivao*, but he was disinherited from the crown.

Children of *Tauiliili i Papa*

Tauiliili i Papa, was the son of *LeAumoana* and *Fuiailelagi* (daughter of *Salima i Papa*) and the great-grandson of La'ulu *Nofovaleane* of SaMuliaga. He had three other sons (besides *Tupuivao*) who were known to have learned how to walk and swim by crawling or floating (*fa'atafetafega*) on the waterfall river rocks at Papaigalagala at Letogo village, Upolu (*tama o fa'atafetafega i vai Papaigalagala*). They were well-cared for by having them crawl on the flat slab of the river rocks at the waterfall in the back yard of Fagali'i village in Vaimauga district, Upolu. The story is told of maternal pride in caring for young boys by exercising them, through crawling and surfing up and down the waterfall on the smooth flat rocks of the river at Vaipapa—*O tama na fa'atafetafe* (floating) *i Vaipapa*, meaning the sons (or princes) that were taught swimming by sliding up and down the slippery rocks of the river at Vaipapa (the name of a small property behind Fagali'i village, in Upolu)—*my translation*; hence the name, *Tauiliili i Papa*.[lxvii]

This story is different from the story of the baby grandsons of La'ulu *Nofovaleane* as these children were already crawling—*fa'atafetafega*—see The Story of La'ulu *Nofovaleane*, page 191—but we should note, *Tauiliili i Papa* is the great-grandson of La'ulu *Nofovaleane,* since he is the son of *LeAumoana,* whose second marriage was to *Tapusalaia,* sister of *Asomua.*

These three sons were:

- *Tupuivao*, whose mother was TuiA'ana TuiAtua *Taufau* (Tafa'ifa *Salamasina's* granddaughter). He turned out to be very cruel and was later banished to Tutuila. Also, he was disinherited from his mother's crown titles. Queen *Taufau* said her future kingdom floated away on the tide of the receding ocean—*Ua tafea* (floated or swept away) *le utu* (the right of succession to royalty[lxviii]) *a Taufau*. The etymology of *utu* is from the fisherman's bamboo receptacle for holding fishhooks, whale teeth, octopus rock bait, etc., used here as a metaphor for inheritance heirlooms—*my translation*.

- *Toilolo*, whose mother was *Sualupe*, the princess of the LeSaena clan of Tuna'i—her mother was *Mualeoā So'oialo*. *Toilolo* was falsely accused by his brother *Tupuivao* of having an affair with his wife *Iliganoa Taulalo'ese*. Thus *Tupuivao* banished *Toilolo* to Tutuila. On his way to Tutuila, *Toilolo* stood on board his vessel and looked back to *Tupuivao* and said, "Today is my day (meaning my punishment); tomorrow will be yours." This became a Samoan proverb, and it came to fruition: *O o'u i le asō a oe a taeao*, meaning "Today, my turn, tomorrow your turn," or "I'm punished today; tomorrow will be your turn"—or elliptically, *O oe le asō a a'u a taeao*, meaning "You're on today; tomorrow's my turn," or "You triumph today, and I tomorrow." The Orator Chief chooses which version fits the message.
- *Vaovasa*, whose mother was *Na'ūimamaia*, daughter of *Segi* of Amoa, Savai'i. *Vaovasa's* lineage would snake through and connect with *Tuiavi'i*, son of TuiToga (living in Faleata), who married Letele *Talaeia*, daughter of *Mata'afa* of Faleata. They produced *Taua'aleto'a* and a daughter, *Unusialeto'a*.

Taua'aleto'a's lineage produced the Tauiliili of Amile TuiAtua clan—i.e. *Tago*, *Taua'a*, *Tupuola*, and *Pafuti*—their Sa'o Tama'ita'i, etc. *Unusialeto'a,* the sister of *Taua'aleto'a,* married *Togia* of Sagafili and bore *Tautalaimoega*. She married *Ugapō* and bore a daughter *Alolenei*. *Alolenei* married *Vaovasa* (son of *Tauiliili i Papa* above), giving birth to *Talaleomalie*, who became the wife of TuiA'ana TuiAtua *Faumuinā* (see *Faumuinā*, page 212) and bore *Fonotī*. This is the lineage that orchestrated the taking of the Mata'afa title from Faleata to the Atua district. So, as one can see, in *Unusialeto'a* the female lineage, combined with *Faumuinā* (a name that originated in Faleata) connecting with *Talaleomalie* and begetting *Fonotī*.

When *Fonotī* became Tafa'ifa, he further integrated the Mata'afa title into the TuiAtua clan genealogy, which justified Mata'afa *Fa'asuamaleui's* claim to the Tupua and TuiAtua titles in Period VII when Christianity was arriving in Samoa.

It should be pointed out that Prince *Vaovasa's* genealogy would eventually establish connections also with that of Paramount Chief

Mata'afa of Faleata district, which explains the reason for the Mata'afa title being located and bestowed by Atua district—this is something I feel compelled to outline here:

For *Vaovasa* married *Alolenei,* daughter of High Chief *Ugapõ* and Lady *Tautalaimoega* of Falealupo, Savai'i. *Tautalaimoega's* mother was *Unusialeto'a*, granddaughter of *Mata'afa* from his daughter Letele *Talaeia* of Faleata (around A.D.1560). *Unusialeto'a's* older brother *Taua'aleto'a,* also known as *Taua'a*, (grandson of *Mata'afa*) became the founder of the prestigious Atua family clan Tauiliili, with his grandchildren including *Tago*, *Tupuola*, Lady *Pafuti*, and, in later generations, *Tauiliili*, Lady *Suluo'o*, *Leilua*, *Ilimatogafau*, and *Tuimavave*. This *Tuimavave* (1740-70) married *Salaina'aloa*, daughter of Prince *Luafalemana*, who was the son of Tafa'ifa *Tupua Fuiavailili* and brother to *Galumalemana*—*Galumalemana* succeeded his father, *Tupua Fuiavailili*.

Tuimavave's marriage to *Salaina'aloa* bore *Fa'asuamaleui* on whom were bestowed the Mata'afa and TuiAtua titles. He fought to prove that he was legitimately a descendant of Queen *Taufau*, first through the Samoan Court in a case eventually settled by the Berlin Act and outside judges. Hence, he is the prince of the SaLeValasi royal family clan. His great-grandson, Mata'afa *Iosefo* was elected to Head of State in 1898, with the TuiAtua and TuiAana Pāpā titles bestowed on him. The Gatoa'itele and Vaetamasoāali'i Pāpā were not bestowed, thus he was not a Tafa'ifa. But his genealogy is connected to the Malietoa family clan, thus he was also referred to as Malietoa.

The *Taua'aleto'a* genealogy would produce *Mata'utia-tu-i-le-to'a* or *Mata'utia-le-to'a* ("standing on the cliff") who married *Autā* of Lufilufi, giving birth to *Mata'utia* and *Magele*. These two chief titles as well as Fonotī and SaLeValasi, are titles in the village of Iva, Savai'i, where a branch of the SaMuliaga clan domiciled.

With this family constellation we have identified genealogical connections with the SaMuliaga, TuiAtua, TuiA'ana, Mata'afa, Taua'a, SaTago, SaTupuola, SaTupua, SaLeValasi SaMalietoa, and, finally, TuiToga *Tuiavi'i*, living at Toamua, Faleata, Upolu, that all started with *Tuiavi'i*'s marriage to LeTele *Talaeia*, Mata'afa's daughter. This family web or network, as we see, comes in handy when a call for war assistance arrives.

Taufau

When Queen *Taufau* was ill in old age, and her health was waning, she desired to decree the throne and titles to her son, *Tupuivao*. Unfortunately, *Tupuivao* turned out to be mean-spirited son who believed in and practiced cannibalism as a way to put fear into the people of Upolu.

Queen *Taufau* sent her servant *Atamaiali'i* to fetch *Tupuivao*, so they could discuss the affairs of the kingdom and her last wishes. However, *Tupuivao* did not want anything to do with her and couldn't care less about her death and her kingdom. So Queen *Taufau* sent word again, and *Tupuivao*'s response to the servant was, "Tell my mother, please, not to interrupt my pigeon-catching contest." Again the queen sent *Atamaiali'i* to tell her son that she was dying and that she wanted to see him. But *Tupuivao* said to the servant, "Tell my mother that I have crossed to the other side of the island to follow the pigeon flock; please don't worry about me." *Tupuivao* didn't want the crowns. He'd rather indulge in his hobby of pigeon-catching—*seu lupe*.

So Queen *Taufau* sent word to her sister, *Sina*, to bring her son, *Faumuinā*. *Faumuinā,* as directed by his mother, *Sina,* went to visit the queen on her deathbed. Queen *Taufau* received *Faumuinā* and decreed that he would inherit the TuiAtua and TuiA'ana thrones and kingdom, and he should "not be afraid of the that rude boy catching pigeons in Upolu."

Queen *Taufau* decreed that *Faumuinā* should succeed her and inherit everything she had for *Tupuivao*, and that *Tupuivao's* genealogy should be banished forever. It is from this story that the Samoan proverb is derived: *Ua tafea le utu a Taufau* meaning "his inheritance has been floating away at sea."

Pigeon-Snaring

There are several legends involving this recreational activity of pigeon-snaring, an exclusive chieftain sport.

We saw that Prince *Tupuivao's* desired priority was to the game, so that he chose to forego his earmarked inheritance of the kingdom from his mother TuiA'ana TuiAtua *Taufau*, granddaughter of Tafa'ifa *Salamasina*.

Also, the well-known champion *Lefaoseu* (who also became TuiAtua) of the Atua district, in Upolu, is said to have defeated all his contemporaries in Upolu and Savai'i until he met the end of his life from his angry contemporary *Ulumu* in Neiafu, Savai'i, according to the Savai'i version of the legend. Eventually, his murder was avenged by warriors from his Atua district.

Malietoa *Toatuilaepa* received his ava cup name, *Seufagafaga,* and his cup bearer or valet's name, *Taumasina,* from pigeon-snaring contests at Ti'avea, Uafato, and Fagaloa villages in the Atua district of Upolu. He also acquired his servants from the same contest and later bestowed them, as orator chief titles, at his residency and seat of government in Malie, Upolu.

TuiManu'a is also known to have been a prolific gamer of pigeon-snaring throughout the archipelago. And many paramount chiefs were participants in this exclusive form of recreational activity. A few paramount chiefs' names were derived from the sport, such as *Seumanutafa* of the Vaimauga district, Upolu, *Seumanufanai* of the Palauli district, Savai'i, *Seumanufilia* of Salelologa district, Savai'i, and *Manua'ifua* of Afega village.

The sport's contributions in the cultural norms and language are equally important. Many new words, proverbs, and metaphors helped enrich the language. For example: The practice of calling out a sound mimicking the pigeon sound, much like a western duck-hunter mimicking the sound of a duck to entice them, leads to the pigeon sound *ae'ae',* which means a bird has entered the cage in the hut—thus *Ae'ae' le manu ua ulu*. Orators would use this proverb, in an oratory introduction, to proclaim the founding of a new morning and day earmarked for the occasion. Another proverbial saying is to call out (announce) the "first catch prize" as in *ua fa'ailo le Lupe Mua*, which is often used, together with the *ae'ae' le manu* proverb to welcome or capture the new day and the occasion, metaphorically, in oratory. Games and recreational activities are sources of cultural norms and practices as well as of language enhancement.

So, the Samoan pigeon-snaring or pigeon-catching contest is a sport practiced by paramount chiefs. It requires young men of resources to support participation in the sport. The preparation for the contest requires building pyramidal rock-mound structures, in the middle of the forest, where plenty of the type of trees that produce fruits desired by pigeons can be found. The contrivance often includes a noose for entangling the birds.

Samoans uses a small net with a narrow opening, affixed to the end of a rod of about twelve feet in length. The chief who holds this is concealed in a small cabin, about five feet high, built with freshly cut branches and leaves for camouflage. On the outside there is a trained or domesticated pigeon, tied by the leg. And near at hand stands an attendant with another trained bird, tied in like manner to the end of a very long line. This bird is suffered to fly out to the string's whole extent while the other end is held by the participant. This bird is allowed to fly around over the mound as though it were a wild pigeon.

With the constant cooing of the support staff, disguised below the various areas of the mounds, a number of wild pigeons are attracted to the neighborhood. When the sportsman calls the trained pigeon, held by his hand, to come and perch on his hand, this attracts the wild pigeons to follow. Thus they are caught. Once caught, a prize is called out to record the catch. There are many prize categories for the contest: for example the first to catch, and, of course, the most catches.

Building the mounds requires many young men to carry rocks and boulders for the foundation levels. The mounds are built upward like pyramids, with a flat landing-space on top. A mound can be 30 to 40 feet tall, and 40 times 30 feet at the base. The apparatus required for the sport is possession of trained birds and the assistance of a few young men to carry out the hard work. It takes time to prepare for a contest and the contest location could move as the flock moves to another place.

The oral history of this elite sport recalls legends from when the first trained tropical parrot (*sega*) was stolen by *Taeotagaloa* and *Lefanoga* from the TuiFiti (see Stories of the Sons of *TagaloaUi*, page 106). It was desired by the Malietoafaigā, and thus the legend has it that *Lefanoga* (though some say it was *Saoluaga*) delivered it as gift to the Malietoafaigā. It appears this is the period when Samoans first took up the pigeon-snaring sport, though the sport of bird-training had long been practiced by Samoans and Manu'ans before the sport of pigeon-catching began.

Adoption

We have seen several adoptions in the stories to this point, and to fully understand the Royal Family genealogy, we must first understand adoption. Adoption is more than just a concept: it's a process that Samoans and Manu'ans employ to accomplish the following:

1. if there is no boy in the family then they must adopt a girl and vice versa in order to maintain a cultural belief that a boy must have a sister and a sister must have a brother; and
2. to continue the bloodline in both male and female lines.

This mirrors the difference between the maternal mitochondrial DNA line versus the paternal Y-chromosome line (as discussed in Book 1, *Navigators Quest for a Kingdom in Polynesia*). So adoption is a completely different structure in the Samoan culture.

For example, if a brother has no daughters, it is an obligation for his sister, who may have more than one daughter, to give one to her brother so that he may have a daughter and his sons may have a sister. The same process operates in the opposite direction. A brother must have a sister, and your two daughters must have a brother.

This is a very common practice with Samoans and Manu'ans, and there is a well-accepted standing for that adopted child in school, church, and society. They are treated, without exception or discrimination, by all family members, as a biological child. In the Samoan family culture, it is an anomaly for brothers to be without a sister and likewise sisters without a brother.

Where this practice becomes a challenge is when adoption is done with children outside the genealogical family tree. The inheritance to titles, land, and family heirlooms can be disrupted and bestowed to the non-biological heir. Some of the royal families have had heirs to the crown that were adopted sons, and, in fact, their bloodline carries the royal title till this day. For example: Malietoa *La'auli* is the adopted son of Malietoa *Uitualagi*, and, as we shall see, Tupua *Fuiavailili* is the adopted son of Tafa'ifa *Muagututi'a*.

We should also remember, Tafa'ifa is a Samoan word equivalent to the English word king, for the Samoan language does not have a true word translating the title *King.* "King" was introduced in the scriptures when the Bible was translated into the Samoan Language.

The story of the adoption of Tupua *Fuiavailili* by Tafa'ifa *Muagututi'a* starts with the first *Tafa'ifa* and also the only female that has held this title in the history of Samoa—*Salamasina* and her genealogy.

Faumuinā

So, *Taufau* passed on, and *Faumuinā* became king and obtained the TuiAtua and TuiA'ana titles. He married three times.

Faumuinā's first marriage, to *Talaleomalie* (meaning "an eloquent tale"), daughter of Prince *Vaovasa* (see Children of *Tauiliili i Papa*, page 205), gave birth to prince *Fonotī*. Her father *Vaovasa* was the son of Paramount Chief *Tauiliili i Papa* of the prestigious and mighty SaMuliaga clan, one of the three young princes (*Tupuivao*, *Vaovasa* and *Toilolo*) who learned how to walk and swim by crawling or floating (*fa'atafetafega*) on the waterfall river rocks at Papaigalagala at Letogo village, Upolu.

It should be pointed out that Prince *Vaovasa's* genealogy connects with the TuiAtua TuiA'ana in Savai'i through his brother Prince *Tupuivao,* whose mother was Queen *Taufau* (see *Taufau*, page 208). Also, (as we saw in Children of *Tauiliili i Papa*, page 205) his genealogy would eventually establish connections with that of Paramount Chief Mata'afa of Faleata district, which explains the reason for the Mata'afa title being located and bestowed by Atua district.

Faumuinā later married *Tu'ua-ma-le-ulua'i-ali'i*, a daughter of Paramount Chief *Manu'aifua,* son of *Saena* of Tuana'i village and descendant of the Malietoa Sagagaimuli family clan in the village of Afega. They begat a girl named *Samalaulu*. (*Samalaulu's* mother was from my village).

Faumuinā's third marriage was to *Atamulau*, daughter of Orator Chief *Segi* of Amoa, and they begat a son, *Va'afusuaga*.

The monarch Paramount Chief *Faumuinā's* reign was marked with peace and harmony across the island's major families and respective district territories. However, the two brothers, *Va'afusuaga* and *Fonotī* were brewing a rivalry for the monarch title, even before their father *Faumuinā* passed. Although the sister, Princess *Samalaulu*, stayed neutral, she nevertheless was inclined to be sympathetic toward *Va'afusuaga*.

The fact that these children had different mothers was a typical source of this kind of sibling rivalry, especially for boys vying for the inheritance of the paramount title.

So, *Faumuinā's* first son was *Va'afusuaga*; his second son was *Fonotī*; and the third child was the girl named *Samalaulu*. And these children caused the country to go into a civil war after the death of their father—the first civil war of Samoa.

The country was torn apart. Greed-induced ambition to inherit the crowns or throne led to competition and jealousy between the two brothers, with the sister favoring *Va'afusuaga*. War ignited at the end of the funeral, when *Fonotī* chose to keep for himself a state heirloom fine mat—this might be similar to refusing to give up a royal heirloom Persian Rug—rather than gifting it to his sister *Samalaulu* as was customary at a royal family funeral.

War parties were recruited from all four corners of Samoa, including Tutuila Island, and from all the respective family genealogies and distant connections, as well as from friends. The war divided families, villages, districts, and islands. It took its toll on the people and after three years *Fonotī* emerged victorious.[lxix]

Fonotī was victorious and inherited the four Paramount PāPā's. He became the second Tafa'ifa of Samoa.[lxx] He won all of Samoa, including parts of Manu'a which was partitioned out into different camps.

The second Tafa'ifa

Fonotī

As a result of his victory, *Fonotī* laid claim to the Tafa'ifa title. The country and Royal Houses agreed and subsequently bestowed the respective crowns—TuiA'ana, TuiAtua, Gatoa'itele, and Vaetamasoāali'i—onto *Fonotī*. He was now the second Tafa'ifa since *Salamasina* three generations ago.

The war resulted in several designations and appointments decreed by *Fonotī* or his sister *Samalaulu* to various warrior chiefs and warrior villages for bravery in fighting. For example,

Paramount Chief *Tanuvasa* was decreed over the other half of the District of TuiA'ana, and Paramount Chief *Alipia* was given the authority over all orators of the whole district of TuiA'ana.

Fonotī became the king, the Tafa'ifa, while his brother, *Va'afusuaga-Toleafoa,* was punished and ostracized to the island of Tutuila. This punishment angered one of the powerful families in Samoa at the time, and they went to Tutuila to bring him back on their own authority.

Va'afusuaga

The Samoan major family that is inextricably a part of Prince *Va'afusuaga* and his son *Toleafoaiolō's* extended family structure is the SaTunumafono of Safata village in the Tuamasaga district in Upolu. *Tunumafono* and his two sisters *Taulapuitaua* (who married TuiAtua *Letauā*) and *Lefe'eonu'u* (who married *Va'afusuaga-Toleafoa*) were the children of *Seuliali'i* of Puipa'a Faleata and *Tapuvaemamatu'u* of Safata. *Seuliali'i* was the son of TuiToga Tuiavi'i, or *Puipuiifatu*, and *Timuipaepaetele*, daughter of Paramount Orator Chief *Ale* or, some say, Orator *Ulu*. *Taulapuitaua* gave birth to a girl *Tete'etamaita'i*, who in turn married TuiAtua *Fotuitama'i*.

The SaTunumafono family clan is a major and powerful clan, also known as the Alataua (the main war-warrior party of Tuamasaga district) of the Malietoa dynasty and the royal Pāpā of Vaetamasoāali'i.

We have to go back to *Va'afusuaga's* mother and her genealogy to shed light on these family connections. Lady *Atamulau*, the daughter of Senior Orator Chief *Segi* of SaMuliaga, was a descendant of *Fuaoleto'elau* (half-brother to Malietoa *La'auli*, and the biological son of Malietoa *Uitualagi*). Specifically, *Asomua* and his sister *Tapusalaia* shared the same lineage of *Fuaoleto'elau*.

Tapusalaia (the princess of Paramount Chief *Asomua*) married a Togan high chief *LeAumoana* (the son of TuiToga and *Maupenei*, daughter of La'ulu *Nofovaleane* of SaMuliaga—see The Story of La'ulu *Nofovaleane*, page 191), who bore a girl *Maupenei*. Lady *Maupenei's* granddaughter *Sapioamoa* (whose father was from the Mano'o and Fiamē family clan of Samatau, in the A'ana district) married TuiToga *Tupoufei'a* and bore a boy, *Latulagi*, and his two sisters, *Latumailagi* and *Taleta*. *Latumailagi* married Orator Chief *Segi* of SaMuliaga of Amoa village and bore *Atamulau*.

Faumuinā married *Atamulau* (see *Faumuinā*, page 212), who bore *Va'afusuaga*. *Va'afusuaga* married *Lefe'eonu'u*, a daughter of *Seiuluali'i i Puipa'a* in Faleata, a major branch of the family SaTunumafono of Safata as described above. This marriage produced *Toleafoa-i-olō* or *Toleafoaiolō*. He married Princess *Taleta* of the SaTunumafono, a sister of his grandmother *Atamulau*. So the connections are seen here between SaMalietoa, SaMuliaga, TuiToga, SaTuiAtua (since *Tapusalaia's* mother was *A'atasilogogoa*, daughter of TuiAtua *Fotuitama'i*), SaTonumaipe'a, and SaTuiA'ana.

And so it is said, in the history of Samoa, that this is the only family so powerful that it single-handedly launched a war campaign to bring back their son, *Va'afusuaga-Toleafoa*, from his banishment in Tutuila (or the Island—*motu*—of Tapusalaia, *Le Motu o Tapusalaia*). It's also said that Tafa'ifa *Fonotī* was worried when he heard about SaTunumafono launching such a campaign to bring his defeated brother home, risking another war. And this further encouraged the Tafa'ifa *Fonotī* to find wisdom to achieve peace over his kingdom. This was so achieved, as evidenced in their decree at Sepolataemo and Lalogafu'afu'a.

How Fortunate the Hen

I recall the famous "sighing cry" of Paramount Elder Orator Chief *Alipia Tausimavaega* of Leulumoega, who accompanied Prince *Va'afusuaga-Toleafoa* in his ostracization from Upolu to Tutuila, after being defeated by his brother Paramount High Chief *Fonotī*. When Orator *Alipia* looked around, to see how many of Prince *Toleafoa's* faithful warriors had joined the trip to his banishment, he saw there were only a few of them, and so he sighed with relief: "Oh, how fortunate the hen that her chicks always follow her no matter where she goes"—*Amuia le tuāmoa e tau mulimuli uma iai lana toloa'i*.

This simple metaphor does not speak fully to the cruel reality of war, let alone a war against brothers, sisters, and extended family members such as this civil war had caused. The "agony of defeat" in war means losing a life or causing severe, often permanent, fractures in the structure of the family organization.

And for Paramount Orator Chief *Alipia* and the Leulumoega Council of Nine Paramount Chiefs (*Faleiva ma o lua Mātua na Ta'i, Ape ma Tutuila*) this was a serious, disunifying event in the history of the archipelago. We cannot mitigate the criticality of these extended families' differences, aligned by the brothers, *Fonotī* and *Va'afusuaga-Toleafoa,* as well as their sister *Samalaulu*. United by genealogical family connections, while the side of victory had their causes for celebrations, both the victorious and the defeated had lost something more important, had fractured the family structure that would take much longer to heal and mend. This became a source of family and village infighting and quarrelsomeness.

As history would tell, making peace between the brothers and sister was not easy or immediately done. It took the mighty family, SaTunumafono of Safata district, of the Tuamasaga district in Upolu, to forge the retrieval and return trip of their Prince *Va'afusuaga-Toleafoa* from Tutuila Island. This, of course, led to the peace decree between Tafa'ifa *Fonotī* and *Va'afusuaga-Toleafoa* and *Samalaulu*. But, as for Orator Chief *Alipia Tausimavaega* (to honor all the decrees), he lived up to honoring his duties as a Paramount Chief of the TuiA'ana monarch.

High Chief Orator *Alipia Tausimavaega* received many honorifics in this civil war, including his ava cup name, *'Aumai Tu'inofo-ua-lavā* or *Tu'inofoualavā*—which means "Bring Orator *Alipia's* Ava cup 'for your suffering you have endured no more.'" And the Princess name *Togitoto*—meaning "to pay the banishment in blood"—was decreed to *Alipia's* daughter.

Muagututi'a

Fonotī had a son, whose name was *Muagututi'a*. We should count six generations to this point, beginning with *Salamasina*, then *Fofoaivao'ese*, *Taufau*, *Faumuinā*, *Fonotī*, up to *Muagututi'a*. Six generations, running at about thirty years a generation, totals to almost 200 years.

Fonotī's son, *Muagututi'a* inherited the throne. But, we know, before his death *Fonotī* made amends with his brother over the civil war. So he bestowed the Tonumaipe'a crown on his brother *Va'afusuaga-Toleafoa* as his royal decree. *Fonotī* declared that the Tafa'ifa crowns would rest with his children.

Muagututi'a had three wives. One of his marriages was to *Fenunuivao,* daughter of Paramount Chief *Leutelelei'ite* of Falefā, Atua, and younger sister to Princess *Fenunuivao Sailau*, who had married *Tapumanaia*-III. They had a childless marriage.

Muagututi'a had several children from two of his marriages. Two of these were a boy, *Fepulea'i,* and his sister *Lagi*. But he had no children with *Fenunuivao*. So *Muagututi'a* asked his wife about the possibility of adoption (see Adoption, page 211). And Lady *Fenunuivao* was so elated and excited to hear they might find someone among their family relations that had a child they could adopt. Then she settled in and began to discuss the subject with her husband.

Muagututi'a said that the implications of this act would surely change the trajectory of history of the Island Nation of Samoa. Historians and oracles say that Tafa'ifa *Muagututi'a* remembered the deathbed edict of *Salamasina* (see Salamasina's Children, page 203) reminding her family and her kingmakers Tafa'i—*Fata* and *Maulolo* (of Gatoa'itele), *Umaga* and *Pasesē* (TuiA'ana), *Fuga* and *Mauava* (Vaetamasoāali'i), and *Tupa'i* and *Ta'inau* (TuiAtua)—to "Remember the boy that was stolen by *Talo* and *Ofoia, Tapumanaia LeSatele*." This boy was her son *Tapumanaia* who was stolen by Orators *Talo* and *Ofoia* and taken to Falealili (see Salamasina's Children). And this child was the second reason why *Salamasina* spent most of her time in Falealili; the first reason being, of course, that her mother, *LeValasi*, was alone at Lotofaga after her husband *Mata'utia Fa'atulou* passed away early in their marriage. For Queen *Salamasina* knew that the crowns needed to return to the rightful heir, the male genealogy—for the genealogy is carried by the female, but the crowns are carried by the male.

By now, *Tapumanaia LeSatele* had grown and multiplied his genealogy in Falealili. *Tapumanaia-LeSatele* had a son named *LeSatele*-II (generation #21). Then *Tapumanaia*-II (generation #22) married *Tatinitamaita'i* or *Tatini-tama'i-ta'i* and had a son, *Tapumanaia*-III*,* who married Lady *Fenunuivao Sailau* and had a son named *Sifuiva*. *Sifuiva*, in turn, had a son named *Fuimaono*, who married *Oilau*, and *Oilau* bore one son, whose name was *Tupuafuiavailili* (Tupua *Fuiavailili*). And *Muagututi'a* knew of this relationship.

Muagututi'a asked *Fenunuivao* if they could go over to her sister's family, to Paramount Chief *Fuimaono*, to ask about adopting his son, his only child Tupua *Fuiavailili*, because *Fuimaono* was the only son of *Sifuiva*, the only son of *Tapumanaia*-III and Lady *Fenunuivao Sailau*.

Like Tafa'ifa *Salamasina*, Tafa'ifa *Muagututi'a* was well aware of his responsibility to the family and culture. He knew all along that this might be the only chance for the female line to hand over the Tafa'ifa to the male *Tapumanaia*-II line. For the matriarchal culture is such that the male inherits the title, and the female keeps the family genealogy.

Muagututi'a now discussed the possibility of adoption from his sister-in-law. He said to *Fenunuivao*, "We don't have a son. What if we go to your relatives in Falealili, to your sister, and adopt a boy there to make our son?" He wanted to be the person to fulfill the dying wishes of his great-grandmother, Queen *Salamasina*. So he sent a messenger to *Fuimaono* and *Oilau* with the news that he wanted to adopt their one and only son. The couple understood why their son was requested and agreed to allow the king to have him.

A huge celebration was held in Falealili over the adoption of Tupua *Fuiavailili,* remembering "the boy that was stolen by *Talo* and *Ofoia*, *Tapumanaia LeSatele*." The young boy was taken to Lufilufi.

Sisters and Family Names

It appears *Fenunuivao* must have been much younger than her sister *Fenunuivao Sailau*. While this author couldn't confirm who her mother is, the Atua clan always refers to her as the daughter of *Leutelelei'ite*.

One of the challenges of Samoan genealogy is that all children of a close family—brothers, sisters, cousins, and uncles—can carry and claim the last name or family title. For example, in the SaMalietoa, all descendants from the first Malietoa *Sāveatuvaelua* to the last, Malietoa *Tanumafili*-II who died in 2008, are all referred to as being of the Malietoa genealogy or children of Malietoa. In my personal genealogy, my mother's great-grandfather, *Saena Poao Tagaloa*, is a descendant of Malietoa *Sagagaimuli* and *Sinalemanaui* (sister of the first and original Malietoa *Taulapapa*).

Unfortunately (see The Gatoa'itele Crown, page 175) Malietoa *Sagagaimuli* lost the war against *Gatoa'itele, Fata* and *Maulolo*, and the Tuisamau; thus his children were disinherited from the Malietoa title, and the Malietoa family clan bestowed it on *Taulapapa*, the brother in-law; his lineage is decreed to inherit the Malietoa title till today. The lineage of *Sinalemanaui*, Malietoa *Taulapapa's* sister, was decreed to carry the Gatoa'itele's genealogy through TuiA'ana *Tamālelagi's* daughter *Tuitogama'atoe*, their mother—Malietoa La'auli, Gatoa'itele, TuiA'ana *Tamālelagi, Tuitogama'atoe, Taulapapa* and *Sinalemanaui*. That's why her grandson *Saena Faigā* was decreed to go to be with *Gatoa'itele, Fata* and *Maulolo*, and the Tuisamau at her residence in Afega and Tuana'i. (*Saena Faigā's* father was also called *Taulapapa*, son of Malietoa *Sagagaimuli*, named after his uncle Malietoa *Taulapapa*; *Saena Faigā's* mother was *Faumuinā's* daughter *Letelesā*.)

Samoans are proud of their identity and their family names and titles. Thus this reinforces a sense of connectivity and cohesiveness in the clan.

Another Adopted Child

Fuimaono and *Oilau* were extremely humble and exceedingly excited when the Tafa'ifa *Muagututi'a* and Lady *Fenunuivao* came asking to adopt their only son Tupua *Fuiavailili*. This feeling of honor and humility overwhelmed them until late that night, when they retired to rest from the festivities and celebration. Then they came to the realization: what about *Fuimaono's* lineage? Who would carry that on to posterity?

They couldn't go to sleep all night, until about dawn when *Fuimaono* said to *Oilau*, "Go ask your brother *Te'o* to bring one of his sons, so we can adopt him to carry the *Fuimaono* family lineage."

Oilau was pleased about her husband's decision to asked *Te'o* for one of his sons. So she said, "I have to go in person to meet with my brother, the Paramount Warrior Chief of all of Atua district, at this period."

It is said *Te'o* single-handedly defeated the Malietoa troops, at the boundary between Atua and Tuamasaga on the southeast of Upolu. He not only captured it, but he moved the boundary in favor of Atua district. And Atua gave him a Salutation which is included in his title name: *Te'o, Na po ai le Nu'u*—Te'o that turned the village sun into darkness—*my translation*—for he is the one that the village went to, in the darkness during the battle that achieved victory.

Oilau was successful when she met with her brother *Te'o* because she knew she was *Te'o's Feagaiga* (the sacred covenant of brother and sister), which means no request from her would be denied by him.

Te'o said to *Oilau*, "Take the boy there, *Liulelagi*."

Thus *Fuimaono* decreed *Liulelagi* (or *Liulagi*) to the title Fuimaono—"the only one" or *Na'oia*—and he inherited the *Tupua ma le Aumaga*, a separate and complete title—leader of the Aumaga that prepares the ava ceremony of the Tafa'ifa. Fuimaono Na'oia is the complete title, but it is shortened to Fuimaono. However, one must remember the complete title and the meaning and origin of the word *Na'oia*.

The third Tafa'ifa

Salamasina's Heir

When *Muagututi'a* was on his death bed, he called all the paramount leaders of the country—*Tumua*, *Pule,* and *Tama Matua*—to Lufilufi. He laid out his will to them and decreed these things as his dying wishes. He stated to them, "You see the boy out there running around without a shirt. He will be the one to succeed me."

In confusion, the leaders replied to the king, "That is not your son. You have a son, *Fepulea'i*, and his sister *Lagi*. We don't understand."

Muagututi'a said, "My son *Fepulea'i* can tautua (serve) and *Tupua* will succeed me."

After this meeting, the leaders returned to the village. The orator chiefs were all somewhat perplexed. Naturally, they thought the king had early dementia or something. They didn't understand why the king would name an adopted son the successor, because this concerned the four titles: the Tafa'ifa. How was this happening?

The king began to hear their rumbling and complaining. The people were saying that he had grown senile. Why would he choose this adopted boy over his biological son?

Then the king realized that Paramount Orator *Tumua* had totally missed the point of his decision. *Tumua* thought the old man was not being logical here. So the king called him and the other chiefs to him, saying, "*Tumua*, I heard that you folks are having a problem with my decision." He continued, "Let me explain to you the family of this boy."

So the old man explained. He broke down this boy's genealogy. "This boy descends from *Tapumanaia*. *Tapumanaia* was the son of *Salamasina* that was stolen by *Talo* and *Ofoia* at birth. He was taken because *Falealili* didn't have a high title. They didn't have a high chief. So they conspired to steal one from the king. They took care of the boy and beautifully renamed him, *Tapumanaia LeSatele*. Then he bore *Tapumanaia LeSatele le lua*. He bore *Sifuiva*. *Sifuiva* became father to *Fuimaono*. *Fuimaono* married *Oilau*, sister of *Te'o*. And now, the only son of *Fuimaono* and *Oilau* is *Tupua*, the boy I adopted."

The leaders were shocked! They stood in awe in their newfound understanding of who this boy really was, for it was now no wonder the king requested this boy to succeed him. In awe, the orator said, *'Oi ta fefe, o le tama o aiga le tama*, or, *e to'atele le aiga o le tama, ua so'o Samoa o le aiga, tama o aiga*—That is the first time that the word *tama-o-aiga* was ever coined. That is our Tupua today, from the beginning until now.

This was the first time these words had been said, *O le tama o Aiga*, meaning, "the son of royalty." Samoan coins carry a most famous quote from this ordeal. *Ole tama o aiga*.

The salutation *Aiga ma latou tama, tama ma latou aiga* means, "The family and their prince, the prince with his family."

When *Muagututi'a* died, *Tupuafuiavailili* became his successor. He was now the Tafa'ifa.[lxxi]

Tafa'ifa *Muagututi'a*'s Decree

When this boy *Tupuafuiavailili* became king, special royal fine mats were given out, following a very famous decree in the history of the Royal House of SaTupua. For Tafa'ifa *Muagututi'a* educated the orator chiefs about how extensive Tupua's royal family genealogy is, and this event shows the way Tafa'ifa *Muagututi'a* explained the Tupua *Fuiavailili* family connections and genealogy. This is also the first time the prestigious title *TamaAiga* appears for the royal prince of the royal families of Samoa and Manu'a. (In Hawaiian the same word is spelled *Kamaaiga*.)

The orator chiefs, and their respective fine mat gifts, evidenced their family connections to Prince Tupua *Fuiavailili*. And the place Falenu'utupu is where the paramount talking chief of the Sa'ofaigā i Lufilufi and Paramount Talking Chief *Manuõ* had to open and gift the heirloom fine mat for the boy prince. For they were the aiga.

Today, if you go to Vainiu, which is a village in Fagaloa, Paramount Chief *Molio'o* has to open and gift his heirloom royal fine mat because of this prince. In Vaie'e and Falefā, Paramount Orator *Iuli* has to open his royal fine mats. And if you go to Vaiiliili, which is a residence of Paramount Royal Chief *Leutele*, then Paramount Talking Chief *Moeonoono* has to open and gift his royal fine mats.

Again, if we go to Salani, in Falealili, a famous orator has to open and gift his royal fine mat—his name is *Ofoia*. Then, after Salani, comes Falefasa, which is another sacred ground and residence, where another orator, named *Taloolema'anao* (*Taloolema'agao* or *Talooma'anao*) or, in short, Orator Chief *Talo*, opens and gifts his royal fine mat. We should remember (see The Children of *Va'afa'i*, page 161) Orator Chief *Talo* is a descendant of *Ise*, son of the illustrious *Manusamoa*, Warrior of Falealili, and his wife *Taua-nu'u-faigā* (war-village-the cruel) daughter of *Va'afa'i* of Tuna'i. (*Tauanu'ufaigā* is a namesake of a cruel, demonic paramount chief ancestor—generation #14—of this *Va'afa'i*—generation #17—in the village of Tuana'i, in the same way as *Letelesā*, daughter of Faumuinā of Faleata, Upolu, is a namesake of the ancient matriarch, *LeTelesā*.)

After that comes Faletoi, where Talking Chief *Fa'autania* will open and gift his royal fine mats. And from there, it goes on to Savai'i, Puleono. And from there to Leulumoega, Tumua, with Alipia, Ape and Tutuila heirloom fine mats to be gifted. From there it comes to us in Afega, Laumua, and the Fata and Maulolo heirloom mats are gifted. And now you have completed the round of all the Royal Houses of Samoa.[lxxii]

It is important to remember that Tafa'ifa *Salamasina's* genealogy stems from all the known royal kingdoms and monarchies of Polynesia, i.e. from TuiManu'a, TuiTele, TuiAtua, TuiA'ana, TuiSamoa, TuiToga, TuiFiti, Malietoa, TuiUēa, SaTonumaipe'a, SaLilomaiava, SaTagaloa, SaMuliaga, etc. Thus, Tafa'ifa *Muagututi'a's* educational narrative, about the distribution of heirloom fine mats, serves to remind the orator chiefs of *Salamasina's* royal genealogy. To commit this to memory is equivalent to memorizing *Salamasina's* extended genealogy. And, almost always, someone is going to ask about it.

The Story of the Warriors *Lutu* and *Unutoa*

TuiAtua Genealogy

The Paramount Chiefs *Lutu* and *Unutoa*, of Aua and Fagatogo/Utulei Village, have titles and salutations that only a few chiefs share. The title Sa'o Usoali'i is a combination of the title *Sa'o* (Head Chief) and *Usoali'i* (Fraternal Brothers). That means they are Sa'o of their respective village family clans, and they are also Fraternal Brothers to other high chiefs in the district of Fagaloa. To put it another way, they are Fraternal Brothers to the Paramount Elder and First Ma'oupū Chief Mauga (see *Mauga*, page 66 in the Period VII timelines).

This means that, in the seating arrangement of the district of Fagaloa Bay, First Ma'oupū Mauga assumes the *Sa'o* post on the right side of the Maota (the paramount chief's house) and *Lutu* and *Unutoa* would sit directly across on the left side posts of the Maota.

These two High Warrior Chiefs, *Lutu* and *Unutoa* (originally called *Solosolo*) are originally from the Falealili district of Upolu Island. They are descendants of the prodigious Tolufale genealogy, the third son of *Pili* and *Sinaaletava'e* (see TuiAtua, page 10 in Period II of the timelines). Their father was *Mata'utiamoelala* of Falealili village, and their mother was *Alaifea*, daughter of the first *LeSatele* or *Tapumanaia*-II (son of Tafa'ifa *Salamasina*—see Salamasina, page 52 in Period VI of the timelines). So their uncle was *LeSatele* (*Tapumanaia*-II).

Lutu and *Solosolo* had a sister named *Alapataume* who married *Alaimoana*, a high chief from Toga Island. They are the ancestors of the prestigious High Chief *Fanene,* whose children include *Te'onapõailenu'u*, *Oilau* (mother of Tafa'ifa Tupua *Fuiavailili,* see Period VI: TuiA'ana *Tamālelagi* and the Tafa'ifa, page 48 in the Timelines), daughters *Avaialiso*, *Taetele*, a son *Tuatagaloa*, and daughters *Meleiseā* and *Leilua*. *Leilua* married TuiManu'a.[lxxiii]

The Story of Paramount Chief *Fanene*

Since we've mentioned the Paramount Chief *Fanene* and his illustrious children, we should add the fact that Lady *Tofono* was the mother of *Fanene*, and we should include his *Alo o Fanene* Salutation as the grandson of *Lutu* and *Solosolo's* sister, *Alapataume*.

Legend has it that *Fanene* was known for his cruelty, and the village of Falealili ostracized him to Tutuila. The title Fanene, in Falealili, was then carried by his cousin *Alaimoana-ia-Titõ,* who married *Poto Sinaaletava'e*, the daughter of Prince *Afoafouvale*, who was himself also banished to Tutuila after being defeated by his younger brother *Galumalemana*. And so *Alaimoana-ia-Titõ Fanene* adopted his wife's only brother, named *Simanu Afoa*, and he was also given the Fanene title.

Concerning the other *Fanene*, the original *Fanene* who was ostracized to Tutuila, he landed in the village of Nu'uuli and was met by the Paramount Chief *Mageafaigā*. And *Mageafaigā* directed and decreed him to occupy the west part of Nu'uuli village, toward the mountains, where the LDS Church is located today.

Thus, this Fanene title is foundational in the Nu'uuli and Fagaloa Bay district's organizational structure. So if you get the sense that this part of Tutuila is homeland to the clans from Falealili, Atua, Upolu, this should shed light on the origin of their migration to Tutuila.

Warriors

The Warriors are an integral authority to the "House of War," *Fale o Alataua* at Sapunaoa, in Falealili, Atua. The two warriors *Lutu* and *Solosolo* were brought over to Tutuila to slay the demonic cruel warrior named *Tuife'ai* (meaning Tui the cannibal) who was causing havoc on the island of Tutuila. Local legend says he was really TuiSamoa from Falealili. The warriors *Lutu* and *Solosolo* came to Fagaloa Bay and pursued *Tuife'ai* until he was defeated, and his head was severed, as was customary in primitive warfare. The head was given to *Solosolo* to take with him to the other side of the Bay (to Aua), and he was decreed to live opposite from the Utulei and Fagatogo properties where *Lutu* would reside. It is on this occasion that *Solosolo's* name was changed to *Unutoa* (*O lau ulu na ma lou toa* meaning there's the head and you, warrior—*my translation*).

The genealogy below is the Tutuila version, after the two Paramount Warrior Chiefs settled in Fagaloa Bay district in Tutuila.

Tutuila Genealogy

TuiAtua *Mata'utia* was a paramount high chief from Atua, Upolu (Western Samoa). His genealogy extends from the first consolidated Tafa'ifa (queen of Samoa), named, as we have seen, *Salamasina*. At this point in time, Tutuila was under the reign of Atua, Upolu.

High Chief *Mata'utia* married a woman named *Fuatino* (of Tutuila) and begat sons named *Unutoa* and *Lutu* and a daughter named *Tulimalēfo'i*. (The high chief was training his domesticated pigeon to fly to his daughter's hand, but the pigeon decided not to fly back to the chief, hence the name *Tu-lima-lē-fo'i*, which means "stand on her hand without returning." This is now the princess name of Paramount High Chief Mauga of the Pago Pago village, Tutuila.)

Lutu married a woman named *La-fala-vave* from the village of Fagatogo. They begat children named *Lutu*-II and *Ma'ilo*. *Lutu*-II married *Utuutumatagi*, daughter of *Savea* from the village of Matu'u located next to Fagatogo. They begat two sons, *Leafi* and *Tuaaumafuamalu*.

Tuaaumafuamalu married *Sivaitafe* (daughter of High Chief *Asuega* from Pago Pago village), and begat two sons named *Asuega* and *Falafuti*. (This was a different Asuega from the father of Tuini—see *Mauga*, page 66 in Period VII—but they appear close in generations, showing the interconnections of *Lutu*, *Unutoa* and their sister *Tu* or *Tulimalēfo'i* with *Mauga* through the Elder Paramount Family *Asuega* of Pago Pago village.) High Chief *Asuega* married *Fa'auliuli* (daughter of *Fano* from the village of Fatumafuti) and they begat a daughter, *Talivale*. Then *Talivale* married *Unutoa* who was *Lutu's* brother five generations before.

So now *Lutu* and *Unutoa's* genealogies became conjoined. *Talivale* and *Unutoa* begat a son named *Tamaolepo*. *Tamaolepo* married *Polova'a* and begat a son also named *Lutu*. This *Lutu* married *Tulimalēfo'i* who was the princess of Mauga, and they begat a son named, again, *Lutu*.

This genealogy begins with a high chief title holder, Tupua *Mata'utia*, and then continues through intermarriage with other family title holders, such as the Asuega clan that extends from the Mauga clan in Pago Pago. So this very last *Lutu* had family extensions from *Mata'utia*, *Lutu*, *Fano*, *Mauga* and *Asuega*.

Lutu married *Fala*, daughter of *Afo*, who was a famous talking chief from Nu'uuli. *Afo* and his brother *Aego* were the paramount talking chiefs from the village of Nu'uuli. They had a sister named *Pulapulalagoto*. *Pulapulalagoto* married a chief from the village of Vatia, named *Suaese*. *Pulapulalagoto* and *Suaese* begat a son and gave him the chief title name *Lutu*. Then *Lutu* married *Mulimatagi*; they begat a son named *Lututatau*, who was alive during the early 1900s.

Lututatau married *Fa'atupuisasala* and begat sons named *Lutu*, *Sione,* and *Taeu'u*, an entire generation that was alive during the early 1900s.[lxxiv]

Conclusion

This completes the history of Samoa from when *Salamasina* established the Constitution of Samoa with the four titles. This is how these families continued to evolve. This Constitution continues to carry throughout Samoa today.

When Samoa decided to become independent, they chose Tupua, *Tamasese*, and Malietoa to be the joint heads of state. Mata'afa surrendered his royal status, and he became prime minister; that's how Samoa is today.[lxxv]

Period VII: The Arrival of Christianity

At this point we are getting ready to process how Christianity came into Samoa and Manu'a. But first we should understand what was happening in the world prior to this event. A history that is set in isolation is not always accurate, because of interpretation. We need to ask questions: Why did people behave this way? Why were the missionaries in a rush (for yes, they were—Rev. John Williams had already given himself the credit for taking Christianity to the Pacific prior to his arrival there; he was in a rush to achieve more)? Then, in asking and answering questions, we can start to make assumptions and change the way we will deliver the message.

When we dive into the way Christianity was carried to Samoa, then we can see why the Samoans wanted more. They wondered why the missionaries arrived to quickly drop information, then departed, leaving them with that desire for more. But the Europeans had turned the business of colonizing the world into a race across the globe. It was a race between existing religious denominations. The Spaniards brought a quick embrace of Catholicism, because Catholics were conquering with the sword or the word of God, whichever came first. The faith of Islam, from its beginning, had been one of conversion by the sword. And the other major religious sects, such as Hinduism, Buddhism, Jainism, Taoism, and Confucianism, all had their challenges in proselytizing the "heathens."

I believe that the Samoans were aware that this invasion was coming. Samoa, at this time, was not an isolated place. Other explorers had been through Samoa, before the missionaries arrived with Christianity. These people must have brought information about their world into Samoa, and that information must have resonated with the people they came into contact with. This may have been the very reason why Samoans knew that there were more people out there. These people would be different in appearance and in behavior. The tools and clothing they used would be different. But, most importantly of all, they would worship differently. So when the "Messenger of Peace" dropped anchor in Sapapali'i, they knew that this was coming.

And they were ready. For Samoa is the one place that has effectively woven the Word of God into its culture. I will continue to compare this to a woven tapestry where, on the flip side, you see the same design. The motto of the country of Independent Samoa is *Fa'avae i Le Atua Samoa*—Samoa's foundation (government) is upon God. And the people have enhanced family communication and relationships by conducting worship together as a family, reading the Bible texts, and having discussions about what they read.

First Missionaries in Polynesia

First Missionaries in Micronesia and Guam

In 1521, under Spanish rule, Ferdinand Magellan introduced Catholicism into the Philippine Archipelago and went on to Guam. So Catholicism, at that time, became the main religion in Micronesia.

First Missionaries in Tahiti and beyond

It wasn't until August 10, 1796, that Captain James Wilson set sail on the Duff for Tahiti with thirty missionaries on board. Not all of these stayed in Tahiti. Some were destined for Togatapu, the Togan Kingdom, and Cook Island.

Arriving March 5, 1797, at Matavai Bay, on the east coast of Tahiti, the passengers on board the Duff included thirteen men, six women, and three children. Eight of seventeen missionaries left on the next British ship to arrive in Tahiti.

These missionaries encountered much difficulty with the natives, due to lack of proficiency in the language and culture, and due to the natives' outright recalcitrance toward Christianity. For the native Tahitians did not initially warm up to the message of Christianity, because of their experiences with previous Europeans who had brought a lot of diseases to the island.

The credit for the establishment of the mission in Tahiti goes to Rev. Henry Nott (1774-1844). Rev. Nott was a bricklayer and LMS missionary who endured the difficulties of preaching

Christianity to the Tahitians.[lxxvi] He eventually mastered cultural acclimation and a proficiency in the native language, into which he began the Bible translation initiative that facilitated tremendously the evangelization of the natives. He gained a solid working relationship with King *Põmare*-II, and the king encouraged and assisted Rev. Nott in Bible translation efforts.

In 1817, Rev. John Williams and his wife, Mary Chawner Williams, established their first missionary post on the island of Raiatea, accompanied by Rev. William Ellis and his wife. Thirteen years later John Williams would drop anchor in Sapapali'i lagoon in Savai'i Island with the Message of Peace for the Samoan and Manu'an people.[lxxvii]

First Missionaries in Hawaii

Henry *'Õpūkaha'ia* (circa 1792-1818) volunteered as a ship's labor boy and ended up in New England in the USA. He received some education there. While in school on the East coast of the United States, he became one of the first native Hawaiians to become a Christian, thus inspiring American Protestant missionaries to come to the islands during 19th century.

Arriving around 1819-20 from New England, USA, they brought a message of peace and the Christian way of life. It was more than just their lifestyle that impressed the new King *Liholiho*, son of *Kamehameha,* and *Kamehameha's* widow *Ka'ahumanu*. When the young King *Liholiho* died, *Ka'ahumanu's* power and influence enabled her to abolish the old rules of discrimination against women and even the worship of traditional Hawaiian gods. *Ka'ahumanu* requested baptism, but Hiram Bingham withheld it, claiming she did not yet show the signs of genuine regeneration. Finally in 1825 she did receive baptism, taking the Christian name Elizabeth.

In the year 1819, before the arrival of Protestant (and, later, Catholic) missionaries to the island kingdom, a high chief *Ali'i, Kalanimoku,* prime minister of the kingdom and a loyal court officer to *Kamehameha*-I, on his own accord made the bold decision to become a Christian. That summer he was baptized into the Catholic faith. The event took place on the deck of a French military vessel, L'Uranie, under the command of Captain Louis de Freycinet, docked at Kawaihae Bay on the Big Island of Hawaii.[lxxviii]

The Mystery of Early Christianity in the Pacific

I don't want to misrepresent this matter of the arrival of missionaries in the whole of the Pacific Ocean region. In particular, I am baffled and curious as to why Micronesian seafaring travelers did not bring Catholicism down to Polynesia, given they had been exposed to it since 1521. For 300 years elapsed between when Captain Magellan introduced Catholicism to the Philippines and the Guamanians, and the arrival of Christianity in the East Pacific. And no mention is made of Catholicism spreading down to the East Pacific. I find this a conundrum, because the Micronesians were also known for their seafaring skills and for being formidable explorers.

The spread of stories and ideas is ubiquitous, and they are carried, as it were, by the wind. So I am suspicious that, perhaps, ideas based on (Catholic) religious theological beliefs might have spread down to Polynesia from Mainland Asia through the Philippines Archipelago and Micronesia. This spread of religious beliefs and philosophy might very well have influenced the Polynesian Navigators, given their physical location in between Western and Eastern Polynesia.

I made mention in *Navigators Quest for a Kingdom in Polynesia* (the first book of this series) of a Franciscan friar, John of Monte Corvino, who headed east, around A.D.1290-1294, as a representative of Pope Nicholas IV.[lxxix] John Corvino would be the first European and Christian to traverse the Malay Archipelago and the Indonesian Archipelago, up to the China Sea, in the modern era. He reached Khanbalik in A.D.1294 by traveling along the South China Sea and the Straits of Malacca through the Yellow River. This means Christian principles had been spreading in Southeast Asia since Islam first traversed the Silk Road back in A.D.700 and finally reached the Asiatic Archipelago in early A.D.1300.

The process of diffusion and the infusion of ideas is ubiquitous, and we cannot stonewall about it forever. So I am suspicious that the cognitive development of the Navigators must have been influenced by this diffusion and infusion of Christian ideas during their sojourn in the Fiji Archipelago for over 800 years.

The Impact of Christianity

The arrival of Christianity added a new paradigm shift to Samoan and Manu'an culture. It added new innovations in the language. And people had to look internally to find the meaning of faith, hope, resurrection, internal pain and suffering, internal happiness and fulfillment, philosophy, and psychology. Also, Christianity reaffirmed the importance of the orator function and methodology, since delivering the Christian message in the Bible uses the same methods of parallelism, examples, parables, metaphors etc.

The impact of Christianity on Samoan cultural norms, customs, and formalities made Samoan society more loving, peaceful, more hospitable, and more open-armed. At the same time, new words and profundity were added to the lexicon of the Samoan language, as a result of the translation of the Bible. And when we look at the difference between the Old Testament and New Testament, we see that the Old Testament is storytelling, and the New Testament is teaching and oratory, reaffirming the oral language. Language ties the culture into a cohesive and sustainably Christian way of life for Samoans.

But what is the difference between Samoan Christianity and Christianity in other cultures? Why were Samoans able to weave the Christian spirit and principles into the fabric of Samoan culture, so they became inextricably inseparable?

Documented History

Early missionaries, together with a few social scientists, were the savants who documented the history and language of Samoa and Manu'a, immediately after their arrival in A.D.1830. Much of their educated guesswork was, of course, based on the available body of science and general knowledge at the time, for conventional knowledge about Polynesian migration across the East Pacific Ocean was very limited and fragmented. So the current, written history of the Samoan and Manu'an kingdoms is based on their limited knowledge.

At that time, their guesstimated date for the origin of Samoan and Manu'an civilization was around A.D.1100-1200, as recorded by Dr. Krämer. That is about 2,500 years later than the estimated arrival of the Navigators' migration, which would be around 1500 B.C. Also, it should be noted that earlier migrations are now postulated to have arrived in the Fiji/Rotuma Archipelago in around 2000 B.C.—the Navigators would have sojourned there for over 800 years before settling the Manu'a Archipelago. These new dates are found due to ongoing excavation and subsequent re-dating (to around 2200 B.C.) of the early Lapita trading network in the Bismarck and Solomon Archipelagos.

My purpose in including the time periods in this writing is to reconcile the chronology of historical events and map them onto the arrival of the Navigators' migration. And, of course, to update the current history of the archipelago.

The Period of Enlightenment

The period from 1650 through the end of 1800 is commonly referred to as the "Period of Enlightenment." The world was looking outwardly to conquer or colonize the world. Expanding trade meant finding new markets for both imports and exports of new products and services from exotic lands and cultures.

While imperialism had an open agenda, proselytizing Christianity was a great "leading motive" of a well-orchestrated mission. Thus, to understand the background of the arrival of Christianity in Samoa, one must first understand what was going on in the rest of the world at that time. A tsunami wave was about to hit Samoa, and, too often, the Navigators of the Pacific had isolated themselves into their own little world and thus lost sight of the bigger world surrounding them.

1400s

During the 1400s, the "Age of the Renaissance" began in Europe. This began the Early Modern Age period that included art beyond iconic Christian art—paintings and sculptures of Christian subjects like the Virgin Mary, and other Biblical figures. Art now displayed emotions that had not been portrayed in art prior to this period. A lot of people may not realize that the new discovery here (in art) was architecture. Art did not credit the architects for their contribution to artwork though; credit was only given to the artist. For example, Brunelleschi built the dome in Florence, Italy, after coming up with the concept of looking at one point with multiple dimensions.

But one thousand years prior to this era, scientists such as Aristarchus of Samos, Heraclides Ponticus, and Philolaus, were already discovering the magnetic structure of the earth. There were many theoretical concepts that these men of science wanted to prove. One of their ideas was the early question of whether the earth is flat or round. Then Nicolaus Copernicus (1473-1543), the Royal Prussian native mathematician and astronomer, formulated a model of the universe that placed the sun rather than the (round) earth at the center of the universe. Copernicus' calculations led to many questions about what is truly out there.

At this same time, Christianity's efforts were being pushed outward in competition with other religions, in particular that of Islam. The Ottoman Empire was at its peak of growth. This sparked Christians to push their message out to the heathens in the far remote cultures of the world. In Portugal, the Portuguese were raising and collecting enough capital to build more ships to discover new lands out there; they reached West Africa and established a fort upon the coast.

1500s

In 1492, Christopher Columbus set out on his venture into the New World. The "Colonial Era" was just beginning, and it continued in the 1500s with the intensifying quest to conquer South America. The Spaniards conquered Puerto Rico, Jamaica, and Central America, moving on to South America. Meanwhile this tsunami of change was moving below China, crossing the Atlantic, moving into North America, and arriving here. All this was happening in this era of A.D.1500.

All these routes were pathways for European ships to move between various countries, imposing their own form of governments upon them. The Pacific Ocean current flowed from Asia, out into the Central and Northeast Pacific Ocean, passing California and heading all the way up to Alaska, providing set paths for navigation, and these routes of Pacific Ocean currents still exist today.

Oftentimes, the ship's captain would stray from those set paths and land on an island. They would use these opportunities to see what resources and provisions, such as food and water, they could gather from these islands. They would never actually document these places along the routes until finally, in 1568, a Spanish navigator, Álvaro de Mendaña, traveled down to the Philippines, went past Australia, and ended up in the Solomon Islands. He was credited with naming the Solomon Islands.

The Portuguese explorer, Jorge Álvares, was the first Jesuit to establish a mission in China, in 1513. The Jesuits were, and still are, a Catholic society. Their purpose was the propagation of the Catholic faith by any means possible, and they really were and are the foremost Catholic teachers.

1600s and 1700s

In the 1600s and 1700s, the focus of the Europeans was to Christianize the Asians. William Dampier sailed to the Northwest of Australia and New Guinea. He is the man said to have discovered Samoa and the Easter Islands. When he passed away, his journals were lost, but fifty years after his death, the journals of his first shipmate, Dutch scientist Jacob Roggeveen, were discovered. Through translating the journals of Roggeveen, it was concluded that Roggeveen, not Dampier, was the discoverer of Samoa.

Into the 1800s

The end of the 18th century ushered in a resurgence of the spread of the Word of God and Christianity to newly discovered nations and countries of the world. England was the epicenter of the movement to deliver the Message of God to the "heathen."

The extraordinary success of the British in subduing the whole of India and entrusting it to the East India Company, in 1757, marked the beginning of the imperial or colonial era in South Asia. The East India Company became the expansionary apparatus of the British Empire throughout the 19th century.

While the East India Company continued to colonize many countries in Southeast Asia—such as Java in 1811, Singapore in 1819, Malacca in 1824, and Burma in 1826—exploration of what "heathen" territories were still available was promoted through funding by the government, wealthy families, and large trading companies.

Captain Cook's voyage of exploration was funded in pursuit of validating the world map coordinates in areas where he landed, observing the transit of Venus across the face of the sun, and searching for a fabled "Great Southern Continent."

European Arrivals

Columbus

Image 3 Christopher Columbus, The_life_of_Christopher_Columbus.djvu: Roselly de Lorguesderivative work: Shooke (Talk me in Spanish, English or Italian), Public domain, via Wikimedia Commons

"And as soon as I arrived in the Indies, in the first island which I found, I took by force some of them in order that they might learn (Castilian) and give me information of what they had in those parts; it so worked out that they soon understood us, and we them, either by speech or signs, and they have been very serviceable. I still have them with me and they are still of the opinion that I come from the sky in spite of all the intercourse which they have had with me, and they were the first to announce this wherever I went and the others went running from house to house and to the neighboring towns with loud cries, Come! Come! Come! See the people from SKY!"

So said Columbus in his *Letter to the Sovereigns on His First Voyage*. 15 February-4 March 1493[lxxx]

Roggeveen

Image 4 Arent Roggeveen, father of Jacob Roggeveen Fitmoos, CC BY-SA 4.0 <https://creativecommons.org/licenses/by-sa/4.0>, via Wikimedia Commons

Many years after the discovery and translation of Roggeveen's journals, a gentleman by the name of Behrens quoted from them, describing chiefs, surrounded by men on the front and back, and making the interesting observation that the inhabitants were mostly white. "I hardly found any difference from us and our European nation except, one was a little redder and the other a little browner, tanned by the sun."[lxxxi] Similar observations of the natives were made by others among the earlier explores.

A small number of Europeans stayed on the island after being stranded; they made a personal decision to stay. And we should remember, in the late 1500s there were fleets of Spanish galleons delivering spices, using the routes from the Philippines all the way to the Americas—mainly to Mexico. I believe that some of those ships may have been stranded by the winds and ended up in the South Pacific, in Samoa; in fact, there are documented journals that cite Hawaii, because Hawaii was also on the route.

Roggeveen's journal goes on to describe the inhabitants as friendly in speech and prudent in behavior, seeming to be an honest people, adding that they were not painted as inhabitants of others he had seen.[lxxxii] "No savage in their nature" is the impression made on observers in 1722, almost 100 years before the arrival of Christianity.

The captain's diary continues, describing how the inhabitants clothed half their bodies in "skillfully prepared silk bast" (the thread of a bark tree) and long fringes. He was speaking of the siapo, tree-bark with native designs, and printed clothing materials. Their conduct on first meeting the seamen was pleasant, and they seemed pleased as if gods had arrived among them, then sad when they left.[lxxxiii]

Discoveries of people who actually came ashore on the island earlier than this period, in the dawn of the 1700s, are few to none. But the peaceful engagement here indicates, initially, the friendlier nature of Samoans as opposed to the reputation of Samoan cannibalism in ancient, primitive history. The respect and generosity of their nature and customs are evidenced in this early interaction with foreigners who, for obvious reasons, looked completely different from them.

Why do you think they would say that they (the Samoans) were thoroughly satisfied with us (the Europeans) as though gods had arrived among them?

Scientific Observation

Let's go back. "No savage nature," and "Nor were they painted..." The Samoans were not, in fact, painted; they were tattooed. The *pe'a* is the thing that might have been considered to be paint, and Samoans do tattoo their bodies.

Remember, these were not ordinary Europeans; these were scientists. When they were travelling, they had to be sanctioned by their country and given a group of ships. It wasn't just one ship that was built for the Dutch; many ships needed permission to come in. And these were men learning about the world. They had to be exact, because they knew that their work would be studied by others. The observation that we did *not* paint our bodies implied that we were not like other islanders in the Pacific.

Also, Samoans never worshiped idols, and the Europeans found this to be very advanced in our development. (The Samoans worshiped spirits.)

From all this we can conclude that, 100 years before Christianity, we weren't running around naked. Indeed, even during the time we were under the Togan yoke, we had clothes. The description of the *titi, na fai ma le lauti* was a description of the skirts or wraps made of tea leaves which were worn. So, perhaps, the question arises: at what point in time did we put these clothes on? Was it as a result of meeting Europeans? Clearly in the 1700s we were already observed to wear clothes. (Again, we should consider the source and the sources are very credible.)

Bougainville

Image 5 Louis Antoine de Bougainville
Konrad Westermayr, Public domain, via Wikimedia Commons

Bougainville, a French admiral and explorer, arrived forty-six years after Roggeveen. For many years he was credited with discovering Samoa. It wasn't until the discovery of Behrens' translated journals that people understood Bougainville was the wrong person to receive credit—a lot of early information on the South Pacific came from the journals of captains or sailors.

Bougainville sailed along Manu'a and made contact with the natives. As soon as the explorers were spotted by the natives, people came running out and even swimming out to sea to help them to shore. The travelers were amazed at how well the natives swam to sea—it is, of course, a prime example of how well the people could navigate the water.

Count Jean-François de Galaup

Image 6 Jean-François de Galaup
Engraving by D. K. Bonatti (d. 1819?) after a painting by Jean François Bosio (d. 1827), Public domain, via Wikimedia Commons

Then Count Jean François de Galaup and his crew were attacked, with many of them massacred in Asu. It has been discovered that a group from Falelatai that was visiting Asu caused a miscommunication, leading to the natives killing these men and officers.

This event occurred in 1787, so at this time we already had knowledge of the outside world. We knew that, beyond these horizons, there were people other than ourselves—of course, we already knew that because of our relationship with Toga and Fiji, but what we didn't know, at first, was that there were people of different colors, with different cultures. The Samoan psyche must have changed with the knowledge of these people.

Another major thing introduced to the Samoan people was the use of iron. Samoans must have observed iron, with the ships and weaponry that the Europeans brought with them. Such things were now being traded with them. They saw different materials that they could use for themselves.

Kidnap and Procreation

1802 is still thirty-one years before the arrival of Christianity. At this time there was an Englishman living in Tutuila. He had drifted from Toga to Tutuila three years before, and today we put his arrival between the years 1795 and 1796.

When he was offered a ride back to civilization, the Englishman declined. There wasn't any mention of him having children, but I suspect he may have many children in Tutuila.

The natives understood the concept of mating with new people coming in, to receive the infusion of new blood into their population. That underlines the genealogical structure that Samoans followed. New blood ensured they did not cross over with each other, because their bloodlines were too close. There had been many stories of relationships between close relatives causing catastrophe, such as the story of TuiAtua *Mata'utia* who married his cousin. Unfortunately, she suffered a miscarriage (see The Story of *LeValasi's* husband, *Fa'atulou*, page 171).

Samoans knew that, over time, relationships between close relatives were not good practice because the bloodlines were too close. So when later, in 1823, another voyager passed by Manu'a, he and his companion were kidnapped by the natives for procreation. And in 1824, an American voyager strayed from a ship called Marlo, that called into Pago Pago, Tutuila for provisions.

John Williams

In 1830, John Williams arrived in Sapapali'i, and Christianity was now in Samoa. So yes, we could have easily jumped straight to 1830, to study the arrival of Christianity. But I wanted to show that wind, that tsunami, that was coming to the Pacific before the arrival of Christianity.

Image 7 John Williams, Unknown author, Public Domain, via Wikimedia Commons

The Wind of Change and Peace

As odd as it may sound, it has been scientifically discovered that records in verbal language are much more accurate than those in written language. Here is the rationale: On the one hand, as you tell stories, you begin to embellish them to make them sound good. But on the other hand, you must remember that these are stories of people, their families, and their land—once these stories are told, to actual people, these people are the ones who would immediately correct you. Especially when you tell the stories of families that may be hearing your version for the first time. If they know you are not telling it correctly, they will stop and correct you. For you are talking about them and their family story.

Let us follow this story:

The wind of peace and love to all mankind began with a lovely breeze in a desert town, in area call the Levant, and it picked up momentum as it made its way, up the northwest land to Asia Minor, and began to split into two trajectories, one turning westward toward Europe, and one turning eastward, moving upward toward the mountain range of the Caucasus, the northern arm of the Silk Road. This trajectory then snaked through the Himalayan range, where "Himalay" means "the abode of snow" in Sanskrit. The eye or core of the wind gathered up speed and turned into a major storm as it moved across the European continent.

Likewise, the trajectory north-eastward and due east produced a wind that slowly, but steadily and unrelentingly, covered the Tibetan Plateau and the Mongolian-Manchurian flatland steppe like a canopy.

The wind of the message of peace was now a message of change—The Wind of Change. And because the Silk Road was a well-established and well-traveled trade route to Asia, it was now a wind tunnel, expediting the spread of the message of peace and love everlasting throughout every town and city on the trade route. The often-combined purposes of the caravan group—for trade activities and for the introduction of the wind of change through religion—created a culture and an approach. Depending on the situation, the method would be to sell people religion, subdue them to worship the new god, and then proceed to conquest and to trade.

We know, from history, that the spread of religion was not always received with open arms. In most cases the "Wind of Peace and Change" encountered fortified wind-blockers of violent resistance, which led to war and disastrous outcomes. The basic methodology—denouncing the old deities and accepting the new Christian God—was always the most challenging part of early missionary work.

The metaphorical wind now snaked through the Indus Valley and across the Mongolian and Manchurian steppe to greater China. It continued on to the east and down to Southeast Asia, into the Malay Archipelago, then finally on to the Pacific Islands. By the time the wind entered the massive Pacific Ocean, this was the last frontier to hear the message of peace and life everlasting.

This wind now created a tsunami that erupted in East Polynesia and swept through all the South Pacific Islands. Much knowledge and experience had been accumulated about the business of proselytizing the Word of God, over the past 1,830 years since the little desert breeze in Bethlehem that forever changed the demographics of the Levant and now of the whole world. Thus, the approach had been honed and came now in a "cookbook" form, when the wind arrived in Polynesia.

The London Missionary Society (LMS) had already been to Africa, India, China, and Southeast Asia, some 150 years before arriving in Samoa. Catholicism had been fully established throughout Central and South America since A.D.1530, when the Spaniards and Portuguese dropped anchor in the Americas, as well as in many parts of Africa and Southeast Asia. Lessons from these missionary works helped hone the "cookbook" of missions to the "heathens."

The Arrival of Christianity in Samoa

History of the Protestant Churches

In discussing Christianity and Samoa, I want to review Protestantism, in particular, because this is what we owe much to, in terms of bringing Christianity to Samoa. So I will give you a background on what was going on during this period, and on the quest to discover the other side of the world.

Martin Luther

Image 8 Martin Luther by Karl Bauer, Public domain, via Wikimedia Commons

In 1534, Martin Luther had now completed translating the Bible into German, and we should not over-simplify or minimize the major paradigm shift in theological philosophy which was brought about by his propositions—in particular that there is no mention in the Bible of payments for indulgences or the accumulation of indulgence credits for forgiveness of your sins at judgment day, either by God or by a priest—this had been a convenient way for the Roman Catholic church to raise money from the membership, particularly the poor people, by asking them to pay for indulgences. But the German-educated, upper-class theologian monk flipped the whole (Roman) Christian model upside-down, with more focus on the literal, written words of the Scriptures, showing that the path to the Kingdom of God is by faith and believing in the word of God. Hence the birth of Protestantism.

This new paradigm shift in religion pushed the already maturing Renaissance period into another paradigm in science and philosophy called the Age of Enlightenment. This was the wave that swept the Pacific Islands.

John Calvin

Image 9 John Calvin. Artist Unknown, but image appears in 1892 book by George Pierce Hays, published by J.A. Hill & Co., Public domain, via Wikimedia Commons

The first university of Sweden had opened. Henry VIII was getting a divorce, going against the Catholic Church—Henry refused to obey the Catholic Church and now got the Protestant Church to approve his divorce, so England now had two religions, Catholic and Protestant. And in 1536 John Calvin, an influential Protestant, published a prayer book in England that solidified the Protestant Church. Queen Mary (Henry's daughter) was the last monarch to practice the Catholic faith at the time. Elizabeth I was to inherit the throne, and Mary made Elizabeth promise that the Catholic faith would continue to be predominant in England.

Against Mary's wishes, Elizabeth I became a Protestant. And she was succeeded by King James I (who sponsored the translation of the Bible now known as the King James' version). Other problems between Catholic and Protestant leadership continued, but England remained Protestant.

John and Charles Wesley

Image 10 John_Wesley_1.jpg: John Faber (1695-1756)derivative work: SteveW, Public domain, via Wikimedia Commons

In the 1700s, Charles and John Wesley founded the Methodist Church at Oxford. All the church hymns were written by them and were later adopted by other Christian religious groups, including the LMS (London Missionary Society).

The LMS arrived in Tahiti and began to establish there in 1770. And the wave of European colonialism continued moving, eventually arriving in the South Pacific in 1797.

When we study how we in Samoa received Christianity, we must also study the forces outside of that. When Samoans started to work together with the missionaries, we started to understand the ways of the Europeans. We saw they were in a rush to colonize the world, whether by the sword of steel or the sword of the eloquence of the Word of God. And they used these two methods to justify each other.

Samoan government at the Arrival of Christianity

Just to recap the developments in Samoan government at the time: Paramount Chief *Tupua* became the Tafa'ifa, the king. His son *Galumalemana* succeeded him, continuing in accordance with the decree of Queen *Salamasina* not to forget the boy, *Tapumanaia le Satele*, who was stolen at birth and taken to Falealili (see the events listed under Period VI: TuiA'ana *Tamālelagi* and the Tafa'ifa, page 48 in the Timelines.)

We should remember, *Fonotī* had a son named *Muagututi'a* who adopted the boy named *Tupua* from the Tamālelagi genealogy (see *Muagututi'a*, page 216). *Tupua* had three sons; two of them were *Afoa* and *Galumalemana*. *Afoa* became the king, but his brother was loved by his people, so they went to war for the kingship. *Afoa* lost to his brother, and *Galumalemana* became the king. On his deathbed *Galumalemana* decreed that his unborn child was to succeed him, but instead, the older son, *Nofoasāefā,* took the throne by force in 1770.

Another paramount chief in Atua was Mata'afa *Fa'asuamaleui*. This was the period when the TuiAtua was taken by *Paitomaleifi*—names that are only three to four generations from the present day. These were the ancestors of my students' great-grandparents. The names were my students' family names and would have begun to sound familiar to them.

TuiA'ana *Nofoasāefā* heard that Mata'afa *Fa'asuamaleui* had wrested away the TuiAtua title from his cousin *Paitomaleifi*. So now, *Nofoasāefā* wanted to take the TuiAtua title from Mata'afa *Fa'asuamaleui*, and he succeeded. After losing to *Nofoasāefā*, Mata'afa *Fa'asuamaleui* was banished to Tutuila, where his salutation now resides in Tula village (in Tutuila, American Samoa). All his children and titles, including the Tupuola, were his gifts to American Samoa.

TuiAtua TuiA'ana *Nofoasāefā* passed away. The other sons of *Galumalemana—Tupolesava* and the son that was originally decreed to receive the title while yet unborn—were now deciding who would be next to inherit the throne. *Tupolesava,* along with a chief from Lufilufi, wanted to receive the Tafa'ifa. But the people of Atua rejected the notion of *Tupolesava* being king; they wanted

I'amafana, the son that the king had decreed to receive the title. So now these brothers went to war. *I'amafana* defeated his brother *Tupolesava* and became the king.

We should notice the timeframe here. It was now 30 years prior to the arrival of Christianity. The Europeans had already had some contact with Samoans. In 1772, Roggeveen had already landed in Tutuila. Samoans had seen these people and must have questioned them about their arrival on the island. Their curiosity may have led them to ask about European clothing, tools, and all the things they saw that were not ordinary to them.

King *I'amafana* decreed to Malietoa *Vaiinupõ* in 1820 that he should take over the throne after he passed on. The son of Mata'afa *Fa'asuamaleui* became the TuiAtua, after the death of *Nofoasāefā* and *I'amafana*. And he died in the war with Malietoa *Vaiinupõ*.

At the same time, another warrior king, *Lei'atauaLesā Tamafaigā*, also known as *Tamafaigā* (a descendant of *Lelāpueisalele*—daughter of *Sinalagilagi* and *Malālatea*—and *Luafataali'i*—the son of *Tolufale*—see The story of *Lei'atauaLesā*, page 180), took stranded European sailors into his home. These sailors began to build double-decker canoes with cannons for the king's navy. He changed his strategy of war with these new weapons. So, with this power, he began to conquer throughout Samoa, aiming for the titles of kingship.

When the missionaries arrived, Malietoa *Vaiinupõ* was struggling with *Lei'atauaLesā Tamafaigā*, who coincidentally came from the same family. Ultimately, it was the murder of *Lei'atauaLesā Tamafaigā* in Fasito'otai that caused the Malietoa to fight. And now came the arrival of the missionaries in 1830.

We recently had the Men's Conference on Championship: Samoan history has many great warriors who led to victory in great battles, and being the "champion" is what warriors strategized to achieve with their troops in many battles over Samoa. So here, *Lei'atauaLesā Tamafaigā* died, and Malietoa *Vaiinupõ* became king, as decreed by *I'amafana*.

War and the Messenger of Peace

The war between Malietoa *Vaiinupõ* and the TuiA'ana from Leulumoega was the most horrific war in Samoa history. Pressure for war had been building up since the passing of Tafa'ifa *Galumalemana*. His son *Nofoasāefā* did not adhere to the decree that *I'amafana* should succeed *Galumalemana*. And the wars that ensued, initiated by *Nofoasāefā*, kept on rolling until Malietoa *Vaiinupō* and his war against the A'ana district. The fact that over 60 years of fragmentation and instability in government leadership (1770-1830) culminated in the message of Christianity, provides a cultural paradigm for the meaning of the word "godsend."

The "Messenger of Peace" must have appeared to the Samoans as a huge and very strange European ship, as it arrived on the shore of Sapapali'i. And, as the ship was approaching the shores of Sapapali'i, sailors on the ship would have seen smoke from villages burning due to this war. But this isn't why the Europeans called the Samoans savages. At the time they arrived, they already knew that there was a political war going on in Leulumoega. Paramount Chief Malietoa *Vaiinupō* was leading this war of vengeance for *Lei'atauaLesā Tamafaigā's* murder. The Malietoa was winning the war against the TuiA'ana. But they were burning everything, including the women and children; there was no mercy shown.

Malietoa Vaiinupō

Malietoa *Vaiinupō's* grandfather was Malietoa *Ti'a*, whose first marriage to *Taufailematagi*, daughter of *Li'o* gave birth to sons, *Sulusulumaivasa* and Malietoa *Fitisemanū*. Malietoa *Fitisemanū* and *Palo*, daughter of *Memea* of Sapapali'i, Savai'i, were the parents of Malietoa *Vaiinupō* (see *Mauga*, page 66 in the timelines, Period VII: The Arrival of Christianity).

Malietoa *Fitisemanū's* second wife was *Fuatai*, daughter of *Gaugau* of Sapapali'i, Savai'i, who gave birth to a son Gatuitasina *Taimalelagi*. *Fuatai* later became the second wife of Malietoa *Vaiinupō.*

Malietoa *Ti'a's* second marriage, to *Lāmanā*, granddaughter of Tafa'ifa *Galumalemana*, from Asau, Savai'i, gave birth to daughters *Tuitofā* and *Aigaevalu*. *Tuitofā* married Tuimaleali'ifano *Suatipatipa*, grandson of Tuimaleali'ifano *Tuitalili*, who was the son of Lilomaiava *Letamaaleāitumaletagata*, son of TuiA'ana *Samalaulu* and Lilomaiava *Nailevaiiliili*. Thus the Samalaulu genealogy connects to the Gatoa'itele through LeSaena and the grandfather *Manua'ifua*.

Tuitofā's son Tuimaleali'ifano *Sualauvi* was dispatched to take the mission to Falelatai, village, in A'ana district, Upolu. And Malietoa *Vaiinupō's* son, Malietoa *Laupepa,* was the first ordained minister of Afega village. *Laupepa* married *Sisavai'i*, daughter of *Niuva'ai* of Palauli—*Niuva'ai's* grandmother, *Sailiemanu* was the sister of Malietoa *Ti'a's* second wife *Lāmanā* (above). Malietoa *Laupepa* and *Sisavai'i* gave birth to a daughter, *Fa'amusami Leuatōivao* and sons Malietoa *Tanumafili*-I (1890) and *Siliva'ai*.

Malietoa *Vaiinupō's* second marriage, to his father's second wife, *Fuatai* (above), gave birth to *Talavou.*

The Family of *Tuimaleali'ifano*, Prince of the Monarchies of SaTupua and SaMalietoa

Tui-ma-le-ali'i-fano (*Tui* stand erected, *ma* and, *le* the, *ali'i* high chief, *fano* died wastefully) was named after the high chief from Palauli, *Ali'ifanovalevale* (high chief died wastefully—see Lilomaiava, page 58). High Chief *Ali'ifanovalevale* of Palauli and his wife *Fililesalue*, daughter of TuiAtua *Fa'aso'utele* (generation #18) were the grandparents of *Tuiavi'i*, *Togia-lelei* and *Puipuiifatu* (sons of TuiToga). And this is the beginning of the Lilomaiava genealogy with *Tuiavi'i's* son *Tuifa'asisina* of Sagafili, A'ana district, Upolu. Thus, genealogical connections of Tuimaleali'ifano to the TuiAtua, TuiA'ana, TuiToga, Malietoa (through his grandmother *Samalaulu's* mother, below), and Tu'uamaleulua'iali'i.

Tuimaleali'ifano's royal genealogy begins with TuiA'ana *Samalaulu*, one of three paramount royal chiefs who were children of Paramount TuiAtua TuiA'ana *Faumuinā*. Lady *Samalaulu's* mother, *Tu'ua-ma-le-ulua'i-ali'i* was the daughter of High Chief *Manua'ifua*, a descendant of the Malietoa and the Gatoa'itele royal house, of Afega village, in Tuamasaga district, Upolu. *Samalaulu* married Lilomaiava *Nailevaiiliili* of Palauli village, Savai'i, and gave birth to *Letamaaleāitumaletagata* (the son of a demon and a human).

The tale is that Lady *Samalaulu* was looking to gather up war warriors, and so she came to Lilomaiava *Nailevaiiliili* in Palauli village, and she asked Lilomaiava for troops. And so Lilomaiava gave her the troops in exchange for her hand in marriage, although the paramount chief was at an old age and already had seven marriages, with many children already young adults. But a sacrifice had to be made for her brother *Va'afusuaga's* kingdom.

It was a shocking news to the village of Palauli when the princess announced her pregnancy. And rumors ran wild: How could this be? But Princess *Samalaulu* had a healthy pregnancy and gave birth to a healthy son. And they named him after the rumor about her pregnancy—"It must have been a son of a demon and a human," they said, because, "How could it be, for he was too old to have a child." Hence the name *Letamaaleāitumaletagata*.

The boy inherited his father's title, Lilomaiava. He also inherited his mother's TuiA'ana title and salutation. Then Lilomaiava *Letamaaleāitumaletagata's* marriage with Taufau *Naifoaiaana*, daughter of *Laumatiamanu* (a grandson of *Va'afusuaga*) produced *Tuimaleali'ifano Tuitalili*.

Tuimaleali'ifano married *Tuitogama'atoe*, daughter of *Tauiliili* of Amile, with connections to the TuiAtua clan, and they had a daughter, *Sauimalae*. Then *Sauimalae* married Tafa'ifa *Galumalemana* and bore Tafa'ifa *I'amafana,* who decreed the Tafa'ifa title to Malietoa *Vaiinupõ*.

Tuimaleali'ifano's second marriage, to *Ulualafā*, daughter of *Pula* of Saleimoa village, bore *Leavaise'etā*, who was decreed to orate the ava ceremony for Palauli village and the Falelatai village Council. He married *Taiai* of Falefā, who bore *Niupulusu* (or *Lilopogi*) and *Leituala*.

Leituala married *Sailiemanu*, half-sister to Malietoa *Ti'a's* second wife *Lāmanā,* and produced *Vavatau* who married *Leativāosalafai*, giving birth to *Niuva'ai*, whose daughter married Malietoa *Laupepa.*

Leituala and his brother *Niupulusu* were princes in Palauli village. *Leituala* was the paramount voice (*Sa'o Fetalai* or *Sa'ofetalai*) in Niusuatia for the Āiga SaTunumafono. And *Niupulusu* (also called *Lilopogi*) married *Taumaunu*, daughter of *Taefu* of Falelatai, who bore *Tuimaleali'ifano Sualauvi*.

This meandering path—through TuiAtua, TuiA'ana, SaTupua, Malietoa, Gatoa'itele, SaLilomaiava, and SaMuliaga—gives the justification for the Prince TamaAiga title and salutation for

Tuimaleali'ifano. Today, Tuimaleali'ifano is really the TuiA'ana and can also claim the Malietoa To'oa title, for remember, he is a descendant of *Tuitofā*, sister of Malietoa *Fitisemanū*, who was the father of Malietoa *Vaiinupō*. This can be referred to as Malietoa Feagaiga. Tuimaleali'ifano is also claimed by Afega village as their royal prince TamaAiga, due to a descendant of TuiA'ana *Samalaulu*. According to R.P. Gilson, the Tuimaleali'ifano who passed away in 1862 was a Tafa'ifa.

Tafa'ifa Malietoa and the Missionaries

The Tafa'ifa Malietoa—the Samoan king from the European perspective—did not get the treatment from the missionaries that he felt he deserved. Once the mission was established and rolled out to the villages, the missionary leadership were executing their standard plans for the development of the Samoan LMS church. In spite of limited teachers and clergymen to satisfy demands from the village chiefs for more resources, the missionaries were in total control of the mission's destiny.

The relationships began to be strained, due to Malietoa *Vaiinupō's* demands for more control of missionary resources and of the implementation schedule across the islands. This created somewhat of a power struggle between Malietoa *Vaiinupō* and the LMS leadership. And this caused fragmentation in the rank and file of the LMS organizational structure, as well as in the chieftain organization. For the value proposition of the European missionaries, as teachers and as a source of access to European goods, tools, and "know how," was compelling to the village chiefs. So the missionaries were clearly the leaders of the church and were listened to obediently by the village congregations, which in many cases were the whole village.

The Tafa'ifa was losing his grip on the population of the island country, and eventually his authority with the church was being neutralized and minimized by the LMS church leadership. The missionaries felt the Malietoa had no real authority over the people. But what the missionaries did not understand was that it was not the king that had the authority but rather the Chiefs Council at the various levels of the village, district, family, and chieftain organizational structure.

Thus, down toward the tail end of his life (A.D.1838-1841) the Tafa'ifa Malietoa decided to leave Sapapali'i village, to relocate back to his primary residence and Seat of Government in Malie and Afega, Upolu. It was the twilight period of his life, and it was the time when my ancestors in the villages of Malie and Afega became more intimately involved with the organization of activities in Tafa'ifa Malietoa's government, up to his last decree before he passed in 1841.

Since Fata and Maulolo were the Tafa'i of Gatoa'itele (also known as the Tafa'i of Malietoa), they were the orchestrators and mediators of many peace offerings among the tribal monarchs. Collaboration with the other six Tafa'i—Tupa'i and Ta'inau of TuiAtua, Fuga and Mau'Ava (or Mauava) of Vaetamasoāali'i, and Umaga and Pasesē of TuiA'ana—was the path to calming the population and maintaining peace.

Tafa'ifa Malietoa *Vaiinupõ's* Decree

Tafa'ifa Malietoa *Vaiinupõ's* "parting words of farewell" decree to Samoa is: When I pass, I return the PāPās to their respective families and custodians for their heirloom authorities. The TuiA'ana and TuiAtua titles shall be returned to their respective families. The Malietoa monarch and the Gatoa'itele and Vaetamasoāali'i PāPās shall be returned to their respective families and custodians. And the title Tafa'ifa shall be buried with Malietoa *Vaiinupõ*. Additionally, Malietoa *Vaiinupõ* asked Tafa'i Fata and Maulolo to please look after his son *Moli,* to ensure he stayed in the church and inherited the Malietoa title.

At the time, the prominent member of the TuiA'ana and TuiAtua family genealogies was also *To'oa* of Falelatai, who was also Tuimaleali'ifano *Sua-tipa-tipa* or *Suatipatipa*.

According to this decree, there would be no more Tafa'ifa title, the source of wars. But this decree was not readily accepted by all the major families and the Samoan chieftain system. While most recognized the idea of eradicating the sources of war, the country was afraid of losing their *Fa'aSamoa* and their dignity and family identity.

Tafa'ifa Malietoa *Vaiinupõ's* decree was made to ensure Samoa would stay Christian and achieve lasting peace. The Malietoa somehow knew that as long as the Tafa'ifa title was to be bestowed there would always be war. And the more war people had to endure, the less Christianity would be practiced, and the more likely would be a reversion back to heathen behavior.

In the end, Tafa'ifa Malietoa *Vaiinupõ's* dream and vision for a peaceful Christian Samoa Nation was finally realized. This goal and objective became the primary motive for the Malietoa monarch and clan to stay in the LMS Church and never again pursue the Tafa'ifa title. A leader's achievement is often summarized down to one iconic idea. For Tafa'ifa Malietoa, this is a Christian Samoa. Today Samoa has a 99% Christian population.

Subsequently, Malietoa *Moli* graduated from Malua Seminary and became Malietoa Gatoa'itele Vaetamasoāali'i. Before his passing, Malietoa *Moli* also asked Fata and Maulolo to take care of his son *Laupepa*, who was at the time the first minister of Afega village. *Laupepa's* brother *Faleono* was married at the time to the sister, *Sala,* of my great-great-grand father, *Saena Poao*. *Laupepa* would also inherit the Malietoa title. Then Malietoa *Laupepa's* son, *Tanumafili*-I, was named after the Malietoa/Gatoa'itele sacred residence, Tanumafili, in Afega and Tuana'i villages, Upolu.

My sources for information on these last years of Malietoa *Vaiinupõ* in Malie and Afega villages are my family's personal diaries and court testimonies, proceedings, and documents.

Tumultuous Period of Wars

Wars fought for who should preside over the country as Head of State were far too many during the colonial period in Samoa. Prior to this period, wars were generally isolated to regional family and clan excursions, often undertaken to solidify the completeness of the Tafa'ifa rulers—that is, for the country's families to unanimously settle on which family was to inherit the Tafa'ifa title. Such conflict occurred at the level of which prince or princess was to be bestowed with the title Tafa'ifa. However, during the European colonial period, this became more complex because the dissenting factions were within and between families—intra/inter-family disputes. This took the paramount major families back to re-fighting the 1500 A.D. wars of PāPās for a new Tafa'ifa title, reimagined by the European colonialists.

Let's go back, prior to the arrival of Christianity in 1830: Paramount Chief *Lei'atauaLesā Tamafaigā* had passed, and

Malietoa *Vaiinupõ*, who was decreed by Tafa'ifa *I'amafana* to follow him as Tafa'ifa, made his move to claim the Tafa'ifa title. The Malietoa became Tafa'ifa. He had the sole authority to dictate his successor, and it could be one of his princes or princesses. In fact, theoretically, the Tafa'ifa title could have stayed in the Malietoa monarch line for an inconceivable period of time. But that is not what happened, after the European colonialists contrived to build a new Samoa country. Thus the tumultuous families infighting that followed for over seventy years (1830-1900).

I choose not to chronicle the minor excursions or major conflicts in 1848, 1860, 1880, and 1893, before the end of the convoluted Condominium and the dawn of the Partition. Tafa'ifa Malietoa *Vaiinupõ* knew all along that his Kingdom, Mālõ, was a gift from Heaven. It had been prophesied in the 1500s. Thus, chronicling the wars serves no purpose other than reopening old battle wounds. War is war. The price of war is death and internal wounds. And healings are for the sick and wounded. While these wars are part of its history, what Samoa achieved from this tumultuous period is a new and a free thing. A different type of freedom. An unconditional freedom. It's a Christian freedom, an unconditional gift and love, afforded to the Samoans from the only God they accepted to be the foundation of their way of life.

Christianity in the Pacific

Tahiti, Hawaii, and New Zealand

Image 11 King Põmare-I, signed "B", unknown, more not stated in source, Public domain, via Wikimedia Commons

King *Põmare*-I of Tahiti accepted Christianity from the London Missionary Society, led by Rev. Henry Nott, in 1797. The same vessel, Duff, transported LMS missionaries to Togatapu, Toga in 1797. In 1822, Methodist missionaries also arrived in Toga with their own mission. Neither of these missions was fully accepted by the kingdom until 1826, when King *Taufa'ahau* finally embraced the Methodist version of Protestantism and was converted to Methodist Christianity in 1831; then he was later known as Tui Kanokupolu and subsequently took the title King George *Tupou*-I in 1845.

The first Protestant missionaries arrived in New Zealand, to take the gospel to the Maori people, in 1814. And in 1820, the first Christian missionaries arrived in Hawaii from Boston, USA.

Image 12 Kamehameha-I, Gabriel Bertram Bellinghausen, Public domain, via Wikimedia Commons

Queen *Ka'ahumanu* converted to Christianity 1825 (see First Missionaries in Hawaii, page 229). She was descended from King *Kamehameha*, and her son became *Kamehameha*-III. The legend in Tutuila, Samoa, about *Kamehameha* is that King *Kamehameha*-I's mother was a Samoan. Her mother, a Samoan, was from the village of Aunu'u, Tutuila. The legend continues with a warrior chief's ship from Hawaii being stranded, by a storm wind, off the coast of the little island of Aunu'u, Tutuila. The people of the village took him and cared for him and his crew. As was customary in the Pacific Islands, preparation for a new boat and provisions had to be undertaken to get the guest chief back home. When the village sent him and his crew off home, a village maiden was already a "common law" wife to the chief. As such, she went with him to Hawaii. And the child from this union was *Kamehameha*-I.

If you go to the Big Island, where King *Kamehameha's* home is located, the documents of his genealogy are found there. And on the Big Island, there are villages named Upolu and Savai'i.

Hawai'ian and Savai'ian History

This tale, about the Hawaiian seafaring warrior blown by the storm to the small island of Aunu'u, Tutuila Island, cannot be confirmed, for the details have been swallowed up by the passage of time. But however it's recounted, the memories exist in the village's oral tales. It could very well have been a Hawaiian, seafaring from the Big Island of Hawaii where the *Kamehameha* ancestral clan resides, that was stranded in Aunu'u island.

The genealogy of Hawaiian monarchs is fully accounted for, in the various genealogies and legends of the kingdom, down to King *Kamehameha*. However, there are strong genealogical connections between this little, beautiful oasis and Olosega, in Manu'a. There are Manu'an legends of their seafaring warriors and explorers such as *Lata*, *Paao*, *Pili*, *Maui*, *Fitiaumua*, *'Atea*, *PapaAtea*, *TagaloaLā*, *Taeotagaloa*, *Mafui'e* (who procured fire), *Wahieloa*, *Tafa'i*, and *Aitagata* in Hawaiian or *Āitutagata* in Samoan. (Many of these are covered in my first two books, *Navigators Quest for a Kingdom in Polynesia*, and *Navigators Forging a Matriarchal Culture in Polynesia*.) These are all names that are very much included in Hawaiian history, and this gives evidence to the relationship between the Navigators of the Samoa and Manu'a Archipelago and the inhabitants of the northern Pacific islands. It evidences also the early explorations of the Navigators.

These Manu'an names are foundational in the various genealogies of the Hawaiian monarchs from the *Ulu*, *Nanaulu-Maweke*, *Puna,* and *Hema* lines, down to *Kamehameha* and *Kalakaua*.[lxxxiv] *Laau* and *Pili* are listed in the 44th and 45th generations on the *Puna-Hema* lines. Also, according to legend, the high priest *Paao* (a Manu'an from Olosega) sent for *Pili* (son of *Tagaloalagi* of Manu'a, and founder of Tahiti) to come from Tahiti to Hawaii to form the government there.

There is also the legend of *Maui* fishing up the islands of the Hawaii Archipelago in the Hawai'ian version of creation. And there are New Zealand legends that claim *Lata* and another Samoan from Savai'i discovered and settled New Zealand—the native Maori did not know any islands located in the far northeast like Hawaii, so they couldn't have mistaken the spelling of Hawaii vis-a-vis Savai'i in the text.[lxxxv] Judge Abraham Fornander (Circuit Judge of the Island of Maui, Hawaii), cites D. Malo, author of the royal Hawaiian genealogy and Kalakaua's history of the Hawaiian islands publication, as well as Sir George Grey's publication of New Zealand legends in giving this information.

So we see that all the names above are integral to Hawaiian genealogy and history.

The Polynesian Triangle

According to accepted history, the Hawaiians were founded by the Tahitians. But the Tahitians were discovered by the Samoans. Also, the Hawaiians discovered New Zealand. But the Maori people were not the natives of New Zealand at the time of their migration around A.D.550-700; there were already indigenous people living on the land.

The Polynesian triangle is formed when mapping a nautical vector from New Zealand to Hawaii, and from Hawaii down to Samoa and Toga, and then crossing over back to New Zealand. In the middle or center of this nautical triangle is the long-standing debate between Samoans and the Togans as to which island is actually the "Cradle of Polynesia."

But, returning to our history: King George *Tupou*-I of Toga, adopted his name from King George of England. He accepted Christianity for Toga in 1831, after the "Messenger of Peace" dropped anchor in Savai'i, Samoa in 1830.

Where America fits in

To understand the history of Samoa from 1830 to 1900, you must understand the events that led up to that critical point of the arrival of Christianity. The world was becoming smaller and smaller, just as today when we are now dealing with what our ancestors must have dealt with in the 1700s. With this newly-found understanding, we must retell our history in light of new historical developments.

The European mood was to colonize the world for their names' sake. The Americans also wanted to get into the colonization business. They knew they were running behind because they were a newly-developed country. They knew they had to do something, because they were basically on the sidelines. So they sent their navies out to parade into the Pacific, beginning from the 1850s.

The American-Spanish war was fought to display that American power far exceeded that of the British. The Americans needed to show the world that they were a powerhouse, and the only way they were going to do that was by sending their navy out to sea. So, the Americans defeated the Spaniards and were awarded the Philippines, Guam, Hawaii, and eventually Samoa in 1898.

During 1830, in Samoa, the arrival of Christianity and other Europeans was already a critical period of our history. There was a juggling act between Christianity and how to form a legitimate, formal, centralized government made up with our own cultural rules. The Europeans were hoping that we would use some of their common laws as a part of our laws to create a solid government. Meanwhile Christianity was being processed into the villages.

Young and Hunkin

When the first missionaries left, Samoans began to "use" anyone who looked European to continue to teach this process of Christianity to the people. Expatriates, such as Young from America and Hunkin from England, came to Samoa as sailors, crewing vessels, and decided to take a risk on making a home and life in the Samoan archipelago. Neither Young nor Hunkin was Christian, but they ended up teaching the Samoans, however cryptic their knowledge of Christian principles was.

Hunkin was the first merchant to be a commercial retailer in Samoa, at Leone village. He was also the first European to marry a native Samoan princess, daughter of Paramount Chief *Fa'ivae* (son of *Tuitele*) in Leone.

Young was a skilled worker, with general mechanical skills. In fact, rumor has it that he and a couple of other expatriates helped build cannon-type guns on the double-hulled canoes of the cruel Paramount Chief *Lei'atauaLesā Tamafaigā,* giving him a naval artillery war machine. This is how Chief *Lei'atauaLesā Tamafaigā* was able to subdue the villages during his cruel campaigns of war.

When Rev. John Williams made a second trip to Samoa in 1832, he stopped in Manu'a, where TuiManu'a needed people to help establish a church. Subsequent to Rev. Williams and TuiManu'a's brief meeting in 1832, the LMS mission expanded the church to Tutuila at Leone village, where Hunkin's father-in-law, *Tuitele*, resided. Hunkin became involved, helping the lead missionary to build the church. Hunkin later became a Christian and was made an assistant pastor in Leone.

Later, in 1843, Arthur Stephen Young Sr., newly converted, arrived with his wife. He was armed with newly printed copies of three books, or chapters, of the New Testament. Young was ordained to be an assistant missionary, to head up the Manu'an mission. And instructions were conveyed to Mr. Hunkin to accompany Mr. Young and family, to introduce them to the TuiManu'a. Hunkin stayed for a period of two years before he returned to Leone village and decided to go back to exercising his commercial merchandising entrepreneurship.

Orator Chief Pa'u

Arthur Stephen Young Sr.'s wife was the lady, Princess *Vitoliomanuoa'ana Felavai* (*Vi-toli-o-manu-o-A'ana* meaning native green apple picked by the birds of A'ana). She was the daughter of Paramount Chief *Leaupepe* of Faleasi'u and Fasito'o (the seat of Paramount Orator Chiefs *Ape* and *Tutuila*). Paramount Chief *Leaupepe* was a descendant of *Tuala*, brother of Tafa'ifa *Salamasina*.

Young Sr.'s son, Arthur Stephen Young Jr., would be given the high "Orator Chief Pa'u" title from the village of Samatau, in A'ana district, Upolu. There is no confirmation of the title bestowment; however, the Samoan custom is that, once your first name is a title or chief name, this means you are a title-holder of that chief title.

The origin of the Pa'u title goes back to A.D.1380, when *Papali'inagauaisavai'i* (a descendant of *Luafataali'i*, son of *Tolufale*) married *Fitimaula* (daughter of Orator *LeTufuga* of SaFotulafai and *Fa'alulumaga*, the daughter of TuiA'ana *Uōtele*—see TuiA'ana, page 22 in the Period IV timelines). They had two sons, *Alalatoa* and *Tu'uma'ai* (see The Story of *Tu'uma'ai*, page 192). *Alalatoa* married a daughter of *Usu* in SaFotulafai, giving birth to *Pa'u*.

However, the name *Pa'u* is mentioned in legend further back, in the time of the first Tagaloa *Funefe'ai*. There, *Pa'u* married Tagaloa *Funefe'ai's* daughter, and he was given the name *Pa'u-mailei-malo* by Tagaloa *Funefe'ai*. *Mailei-malo* means "conspired against the Mālõ" (or against the government), hence the name means "Pa'u who conspired against Tagaloa *Funefe'ai's* Mālõ." (*Funefe'ai's* time period is the time of *Tagaloalagi* whose daughter *Sinalagilagi* is the progenitor of *Va'afa'i, Fata, Maulolo* and *Luafatasaga*, around the *To'o* and *Ata* generation.)

The argument for Pa'u's chief title is similar to that made for the Tupuola title at Fagasā village. His mother's genealogy is absolutely the correct one, going back to TuiA'ana *Uõtele* and *Tamālelagi* via *Leaupepe*. Also, her mother's family name is *Felavai* of Fasito'o village, and that is how Chief *Leaupepe* of Faleasi'u village went to marry her.

The foundations of every chief title, bestowed by a family, and the legal test of the legitimacy and authority of such a title, are:

- There must be a genealogical relationship.
- The title origin must be in the family history.
- The title must have "land" or property rights to the family's real-estate property. That is, it must be defined in a specific village structure and salutations. Thus, every title has a piece of land, village, district, or island that defines it.
- And the title must be bestowed by the appropriate family authority and village Chiefs Council.

Thus the title, Paramount Orator Chief Pa'u, is of one of three senior orator family titles in the structure of the village of Samatau, in the A'ana district in Upolu—that is, "The Honorable Pāpā of Paramount Chief Fiamē and the Orator Chiefs, the Mātua Telei'ai (or Telea'ai), SaMano'o, SaPuni and SaPa'u."[lxxxvi]

It should be pointed out that the ancient founding Elder Telei'ai is the same Telei'ai title as in Princess *Samalaulu's* female lineage of the TuiManu'a, in which *Leasaū's* son, *Telea'ai* and a daughter of Orator To'oto'o *Fa'amausili* brought forth a son, *Tauoti*. *Leasaū* is a descendant of TuiManu'a *Salofi,* and he is one of three princes—*Leasaū, Moliga,* and *Nuanua*—together with their adopted brother—*Lefiti*, the Fijian—of Tau, Manu'a's Salutations: Honorable *Le-fiti,* or *Lefiti ma le Pupu* (three) *Ali'i's* (*Pupuaali'i*, which is the Manu'an terminology for *Aloali'i*). *Telea'ai* would be in generation #26, or around A.D.1670 according to Dr. Krämer's calculations. And *Tauoti* married *Sina*, the daughter of the Paramount Chief *Tuiolosega* in Olosega Island, Manu'a, giving birth to a son, *Sava*. *Sava* married *Tapu*, the daughter of Orator To'oto'o *Tulifua,* and she bore a daughter *Amipelia* who married Pa'u Young Jr. (A.D.1872-1895).

We should remember here that you cannot speak in the chief council without a chief title. This really made the case for Young Jr. being a Pa'u titleholder. Also, it would be totally impolite and, in some circles, prohibited to have an untitled young man wed a princess of the TuiManu'a lineage, and, as we have seen, Pa'u would later marry *Amipelia*, daughter of *Sava* (son of *Tauoti Telea'ai Leasaū* and *Sina* daughter of *Tuiolosega*,[lxxxvii]) of the prodigious TuiManu'a lineage. This union gave birth to three daughters: *Matelita*, *Taliota* and *Ane*. *Matelita*, the first born, would become TuiManu'a in 1890; she died in the prime of her young life in 1895. So we see, it is important and appropriate to disclose Pa'u's Samoan royal paramountcy pedigree.

The Honorary Missionaries

The "honorary" missionaries, including Hunkin and Young, are credited with helping establish the mission at Leone village and the Manu'a Archipelago. Young, Hunkin, and the missionaries established the first church in Leone—but not in Pago Pago; *Mauga* had to argue his case, much later, to finally get a church established in Pago Pago, because everything was controlled out of Leone.

Hunkin later left the mission to pursue his entrepreneurial career. And Pa'u Young lived in Manu'a.

As you begin to hear these European names, you can see that they played a major role into the history of Samoa; Hunkin was one of the earlier entrepreneurs in Samoa in 1848.

A lot was going on in Europe then, and I would ask the question: Why Protestant? Why LMS? Through this research, I believe I've discovered answers. England adopted the Protestant faith because of the divorce King Henry VIII—he wanted a divorce and the Catholic Church told him no (since the Catholic religion does not practice divorce). In the early 1700s, English Protestants formed the LMS organization. LMS was a non-denominal organization, raising money to send missionaries into the world, including Africa, South America, and the Pacific. And John Williams was chosen for the Pacific. His aggressive nature was fully focused on this initiative to carry out the mission to the heathens; and for Johns Williams this meant the Pacific.

So, to understand that origin is to understand how we will continue to carry out the mission to our people. This is the introduction of European ideals into our society, beginning the process of a centralized government, and finally concluding with the marriage of Christianity and our government.

First Religious Organizations

1828-1829: Wesleyan (Methodist)

Paramount Chief *Lilomaiava* (a very close relative of Malietoa *Vaiinupõ's* family genealogy—see *Vaiinupõ*, page 69 in the Timelines, Period VII: The Arrival of Christianity) had traveled to Tongatapu around 1828. Wesleyan Christianity had arrived there from Sio-Vili via sailors, deserters, and other Europeans. So *Lilomaiava* was introduced to Methodism while he was there, before returning to Savai'i.

The London Missionary Society established their mission in Sapapaali'i in 1830. When Rev. John Williams went back to Tahiti for more provisions, the mission in Sapapaali'i was left to the care of the Malietoa and a few teachers.

Lilomaiava went to the Malietoa to ask for a missionary teacher but was turned down due to insufficient teachers being present. This made *Lilomaiava* angry and led to his establishing Wesleyan missions at the villages of Satupa'itea, Palauli and Safotu, because these villages are genealogically all related to the Lilomaiava Family.

1830: London Missionary Society (L.M.S.)

Rev. John Williams was designated by the London Missionary Society to carry Christianity to the Polynesians. As we have seen, he had already taken the Christian message to Cook Island, Tahiti, and Togatapu before coming to Samoa, at a time when Malietoa *Vaiinupõ* was fighting a war against A'ana because of the "murder" of *Lei'atauaLesā Tamafaigā* (see War and the Messenger of Peace, page 247).

It was *Tamafaigā's* cruelty that got the best of him. His regular practice was to ask the princess of a village to lay with him, even if by force. The village of Faleasi'u was prepared for his cruelty when he sojourned in their village. As expected, he asked for the princess of the village, in spite of her violent disapproval. So the aumaga planned out his assassination and took *Tamafaigā* and his warrior party by surprise. *Tamafaigā* was chased into the ocean in the middle of the night, then he was he was caught and his body cut to pieces by aumaga warriors.

Image 13 Rev. John Williams, Public domain, via Wikimedia Commons

The "Messenger of Peace," the vessel carrying John Williams, Charles Barff, and eight other teachers, dropped anchor at Sapapali'i, Savai'i in mid-July 1830. Malietoa *Vaiinupõ* spoke to John Williams through *Fauea*, a Samoan talking chief who was living in Tongatapu at the time when John Williams was preparing for the trip to Samoa. And John Williams spoke through John Wright, a European resident of Apolima, when conversing with Malietoa.

When John Williams left Samoa and returned to Tongatapu and other island stations, he entrusted the missions at Sali'i, Mulifanua (a village of the Taimalelagi Natuitasina title), and the village of

Malie in Upolu (the official ancient residence of the Malietoa title and throne) and their teachers to Malietoa *Vaiinupõ*.

In 1832, John Williams returned to Samoa to discover the earlier, Wesleyan mission growing at twice the rate of the LMS. He attributed these conversions to the untimely death of *Lei'atauaLesā Tamafaigā* of Manono and Apolima Islands. Williams had assumed that *Tamafaigā* would have been an adversary of the LMS, because he was already affiliated with the Wesleyan mission.

Chieftainship and the LMS

The missionaries had to maintain a delicate balancing act between Samoan chieftainship and the LMS and Christian dogma in order to win over the indigenous Samoans. Rev. John Williams noted a major Samoan advantage, in that Samoans lacked the idols, temples, and powerful priesthood which had been encountered in Eastern Polynesia. But he saw the chiefs as a double-edged sword. On one hand, he observed the suppression of personal liberty, versus the association of religious sanctions with the privileges and maintenance of rank. Frequent wars were plaguing the population and causing havoc in the family structure. Families were torn apart because of family members siding with different family relations and loyalties, with brother turned against brother and against father and in-laws, etc. On the other hand, chieftainship represented the protection, patronage, and power needed to open up heathen lands, to stimulate mass conversion, and to punish the wicked and repulse enemies.[lxxxviii]

The Malietoa bestowed the Sūsūga title on the ministers from the London Missionary Society. He clearly understood the role of the minister as a *feagaiga*. He knew that the minister was the ambassador between God and the people. Malietoa knew that the people of God must be appropriately addressed and could not be referred to as a servant, *'au'auna*. It wouldn't make sense, since they were the servants of God, the one who created us. That's why Malietoa said, "We need to change your title, because you are the *feagaiga* of the Lord—Lord of the people of Samoa." Therefore Malietoa bestowed the Sūsūga title salutation on them, so that all of Samoa would know. It's called *Ao ole fa'alupega a Samoa*. For the minister could not sit in the chief council if he didn't have a title.

Rev. John Williams and the LMS decided to retain Samoan customs and practices while promising all the blessings of Christianity and more.

1835: Rev. Turner and the Conversion Strategy

In 1835, Rev. Peter Turner and several other teachers arrived in Samoa. By 1836, Turner had established churches in 68 villages, including several in Tutuila.

The conversion strategy was simple but effective. It was something the LMS missionaries had honed for one hundred years, since John and Charles Wesley founded the Methodist way (eventually the Methodist Church) in Oxford, in England, in 1730.[lxxxix] The strategy was:

- Teach them the Word and the way of God.
- Ensure retention and maintenance through repetitive practices.
- Have them embrace the Samoan cultural system that is consistent with Christian values.
- Follow the village and district hierarchical structure, because it follows Samoan family structure and genealogy.
- Build churches in the villages, for they follow village ordinances and chief council authority, and they are often grouped into district authority.
- Follow the cultural protocol of using district sacred meeting grounds (*Malae*) for major mission meetings.

The implementation of this strategy really evidences the lessons learned by the missionary administration from years of mistakes they had made around the world—for example, the well-known problems with the approach taken in South America and North America with the Indians, where they gathered them up and moved them into settlement compounds, keeping them away from their extended families and friends and from the property which defined them. When diseases hit these compounds, they were quickly spread and could be devastating to the highly confined communities. Also, separation from their culture and social community disconnected people from their ancestry and historical identity. This turned out to be disastrous for the native converts and for the mission.[xc] So, when the LMS missionaries came to the South Pacific, they had learned that "blending in," or incorporating indigenous culture and family traditions into religious teaching and practices, are key to proselytizing religion.

The training of teachers was the initial focus, until 1845 when the Malua ministering school opened for Samoans to train to be ministers. It was a train-the-trainer approach. Samoans are quite familiar with such an approach—it's the same one they use in teaching how to use the fishing net, for example.

This deliberate strategy was brilliant for the LMS and the mission of God, for the LMS knew, from the warrior constitution of the Samoans, that they would make great missionaries to the more violent Melanesians, such as those on Solomon Island, Papua New Guinea, Ellis Island, Tokelau Island, Vanuatu, and others. Today, if one would visit any of these places, one would find names of people and places and churches that are Samoan names, in memory of Samoan missionaries.

1835-1836: Wesleyan and Togan Methodism

Joel Tupou was brother to King George Tupou *Taufa'ahau* and carried on the mission. *Latuseu* was another relative of the king but was an early Christian convert in Toga and became a missionary for Church of Toga (the *Lotu* Toga). In September 1835, Rev. George Pratt and Rev. Samuel Wilson (son of the missionary Charles Wilson of Tahiti, who later stayed on in Samoa) continued with the mission at the Lotu Toga. This led to a point of contention with the Samoans, because they preferred to have a European missionary as their teacher or preacher, as opposed to another Polynesian—let alone a Togan, a long-time enemy from Samoa's olden days.

In June 1836, the first contingent of the LMS arrived in Samoa from England, led by Rev. Barff and Rev. Buzacott. They came to prepare the way for resident missionaries due from England. They began to learn the language and started work on the development of a written language, in order to begin the translation of the Holy Scriptures. There were five missionaries altogether, soon to be joined by a sixth, so that, including visitors, the London Missionary Society now had nine Europeans on hand to set its future course. In addition, the staff of Polynesian teachers was augmented.

1839-1841: The Tutuila Religious Revival

The Tutuila Religious Revival of 1839-1841 caused a lot of concern, because of claims of being possessed by the Holy Spirit. There was the tendency of converts to show, periodically, intense religious excitement or enthusiasm. This often led to spirit possession in trances, dreams, or delirium.

The conduct of a medium may manifest as "hysteria" or, in other times, might also be contagious, leading to outbreaks of weeping, shouting, and fainting among spectators or worshipers. There was no confirmation, but it was noted that Rev. Murray had some background in revivalism in Britain. There were some clues that he was known as the toughest disciplinarian, relentlessly hard on sin and always on the watch for it, and adamant in requiring repentance. The LMS concluded that this kind of dogma often led to this level of religious excitement and enthusiasm.[xci]

1845: Catholicism

In 1845 Catholicism arrived in Samoa. Its messengers were French Marist missionaries, Fathers Roudaire and Violette. They came aboard "L'Etoile de la Mer," from Wallis Island, and initially dropped anchor at Falealupo in Savai'i. From there they followed the north coast around to Fa'asaleleaga, finding only one opening. That was in Lealatele (Itu-o-Tane on the Male side), where Paramount Chief *Tuala*, of a major family of Samoa, accepted the new church (*Lotu*). *Tuala Pope*, descendants of Āiga SaTuala, received and accepted the Catholic Missionaries in Savai'i.

Apia Bay was the next call and, the priests hoped, the future site of their second mission center. Rumor had it that the French wanted more than just a mission. They wanted to colonize Samoa, in a similar way to Tahiti, with a French warship carrying a large contingent of marines. But the threat never materialized.

Mata'afa *Fanamanu* (or *Fagamanu*) was the holder of the TuiAtua title then, and one of the contenders for the crown of Head of Samoa. He was a Wesleyan. But, to his amazement, he was the preordained sponsor of the Catholics in Samoa!

An anecdotal account of his sponsorship comes from ten years earlier, when his ship was stranded en route to Tutuila Island, carried by a storm wind to land at Wallis Island. The paramount chief of Wallis, *Lavelua*, took care of him and provided a new ship and provisions for him to go back to Samoa. This same High Chief *Lavelua* was converted to Catholicism in late 1842 by the French missionaries from French Polynesia (Tahiti) when they came to his island.

When the High Chief *Lavelua* inquired as to the French missionaries' next port of call, the missionaries said Samoa. Then they asked the chief if he knew any person or family connection in Samoa from whom they could seek assistance with their work in Samoa. It was at that moment that Chief *Lavelua* began telling them how he had hosted a chief from Samoa, Paramount Chief Mata'afa *Fanamanu,* a few years before the arrival of Christianity in Samoa. He did not know how high his title was, but said they should be sure to tell him *Lavelua* sent them, and also to give his regards.

The Catholic missionaries received the Afioga title, so you would refer to them as: *Lau Afioga le Pope*, *Lau Afioga le Pakele.* The Methodists in Alataua, Manono, and Apolima Islands also received the title Afioga and likewise the salutation.

Mata'afa *Fanamanu*

Fanamanu vouched for the Catholic church's relocation from Lealatele, Savai'i to Apia, the main town and capital of Samoa in Upolu Island, in the early years of the mission in Savai'i and Upolu. They needed land to establish a main church and headquarters in Apia, to begin recruiting membership in Upolu.

Subsequently, from 1902-1911, persistent volcanic eruptions on Mt. Matavanu at Gagae'mauga district in Savai'i,[xcii] caused the migration of several communities—Sale'aula, Mauga and Samalae'ulu—to Upolu. The village people of Sale'aula permanently relocated to a new village named Salamumu at LeFaga village in the district of A'ana, Upolu. The populations of Mauga and Samalae'ulu were relocated and resettled at the Afega and Tuana'i village property, with their newly formed village called Le'Auva'a.[xciii]

Originally about 450,000 acres of land (now over 700,000) of Afega and Tuana'i villages property were (and are) granted for the Le'Auva'a community to occupy and settle. This was negotiated by the Head of State Mata'afa Tupua *Iosefo* with Fata and Maulolo and the Tuisamau Chiefs Council, under the auspices of the genealogical lineage of these people as descendants of Tuala, elder son of TuiA'ana Tamālelagi—and thus of Gatoa'itele, Malietoa, and Fata and Maulolo and Tuisamau—to occupy and settle land on the property commonly and legally referred to as the "Fata & Maulolo Property Estate Square," or *Fa'atafafa-a-Fata-ma-Maulolo*, one of the largest single contiguous acreages that cut across the land of the Tuamasaga district. This was decreed to them by Malietoa *Uitualagi*, son of *Fata* and *Maulolo's* nephew Malietoafaigā *Uilamatutu*.

We should note, at this point in the leadership of the country, Mata'afa *Iosefo* was related to the Malietoa, and some still remember that Malietoa *Laupepa* had given Mata'afa the Malietoa title while Mata'afa had already titled himself To'oa, before *Laupepa* was banished and taken away to Micronesia. Also, the Saena of the Tuna'i clan is, of course, a descendant of *LeTelesā* of Faleata district and closely aligned with Mata'afa *Iosefo*. But the legal property rights of these acres were not and are not deeded to the Mauga and Samalae'ulu village communities, now called Le'Auva'a.

Decreed lands cannot be sold or deeded to any parties without the consensus of every member of the village(s) at home and abroad. This is virtually impossible, because it changes the legal definition of the village structure, which will affect their salutations and family identity. The Le'Auva'a Chief Council have been unsuccessful in their legal attempts (five or six times in the past 60 years, since I can remember) to have the government Court of Lands and Samoan Titles issue a final decision allowing the land to be permanently and legally deeded to the native population of the Le'Auva'a village. But at no avail.

Early during the settlement, the Catholic Church of Samoa Administration Headquarters was relocated to Le'Auva'a or Leauva'a village as it's today.

Mission Station Distribution

The following is a list of Mission Stations:

Tutuila
- Leone (Tuitele and Fa'ivae)
- Pago Pago (Mauga)

Upolu
- Apia (Seumanutafa Pogai)
- Malie (Malietoa Vaiinupõ)
- Falelatai (Tuimaleali'ifano)
- SaLuafata in Atua (Sagapolutele and Tagaloa)

Savai'i
- Sapapali'i (HQ)
- Safune, Itu-o-Tane
- Palauli (Itu-o-Fafine)

By 1839, more stations were established:

- Ta'u, Manu'a (Assistant Missionary Matthew Hunkin, the Englishman who married a lady from high Chief *Fa'ivae's* family, was sent to spearhead the mission at Ta'u.)
- Matautu, Savai'i
- Lepa, Salevao sub-district, Atua, Upolu
- Fasito'otai, A'ana, Upolu
- Leulumoega, A'ana, Upolu
- Falealupo of Vaisigano and of Asau district in Savai'i

A question arose as to the choice between centralized and decentralized churches—Mission Headquarters vs. Village/District churches. By 1840, village churches were being supported by Samoan pastors, ordained from the Maula Institute, and deacon-chiefs. And by 1860-70 the mission was totally relying on the appointed pastor and deacon-chiefs.

Religion and Culture

Cultural Loss

As we saw in my first book, *Navigators Quest for a Kingdom in Polynesia*, the limited archeological evidence available, most recently discovered in the 1960s and '70s, presents a serious challenge as we try to firm up or confirm the timeline of Manu'an and Samoan ancient history. Now we will see, compounding this dating problem, the missionaries' deliberate policy when they first arrived with the message of Christianity in 1830, whereby they vehemently discouraged the indigenous people from practicing or continuing the storytelling and memorization of those myths that are so important to ancient history.

The missionaries were concerned about the risk of competing ideologies. And this reminds me of the status of Christianity and Catholicism in the period after Emperor Constantine the Great, in A.D.324 to 337. Constantine became the hero of the Christians up to A.D.1273, when St. Thomas Aquinas published his famous *Summa Theologica*, writing against the conventional dogma of the time, and making the case for the value of culture in a Christian society. Aquinas promoted acceptance of the erudition and tenets of the classics—in particular, the study of Greek (Hellenic) culture as proselytized by Alexander the Great. To paraphrase the King James version of the Holy Bible, we should give that which belongs to God to God, and that which belongs to Caesar to Caesar; the role of culture is, in essence, just another side of the same coin, with the first side being Christianity.

Once the Manu'ans and Samoans fully embraced Protestant Christianity—given, of course, the similarity of the spiritual basis and the single God to *Tagaloalagi*, god of all Polynesia—this marked the beginning of a slow erosion from memory of their ancient history, told orally through their mythology.

We can compare these cultural stories with Biblical stories. For example, one might ask about King David and when he came to the throne. Maybe it was 1000 B.C. But I've read four different accounts in literature, including Freud who did a completely separate analysis. They all seem to arrive at a date from either 1300 B.C to 1220 B.C. But there is enough archaeological evidence to put King David on the throne in the year 1000 B.C, so what do we believe? There is enough evidence from the rebuilding of the Temple to show King Solomon taking over the kingship from 962 to 925 B.C. So these are not mythological people, nor purely spiritual names. We can fix the timeframe, and we know these are real people.

In the same way, before Christianity first came to Samoa, there was a real Samoan history with stories of real people too. This is the part that the missionaries didn't want us to deal with. And this is where we start to venture out into the spiritual world.

Once we started talking about *Tagaloalagi* being the first, the god, and the one from where we descended... once we talked about the nine heavens, where *Tagaloalagi* lives in the 10th heaven... and then we went from nine heavens to the first available evidence, to where normal human beings live... once we followed that route, then Christianity, or the missionaries, didn't want us to carry on with that history, because it didn't make sense to them. That history was seen as competing with the Spirit, the Word of God, until now.

Now there is more factual evidence, and more available research. Given the connection of the genomes—the evidence of DNA—all of this history is factual now.

We're surely splitting hairs when we start to ask, did Moses actually deliver the children of Israel in 1350 B.C, as some believe, or was it in 1275? Did "somebody" really deliver the children of Israel? And were these people Jewish? All seem to agree that this is so. It actually happened, and so did Samoan history.

Cultural Transformation

The message of Christianity brought cultural disruption and a paradigm shift that forced the most rapid transformation of cultural principles and practices, and of Samoan cultural norms and rituals, as well as altering the organizational and leadership structure to reflect a Christian approach. The psychological and sociological impact of this rapid transformation changed the Island Nation's culture forever. And an understanding of this profound change in Samoan culture is a treasure, to be acquired and made accessible for many important reasons besides preserving the story for posterity.

Applying science to transformational cultural or technological shifts, to understand the major disruption of such a paradigm shift, requires first an understanding of both the initial culture and the propositions of the new paradigm, because such a shift disrupts everything, from the bottom all the way to the top, and in every possible way. Many areas of the current system or culture pose challenges to understanding this, starting with people, human aspects, norms, rituals, ordinances, governance, history, beliefs, mythology, protocols, clothing, art and entertainment, economics, division of labor and responsibility, identity and freedom of individual and family clan, and security. It's a complex and intricate process, and a scientific discipline has recently emerged, induced by the disruption of the modern paradigm shift caused by the technology of the internet.

Looking at the internet, I couldn't help but see the analogy with how Samoans went through exactly this major and profound transformation process, as the Christian ethos and way of life was implemented into its culture. And fundamental to this transformation process was the translation of the Bible into the language of the existing culture. For if culture gives us the bones and flesh of the ancient Samoan ethos, then language, metaphorically speaking, would be the marrow in the bones.

Language is the key that brings a culture to life in a cohesive system of norms and rituals. John 1:1-2 in the Bible says, "In the beginning was the Word, and Word was with God, and the Word was God. He was in the beginning with God" (NRSV), as I mentioned in "The Gift and the Miracle" in *Navigators Quest for a Kingdom in Polynesia*.[xciv] Thus, the forced transformation of the culture was only made possible through the translation of the Holy Scriptures.

As with any change, in any system or culture, resistance would be a natural occurrence and had to be expected. But, as in this case, a change that comes from the king downward is usually accompanied with dictatorial enforcement. Thus we find the idiom of "the word or the sword"—accept the "Word of God" or die in your old ways.

Impact of the Bible on Language

The translation of the Bible into the Samoan language was the single most transformational disrupter of Samoan culture in over 3,000 years. Its impact was most significant and profound, because it infused words describing very deep feelings and spiritual experiences and philosophical concepts into the language, in areas where perhaps the language was initially impoverished. At the same time, it reaffirmed the already existing lexicon of the culture's norms and protocols. It introduced a multidimensionality of meanings for many words, and particularly for the Christian principles of God as the Spirit, the Son, and the Father, all in one. For certainly, *Tagaloalagi* didn't have this sort of power and authority, to be manifested in a multidimensional body.

So, to infuse new blood into the language—through the bone-marrow, metaphorically—was sure to cause a tremendous, revolutionary change in the culture's anatomy. The nature of this cultural transformation was accelerated and pressurized by the way in which Christianity's culture (its religious practices and principles) was being implemented from the top down, legislated by the Tafa'ifa downward through the chieftain system, and on to the organizational structure at the grassroots. But perhaps more important was the way in which the "whole of Christian culture," as opposed to small parts added incrementally, was being implemented into Samoan culture. Hence my analogy of a "firehose"—the forced drinking of holy water, metaphorically speaking of course—as I refer to the problem of the risk of drowning from an improperly managed flow, and from the speed of consumption of a good thing.

The Impact of Language on Culture

Looking at today's disruptive technological paradigms, we come to realize and be humbled by the complexity of integrating major cultural paradigm shifts into the multiple layers of existing technologies that are critical to today's culture and way of life. So we can begin to understand the science of transformation implementation. And this is my whole purpose, to make the case for the multiple layers of culture, laid down over 3,000 years of evolutionary cultural development among Samoans and Manu'ans, honed up to this critical point of accepting Christianity.

We have already seen how Samoans and Manu'ans integrated many incremental changes into their culture, to make it work for them during thousands of years. But the "secret sauce" (to borrow a metaphor from the business lexicon) is the translation of the Bible, because it resulted in deep-rooted changes in the overall Samoan language. And, since language is so crucial to life itself, these changes added threads of a new weave that would forever carry the profound meaning of Christian culture in the life of the language.

The invention of the moveable-type printing press by the German inventor, Johannes Gutenberg, accelerated preaching and education in the Scriptures across the globe. But it is language that made this possible, not the moveable-type press, for the press is only a vehicle to carry language. And the Bible now proposed a new paradigm in culture, or religion, to the Samoans.

Language and the Orator

St. Thomas Aquinas lobbied tirelessly to convince the Church to accept culture as the other side of a single coin, where one side is religion and the other is culture (meaning Classical Greek culture at the time). I discussed this in my book, *Navigators Quest for a Kingdom in Polynesia*.

If changes are implemented into a culture's language, then these lead to a major paradigm shift within the language. And a paradigm shift in the language leads to a paradigm shift in the culture. In fact, a paradigm shift in culture can only be effectively achieved if it starts with a shift in the language.

The Samoan chiefs cleverly and intuitively picked up on the idea that Christ was really the "First Matai" (chief)—not the same as using the title of chief in European culture. Chief, to the Europeans, meant a clan leader and usually implied a native, barbaric (barbarian) leader, perhaps even the leader of a native, savage clan or a family practicing cannibalism. But the early Samoan converts saw changes in the language as promulgating the orator role of the chiefs, or Matai, into instruments of Christianity. Mimicking the oration and teaching of Christ and his disciples reaffirmed the importance of oration of the chiefs. And this became foundational to the Samoan ministry's pastors and clergymen.

The missionaries did not catch on to this until the Samoan clergy educated them about it. Samoan missionaries and teachers were rated by their ability to deliver sermons and lead the church members. That this was ordained by God was as natural to Samoan culture as the presence of natural orators. So embracing the new changes to the language (the paradigm shift via translation efforts) became a God-given gift to Samoans, hence their overarching translation efforts.

Translating the Bible

New words—depicting deep, profound, spiritual experiences and ways that change human behavior and customs—gave richness and new life to the Samoan language. For example:

- *lotofuatiaifo* (heartfelt opinion, spirit, conviction, love, empathy, passion, etc.)
- *alofa-tunoa* (unconditional love, which stands erected, alone, independent; it does not lean upon anything or anybody, and it is only used to refer to the unconditional love of Christ)
- *fa'atuatua* (to trust, to have faith in someone or in their efforts or organization)
- *manava-alofa* (the love that's remembered every time you breathe)

In this paradigm transformation, Samoans exploited the method of gluing words together—adding words together to form new words—as in the examples above. Hence the "agglutinative" classification of the Samoan language. The depths of understanding of the authors of Bible translations—into Greek, Hebrew, Aramaic, Latin, Arabic, Islamic, and finally the English language—gave the Samoans clarity in their efforts to translate the Scriptures into the Samoan language. But this was more than just a translation effort; it was a study of a major paradigm shift in a primitive language, one that had been used in isolation for over 3,000 years up to the 20th century.

Observe the development in how Samoans used verbal participles to accommodate the development of new words and agglutination. The verbal participles (which were discussed in Volume I of this work, *Navigators Forging a Matriarchal Culture in Polynesia*) are two to three letter words, where each must contain a vowel, and two vowels must not be together. These were used in a transformation that began with translation and was then delivered to the field, for Samoan clergy to compose their sermons and hence introduce them to the Samoan people. These new words were picked up and woven together by the chiefs and orators in their public speeches and orations.

This linguistic paradigm shift changed the DNA of Samoan language and culture forever. It infused life and further cognitive development into the people's way of thinking and living. This implementation, from the newly published Scriptures using the modified language, accompanied the mission infrastructure and organization as it was rolled out across the island. And, in this process, one of the wisest decisions the LMS missionaries made was to incorporate the local mission into the village infrastructure. This allowed the village chief council to provide security and to chaperone the church and its members. For the missionaries knew that deviation from the village and district structures would immediately be a cause of dissention.

Culture and Morality

The objective of the London Missionary Society's teaching and preaching was to Christianize the law of the land. They placed a ban on activities and relationships, social and personal, that, by mission standards, were immoral or tainted by "heathenish" associations. And they prescribed that the ethics and conventions of Puritanism were essential.

For the sake of godliness and decency, Samoans would have to change many of their ways: changes, for example, in sex and family relations, polygamy, divorce, certain customary marriage rights including the exchange of goods and the public test of virginity, adultery, fornication, prostitution, use of obscenity in word and action, new standards of dress for women including "full coverage," hair styles for both men and women to de-emphasize sex, and the partitioning of houses to ensure separation of sleeping areas. All these physical changes in the culture could only mean major behavioral modifications. But again, the "secret sauce" was the transformation of the language, induced by the translation of the Bible into the Samoan language.

So now, a social scientist goes to Samoa and Manu'a, and spends a year or less studying Samoan and Manu'an culture, and then writes about it, without practicing it, and is often heralded as being the "expert"! This is the very reason why I decided to write my books on Samoan and Manu'an history and culture, after living and learning for over 40 years. It is my journey. If you don't know in detail where Samoans and Manu'ans came from, how they got here, and exactly how they survived in isolation for thousands of years, you are probably not an expert on Samoan and Manu'an history and culture.

The Written Language

So, the written Samoan language was developed when European missionaries gathered nine Samoans, proficient in the verbal language, in Savai'i. These nine people, including six Samoan paramount chiefs, tasked with developing the first translation of the Bible into a Samoan written language, were:

1. Afioga *Mala'itai Leuatea* of (or o) Safune, Savai'i
2. Afioga *Maiava* of SaPesetā clan of SaTo'alepai, Savai'i
3. Afioga *Leota Penitala* of Avao, Savai'i
4. Le Sūsūga *Talavou* Malietoa of Sapapali'i, Savai'i
5. Le Sūsūga *Va'aelua Petaia* of Lalomalava, Savai'i
6. Le Sūsūga *Laupu'e Gagaimalo* (his full name) of SaMauga
7. Reverend George Pratt
8. Reverend M.S. Turner
9. Reverend J.E. Newell

The team presented here is tremendously remarkable, for they had to be able to understand several languages to compose a written language for their native tongue—a stupendous challenge indeed.

The purpose of developing a written language was to translate the Christian Bible—the Christian message. In order to develop such a rich language, the missionaries exposed the nine to Greek, Latin, Hebrew, Aramaic, Indonesian, Malaysian, and Tagalog, to translate the meanings of each Bible story. From these, the Samoans understood the meanings and provided their verbal translation.

For example, the Samoans were able to define "sin," based on the Greek definition, which described sin as anything outside of a bullseye. The nine Samoans took this idea and related it to catching birds, where the bird is the mark and anything outside of that mark is sin. The Samoan word then is *agasala*; *aga* meaning traditions, *amio* meaning behavior, and *sala* meaning to be penalized. Then, in those ancient days, Samoans referred to Jesus Christ as *O le manulauti o Iesu Keriso*, meaning "just as the bird sitting atop the ti leaf, so is Jesus our target."[xcv] Jesus is the ultimate faith which one does not deviate from.

Through studies and exposure to different languages, the nine compiled a written Samoan language. Phonetically they developed the vowels and later consonants, then phrases, and eventually sentences. They began the work in 1832 and selected the Falema'a hamlet in Falealupo village as their working place, due to several wise and capable orators who resided there. Because of the difficult terrain, however—they had been canoeing and hiking to get to Falema'a—their workplace was relocated to a sub-village of Safune named Leagiagi. However, Avao was selected as the final village in which the translation team was housed.

The team translated based on concepts and phrases, rather than word for word. They began with the book of Matthew in the Christian Bible. They dissected passages and explored their meanings in Greek and Hebrew, from which they were able to orchestrate a similar Samoan meaning.

Once the book of Matthew had been translated, in 1842, missionaries sent a copy to London. Later, several copies were printed and delivered to ministers in Samoa. By 1845, a complete Christian Bible had been translated and sent off to London for final printing. Later that year a final version of a translated Samoan Christian Bible shipped off to Samoa.

Conclusion: Religion, History and Titles

There is a deep connection between Samoan history and Biblical stories. The general public often assumes both to be mythological and not factual. However, science is proving that both Samoan history and the Biblical stories are true.

Samoan culture is founded on the family structure, devoted to God. This structure had within it certain roles and responsibilities to be carried out by its members. With vast multiplication over time, the family became a village, which became a district, which became a country.[xcvi] Thus, if we read the various village salutations, we will note the paramount chief title and the honorific salutation: "He is the half-human half-spirit," as found, for example, in the Luatua title of Saleimoa village, the Amituana'i of the village Lotofaga, the Lualemana of Aoloau village, American Samoa, and several others throughout Samoa and Manu'a.

The question arises, why are these titles and salutations still in existence today, after over 200 years of Christianity? And the Samoans answer is that this is their history, from the beginning till the end of the world. Their legends, mythology, and folklore are the sources of Samoan history. Through the imagination of the storyteller comes the justification for how the legend ends.

Period VIII: Forging a Modern Government

History and a New Samoan Nation

I have covered the mission of Christianity in Samoa in my writing on Period VII. Here, I will focus instead on the political process leading up to formulating a new Samoan Nation.

Drawing from R.P. Gilson's comprehensive 1970 study in of this period in Samoan history,[xcvii] I would like to summarize events in an outline format for historiographical purposes. I believe Gilson's chronology of the colonization period and process in Samoa is factual, clear, and fair, and offers a balanced perspective. His research shows the characteristics of a committed, honest, passionate historian, with an insatiable appetite for detail and precision. His assiduous efforts compiled a phenomenal library of research materials, gathered from England, New Zealand, Australia, and Samoa, documenting Samoan colonization by the world's Western powers. He committed himself, with academic passion, to seeking an unbiased truth in chronicling Samoan history since the arrival of Christianity and the ensuing colonization throughout A.D.1800 to 1900.

J.W. Davidson of the Australian National University, comments, in his introduction to Gilson's book, that the sources on which the book was based were particularly extensive and complex. He points out that it can be difficult to use documents written by Europeans to understand the realities of non-Western societies, but it's also difficult to interpret documents written in a different language (such as Samoan) when looking at intricate issues of law and politics during periods of profound social change. So I will leave the details to R.P. Gilson, and I shall provide a searchlight for readers and students of Samoan history.

Not Just a European View of History

I have set out to write about the history of Samoa in a balanced way. But up to this point, almost all the available historical literature about Samoa is written by Europeans and has an exclusively European point of view. This was the only perspective that mattered in the epoch of European colonialism. Thus R.P. Gilson's chronicles of the anatomy of the colonization of Samoa, during this critical period in its modern history, should be considered "prima facie evidence," judging the competency of the colonizers of Samoa. Gilson laid it out in such meticulous detail that one can only conclude this was clearly not the best experience of colonization by Europeans in Polynesia.

Instead of analyzing this, I am more interested in the role the Samoan leadership played in negotiating through these convoluted conundrums in their newly emerging multicultural society in the Navigators' Archipelago. It is their history. That's why I have labored to show how much of their culture and history was already established before European colonization began.

I needed to answer the question of what Samoans and Manu'ans already had—relating to culture, history, government organizations, taboos, and ordinances—before the Europeans began introducing the ways of the "civilized" world. Establishing this will facilitate the measuring task, because it gives a clear boundary of changes, from before and after, to use as a yardstick.

Obviously, I don't believe enough clear vision has been focused on the early history and cultural development of Samoa to draw a valid contrast and comparison. Thus we have several generations that have grown up with the belief that Samoan history began after accepting Christianity in 1830.

Kudos to the missionaries, that they did such a good job preaching Christianity that Manu'a and Samoa have a 99% Christian population today! But the missionaries might also take some of the blame for the botched colonization. They insisted on pursuing an arms-length policy, keeping them from guiding Samoan leadership through the difficult formulation of a government organization structure. The missionaries were staffed with some very well-educated and intellectually competent theologians, who could have effectively and easily guided Samoans through this process; they had already established credibility and gained the confidence of Samoan people at all levels of the culture.

So the initial value of R.P. Gilson's detailed report, describing how Europeans botched the colonization of Samoa, is for history students to pore over, studying events in history. But the real value is in helping understand the roles of Samoan leadership in the construction of the new government and nation. There is plenty of evidence from European intellectual contributions, in documenting the culture and history for future generations of Samoans to examine. But a Samoan viewpoint should also be included.

Samoan Leadership at the Arrival of the Missionaries

I have sedulously described the development of Samoan culture through history, from settlement of the kingdom in the archipelago to the arrival of missionaries with their message of peace. Samoans were already accustomed to having a single ruler, known as the Tafa'ifa. As we have seen, at the time of the arrival of Christianity, Malietoa *Vaiinupõ* was the reigning Tafa'ifa, the seventh Tafa'ifa since Tafa'ifa *Salamasina*. With the exception of the reigns of TuiAtua TuiAana *Fofoaivao'ese*, *Taufau,* and *Faumuinā*, the Tafa'ifa had ruled over all Samoa for about 420 to 500 years. So, in the minds of the Europeans, Samoa had already achieved a ruling authority in the kingship of its monarch. But the interpretation of this political governance was the cause of confusion and convoluted chaos with the dawning of a new government in Western Samoa.

At the arrival of Christianity in 1830, Samoa had endured over 100 years of tumultuous conflict between royal princes and siblings. This was a period plagued by war, from Tafa'ifa *Tupua Fuiavailili* to his grandson Tafa'ifa *I'amafana* who bequeathed the Tafa'ifa title to Malietoa *Vaiinupõ*. Thus Samoans were very much accustomed to such infighting and conflict before the Europeans invaded the Island Kingdom. So Europeans did not introduce the Samoans to war, but rather they exacerbated conflicts in order to achieve the goal of a single monarchical dynasty.

European Choices for Leadership

It's much easier to influence a single authority, rather than having to negotiate with different paramount chiefs or groups of chiefs. The salient issue for the Europeans was who they should choose to lead the country, someone who they could work with or control. This was where each council of foreign government representatives had their own candidates they believed they could control and support.

What the Europeans did not clearly understand or appreciate about the Samoan organization, structured on major families, was the complexity of the genealogical system of the monarch family. The Island Nation is very tiny, and its genealogies, close and closely intertwined, are foundational to the Samoan psyche. So divisiveness meant tearing the family apart. Dissension between family members caused infighting, pitching family members against each other, and thus family against family, and district against district. This only perpetuated and prolonged the struggle to find a consensus choice for a leader to rule the country. It shouldn't have been necessary to prolong the suffering of the leaders by banishing them through extradition to the major Western country's colonies, but Malietoa *Laupepa* was sent to Saipan, and others to other German colonies.

Samoan Choices for Leadership

There are plenty of colorful characters in the history of the colony, and a few who, while not successful in their conniving schemes, nevertheless add a colorful dimension in the annals of the Samoan colonial history. But the main cause of the fragmentation of leadership in governance of the Island Nation was the fact that there were now three major world powers—Germany, Great Britain, and the United States of America—each with an appointed councilor present in Samoa. This increased the challenge of getting consensus on standardized policies, rule-making, and authority for enforcement. The British were just as happy to keep the French out, because of competition from Catholicism. However, the Catholic church was already in the kingdom, centered in Savai'i in the Lealatele district, and the Marists' schools were very popular with expatriates and with members of the Catholic church.

The internal divisiveness of authority in Samoa's major ruling families became problematic due to instability. The official representatives from Great Britain were very much supported by missionaries from the London Missionary Society (LMS) and, of course, by Samoan LMS Congregational Church members. Also they were very much loyal to the Malietoa dynasty.

The fact that Malietoa *Vaiinupõ* had sworn an oath to have his children committed to the LMS ministry, to study at the Malua Seminary and the Seminary College in Fiji, was exactly what the LMS missionaries wanted for sustainability of the Protestant denomination in Samoa. His family—*Moli*, *Talavou* (a member of the Bible translation team), *Laupepa* (*Moli's* son), *Tanumafili*-I (*Laupepa's* son) and *Tanumafili*-II—were pledged, by decree, to LMS roles of custodian.

Also, Tuimaleali'ifano represented the royal princess title for both the Malietoa dynasty (through *Tuitofā,* sister to Malietoa *Fitisemanū*, father of Malietoa *Vaiinupõ*), and the TuiA'ana and TuiAtua or SaTupua dynasty (through TuiA'ana *Samalaulu,* mother of the first *Tuimaleali'ifano*).

The SaTupua monarch title and authority was being contested by *Tamasese*, and a tug-of-war was coming between the SaTupua monarchy and the SaMalietoa monarchy. Mata'afa *Fanamanu* acquired the TuiAtua title and was now contesting for the Tupua title. At the same time, *Tamasese* had acquired the TuiA'ana title and went to war with the Mata'afa for the Tupua title. These two were both contesting to be the "King" of Samoa, but there was no Tafa'ifa after Malietoa *Vaiinupõ*.

These families were also very much LMS Protestant church members. However, when the Catholic church was established in Savai'i and later moved to Apia, Upolu, Mata'afa became a major supporter of the Catholic Church. The Catholic missionaries had come to Samoa via Wallis Island, where Mata'afa *Fanamanu* had been shipwrecked a few years before, and the high Chief of Wallis Island had given instructions that they should seek the Mata'afa out if they should need assistance (see 1845: Catholicism, page 267). Mata'afa *Fanamanu* later became a candidate for the kingship of Samoa, with considerable influence and authority. Also, later, the SaTupua monarch continued to embrace both the LMS and Catholicism.

The clan of Paramount Chief *Lei'ataua* held onto their loyalty and leadership in the Methodist Church, which was brought over from Toga by King George *Tupou* of Toga (a namesake of the English king).

So these were the Island Nation's major contestants for the ruling monarchy of Samoa, from 1830-1900.

Samoan Innovations in Government Structure

We should keep in mind that the government structure of Tafa'ifa *Vaiinupõ* during this period followed, exactly, the National Salutations structure of the *Tumua* and *Pule* authorities. This represents the first Samoan innovation in construction of a modern government organization. It automatically eliminates the gerrymandering of borders and boundaries to geographical districts, a major cause of war in many societies.

The central government, called the *Mālõ*, consisted of Tafa'ifa Malietoa *Vaiinupõ* and his *Tafa'i* senior orators, totaling eight chiefs. Additional were the *Tumua* (three in Upolu) and *Pule* (six in Savai'i) authorities at their respective districts, and one additional authority, the *Aiga i le Tai* (family at leeward islands) in Manono Island. Their respective authority and protocols were an integral part of the culture. And communication protocols were also embedded in the culture.

This was the *Mālõ* government organization at the time of the arrival of the missionaries and their message of Christianity. The transition to a new, modern form of central government was really a transformation initiative from this culturally based organization and structure of government.

A second Samoan innovation was the incorporation of the district's paramount chiefs into the "House of Nobles," the *Ta'imua*, to show understanding of the hierarchical structure of Samoan culture.

The third innovation provided a district governor position to deal with district affairs. Later, they created a government-sanctioned village "mayor" as a representative of the government in village council affairs.

This was the structure the Samoans wanted, and the Steinberger regime (see 1873: The Steinberger Regime, page 298) recognized this and wisely embraced it.

By the way, the LMS mission leadership also recognized this structure during the building out of the mission to all of Samoa and Manu'a. The lesson learned from the Mission Authority was to weave the Christian way of life into the cultural *Fa'aSamoa*—the "fine mat," metaphorically speaking—and let the people adhere to it just as they did to their cultural norms and rituals.

So... Work with the existing system and reduce behavioral modification efforts. That is, of course, easier said than done.

The Colonial Period

Christianity and European Civilization

The colonial period was ushered in by the missionaries. It was again a case of a coin with two sides: Christianity on one side and colonialism on the other. This tiny kingdom with its innocent way of life was about to get a rude awakening to the world's "civilization" paradigm.

The lateness of the island's discovery by the civilized world meant that absorbing the ways of the civilized world would be analogous to "drinking out of a firehose." But how exactly did Samoans partake in consuming, not just Christianity, but also the new ways of European civilizations? For the two worlds, of Christianity and European civilization, came into the Island Kingdom simultaneously, because they were delivered to the people by the same teachers. Sometimes, some missionaries even confused the two and forgot which came first, the way of God or the ways of "civilized" men.

The Samoans had contemporary reference points—the Kingdom of Hawaii, the Kingdom of Tahiti, and the Kingdom of Maori, later known as New Zealand, were all in the midst of colonization and Christianization, though they'd been in that process for as much as fifty years before the Samoans. So, fragmented information had blown in on the wind from the Western Pacific coming into Samoa. The wind of change, or chaos as some would refer to it, brought this collective experience into the island culture.

Samoans were well aware of the struggles these other island nations were in the midst of, as they tried to contemplate the future and decide which way to turn. The European model of colonization was at best a type of freefall, a model made up as it went along, depending on the level of absorption or tolerance of the people to accept these major changes to their innocent way of life.

Samoans were aware of the conflicts between the missionaries, or God's people, and the colonizers or entrepreneurial merchants seeking a kingdom for themselves. They were aware of human motivations and human desires to get things done. The chaos lay in the process of internalizing the acceptance of God's will and rationally consuming the overwhelming new ways of the civilized world. For as we now know, in the history of the civilized world, Christianity, Islam, or almost any other religious faith is proselytized with Holy Books in one hand and the sword in the other. For the Christian, either you died in the Lord, or you died in vain.

These points of reference, provided by the struggles of these other island nations, were of tremendous help to the Samoans. But it was like a race to determine if you either died of drowning from the firehose or found an orderly way to take in the changes, to the betterment of people and country. Plenty of overly ambitious Samoans were looking out for themselves and their families. For human fallibility is universal and does not discriminate against any ethnicity or nationality—Samoans weren't any different.

The Colonial Experience

Samoans are masters of weaving multithreaded "fine mats" to their own design, to ensure cohesiveness and to work in a practical manner in their culture. In this same way, they incorporated Christianity into their culture, to ensure adaptation and consistency in the people's Christian way of life. So now, today's generation has the luxury of looking back into their history, because they are standing on the land of freedom—that is, because they have already achieved independence and can reaffirm the freedom that their ancient ancestors searched for over thousands of years.

Samoan ancestors, or the Navigators, had long ago mastered colonization before the colonial period arrived. But for the current generation, they hadn't really colonized any further for several hundreds of years, so their knowledge of the ancient events of colonization lay in oral memory of the past. None of the 1800s generation had any hands-on experience of colonization to use in regression (working forward from memory) for help. For once the Samoans had founded and settled their kingdom, they immediately curtailed their exploration activities in favor of developing their newly colonized home.

Samoans were really innocent in so many ways, since the time their ancient ancestors founded the Island Kingdom. But this experience with Christianity and with absorbing the outside world's civilizations would forever change their life—their culture, religion, DNA, governance—leading them to become a new Island Nation.

This colonization experience was not really physical or a result of aggressive force, but it generated philosophical and cognitive development, based on the abundance of information that arrived with little or no precursors to help in digesting it all at once. This was an experience in learning and internalizing new philosophical ideas about life—ideas that the Europeans had developed and honed for several thousands of years and that, now, the Samoans had to adopt and reweave into their cultural norms and religious rituals, to build or shape a new kind of country.

Arrival of the World Powers

The consuls of world powers, representing Great Britain, Germany, and the United States of America, arrived on the island not long after the missionaries descended on the kingdom. These respective consuls resembled a revolving merry-go-round, with different characters appearing at random points, claiming appointment by respective powers of government, only to be discovered later to have been self-appointed, after being suspended from missionary work in another island kingdom. Confirmation—to distinguish between these government appointees and self-promoted characters—took time to arrive, and it usually had to be dispatched by naval vessels or by the head of the church coming from headquarters to introduce the government representative.

There was evidence that the world powers' attitudes were very lackadaisical about Samoa. This was due, mainly, to the lack of significant resources or mineral wealth, and the lack of abundant cheap labor or enough land to be used for commercial farming for export purposes. The economic potential of the Navigators' archipelago was very limited. Also, for the United States, the main reason they were preoccupied at this time was that they were fully occupied with their Civil War.

There was, however, something special about Samoa that enticed thrill-seekers and adventurers to find their own "piece of the rock" in a kingdom in Polynesia. All three powers seemed to find themselves trapped in this corner of the largest ocean in the world, in the kingdom of Samoa. Somehow the three powers could not freely and deliberately untangle themselves out of Samoa, and thus came the appearance of an impasse. As we will see later, they, being the world's largest powers, had to invent a whole new form of government structure, called "the Samoa Condominium," enacted in Berlin on 14 June 1889 by the Three-Power Conference, evidence of creativity and inflectional characteristics in usage of the English language (see 1889: The Treaty of Berlin, page 311).

There are several countries that have been partitioned into two ruling powers, such as the Virgin Islands, New Guinea and Papua New Guinea, and others, but none is called a "Condominium" other than Samoa.

Who Came to Samoa?

The time was, of course, one of large-scale migration and fortune-hunting in many parts of the world, led by missionaries bringing their message of Christianity to the innocent jungle of Africa, the land of the rising sun of the Asian continent, and the tropical rainforests of the Amazon and the Andes mountains. But what was Samoa's special attraction?

Thomas Trood asked this question in his 1912 book, *Island Reminiscences*.[xcviii] Gilson says that Trood supposed Europeans were captivated by the prospect of the "easy life," which doubtless attracted many others too. But Trood's lingering question is why did they go to Samoa in the first place? For the Pacific Ocean was the last frontier to be conquered.

One of the dominant powers in the world's race to colonization was the British, with its naval power at its peak, while Portuguese and Spanish colonial reach was beginning to wane. Germany was holding onto its colonies in Africa and Southeast Asia and had started retreating back to the European continent. And the United States of America was the "Johnny come lately" member of the party for territorial acquisition, flexing its muscles and power in the world at the Pacific rim. The Americans were, however, preoccupied with their Civil War, as I have mentioned. Also, the

Mexican-Spanish American conflict that led them to the Pacific at the Philippines evidences their policy of "Manifest Destiny" in action. And the French were holding on to what they had, in Africa and the Asian continent, and were struggling with the geopolitics of Tahiti in the region of the South Pacific.

Missionaries were trained teachers in the Word of God and in academic studies, and a few were scholars in literary science. A few trained scientists followed the missionaries to undertake social studies and field work. We owe a lot to the work of these scientists or trained academics for beginning the documentation of the Island Nation's environment, history, and way of life.

Merchants and independent adventurers and entrepreneurs, "seeking fame and fortune," descended on the island shortly after the missionaries arrived. By 1837 there was a group of expatriates in Apia town proper.

A lot of the European population were immigrants of all kinds carrying very few or no traveling documents, so there was no way to control or police incoming expatriates. The missionaries became the major help to the chiefs of families or villages, in matters of trade and of spreading Christianity to the village people. And it became evident immediately that law and order must be established in a standard manner, in order to provide order in how the European guests and local populations should coexist.

A Need for Laws and Standards

As we will discuss later in detail, the development of governance, using European forms of rules and ordinances to satisfy both the expatriates and the local Samoan population, started with port administrations and immigration protocols, followed by the orderly and controlled governance of European communities and the surrounding villages.

Samoans learned to charge for port and docking fees for incoming schooners. The major port villages saw opportunities to earn a stipend or income by levying docking fees on boat owners. Paramount Chief *Mauga*, of Pago Pago village, Tutuila, was the first to standardize fees and services for the harbor in Pago Pago. Apia harbor also had port charges, but they were not standardized.

The concept of standardized rules was an alien paradigm that expatriate Europeans were trying to introduce to Samoan leaders at various levels, starting with the village and then escalating to the national paramount chief leaderships of major families. They wanted to get Samoan citizens to understand the concepts of ordinances, governing the boundaries of rights of property ownership, and also the ideas of punitive punishment for violating any ordinances governing the expatriates' residences and property.

Reciprocity and Property Rights

The expatriates were struggling with what they viewed as Samoan thievery of their personal property. Hence the push for standard ordinances and the ability to enforce such rules to discourage "uncivilized behavior." But the expatriates didn't understand, nor did they care to appreciate, the basic Samoan altitude which is "we are all one family." With this attitude, real-estate and property is something that you cannot take with you but, if you can defend the genealogical connection to it, you can help yourself to—picking the fruit of the land, like bananas and fruits of all kinds, and chickens and pigs as long as you tell someone, like the property owner, who you are and the reasons why you need to have this. Then, one day you can come back with something like a fish, pig, chicken, or cooked food, "umu" in "reciprocity," in return for the generosity.

The trading currency for Samoans was reciprocity: You give, and they give. You give to them, and they give to you—that's reciprocity. Animals, fruits and vegetables, and puka shells were used for trade-offs. This doesn't mean there was no stealing in the culture. But theft occurred when the culture was being taken advantage of by some bad actors.

Personal property became the catalyst leading to a push to introduce European tort and common law into Samoan culture. This was the colonizers' modus operandi, for the sooner European tort and common laws were in force, the sooner they could control the behavior of the population.

Then came the introduction of parliamentary forms of government, followed by legislative initiatives, and on to greater influence over the indigenous leaders, direction, and control.

Access and Intermarriage

While the expatriates failed to understand Samoan attitudes to property and ownership, Samoans struggled to get access to European merchandise and tool products. Access was limited to those who had connections to the European merchants or to trading vendors. Unfortunately, this was exclusively the privilege of paramount chiefs and personal relationships. So yes, intermarriage of the paramount chief's daughter could give, not only access to foreign goods, but more importantly the chance to gain knowledge and information about the outside world. And this created an environment of haves and have-nots in the local community, which eventually grew throughout the district—the more European goods accumulated, the more material wealth a family had, and thus the more authority in the community. This led to an eventual divide between Europeans or expatriates and their now-Samoan, interracial families that were more accustomed to a European style of life vis-a-vis the native Samoan life.

It is *tapu* to marry your relatives, or especially your siblings, so, contrary to observed incidences of incest, Samoans were careful to avoid such marriages. Samoans' guiding "North Star" points to the geographical locations of their relatives or homestead. And so there is a simple explanation for the often-observed pattern of Samoan intermarriage among members of a family's genealogical connections: Samoan and Manu'an family clans visit their relatives, no matter how far back the genealogical connection. Then, in the course of visiting their relatives, they end up marrying within their relationships.

As I have often said, Samoans don't have or need a European compass to guide their long-distance travels. They only need to know where their relatives live. This gives a very deliberate approach to inter-island travel. There is no such thing as leisurely sightseeing. And this takes us, again, to the issue of village property boundaries.

Since all Polynesians are related, they all know where they live. And so, to Captain Cook's amazement when he allowed—or ordered—a young Tahitian crew member to set the course of their vessel toward Sandwich Island, Hawai'i, without a European compass, the young Tahitian intuitively pointed out a direction.

Then, at night, he navigated using the movement of celestial bodies, and magically they arrived successfully in Hawai'i.

So yes, Polynesians are related to each other. Even though time elapses and they may be many generations apart, Polynesians always remember their blood runs deeper than the ocean deep.

Negotiation and Challenge

Intermarriage with Europeans led to the first situation involving racial discrimination experienced by Samoans, discrimination between the inter-married part of the population versus indigenous Samoans. As we observed throughout history, Samoan disapproval of other races, such as Fijians and Togans, was well-established. It was an attitude that had been part of the Samoan and Manu'an Polynesian origin—the idea of keeping to one's own kind. They journeyed through thousands of miles, thousands of years ago, keeping to themselves with a minimum of intermixing with other native, indigenous populations—though those of Togan nationality and the Fijian Melanesians were reluctantly accepted by Samoans, by force of paramount chiefs like TuiFiti or TuiToga.

As we shall see later in the struggle for self-governance, this subtle interracial situation needed to be resolved on the way to free government. The "tug of war" negotiations—between Samoan leaders and the self-appointed representatives of the Europeans, acting on behalf of the major powers—were convoluted and selfishly designed to their advantage, often on both sides of the issue. As a result, opportunities were clear for self-appointed representatives to begin to propose their own version of a constitutional form of government.

The challenge for the missionaries was not so much controlling the indigenous Samoan population, as controlling the increasing numbers of sailors, adventurers, escaped prisoners from Sydney, and deserters from various military naval vessels crisscrossing the South Pacific region. These newly incoming immigrants, without any formal immigration protocols, represented a drastically different profile of European guests, and made a different first impression on the native Samoans. Their not-so-becoming behavior gave Samoans a bad impression of Europeans, one completely contrary to the impression the missionaries were trying to establish to help sell the Christian way of life to Samoans. So the missionaries' objective was to control the behavior of the expatriates, and to suggest an orderly governance process in trading and bartering activities with the Samoans.

Commerce and Trade

The missionaries were very careful not to get involved too much in commerce, or they would jeopardize their preaching of the Gospel. But the head missionary, John Williams, did actually voice his conviction—at an 1838 fund-raising campaign in London's Guildhall—that evangelism by taming and sophisticating the savages was creating the conditions most essential to commercial progress in the Pacific.[xcix]

Not all the merchandise traded was legitimate or of good quality. Different colored beads of no value, poor quality tools, and poor used-clothing materials were all traded with the Samoans without their ever knowing they were being deceived. But at the same time, the missionaries were somewhat over-protective of the Samoans, protecting them from expatriates more experienced in the ways of the outside world.

Adding order to this process led directly to a more complex and comprehensive standard set of laws, which turned out to be more difficult than originally conceived. Thus, it made perfect sense to start with port rules and fee receipts, to show the benefits of these to the village chiefs, and therefore to ensure a willing adherence by all parties involved.

Laws and Constitution

Port Authority Rules and Fees

The port at Pago Pago harbor bay was very popular and busy, with ships from Europe and all over the Pacific. So Paramount Chief *Mauga* of Pago Pago village took it upon himself to negotiate the rules and fees for a few of the early, incoming vessels. Chief *Mauga* was willing to negotiate to find a standard fee that would be acceptable to the vessels.

The next port was Apia, and Paramount Chief *Seumanutafa Pogai* and Fraternal Chief *To'omalatai Toetagata* (an early convert to Christianity in around 1835) took up efforts to develop a set of rules and fees, following the example of the port at Pago Pago harbor. Also, since Apia was the main town where resident expatriates were located, Chief *Seumanutafa Pogai* saw the value of standard rules and orders. So he took the initiative to develop rules of governance for the district of Vaimauga, which includes Apia proper.

The British vessel Conway, captained by Charles Bethune, was the second vessel from Great Britain in several months, since the arrival of the Pandora. It docked in Pago Pago harbor around 1837 or 1838. Captain and commanding officer Charles Drinkwater Bethune negotiated and accepted Chief *Mauga's* verbal terms and fees. The British naval vessel had come to recapture escapees from Australian penal colonies.

Captain Charles Drinkwater Bethune requested the paramount chiefs of the Tutuila Island harbor bay to meet, so he could share with them this documented set of rules and fees, and so he could get a consensus from the chiefs to sanction the agreement. While this was not a national agreement, it nevertheless represented a complete set of rules and fees for the Pago Pago harbor bay. This would be the model for the Apia harbor regulations and for immigration policy.

Community Ordinances and Regulations

After the port authority rules and fees agreements, the next step was to develop community ordinances and regulations governing the expatriates and village populations. These were promulgated in Vaimauga by High Chiefs *Seumanutafa Pogai*, *To'omalatai,* and *Tofaeono*. This also became a model for other districts to study and copy.

Samoan nature says that nothing someone else has created can be accepted without immediate opposition. But, in the end, the rest of the northern Tuamasaga district adopted such regulations (which now included tort and common laws), to the approval of the European residents. Also included were agreements on enforcement of regulations, and provisions for punitive damages and penalties.

The naval vessels from the U.S.A., Great Britain, and Germany were often called upon to act as law enforcement and mediators, and to administer justice to the expatriates and the native Samoans. They mostly favored the European residents, of course. And a chorus arose, in unison, to push the Samoan central government into a more European, parliamentary form, with the complete adoption of European laws and torts—common, commercial, and criminal.

The commanding officer of the naval vessel often served as the default judge and enforcer of European laws that native Samoans had to understand and adhere to. The commanding officers of these vessels were pioneers in establishing orderly conduct and starting legislative efforts in Samoa, a process that eventually led to the transformation and organization of the legal government. But for now, there were several attempts to derive a framework for a constitutional doctrine, to no avail.

1860: The Vaimauga District Code

The 1860 Vaimauga district code was inspired by the initiative of J.C. Williams, the British consul, to formalize *Seumanutafa Pogai, To'omalatai Toetagata, and Tofaeono's* work during the period 1858-1859. At this time J.C. Williams was the acting commercial agent for the United States, a position he would occupy until 1864.

The Vaimauga district code contains seventeen "simple laws" relating, among other things, to property and trading rights, land sales, shipping, marriage, adultery, keeping of the Sabbath, assault and murder, the carrying of lethal weapons, disorderly conduct, and the regulation of liquor sales. No provision was made at this stage for the levying of duties or taxes, but fines were, of course, to be collected for offences, part of the revenue from which was to be spent on public works.[c]

J. C. Williams was successful in getting the code approved by the district village chiefs with minor alterations. In additional to getting the code approved, Consul Williams got approval and agreement to appoint executive and judicial officers to administer the newly established code of laws. This law-making effort was emulated and replicated across the rest of Tuamasaga district (the district of the Malietoa dynasty and clan) thus becoming an example for Upolu and eventually for Savai'i, Tutuila, and the Kingdom of Manu'a.

1873: The Steinberger Regime

The 1873 Steinberger regime—or, more accurately, scheme—came very close to successfully coming up with a genuine government constitution. Acting on behalf of the United States government, under appointment by President Grant, Steinberger had not yet been processed by the Secretary of State Hamilton Fish up to Congress, but instead he sat in on Congress for some time.

In the meantime Steinberger, with somewhat overzealous enthusiasm, continued pushing his initiative with the chiefs, expatriates, consuls and their representatives, and the *Mālõ*, to solidify the drafting of a "constitution" document. This actually gained some credibility with the Samoan chiefs and the population at key major villages.

Steinberger's regime made some significant progress that is worth mentioning:

- The creation of a structure that allowed participation of villages and their respective populations, modeling the parliamentary structure and system.
- The creation of the "Upper House" or "House of Nobles," the *Ta'imua*, and the "Lower House" or "House of Representatives," called *Faipule*. Members of the *Ta'imua* were to be elected by the people of the district and approved by the "King," a title equivalent to Tafa'ifa and introduced by the Europeans.

This political structure gave the people much-needed participation in how the Island Nation was transforming, how their country was transforming into a new nation.

The framework of the constitution's contents was very much borrowed from other island countries' documents, with modifications as they saw necessary, given the lessons learned from other countries' experiences—Hawaii, New Zealand, Tahiti, Fiji, Toga, Niue, and others. For example, they observed the Hawaiian treatment of indigenous landholdings and property rights over family lands. They saw how New Zealand's Maori were struggling with the same land and property rights issues. So the Samoans were very apprehensive about these types of documents, seeing they were a far cry from oral-based agreements.

The only exception the LMS missionaries made to this "constitution" was that there were no specific provisions covering the sale of liquor on the Sabbath. The other major component of the Steinberger regime is that he nominated himself as the premier of the Island Nation.

The *Ta'imua* and *Faipule*

We should not minimize Steinberger's catalytic efforts to pursue the development of a constitution that the Island Nation needed desperately if it was to move forward in building a new government and a modern society. But I want to highlight the Samoans who were struggling to learn a new language, new ideas, new methodologies and science, and to understand European people and their behavior, political structures, trading and commerce techniques, globalization, colonialism, technology, and a whole new way of life.

So, the Steinberger *Ta'imua*, and some of the *Faipule,* material to the development of the new government in May 1870, were as follows:

- Tagaloa Apela, from Saluafata, Atua
- Fuataga, from Aleipata, Atua
- Misa, from Falelatai, A'ana
- Lemana, from Leulumoega, A'ana
- Sāmoa, from Vaimauga, Tuamasaga
- Mata'afā, from Malie, Tuamasaga
- Taupaū Sailusi, from Manono Island
- LeTufuga, from SaFotulafai and Fa'asaleleaga, Savai'i
- 'Aufa'i, from Sale'aula, Itu-o-tane, Savai'i
- Lavea, from Safotu, Itu-o-tane, Savai'i
- Asiata, from Satupa'itea, Itu-o-Fafine, Savai'i
- Ti'a, from Fa'asaleleaga, Savai'i
- Tuiā, from Safata, Tuamasaga
- Mata'utia, from Fa'asaleleaga, Savai'i
- Letuli, from Tualauta, Tutuila
- Le'iato, from Sua ma le Vaifanua, Tutuila

The Faipule authority under Steinberger consisted of:

- Matai'a, from Vaimoso, Tuamasaga
- Tufuga, from Itu-o-Tane, Savai'i
- Leala'iauloto, from Itu-o-Tane, Savai'i
- Mamea, from A'ana
- Aiono, from A'ana
- Tuisalega, from Itu-o-Fafine, Savai'i
- 'Ape, from Fa'asaleleaga, Savai'i
- Fiame, from Atua
- Tupa'i, from Atua
- Amoa, from Atua
- Alapalelei, from Alataua, Tutuila
- Le'aneo, from Itua'u, Tutuila
- Mulipola, from Manono Island
- Tuatagaloa, from Atua
- Masua, from Atua
- Leapai, from A'ana

The district governors under the 1875 Steinberger Regime were:

- To'omalatai Patiole, from Tuamasaga
- Afamasaga Moepa'ū, from A'ana
- Mata'afa Isosefo, from Atua
- I'iga Papali'i, from Fa'asaleleaga, Savai'i
- Tuitele, from Tutuila
- Lei'atauaLesā, from Manono Island

These representatives were selected or elected by their districts, following the already established district structure of Samoa, as evidenced in its national and district salutations. So here we see the incorporation of the paramount family clan and paramount and orator chiefs' structure in the decision-making process.

However, it is important to note that these are just few of the many Samoans who labored to build the new government.

Treaties and Friendships

End of the Steinberger Regime

The ephemeral Steinberger regime came to an end with Steinberger's self-appointed premier being exiled to Auckland, New Zealand—a move orchestrated by the British and American consuls, J.C. Williams and S.S. Foster respectively. These two consuls were never comfortable with the lack of support from the United States government for Steinberger's legitimacy as a Congress-approved representative to Samoa. The land-grab schemes of the various parties in Samoa were the primary motivation of many regimes, including Steinberger's. And the consuls were not in agreement with Steinberger's approach to legalizing real-estate sales, deeds of trust, property rights, and taxes. They were both suspicious of Steinberger's schemes.

While Steinberger's regime seems to have been built on shaky ground, it nevertheless became a catalyst for major forward movement of the Samoans toward a new initiative in government construction. There was evidence that indicated Steinberger had gained the ears and acceptance of the Samoan chiefs in leadership positions. His ideas helped the Samoan leadership hone their own design of what they wanted in the formulation of their new government. Samoans had their differences and their own ways of negotiating to their satisfaction, but they relied on old wisdom to guide the decision-making process.

Designing a New Form of Government

The movement to create a sound and mutually beneficial and acceptable constitution picked up momentum and urgency after the failed Steinberger regime.

The major problem was fragmentation of the different initiatives by various authors. It appears that every time a naval vessel appeared in a Samoan port, there would be a tribunal or court hearing to resolve criminal charges brought by European residents against each other or against Samoan natives.

Throughout these legal disputes, resolution efforts by the commanding officers of the naval vessels—from the militaries of Great Britain, Germany, and the United States—provided a vetting process for the construction of laws relating to real-estate, property rights, and how to get the responsible chief to pay punitive damages for property loss among European expatriates. All through this colonial period, these military naval vessels (fully equipped with weaponry) provided military reinforcements and, in a real and practical way, policing for their respective interests in the colony.

Thus the navies' expanded power of justice administration in the colony became the prevailing principle of colonialism. But this also meant that naval officers became contributors in the law-makings efforts of the Samoan's new government. The onus was on the consuls and the *Mālõ* in Mulinu'u, the seat of government in Apia, Upolu, Samoa. The consuls were all part-time shipping or commerce agents as well as government consuls for their countries, and the challenge was twofold:

- first, funding was needed for the government to pay for help and technical support, and
- second, competent staff were needed to help.

Through trial and error, they struggled forward. The Steinberger constitutional framework was far from comprehensive and workable, but it became a document that could be reshaped to incorporate their ideas and vision. And, with the guidance of the consuls, missionaries, naval officers, and business enterprise leaders, the *Mālõ* (consisting of *Ta'imua* and *Faipule* and the "King") continued development of the constitution through this tug-of-war until it became a work-in-process, living document.

1878: The Treaty of Friendship and Commerce

American involvement in the colonization of the islands of Samoa and Manu'a in the archipelago was a deliberate, long-distance courtship at best. This was conducted initially, under President Grant's administration, through representatives that were a combination of businessmen, tradesmen, and consuls (later, in 1879, the Consul-General of the United States) such as Steinberger, authorized to act on behalf of the department of the United States government Secretary of State.

Limited opportunities within the Samoan territory made it difficult to determine the value of complete commitment, in sending a fulltime representative in Samoa. However, given that Great Britain and Germany were already engaged in the colonization of Samoa, the potential for the U.S. to gain a footprint in the South Pacific made a compelling argument for engagement.

President Grant was pleased with the arrangement for the use of Pago Pago harbor on Tutuila Island, and Paramount Chief *Mauga* was astute enough to recognize that the American president was quietly approving and pleased with the harbor agreement. God's fortuitous creation of the harbor now determined the future of Tutuila's American Samoan population.

Manifest Destiny

The U.S. was going through its post-Civil War healing, and it was now implementing the ideology of Manifest Destiny (isolationism) toward forging a westward migration, simultaneously recognizing they were late comers to the business of territorial acquisition.

With Hayes' new administration following Grant's, there were welcome overtures that gave hope to the Samoan *Mālõ*, the government in Mulinu'u. Consul Griffin, who replaced Consul S.S. Foster (part-time), took a risk to see if he could get a better reception from President Hayes' administration. He left for Washington D.C. in mid-1875, and he met with members of the State Department, presenting to them the case for Samoa providing an American footprint in the Pacific region. He secured an opportunity for the State Department to receive a representative from the Samoan government, to hear their desires.

Laying down the foundation for this dialogue was critical for the Samoan government. Consul Griffin arrived back in Samoa in early 1876, after tending to business in San Francisco, California. Apparently, he knew that the United States government was obliged to forego imperial commitments in Samoa, but he continued, none-the-less, to plug for status as an American Protectorate, as an emergency measure.

The Treaty of Friendship and Commerce

After much debate at the *Mālõ* in Mulinu'u, the Samoan government selected High Chief M.K. *Mamea* from Lefaga, in A'ana district, as the government's emissary to the United States government. He was fluent in simple English. Assistant Consul Colmesnil (the business consul) chaperoned Chief *Mamea*, known as *LeMamea*, to Washington D.C.

Their journey stopped in San Francisco, California, where they prepared for the train ride east to Washington D.C. Colmesnil realized that an appropriate title must be used in meeting the Secretary of State and potentially, also, President Hayes. So before departing San Francisco for Washington D.C., M.K. *LeMamea* became "Secretary of State for the Kingdom of Samoa." And it worked, because he was afforded meetings with the U.S. Secretary of State and, later, a brief meeting with President Hayes.

An agreement, the "Treaty of Friendship and Commerce," was signed in Washington D.C. in January 1878. By the terms agreed to, the United States promised, in addition to the maintenance of perpetual friendship for Samoa, the use of its good offices in adjusting differences that might arise between Samoa and any power in amity with the United States. In return, the American Government secured the first (and, if it wished, sole) right to establish a naval station at Pago Pago, a guarantee of duty-free trade through Samoan ports, the privilege of "most favored nation," and certain extra-territorial concessions—namely, exclusive jurisdiction over disputes between Americans, joint jurisdiction with the Samoan Government over cases between Americans and Samoans, and the observance of American law on matters pertaining to the punishment of American offenders.[ci]

To see this rather one-sided treaty put into effect, the State Department detailed a commissioner, Gustavus Goward, to go with Chief *Mamea* to Samoa, and the navy provided transport for the party aboard the U.S.S. Adams, whose commanding officer was under instruction to locate a suitable site for a refueling depot in Pago Pago, on Tutuila Island.[cii]

Post-Treaty Relationship between the U.S. and Samoa

This one-sided treaty formed the foundation of the relationship between the United States of America and Samoa, which eventually evolved into the current status of American Samoa.

The *Mālõ* in Samoa immediately saw it as a one-sided treaty but, to some extent, they were able to commit to the United States government in the archipelago, to balance the other major powers. Obviously the *Mālõ* were hoping to get more from the Americans but, nevertheless, they achieved the goal of engaging the United States government in providing security and assistance with their navy.

This treaty cemented Paramount Chief *Mauga's* objective to move closer to and embrace the United States and to, potentially, break away from the *Mālõ* and orchestrate a government under the United States.

Twenty-five years later, that partition came to fruition. In the end, all the tug-of-war between those European expatriates and the Samoan leadership and Samoans seemed to have gravitated toward partition and a permanent split in the Island Nation culture.

The Samoan Dilemma

What Samoan leadership had to endure at this time is phenomenal, trying to absorb as much information as possible, and trying to make sense of it all, while negotiating with different types of people who had different motivations, greater resources, and more experience in the ways of the "civilized world." Not knowing who could be trusted or believed in, and distinguishing honest partners from the conniving and fraudulent ones, was a major challenge. Understanding technical methods, philosophical ideas, and principles dealing with modern government, economics, and business management, all posed further challenges to the leadership.

All of these issues, plus dealing with a demanding group of multicultural, international, part-time consuls of three major world powers, must have been exhausting. So the way in which Samoa was colonized, or not colonized, in spite of all this, is amazing. The fact that they navigated themselves between three major powers of the world is incredible. And so it's clear; and so I have chosen not to enumerate all the details of this political nightmare. The salient issue is for Samoans to realize that their ancient ancestors made that migration, 3,000 years before, to find a kingdom and freedom, and this colonialism was only a phase of their history—if a nightmare phase at that.

1879: The Bismarck Constitution

The transition to legalizing the relationships of the three world powers with the Samoan *Mālõ* government came about through various agreements, proclaimed through treaties of friendship. The United States government's treaty of friendship with Samoa, in January 1878, motivated Germany to sign their own treaty of friendship in January 1879. Germany's agreement encompassed a condominium, in which all factions would support previous treaties and abide by municipal convention. This was signed on the German warship, SMS Bismarck, in December 1879.

The agreement with Germany named *Talavou* (the Malietoa *Talavou*—see *Vaiinupõ*, page 69 in the Period VII timelines) as "king for life." In keeping with the spirit of compromise, Malietoa *Laupepa* was given the title of "regent."

It should be noted that Malietoa *Talavou* expressed a desire for Samoa to be protected under the authority of the three world powers. His wishes were clarified in the re-negotiated version of the agreement, by authorities of all three powers, in March 1880. Unfortunately, eight months later, on November 8, 1880, *Talavou* died, suddenly and unexpectedly, leaving the *Mālõ* to Malietoa *Laupepa*.

The *Mālõ* in Mulinu'u felt that the agreement expressed in the "Bismarck Constitution" had put the Malietoa lineage above all other titles. Members of the *Faipule* began to search for a new leader on whom they could cast their support. They found TuiA'ana *Tamasese* to be the man they were looking for, for in his veins flowed another line of "royal blood." He was a descendant of Tafa'ifa *Galumalemana*, through his son, TuiAtua TuiA'ana *Nofoasāefā,* whose brother Tafa'ifa *I'amafana* bequeathed the Tafa'ifa title to Malietoa *Vaiinupõ* (see Salamasina, page 52 in the Timelines).

In the meantime, Malietoa *Laupepa* was crowned to succeed *Talavou* as "king."

1879-1889: The Tripodal Tug of War

Great Britain concluded its deliberations with the *Mālõ* in August 1879, under the direction of Sir Arthur Gordon, and Malietoa *Talavou* signed another Treaty of Friendship with the Samoan Government. This became the foundation of a formal condominium organizational structure for regulating affairs of the Samoan Islands government. It perpetuated the multi-national character of foreign influence, canceling out differences in imperialist outlook among the world powers, and suspending Samoa in a neutral, semi-autonomous state.

Integral to this three-way tug-of-war form of colonial management was the infighting between the Malietoa sibling princes (*Talavou*, *Moli*, *Laupepa*, and *Tanumafili*-I), as well as between *Tamasese* and the Mata'afa. Each power had their own favorite to be King of Samoa, and the manipulative influence on these leaders, coupled with their own motivations, exacerbated the already complex conundrum of their situation.

This situation persisted until the Three Powers Conference on Samoa was moved to Berlin in April 1889, and a General Act of 14 June 1889 evidenced an agreement, subject to final approval and signature by the king of Samoa.

Legalizing these relationships now meant that a proposed ordinance by one party must be delivered and approved by each of the major powers—a logistics nightmare. In case of emergency, they still had to deliver their initiative to each consul to get their approval. In some very critical policy issues, they had to get approval from heads of government—from Washington D.C., London, or Berlin. The process was inefficient and archaic. But it illustrates the challenges the Samoan leadership had to manage and endure.

As one can observe, this tripodal parliamentary structure for politics in this tiny little corner of the world was boiling toward imminent evaporation.

1887: The *Tamasese*-Brandeis Regime

The Germans were more ambitious in colonizing Samoa than both the Americans and the British combined, for the Germans seemed more enamored with the idea of colonial accumulation than with the actual value of the colony's potential economic assets. Samoa did not have sufficient land for large-scale plantations. It did not have an abundance of natural resources, such as minerals to be mined. And there was an insufficient supply of willing laborers to build large plantations or farms.

In early 1887, Eugen Brandeis, a former Bavarian cavalry officer and a local employee of the DHPG—the German Trading and Plantation Company of the South Sea Islands of Hamburg—was directed by Theodore Weber (Hamburg consul and manager of Godeffroy in Samoa in 1864) and the new German consul, Becker, to go to Leulumoega, the seat of the A'ana district, and orchestrate a new government based in Leulumoega, in opposition to the *Mālõ* at Mulinu'u. This government was to be under *Tamasese*, the Tupua monarch, whom they recognized as king though he only held the title TuiA'ana. Brandeis would be the premier to *Tamasese* and the organizer of the new government.

Unlike the Steinberger regime, the Brandeis-*Tamasese* regime involved a legitimate *TamaAiga*—a title that means "sons of the Monarch families." *Tamasese* held the TuiA'ana title and had considerable support from the Atua district and parts of the A'ana district and some major village districts in Savai'i.

This ephemeral regime is known as "The *Tamasese*-Brandeis regime,"[ciii] and this initiative appeared to be an "urgent salvage operation on Germany's part," as author R.P. Gilson puts it.

Tamasese's ambition to be head of the country's government went back to the candidature of his father *Moegagogo* to the TuiA'ana and "TamaAiga," and was heavily supported by family and clan, including the Faleata district and *Aiga o Mavaega* in the A'ana district and Savai'i, as he contested for the *Ali'isili* (highest chief) title of Samoa.

Tamasese's* claim to *TamaAiga

TamaAiga refers to the genealogical princes contesting to be head of the monarchy, whose genealogy is of monarch blood. This title is also same in Hawaii but is held by only few—those who became Tafa'ifa—*Tupua* and his children and grandchildren; those who made it to the Tafa'ifa title. For example, *Faumuinā,* even though he was not Tafa'ifa, held the TuiAtua TuiA'ana PāPā (see *Faumuinā*, page 212 in Period VI); Tafa'ifa *Fonotī*, *Muagututi'a*, *Tupua*, *Galumalemana* and his children (Tafa'ifa *I'amafana*), *Tuimaleali'ifano*; and Malietoa, TuiAtua, TuiA'ana, Gatoa'itele and Vaetamasoāali'i. Not every paramount chief can be addressed as TamaAiga.

So, TamaAiga is a salutation referring to these titles and people, descended from monarch families. The TuiA'ana title and PāPā allow a candidate to fight for the Ali'isili (a European title innovation which stands in lieu of "king." The Germans created this title from their translation of the *Ali'i* or paramount chief; they added the word *sili*, the number one. Hence, "*Ali'i* number one").

Tamasese *Moegagogo* claimed he was TamaAiga from his ancestor Tafa'ifa *Galumalemana* and from his grandfather TuiAtua TuiA'ana *Nofoasāefā*. *Tamasese* took the lead from his father in contending for this title, and of course family support was necessary for a candidacy to head the country. For Tamasese *Moegagogo's* father was *Leasiolagi*, the son of TuiA'ana TuiAtua *Nofoasāefā* and Lady *Tusoloimalie* (daughter of Paramount Chief *Matai'a* of Faleata district). *Nofoasāefā's* father was the elder son of Tafa'ifa *Galumalemana* (1740) who succeeded his father Tafa'ifa *Tupuafuiavailili* (1710).

This same Lady *Tusoloimalie* also married TuiAtua *Paitomaleifi*, cousin to TuiA'ana *Nofoasāefā*. TuiAtua *Paitomaleifi* was defeated by his nephew, Mata'afa *Fa'asuamaleui*, and thus the TuiAtua title went to the Mata'afa. Then, shortly afterward in the same year, TuiA'ana *Nofoasāefā* heard about the nephew Mata'afa *Fa'asuamaleui* defeating the uncle *Paitomaleifi,* and he was unhappy about it. He brought a war party campaign to Mata'afa *Fa'asuamaleui,* and it didn't take long before Mata'afa *Fa'asuamaleui* was defeated and, of course, banished to Tutuila Island. *Nofoasāefā* took the TuiAtua title with him back to A'ana and his home in Asau, Savai'i. Unfortunately, his cannibalism practices caught up with him and he was assassinated in Auala, in the Asau district of Savai'i.

Leasiolagi also married Lady *Usipua*, daughter of *Nonumasesē* and a descendant of the Sa'o Tama'ita'i *Falenaoti* of Tafa'ifa *Fonotī* and the SaTuala family clan in Savai'i, and the origin of the *Aiga o Mavaega* in Faleasi'u village in the A'ana district.

This summary genealogy of Tamasese *Lealofi* (1898) and his father TuiA'ana Tamasese *Titiamaea* (1860), the son of *Moegagogo* (1830) should give an idea of the relationships involved at the time.

The Failure of the Coup D'état

The unsuccessful coup d'état of the *Tamasese*-Brandeis regime in August 1887 came as a bad omen to the Germans, due to the long-awaited international conference on Samoa, which was then in progress in Washington D.C. This turned out unsatisfactorily for Germany, the United States having continued to insist upon opposing the control of Samoa by a single power.

This turned out to be the beginning of the most trying and tumultuous period in the negotiations for a head of the government of Samoa. It shows the extreme fragility and fragmentation of the Samoa Condominium's organizational situation. The German's insistence on creating a king for Samoa became a major obstacle, because there were no laws providing for such a title or position in Samoan culture. The position of king is similar to that of Tafa'ifa, but there are no decrees to provide for a single office called "king"—the Tafa'ifa is achieved through the accumulation of the four PāPās by the families that are custodians of the respective PāPās.

The resulting civil war between Malietoa *Tanumafili*-I (who succeeded his father Malietoa *Laupepa* in 1898) and the TuiAtua Mata'afa was short-lived. It was almost a godsend that the TuiAtua Mata'afa, when first presented with a peace proposal, immediately accepted it, leading, as a result, to a new morning and a new day of peace for Samoa.

Malietoa *Tanumafili*-I was encouraged by the consuls and senior elder chiefs of the *Mālõ* to continue his mission to be educated abroad—after all, he was only 18 years of age. This was a recommendation that *Tanumafili*-I accepted without hesitation. And further to this arrangement, the people of Samoa rallied behind TuiAtua Mata'afa's candidature, for his experience and service to the country. The tripartite consuls also accepted him to be head of state for the country. This was the resolution for peace and leadership in Samoa, going forward to the partition phase of the government of Samoa.

Another significant development in this peace-making process was the establishment of districts and political representatives throughout the country, following the geographical divisions and subdivisions of the *Tumua* and *Pule* authorities, and the new office of governors. This partitioning with district representatives became foundational to the political structure of the Samoan government.

1889: The Treaty of Berlin

The Treaty of Berlin, signed on 14 June 1889 offered a major innovation in the establishment of a Samoan Supreme Court with a single judge, the "Chief Justice of Samoa," who was to be nominated by the three world powers or, failing agreement among them, by the monarchs of Sweden and Norway. The chief justice, as well as having civil and criminal jurisdiction, was also to act as adviser, arbiter, and even administrator in certain affairs of government and state. Additionally, the Berlin Act established mandatory public finance to fund these services.

Given the complexity of Samoa's Condominium (the joint protectorate), the chief justice became the single most important apparatus of the government promulgated by the Berlin Act of 1889. Embedded in the act were processes governing the employment of competent government executives to deal with technical administrative duties. This was, perhaps, a real management improvement, moving their colonization effort forward.

The Role of the Chief Justice

The real test of the role and authority of the chief justice came in ruling over the kingship of Samoa, after Malietoa *Laupepa's* passing 1898. The two contenders were *Tanumafili*-I—the eighteen-year-old son of Malietoa *Laupepa*—and the more senior and experienced TuiA'ana TuiAtua Mata'afa *Iosefo*.

Chief Justice William Lea Chambers, an American, declared for *Tanumafili*-I on December 31, 1898, based on the protocol of the Berlin conference, as the only eligible candidate and therefore king of Samoa.

While the legal decision declared *Tanumafili*-I as king of Samoa, the overwhelming consensus of the *Mālõ* and the world powers was that the best and most practical leader would be Mata'afa *Iosefo*, given his seniority in government affairs and his experience with the *Mālõ* leadership. Thus, as we have mentioned above, the consuls and leaders of the *Mālõ* tried to convince *Tanumafili*-I to continue his seminary schooling in Fiji and leave the government to Mata'afa *Iosefo*. *Tanumafili*-I and the Malietoa clan and supporters were united in this decision. *Tanumafili*-I would not return to Samoa until after the Mata'afa's passing, when he succeeded Mata'afa as head of government and was followed by his son *Tanumafili*-II in 1939.

The Road to Partition

The Real Prophetic "Wind of Change"

The Samoa Condominium, established in the 1889 Treaty of Berlin, was legal and formal, and the three-way tug-of-war had now gotten the attention of the world powers' decision-making authorities. The German government was comfortable with colonizing Samoa, just to add it onto their lists of territory. Great Britain had a portfolio of territories in the Pacific region that they were farming out, to either New Zealand or Australia, for administration. The Americans were simply content with a refueling place in the South Pacific region. So no matter how big or small the "value propositions" were of Samoa to each of the powers, the Condominium was becoming a source of aggravation and irritation to all parties.

The traffic of naval ships, canvassing and congregating in the Navigators' Archipelago, was frightening to the Samoans. By February to March 1889, Apia harbor had, at a minimum, two or three naval vessels from each of the world powers, each trying to manage and calm the warring *Mālõ* and deal with the logistics of the tripartite governing Condominium. These often used naval artillery to subdue the warring Samoan tribes.

By the same token, the tug-of-war intensified, and Apia harbor now docked three naval vessels from Germany (the Adler, Eber, and Olga), while outside the harbor three U.S. naval vessels (Vandalia, Trenton, and Nipsic) were anchored, as well as Great Britain's naval vessel, the HMS Calliope.

On the morning of March 15, 1889, the weather turned ugly. The sky was covered with dark clouds, and there was dead silence, without a breeze. Samoans had experienced these signs of the weather many times before, and they immediately began to break off any war engagements so they could prepare their homes for the impending storm. In the meantime, the captains of the respective naval vessels didn't have a clue.

By early evening, the storm was a typhoon picking up momentum till, around 8 p.m., the German vessel Eber was on the reef shore, totally destroyed, with 50 sailors dead. Before midnight, the Adler was also ripped to pieces on the reef, with 20 sailors dead. This was the violent fate of all vessels, with the exception of the Calliope that managed escape early the next morning. In total, six naval vessels were destroyed, and 146 sailors died.

The Samoans believed this was a "parting of the Red Sea moment" in saving the freedom of the Samoan government. For in the following 10 years, the world powers would begin the transition to partitioning Tutuila into American Samoa and Western Samoa, which was under German authority until Germany lost the First World War and the British took it over; the British assigned it to be administered by New Zealand, leading eventually to self-governance for Western Samoa.

British "Horse-Trading" with Germany

All along, in the affairs of the Condominium and the three world powers, there was the question of partition, both as an isolated problem for the two European powers and for the United States of America, and also as a broader redefinition of the European sphere of influence around the world, through all their respective colonies.

Around the same time period, September to November 1899, the British Government was in the midst of the Boer war in South Africa. The Germans being sympathetic to the Boer side gave impetus to the British to perhaps trade territories with the Germans in the Pacific region.

Before the German emperor arrived in England, in November 1899, the two countries had been busily trading territories. Now, under this agreement, all of Samoa west of longitude 171 degrees West would become German. In return, Germany transferred to Britain her treaty rights in Toga, agreed to shifting the boundary between the British and German spheres in the Solomon Islands, and made a few more concessions in Papua New Guinea. This Anglo-German agreement really determined the future status of Samoa.

Partition

A tripartite convention was signed on behalf of all three world powers on December 2, 1899. And in early January 1901, Germany and the United States of America established administrative control in their parts of the archipelago.[civ]

The Germans immediately installed Dr. Wilhelm Solf as president of the municipality. The first act of the Germans, before hoisting their flag, was removing King Mata'afa *Iosefo* from the position of king. They gave him instead a new title "Highest Paramount" Chief (*Ali'i Sili*) and named the Kaiser of Germany as King of Samoa!

Samoan leaders were resentful that their country had been partitioned, let alone they were also annoyed at the initial act of not honoring the kingship structure they had negotiated for seventy years (1830-1900). The citizens of Western Samoa were not happy that it should be Germans who were their new rulers. They had lost their will to strive for independence during the Condominium but, as the future was to show, they had lost none of their will to retain their own culture or to struggle for control of their own affairs. This would be the catalyst leading to the birth of a national protest organization, one that would lead to their attaining self-governance.

The acrimonious relationship between German rulers and Samoan leaders and citizens, during the fourteen years of German colonization, lasted until Germany's defeat in the First World War which brought the British in, with the introduction of New Zealand into the colonial management process.

Why were Samoan leaders not happy with the Germans? Samoans had had over 60 years of experience with Germans, 70 years with the British, and 50 years with the Americans. But they had accumulated experiences with the British first, initially with missionaries, followed by the diplomatic corps.

When the British came to Samoa, they were constantly being advised by the missionaries and, whether they accepted the advice or not, they were getting good data, because the data were gathered from the ground upward, through all demographics.

Samoans relied heavily on the teaching of the missionaries and thus put their trust in them. But the inextricable relationships between the British Government, the LMS, and the Samoans was totally undermined by Britain's "horse-trading" geopolitics with Germany. And thus, Samoan attitudes toward foreign powers became confirmed in their determination for self-governance.

Eventually a military conflict between Germans soldiers and Samoan protesters, organized by none other than TuiAtua TuiA'ana Mata'afa *Iosefo*, resulted in the defeat of a German squadron of 60 soldiers. Many were wounded and several died.

This was an embarrassment for the German naval command.

1900: American Samoa, Deed of Cession

The United States of America, under President McKinley, signed an Executive Order in February to March 1900, giving authority to Commander Benjamin Franklin Tilley. McKinley's signed authority arrived in American Samoa on April 4, 1900, and American Samoa became, legally, a "Possession" under "Deed of Cession" to the United States government on April 2, 1900. The Tutuila Declaration of the Form of Government proclaimed that the laws of the United States of America were in force in the territory, and those Samoan laws and customs not in conflict with the laws of the United States would be preserved.

The American Samoan government is organized in a manner similar to that of the United States government. There is a house of Legislative authority and a house of Senate authority. The territory reports up to the United States government Department of the Interior. A non-voting representative to the Congress of the United States government is elected every two years.[cv]

Tilley was the first U.S. naval governor of American Samoa, and the person to whom the Deed of Cession was addressed in 1900. Thus one people, one culture, but catering to two different masters, became the new way of life for Samoans and Manu'ans.

An advantage for the Americans was that the United States government already had plenty of experience in dealing with indigenous populations, for better or worse, with the Native Americans. The American government had already had to deal with indigenous family and tribal lands, and with property rights. Native Americans already had their own justice system, and their titles and lands court system.

Manu'a gave up their (King) TuiManu'a crown to the U.S. Constitution, in a manner similar to that of the Hawaiian Kingdom. But they kept their chief titles and family lands and culture. So American Samoans can travel freely into the United States and can file for citizenship once they set foot into any state of the union. They serve in the U.S. military at will, and they are known for their loyalty in their military commitment. American Samoans believe this is another major area where they can show their loyalty to the United States of America, through serving in the military and seeing the world. For example, according to military statistical data, American Samoans had the highest per capita death rate in the Desert Storm conflict of any city or town in the U.S.

1921: The Samoa Act

From 1900 to the First World War in 1914, Samoa was a German colony. On August 7, 1914, the New Zealand government, orchestrated by Great Britain, seized a wireless station in Apia, Samoa, which was being used by the German East Asia Squadron. This constituted an act of war and was followed by New Zealand's Samoan Expeditionary Force landing on August 15, 1914, claiming Samoa as a British colony under the administration of the New Zealand government.

On December 17, 1920, the League of Nations formally conferred a Class C mandate over the former German Colony of Samoa to the Dominion of New Zealand. The mandate was supported by Samoan Constitution Order 1920, which replaced the military occupation with civil administration on May 1, 1922, when the Samoa Act of 1921 came into force.

Under the Samoa Act, the New Zealand governor-general appointed an administrator based in Apia, Samoa, to hold executive power and to report to the New Zealand Minister of External Affairs in Wellington. Lawmaking power was held by the administrator and the local legislative council, although Wellington, New Zealand, had final authority.

After 1945-47, the classification of the mandate was changed to a United Nations Trusteeship Territory. This became a transitional government until Samoa successfully gained their independence in 1962.

The Road to Self-Governance

The Testament

1908 saw the establishment of a Samoan Protest Organization called the *Mau,* or the "Testament" to self-government. This would guide Samoans to independence within the next 60 years. The full initiative of the *Mau* is: *Mau a Pule* (Savai'i authority) *Mau Tumua* (Upolu authority), as in the country's Salutations.

The word *Mau*, according to Rev. Pratt's *Grammar and Dictionary of the Samoan Language,*[cvi] means testimony, which, in the American Heritage Dictionary, means "evidence from a witness." But the word testament also means "tangible proof of evidence." Merriam-Webster Dictionary suggests tangible proof or tribute; an expression of conviction; a creed, as in a witness to the carrying and positive public planning of public goods. This expresses the essence of the profundity of this Samoan protest.

To assess the value of the word *Mau* to the Samoan cause or initiative, we should affirm that it truly means "testament or profound conviction" to pursue self-government. For the word *Mau* does not mean a "strongly held opinion." I saw this translation on Wikipedia in an article on Samoan history, and I feel compelled to make this correction, else we continue to perpetuate an error as it reflects on us throughout the generations.

No revolution was fought for freedom and self-government based on an "opinion." You do not ask citizens of a population to die for an "opinion." People fight and die for their "conviction," for a testament, for a creed, for religion, for Christianity, Islam, Communism, Capitalism, Taoism, etc. This is why I try my best to derive a close translation, giving the essence of the Samoan word's meaning, not just what it means on the surface, because otherwise we lose the intrinsic value of the Samoan meaning.

(For example, I refuse to use the European translation of the *Fue* to mean "flyswatter." The *fue* is evidence of authority in the Samoan chieftain structure and protocols. It's the same as the Egyptian's scepter or the Greek's caduceus or, at a minimum, of the word "flail." For this is what Socrates warned us about, the way we repeat errors just by citing references. How does an orator deliver a speech while the audience is thinking "flyswatter"? It's a joke.)

Remember, Samoans define themselves through the land, because that defines their property rights. So any ruler that didn't understand this principle would most likely misjudge and mismanage Samoans. And this was the problem with colonization by Europeans. Samoans saw and experienced the way the German ruler, Governor Solof, played favorites with the German company, Deutsche Handels und Plantagen Gesellschaft or DHPG, which was dictating the price of *copra* (the harvest of dried coconut meat for oil and perfume) by manipulating the supply and demand through price-gouging. So, led by Orator Chief *Lauaki Namulau'ulu Mamoe* of SaFotulafai, Savai'i, the *Mau* organization was the first organized protest, in an initiative to galvanize the country's support to fight for better treatment—better treatment in wages for labor and in crop pricing, and an end to poor treatment of Samoans vis-a-vis European expatriates. Samoans were not slaves, nor were they accustomed to that kind of treatment.

Orator Chief *Lauaki* was exiled by the Germans to Saipan in Micronesia for five years, and the esteemed orator chief and leader died in Saipan in 1915, while getting ready set sail for Samoa. The *Mau* was revitalized in early 1923, and in 1929 Tupua Tamasese *Lealofi-o-a'ana* took over the helm. By this time, the foe was the New Zealand dominion.

On December 28, 1929, Tupua Tamasese *Lealofioa'ana* led his uniformed *Mau* in a peaceful demonstration in downtown Apia. The New Zealand police attempted to arrest the paramount royal chief.

When he resisted, a struggle occurred between the police and the *Mau*. The officers began to fire randomly into the crowd, and a Lewis machine-gun, mounted in preparation for this demonstration, was used to disperse the *Mau*.

Royal Chief Tupua Tamasese *Lealofi*-III was shot in the back and shortly died. With his last strength, he continued to yell out, "Peace," "Peace," "Samoa," and then his voice stopped; he was dead.

There were seven other warriors who spilled their blood in this peaceful protest march. They are: High Chief *Tapu* of Auala village, Savai'i; Paramount Chief *Faumuinā* of Safotu, Savai'i; *Ainoa* of Tuana'i, Upolu; Senior Orator *Vele* of Lepea, Upolu; Chief *Migao* of Vaimoso, Upolu; Paramount Chief *Leota* of Lealaali'i, Savai'i; and Paramount Chief *Tuiā* of Vaimoso, Upolu. In addition to the deaths, there were fifty-five wounded, one of whom died a month later. Paramount Chief *Faumuinā* of Lepea, Faleata district, Upolu, assumed the leadership role of the *Mau* going forward. Only one police officer died, by the name of Abraham, a native of New Zealand.[cvii]

This is known as "Dark Morning" in the edicts of Samoan history. This sad event cemented the *Mau*'s purpose in the hearts and minds of Samoans, so that they must, at all costs, work toward their independence. The 1945-46 transition to United Nations trusteeship set the stage for a move toward a deliberate plan of self-government. In 1955, the New Zealand Dominion agreed to a deliberate transition to Samoan government over their domestic affairs, under the assistance of the New Zealand Dominion governor-general, a prerequisite to universal suffrage.

1959-61: Final Constitution

The final constitution represents an evolution from previous attempted efforts and frameworks, with an absorption of Western world ideologies helping in its final framing.

The latest Steinberger proposal was far from complete, but it had a structure and section outlines that could be studied and modified according to the desired contents and input from various groups. The *Mālō, Ta'imua,* and *Faipule* were the major benefactors of Steinberger's proposed constitution, because they had learned about what it really meant as a testament document that would spell out the foundation of people's freedom, rights, laws, governance, and protections, with guarantees for their culture as an integral part of their content.

Training in Christianity and understanding of Christian doctrines, principles, and way of life was fundamental to the development of the document. But perhaps even more important, on the personal, cognitive-developmental level, was the absorption of ideology from the outside world. In particular, there was a need to see how new laws and systems of governance from the Western world impacted understanding, on a contextual level relative to cultural norms and practices. This was far more important than getting a PhD as a prerequisite to drafting a document that, in principle, defined their legal and cultural way of life.

At this point the Samoan cultural authorities were the *Tumua* and *Pule* at the local and district levels, followed by representatives from these two-level demographics in the house of the *Faipule*. Then came the *Ta'imua* representatives, at the district level, as well as the governor at a direct managerial level. Also, European expatriate citizens and community were incorporated into the structure.

This body of representations was organized into a European form of parliamentary system. And, with the guidance of the consuls for the world powers, a more balanced content was achieved.

The structural outline of the principles is as follows:

1. Christian rules and principles.
2. Samoan cultural norms and practices at the base.
3. Modern laws.
4. Cultural ordinances and *tapu*.

This was the structure and content of the Samoan constitution, as promulgated by the *Mālõ* at Mulinu'u in 1895. It was still subject to negotiations, up until the early 1950s. Then in 1959-61, a final draft was made of the self-governing constitution.

This would be the framework of Samoa's independent constitution, and a derivative of its national motto, "God's Design of Samoa's Government and Nation"—*my translation*.

The Next Period and the Future of Samoa

Samoa is counted among the 22 Pacific Island Countries and Territories (independent island countries, called PICT) which cover in excess of 10,000 land islands and atolls in the Pacific Ocean, and form a significant force in the region. Thus, as we move on from the past and look toward the future, I am returning to my aerial survey point of view that I put forward in my first book. I will attempt to draw out the relative importance of this region to global geopolitics. But first we should look at the "local" geopolitics of ordinary people in the present day, creating rules for sustainable and equitable management of shared resources.

Natural Resources

Ownership of Land

As we have seen, one of the sources of disagreement and retaliation in Samoan relationships with Europeans was the aggressiveness of Europeans and their expatriates in acquiring Samoan land.

Here is a summary of land-claim cases investigated and confirmed by the Samoan Commission, 1891-4, showing cases confirmed by the Commission court to be valid.[cviii]

Nationality	Area Claimed	Confirmed
German	134,419 acres	75k or 30% of claim
English	1,350,270	36k or 3%
American	302,746	21k or 7%
French	2,307	1.3k or 57%
Others	2,151	2k or 93%
Grand Total	1, 600,893	135,300 or 8%

We have learned from Volume I of this book, *Navigators Forging a Matriarchal Culture in Polynesia*, that the land is foundational to a person's identity or *fa'asinomaga*—to the family property rights that define the family and clan. We also learned that every family's member inherits a "piece of the rock," as the saying says. Thus in essence, to put it in European legal terms, everyone's name is on the deed of the land. However, these family land-holdings have been decreed orally from ancient ancestors. There are no documents substantiating these property rights, as the European and expatriate residents found out the hard way.

In very few families can one person, such as a *Sa'o* Paramount Chief, make decisions on behalf of the whole family. Hence the conflict between a European understanding of real-estate property rights and the Samoan oral, or cultural, family-land identity. This became a source of legal disputes over land acquisition—disputes between the European land management company and the native owners of the disputed family real-estate or property.

The land of the islands was originally surveyed by the United States Exploration Expedition, led by its commander, Lt. Charles Wilkes, in 1836-42.[cix] The unclear identification of title ownerships, due to orally transmitted decrees, coupled with the lack of clear definitions of boundaries and legal surveillance of property, caused disputes. And the authority structure of the Samoan family, defining property rights, became the core issue with the island's real-estate property and intellectual property rights.

As we noted, in the process of cultural development and structure, as described in Volume I of this work, there is no single authority that can decide to sell a family's customary land-holding. It must be sold by consensus or not at all. This is integral to the individual identity, family identity, clan identity, and village and district identities. This is all to be expected, given the infrastructure of virgin islands.

While Europeans and expatriates struggled to force acquisitions of land, in spite of these technical problems, Samoans were more concerned about losing their homeland to land-grabbing companies. This was a source of aggravation and a battle initiative for the Samoans. The major players were the J.C. Godeffroy Central Polynesian Land and Commercial Company (CPLCC) in 1870-1894, Deutsche Handels und Plantagen Gesellschaft der Südsee Inseln zu Hamburg (DHPG) in 1870-1894, W. McArthur & Co. in 1870-1892, and Cornwall in 1872-1894.

Samoans had already heard land-grabbing tales from the Maori in New Zealand, Tahiti, and Hawaii, and were well aware of the challenges they faced in protecting their homeland. So, while there was a temptation to sell the land for cash to acquire tools, weapons, and ammunitions for war, the reality was that not everyone in the family clan was in agreement. Thus the need for an effective mechanism to render justice over these land claims, which in 1890 exceeded 4,000 claims.

The need for a commission or function for legal mediation had been suggested back in the early 1870s when the land rush started, thanks to Steinberg and his schemes that attracted other land-grabbers to take advantage of the earth of Samoans' limited homeland.

The Berlin Act of 1889 included a provision for the creation and administration of a land commission or tribunal, to provide legal remedies for the excess of 4,000 land-claims resulting from land-contracts that stemmed from the land-rush of 1870s. The structure consists of representatives, appointed and approved by the tripartite, and Samoan representatives, appointed and approved by the head of state and the Samoan supreme judge. All judgements need to be approved by the head of state and the supreme judge of Samoa. Thus, of the 1.6 million acres claimed, only 135,300 acres have been confirmed by the Commission court. The chart given earlier is a summary of the net results of the Land Commission Tribunal of 1891-94.

Ownership of the Sea

Dividing the Waters

But today, it's not just a question of who owns the land. Ownership of the world's oceans was first "defined" in 1494, two years after Christopher Columbus' first expedition to America. Pope Alexander VI met with representatives from the two main maritime powers, Spain and Portugal, and pronounced a Papal Bull giving Spain everything west of an imaginary line drawn down the Atlantic Ocean, and Portugal everything east of it. Thus the Pacific and the Gulf of Mexico were assigned to Spain, while Portugal was given the South Atlantic and the Indian Ocean.[cx]

But there was disagreement, way before Pope Alexander VI's decree. The Egyptians first plied the Mediterranean in papyrus rafts, transporting large slabs of stones to build the pyramids around 2500 B.C. According to Herodotus, the Egyptians did not know how to sail the rafts back up the Nile, so they had to dismantle them, carrying them back up the river. Then disputes between the people of Mesopotamia (the Sumerians) and the Phoenicians and Greeks, on who ruled the Mediterranean Sea, led to war and conflict, as described by the ancient writers Diodorus, Virgil, and Plutarch.

Treaties continue to be made, and the South Pacific peoples have always had a belief that, since they were first to colonize the Pacific Ocean, they can lay claim to it as an integral resource upholding their way of life.

The world's effort to better control and manage this critical resource for human life was assigned to the United Nations Convention on the Law of the Sea, signed on December 10, 1982. It is a complicated law, based on a set of treaties from the past that needed to be renegotiated, reconciled, and redefined, governing all navigational rights, territorial limits, economic jurisdiction, legal status of resources on the seabed beyond those limits of national jurisdiction, passage of ships through narrow straits, conservation and management of living marine resources, and protection of the marine environment of all nations concerned. In addition, binding procedures for the settlement of disputes between states were agreed upon as critical to the treaty.[cxi]

Who Owns the Ocean?

The critical importance of the quality of the Pacific Ocean to the survival of the Pacific peoples cannot be emphasized enough. These tiny island nations are only pawns in the geopolitics of the largest and most powerful nations' chess game, involving the Pacific Ocean's resources.

The real problem with the current interpretation of rules and practices is that the majority of the Pacific Ocean is defined as giving fishing rights to almost every major country in the world—China, Japan, Vietnam, Australia, the USA, Russia, Chile, Canada, Argentina, and others. The fishing lanes available to each of these major countries, when added together, cover the total area of the Pacific Ocean, and thus cover the bulk of its economic value from the supply chain. If, on the other hand, the Pacific Island Countries and Territories could collectively combine their 200-mile radii, that would equate to a region of radius 4,400 miles. That would be a significant-sized ocean to control and would offer significant bargaining power.

The focus is the aggregate of Pacific Ocean revenues from the supply chain, rather than locally generated production. The World Bank, citing OECD estimates, values global ocean revenues from the supply chain at $1.3 trillion USD. If you just divide this evenly between the Atlantic, Indian, and Pacific Oceans, that will come to $433 billion USD revenue for the Pacific Ocean—an amount far greater than the amount these Pacific Island countries and territories receive; meanwhile they are trying to squeeze every penny out to make a living. There is enough money to go around.

Who Benefits from the Ocean?

Study 1: FAO Fisheries

The 2006 paper, *Revenue Distribution Through The Seafood Value Chain*—by Eyjolfur Gudmundsson from the Faculty of Business and Science, University of Akureyri, Akureyri, Iceland; Frank Asche of the Department of Industrial Economics University of Stavanger, Norway; and Max Nielsen, Adjunkt at Fødevareøkonomisk Institut, Frederiksberg, Denmark[cxii]—mentions that the total economic value chain of global fisheries was about $68 billion USD in 2005-2006. Today's number is $1.3 trillion USD worldwide[cxiii]—a change that took place in 15 years, which means the value chain of Pacific Ocean catches could easily be around $450 billion USD annually.

Major progress is being made in the worlds of ocean aquaculture development, governance, and management, but progress comes with major challenges. The differences in culture and government objectives make it always difficult to find points of compromise, and so it takes major efforts to negotiate policy and standards and, of course, to enforce compliance.[cxiv]

Study 2: International Union for Conservation of Nature

The Pacific Ocean is indeed vast, but its resources are not endless, and the sharing of those resources is not always consummate with the rights and needs of the people.

The following economic data, taken from the International Union for Conservation of Nature (IUCN) July 2010 paper,[cxv] relate to the fishing Gross Value Product (GVP) for the 22 Pacific Island Countries and Territories (called PICT):

1. GVP for the PICT is $3.32 billion (USD) annually in 2008.
2. If you add the value of industrial tuna catches of $1.2 billion, this brings the total economic value to $4.52 billion (USD) annually in 2007-2008.
3. Of the $1.2 billion (USD) from industrial tuna catches, $78 million (USD) was received for fees and other charges.
4. Of the total GVP of $3.32 billion (USD), $2.30 billion (USD) is attributed to tourism in the region.
5. The remaining difference ($1.02 billion USD,) is attributed to locally generated fishing production.

These numbers are not impressive at all. The study and the data evidence an approach using the typical mantra: collect the data from PICT to monitor their progress, and keep them busy doing as much as they can to improve their economic development. Keep them contained in their respective lane, as it were.

The UN Law of Sea Committee and the Agreement on the 200-mile radius for each country, as measured from its shores, would in theory be plenty for each Pacific Island Country. But here's what is wrong with this rule: the physical size of an island makes the radius of the available ocean space absolutely inequitable for the PICT. To go out 200 miles fishing requires a well-equipped fishing vessel, with all the technology necessary to survive that far out in the ocean. This requires significant capital investment by the local fishermen—something only a very few can afford.

So, as an alternative, the PICT is leasing the 200-mile radius of ocean to commercial fishing companies from capital-rich countries. While this seems like a good alternative, it's a double-edged sword. On one hand the PICT is always at a disadvantage in negotiating with large fishing fleets and aggregators of fish-market buyers and sellers. On the other hand, the PICT risks the danger of over-fishing and severe environmental consequences. American Samoans have been feeling both sides of this metaphorical double-edged sword for some time now.

Conversation with local fishermen in American Samoa indicates that the production of fish at a 10 to 15 miles radius outside the shore is totally depleted. The commercial fleets have totally over-fished it. The tiny motorboats of the local fishermen can't get too far without navigational equipment. So now they're buying fish from the StarKist Tuna manufacturer on the island!

Study 3: High Level Panel for a Sustainable Ocean Economy

Added to this, the article *Illicit Trade in Marine Resources Keeps Billions out of Pacific Economies Every Year,* on 12/05/2019,[cxvi] indicated that about 24% out of 62,800 million tonnes of fish—i.e. 15.07 million tonnes—goes unreported in the data. Of this unreported amount, about 3.2 to 7.2 million tonnes are illegally traded in international markets. That amounts to $4.3-8.3 billion (USD) of revenue, lost every year to the formal economy—let alone the amount lost to the Pacific Island Countries and Territories (PICT).

According to the latest World Bank report, illegally traded fish catches have gone up to around 26 million tonnes, or $80 billion USD of lost opportunity. This is on top of the increased contribution of the Blue economy—an economy that defines the sustainable use of ocean resources for economic growth, improved livelihoods and jobs, and ocean ecosystem health—of $1.3 trillion USD.[cxvii]

These economic value chain numbers are derived from grossly under-reported data, as I mentioned above. And the catches from the Pacific Ocean of six countries (China, Vietnam, the USA, India, Chile, and Indonesia) totaled $37 billion USD in 2012-2013.

Food from the Sea

Overfishing

Today, the Pacific Ocean is a source of seafood to virtually the whole world. Currently the largest seafood processor, supplying major consumers of seafood globally, is China. It makes its living almost exclusive from the Pacific Ocean, a $14.1 billion USD industry in 2013. Others are Vietnam with $5.8 billion USD, the United Sates at $5.1 billion USD, and India with $4.6 billion. Chile exported $4.0 billion in 2013, and Indonesia $3.11 billion in 2012.

I have highlighted these countries because they represent the major fishing fleets currently fishing throughout the whole of the Pacific Ocean. As noted above, these countries have harvested the wealth of the Pacific Ocean exclusively for their own benefit, while the claimants of the Pacific Ocean—the Polynesians, Micronesians, and Melanesians—are left with the crumbs from the blessing provided to them by their deity. This is a well-known area of concern with environmental scientists, policy makers, and managers of all nations.

As we have seen (see Study 2: International Union for Conservation of Nature, page 326), overfishing by these large fishing fleets is draining the life from the water. The ocean's most important predators are being killed at an alarming rate, and when a major predator is taken out of the loop, it's usually the case that species lower on the food chain start to overpopulate their habitat, creating a destructive downward spiral in the ecosystem.[cxviii]

Coral Reefs

Reefs are the boundaries between the ocean and the landmass. They protect the coastlines and provide habitats and shelter for many marine organisms. They are where the ocean meets the land.

The three most common types of coral reefs are fringing reefs, barrier reefs, and atolls. The majority of reefs in the Samoa Island chain are fringing reefs. If we think of the ocean as a source of the food supply chain, sustaining the life of the inhabitants of an island, then the reefs have to be the factory or manufacturer of the seafood supply. It is a simple metaphor. Thus, if we neglect to care for the reefs, the effect will be to destroy the seafood supply. Likewise, if we pursue policies that undermine the health of the reefs and ocean at large, the food supply will become less sustainable, ultimately affecting human survival.

Study 4: Global Coral Reef Monitoring Network

The human impact on coral reefs, through neglect and environmental mismanagement, is significant. Damaging activities include coral mining, pollution (organic and inorganic), overfishing, blast fishing, and the digging of canals changing access into islands and bays, all of which have exacerbated the demise of the reef ecosystem.[cxix] A worldwide study in 2008, by Clive Wilkinson of the Global Coral Reef Monitoring Network, estimated that 19% of the existing area of coral reefs had already been lost, and that a further 17% was likely to be lost over the coming 10 to 20 years.[cxx] Only 46% of the world's reefs could be currently regarded as being in good health, and about 60% of the world's reefs may be at risk due to destructive, human-related activities.

Interestingly, the threat to the health of reefs is particularly strong in Southeast Asia and the East Pacific Ocean, where 80% of reefs are endangered according to Wilkinson's study. The factors that affect coral reefs include: the ocean's role as a carbon dioxide sink; atmospheric changes; ultraviolet light; ocean acidification; viruses; the impact of dust storms carrying agents to far-flung reefs; pollutants; algal blooms, and more.

Study 5: National Oceanic and Atmospheric Administration

Reefs are threatened well beyond coastal areas. It's evident that climate change and warming temperatures cause coral bleaching and, where severe, destroy the coral and the whole of a reef.[cxxi] Studies from NOAA (the U.S. Department of Commerce's National Oceanic and Atmospheric Administration) in their Coral Reef Conservation Program (CRCP)[cxxii] indicate that the current condition of coral reefs in American Samoa and the Manu'an Islands is as follows:

- Good condition overall: corals and algae, fish, climate, and human conditions

- Doing well: Benthic cover and coral populations
- Moderate to severe impact: environmental situation impacting the fish
- Depleted: Sharks and other predators throughout the world, and American Samoa is no exception.
- Negative impact: Climate negatively affects coral reefs due to temperature stress and ocean acidification.

The study also confirmed the active participation of local communities in resource management plans, and in ordinances to govern the health of the coral and reefs, as well as the beaches and costal shores.

Study 6: Tara Pacific Expedition

In another study, the 2016 Tara Pacific Expedition, looking at the Samoan Islands (Upolu, Savai'i, Apolima, and Manono), found that coral cover was extremely low (1%) at approximately half of the sites, and below 10% at 78% of the sites. Acanthurus (a colorful fish found in tropical ocean near coral reefs) and Zanclus Cornutus (the Moorish Idol fish), were significantly (10%) smaller near Upolu than around nearby islands. But marine protected areas had higher coral cover, so local action in managing the reefs is a useful tool in supporting the ecosystems and reducing anthropogenic impacts.[cxxiii]

The message from these studies is a cautionary sign for reef ecosystem health in remote locations on this planet, reinforcing the need to immediately reduce anthropogenic impacts on global sites.

Ocean Pollution

The Great Pacific Garbage Patch

Yet, while the world continues to "consume" the world's biggest resource for life on earth—the ocean—it also continues to dump more trash in the largest "landfill" on earth to destroy it.

Pollution in the Pacific Ocean has reached catastrophic proportions. The "Great Pacific Garbage Patch" was discovered by a racing-boat captain by the name of Charles Moore, during a yachting race from California to Hawaii, and inspired David de Rothschild to found Adventure Ecology in 2014. Effectively, the Garbage Patch is a collection of marine debris in the North Pacific Ocean, forming a "trash vortex." It spans waters from the west coast of North America to Japan. The Patch consists of the Western Garbage Patch, located near Japan, and the Eastern Garbage Patch, located between the U.S. states of Hawaii and California. According to this article, these patches of spinning debris are linked together by the North Pacific Subtropical Convergence Zone, located a few hundred kilometers north of Hawaii. Warm water from the South Pacific meeting cooler water from the Arctic creates a kind of highway where garbage moves from one patch to another.[cxxiv]

According to the European Commission, the "World's Largest Landfill," as it is sometime known, is comprised of about 3.5 million tons of trash. It is often compared to the size of Europe, 3.45 million square kilometers. Its impact on the marine food chain in the Pacific Ocean is catastrophic and is spreading to endanger human life.

Researchers at the University of California San Diego Scripps Institute of Oceanography found that fish ingest an estimated 12,000 to 24,000 tons of plastic per year in the Pacific Ocean. The study also collected 141 fish from 27 species and found that 9.2% of the fish had small bits of plastic debris in their stomachs.[cxxv]

It is estimated that 20% of Pacific Ocean garbage comes from ships at sea that may dump waste or cargo. Other sources of garbage include leftovers from storm drainage systems, and trash from other countries—not just the United States—connected to the Pacific Ocean, including China, Japan, and Mexico.

Other Sources of Pollution

Mercury pollution, resulting from coal-fired power plants, also contaminates water bodies that flow into the Pacific Ocean waters. The Environmental Protection Agency reports that small organisms at the bottom of the food chain absorb the mercury, then as bigger fish eat smaller fish, it works its way back up the food chain to humans.[cxxvi]

The Ocean Floor

And now, while we continue to consume and pollute the resources of the ocean, the world powers are gearing up to excavate the Pacific Ocean floor. Property rights and resources harvested this way will redefine the Pacific Ocean and its 25,000 island nations. This should already be a national priority in every island nation. The amount of employment required will be significant, and this should even serve the Pacific Islands Nations.

Economic Potential

The Pacific Ocean offers some 100 trillion dollars in potential opportunity, according to some successful venture-capital investment managers. But it must be viewed in its totality. The body of saltwater, the ocean waves and currents, the bottom floor and below the crust, the species, the coral reefs, the boundary landscapes—sandy beaches, minerals below the ocean floor, and vegetation in the ocean. Also, any environmental impacts of climatic changes on the ocean should be viewed in the ocean's entirety, to simplify the economic balancing act of the ocean's potentiality.[cxxvii]

The Pacific Ocean has been home to the Pacific Island peoples of the Polynesians, Micronesians, and Melanesians for thousands of years. It spans over 60 million square miles from California to China, and 12,300 miles from Indonesia to the coast of Colombia in South America. And in certain regions it extends tens of thousands of feet below the surface of the water.[cxxviii] The Pacific Ocean was a deity for the Polynesian Navigators, as I noted in *Navigators Quest for a Kingdom in Polynesia*.[cxxix] And a moral question arises: does this most venerated deity have any "rights"?

Throughout these many years, very little has been known about the ecosystems below these millions of square miles of ocean floor—let alone the species, minerals, and chemicals that are found in the ocean. The technology that would allow man to explore and occupy the ocean floor as a permanent homestead has not yet been made feasible. However, our knowledge of the potential resources or assets on and under the ocean floor is growing, and that potential is enormous.

However, as world powers descend upon the Pacific Ocean to explore, exploit, and harvest its resources and assets, the indigenous peoples of the Pacific Island countries are, once again, being sidelined into the role of spectator rather than owner-participants of this pioneering exploration of the world's last frontier. But this represents the signal, most critical resource for the survival of the Pacific Island people. Thus, it represents their greatest hope and ambition for sustainability.

Sharing Resources

Today, the world continues to consume the resources of the ocean; it also continues to dump more trash into the ocean; it also continues to pollute it. But the ocean, as we have seen, is an invaluable shared resource, not just for the Pacific Island Nations, but for the whole of the world.

The recognition that shared resources must be collectively maintained and managed is fundamental in Samoan and Manu'an culture. The whole division of labor and definition of boundaries allows government to function effectively at the individual, family, village, and district levels. And the beauty of Samoan and Manu'an cultural "structuralism"—to borrow a term from social scientists of the "enlightenment" period—is that it's all-inclusive, fully integrated within their culture. The lesson learned, from observation of a culture's application of collectivism, is that cohesiveness and structural sustainability go together, a lesson confirmed by a more recent series of social science research studies on animal behavior, related to selfishness and selflessness.

Selfishness and Altruism

Dr. Elinor Ostrom is a professor of economics and political science at Indiana University and the first woman to win the prestigious Nobel Memorial Prize in Economic Sciences. In 2009, Dr. Ostrom's groundbreaking research demonstrated that ordinary people are capable of creating rules (or norms) and institutions that allow for sustainable and equitable management of shared resources (or other issues of collective concern), such as the ocean, fisheries, clean air, drinking water, Wikipedia, poverty, healthcare, domestic and intimate-partner violence, etc.

Ten years later, in 2019, Dr. Esther Duflo became the second woman (and first woman economist) to receive the Nobel Memorial Prize in Economic Sciences, for her creative experimental approach to alleviating poverty.

Throughout the evolutionary development of economic systems across the civilized world, a prevailing, fundamental belief has been the assumption of mankind's selfishness or characteristic of innate self-interest. Every enterprise, whether for profit or nonprofit, is fundamentally developed based on objectives of self-interest or self-motivation—i.e. on profit maximization or selfishness. However, the study of reciprocal altruism (or reciprocity) goes back to the early 1970s.[cxxx] It picked up momentum in the 1990s and is now an accepted field in economics. So today, more studies point out, to the contrary, a behavior pattern that shows unselfishness among various animals, such as honeybees, rats, vampire bats, and others.[cxxxi] Research shows that the more they communicate with other members of the colony, the more selfless they become.

The key takeaway from these later studies is that the frequency of communication between members has a direct effect on the level of selfishness, vis-a-vis selflessness. That is, the more the individuals interact with relatives, the less selfish they become. So in human terms, the more you speak to your siblings and family members, the less selfish you become, and so you become concerned with the needs of others more than with your own. This carries an opposite implication as well—the less communication occurs with siblings and relatives, the more selfish one becomes, and, most likely, the more isolated.

Communication and Cooperation

My focus is that solutions must be relevant. The development of the modern way of collective management of shared resources (or modern econometric models) is built around cooperative and collective efforts, with elements of reciprocal altruism from the owners of the resources. Sharing can be managed collectively using the rules and norms, established by a governing body or by institutions that the owners agree on, as ways to manage the consumption of resources and their usage levels. This confirms the value of long-established, collective, cultural norms maintained by indigenous peoples, such as Polynesians and other societies around the world.

Mobility (such as moving to wherever the job is located) is encouraged and promoted in United States' culture because it means better opportunities, but it also puts a distance between family members and the core of the family, thus discouraging daily communication with family members and causing fragmentation in the family structure. The salient part of this, for me, is that the foundation of Samoan culture, through its oral, repetitive traditions, reinforces communication among family members. By doing things together, collectively, we reinforce communication, thus achieving cohesiveness in the organizational structure which, hopefully, makes the population more selfless and encourages more generosity.

Politics

As we have seen, Samoan culture collectively organized its structure to provide effective governance (norms, rituals, and protocols) and a system of rewards, together with punitive and corrective measures. But Samoa is no longer isolated, and what happens in the rest of the world can profoundly affect the Island Nation.

For example, the current crisis between the United States of America and China creates a geopolitical divide and competitiveness that could lead to a more disastrous combination of Cold War attitudes and scattered military conflicts across the Asian and Pacific regions. An outright military war in this region would devastate the environment and the people of the Pacific Island countries. The battle of "Armageddon," in the Pacific, would be fought in the realms of Artificial Intelligence, information technology, economic strongholds, and of people and their environment. And the geographic battlespace would be the Pacific Ocean.

The (Dollar) Cost of War

Americans have buried many of their citizens in the Asian Pacific Ocean region, through several conflicts in the region, since the Manifest Destiny doctrine that got them into the Philippines.

Follow this with World War II, the Korean War, and the Vietnam conflict. In World War II, the dead and wounded totaled over 200,000. The Korean war total was 140,000 dead and wounded United States soldiers, and the Vietnam conflict led to 58,220 deaths and 304,000 wounded, meaning 362,220 spilled their blood in the Asia Pacific Islands region.

The sacrifice Americans have made in the Middle East is about 7,000 American soldiers' lives, with about 30,000 wounded out of about 1.2 million U.S. soldiers deployed, at a total cost of $8.6 trillion dollars in U.S. taxpayers' money. That represents about $914 million per dead soldier. By comparison, of the $4.1 trillion total cost for WW-II, about $1.8 trillion is attributed to the Asia Pacific region. Vietnam's $844 billion cost, according to USA Today, divided by 58,000 deaths, equals $14.5 million per dead soldier. And the $390 billion cost of the Korean conflict, again according to USA Today (in 2019 dollars), gives us about $10 million per dead soldier of about 40,000.

My point is that cost of the Middle East conflicts is exorbitant, with nebulous real benefits accrued. Propping up allies is, traditionally, a necessary action but, unfortunately, the cost of it is not necessarily equally shared. The amount of oil and gas under the ground, compared to the potential for clean energy and the available energy resources in the United States of America, challenges the wisdom of spending this kind of capital in war in the Middle East.

The (Attention) Cost of Peace

So here instead is the case for spending the necessary amount of attention on the Asia Pacific Islands region, rather than rushing to war:

1. China is well ahead of the U.S. with its influence on nations across Asia and the Pacific Island countries.
2. China has been using its financial prowess to help the Independent Island nations get into debt—building their infrastructures so they slowly become more indebted to the Chinese government, while giving concessions to the Chinese government to build ports which their naval ships can use.

3. China has been expanding trade agreements with every independent nation in Asia, Australia, New Zealand, and all the Pacific region. Economic prowess is powerful in dictating policy matters in the region.
4. The economics of fishing in the Pacific Ocean leads to areas being carved out in which China already has the lion's share of the catches. 32% of the world's fish consumption comes from the Pacific Ocean.
5. Economic rights to all the minerals under the Pacific Ocean floors will dwarf the oil in the middle East.
6. The largest pollution disaster in the world is trash in the Pacific Ocean. This has to be a priority in environmental cleanup initiatives. We're killing our food supply chain.
7. Policies concerning shipping lanes and their protection are critical to international trades.
8. The Laws of the Sea must be a priority for reexamination, because they severely affect the Independent Pacific Island countries (IPSC). The 200-miles-radius laws of the sea provision will have powerful political implications for the IPSC.
9. The United States of America should make a concentrated effort to provide leadership to both American Samoa and the Independent Island Nation of Samoa, as an American ally in the Pacific Island countries.
10. As we have seen, the U.S. has been involved with Samoa since the period of colonization. So both parts of Samoa assist the U.S. with military port stations and monitoring stations for the region. The U.S. should take steps to replace the dependence of the Independent Samoa government on the Chinese government. The U.S. has more history with Samoans than the Chinese have. A cohesive collaboration of the two Samoas will be much more productive than an arms-length policy.

Sharing and Saving the Pacific Ocean

Misusing Science

Evidence of how the world is turning its attention to rebuilding this critical Pacific Ocean food resource is mounting, and the momentum for change is accelerating according to the World

Bank and the Organization for Economic Co-operation and Development (OECD).[cxxxii]

Authors Garland and Nickson, in their *Netting billions: A global valuation of tuna* article,[cxxxiii] confirm the challenge posed in balancing the needs of politicians, government administrators, regional fisheries management organizations, scientists, business owners, and lawmakers and others.

What we do not always appreciate is that many of the ocean's species—for example, tuna—are migratory in nature. That is, they travel or migrate in some period of their lifecycle. In some specific cases the migration is seasonal, and scientists can trace the place of birth and spawning and the migration path. This precise information can substantiate the claim to ownership by the country of origin of the species, which of course leads to legal battle. For example, a specific type of tuna spawn in San Diego but roam the Pacific Ocean and are often fished in the area southwest and southeast of Polynesia. But the USA claims ownership, even though the tuna are fished several thousands of miles from San Diego. And the USA looks for compensation.

Other nations have done the same with their own species. Thus the role of scientific research in fisheries is critical, for very obvious reasons. The more you know about the species in your ocean-space, the more you have control over it, and the greater your ability to lay claim to the resource.

But the reality is that Polynesians, Micronesians, and Melanesians live on top of the Pacific Ocean, while the powerful nations have cleverly dissected the anatomy and behavioral patterns of species, and have negotiated their ownership using scientific data as justification. The world's most powerful countries continue to create and negotiate ocean treaties at the United Nation's Law of the Sea Committee, but this doesn't alter the Pacific Islanders belief that the Pacific Ocean, where they live, is their heirloom.

Mistaken Policies

Another issue is the dispute over rules for defining shipping lanes and disruptions of them—a dispute against policies that are defined by the largest, wealthiest nations, without any economic considerations made for the Pacific Island Countries and

Territories. It's common knowledge that China is very aggressive in protecting its "shipping lane," because of its strategic disadvantage in the region caused by not owning an ocean that has direct access to open water for its trading partners. The Chinese are boxed in by Russia, Indonesia, Malaysia, Japan, Korea, the Philippines, and many other small Pacific Island countries. This gives China the impetus to invest in rebuilding the Silk Road to access Europe, the Middle East, and the African continent by land. So it makes sense for the Chinese government to pour financial aid into the Pacific Island Countries and Territories, even if PICT can't afford to pay back the loans.

Let's not forget the value of these independent island nations in the "one nation one vote" rule at the United Nations. There are about seven UN votes assigned to these Independent Island Nations (Samoa, Fiji, Toga, Solomon Island, Vanuatu, and Papua New Guinea). If you look into the past 25 years, when China proposed an executive referendum and it passed in spite of opposition by the USA, you should note that almost all the independent island nations voted on the side of China. So, do you now understand the game—rather like football or rugby—that's being played out there by the super-powerful nations? It's the opening of shipping lanes and fisheries inventories to the UN vote.

I believe the Pacific Forum, the Organization of Pacific Island Countries, can accrue significant negotiating capital to get a better and more equitable share of the economic value chain of the Pacific Ocean by leveraging these factors.[cxxxiv]

The Way Forward

To save the Pacific Islanders' homeland and way of life we must save the Pacific Ocean. The focus should be on the Pacific Ocean, a macroeconomic environmental problem. By saving the Pacific Ocean we will, in effect, save all the people of the Pacific.

Pleading moral standards and playing on emotions and empathy to help these Pacific Islanders just doesn't work. It's just like an ocean wave that swells but never breaks, to use Samoan phraseology. Rather, this is a collective world problem, and it demands the attention of the world's citizens. However, the case must be made in economic terms—it's the best way, and it's a universal approach that has the impetus to attract and aggregate major human and financial capital investments, to get the clean-up job done.

A paradigm shift is required: applying private capital to attract creative minds, to collaborate in using already proven technology to solve the Pacific Ocean's "Garbage Patch" catastrophe. Spending capital to just gather data, analyze it, and write reports to tell people who have already known the problem for centuries, is an exercise in futility. We need to deploy capital to solve this disastrous situation, based on economic merits.

If, and when, we solve the environmental disaster occurring in the Pacific Ocean, we will, in effect, save the people of the Pacific Ocean. The cleaner the ocean, the healthier the fisheries' ecosystem, and the healthier the fish we consume. This would lead to increasing the economic productivity of the Pacific Ocean and its contribution to the world economy. It's a kind of rising-tide approach which will float every boat, whether it be canoe, luxury yacht, super tanker, or freight container, metaphorically speaking.

In addition to solving the disaster of Pacific Ocean pollution, we should also think about creating and incentivizing entrepreneurship programs to develop fishery farms and management programs, to assist the Pacific Ocean islanders in improving food supply and economic development. Entrepreneurs are doing this in the Netherlands and other Nordic countries.[cxxxv] These kinds of economic development programs—for example, using lagoons and deep-water reefs to build fish farms—should be done in collaboration with PICT. This should encourage business startups; it would lead to an improvement in skills and would promote economic development and greater productivity.

Defining the Problem

The Samoa Island Nation's future is inextricably dependent on the Pacific Ocean's health and sustainability. And we know, it is the human factor that dictates the future of the Pacific Ocean and, thus, the future of the Pacific Island countries' populations. How the world continues to pollute the Pacific Ocean, how climate changes are exacerbating the ozone layer, how overfishing is depleting the fishery population, and the impending exploitation of resources underneath the ocean floor all have an impact on ocean ecosystems and environmental conditions.

Opportunities can be found in problem-solving areas. Wherever there is a problem impacting the Pacific Ocean, such as pollution or overfishing, then there are potential opportunities for economic development that could influence the economy of the Pacific Island countries.

A well-known problem with the Pacific Ocean is the calamity of pollution. Cleaning up this environmental catastrophe demands labor that's knowledgeable about environmental and oceanic sciences. This is where the future economic development of the whole Pacific Ocean region lies.

Also, the disaster of overfishing affects the livelihoods of all Pacific Island countries. And the impending exploitation of the depths of the Pacific Ocean for mineral resources—without clear examination and accounting of the species, minerals, chemicals, and vegetation in and below the ocean floor, let alone analysis of the impact of violent disruption caused by such excavation—represents another place where significant efforts must be undertaken to move this initiative forward. Efforts are imminent in a comprehensive scientific inventory and impact analysis of species, minerals, gemstones, and vegetation. And this will give rise to opportunities for the Pacific Island countries to provide human resources and ocean property rights collectively to these exploration ventures and enterprises.

Technological Needs

As we have seen, the ocean is the only resource that the two Samoas own, at least within their 200-mile radius perimeter, that can help build economic value. This includes not only the fisheries, but also the minerals at the bottom of the ocean. But to benefit from this takes knowledge about who is doing the research and who is exploring the resources, as well as who is extracting and selling them.

The impending excavation and harvesting of valuable resources in and below the ocean floor represents the most significant economic development for the Samoa Island Nation and the rest of the independent island countries. The very simple, salient question is: how can we take advantage of the greatest asset we have, in terms of our respective property rights, to assist in our economic survival? The answer is that opportunities lie in the area of technologies impacting the economic development and environmental and energy sustainability of ocean.

If you have a vision that, in the next fifty years, mineral extraction will drive the biggest economy in the region, then getting your labor force ready for it, in terms of education, starts now. Students must all be educated about oceanic sciences and environmental sciences.

So, there is a real economic development opportunity in areas of technological developments and deployment. While this is a long-term vision, it absolutely needs to be included in any strategy for economic development of an Island Nation. The opportunity for Samoa is in educational development in the use of technology for these enterprises. This is commonly referred to as "soft intellectual" knowledge leading to skill-based careers, and this is an affordable option for Samoans and other small island countries. The challenge lies in developing the entrepreneurship curriculums and practices to find enterprising opportunities in these oceanic economic developments. This requires an investment in education and intellectual capital, analogous to the commitment made by country of Israeli in the early 1990s, to transform its economic foundation from heavily agricultural to what is now technology driven.

Education

Education will allow the transformation of the Pacific Island Nations from manual labor to "soft" skills and intelligent labor. Exporting skilled and intelligence-based labor yields the most economic benefits. Instead of exporting manual labor to harvest agricultural crops, you can export skilled labor to provide services such as customer services, computer programming, tech support, healthcare services, etc.

This requires students and an educational system. Investment in the educational infrastructure includes low-cost broadband and electricity. Encouragement of students could start with incentives, giving away electronics, toys, and computer games, to allow the kids to play with them.

I read a story about ten years ago where a laptop computer company gave about 200 laptops to third grade (or equivalent) school students, in a school in some middle-African country. They just let the kids have at it, with no instructions or training. In two weeks, the kids were using their laptops to play games. The cognitive process is intuitive—that's how we all learn to speak and do things, just by observing and mimicking others' actions.

The development of an intelligence-based labor force is important because, if the country does not have a lot of valuable resources to export or trade with, economic prospects are reduced down to human resources. And if the country is an island with a small population, it becomes even more difficult to earn a good gross domestic product (GDP).

Examples

Just look at countries like Israel. My first banking-payments software company was exclusively funded out of Israel under, at the time, a very newly-developed venture capital industry and the government's chief scientist startup funding initiative (Israel's Small Business Administration). Our development operations and board of directors were based in Tel Aviv. So I spent considerable time in Tel Aviv in the 20 years I was active with the company. I used to enjoy taking tours, during the weekend, to various plantations, like banana and pineapple plantations. That is how I learned to appreciate the country's agricultural industry and, more importantly, the Israeli psyche.

They started out in 1948 building a country based on an agricultural economy—except, the land lies on sand dunes and desert, with no water resources. That's a contradictory set of facts. So they had to get access to and control the water source, the Jordan River. Hence the 1967 war.

Today Israel is an example of soft skills or intelligence-based labor. They have successfully transformed the economy from being heavily dependent on agriculture, to being almost 70% technology-based. From a new nation, in the middle of a desert, with immigrant labor that arrived with very few resources, they then built a country that stands healthy and wealthy among the nations, and that's incredible.

There are many other examples like Israel, such as Vietnam, Thailand, Indonesia, and many more. For both Samoas, transforming the manual labor force to a soft-skilled, intelligence-based labor force is critical to building a healthy and wealthy, sustainable economy and nation. It takes vision and determination from those who are given the responsibility to serve the country. And it is education that can help in self-healing and in making a living.

Investment and Employment Opportunities

The following is a breakdown of investments and employment opportunities relating to Pacific Ocean initiatives: It's centered on the application of technology in virtually every initiative.

- Harvesting technology paradigms and innovations to drive solutions for assessment and impact analysis of resources opportunities.
- Paradigm innovation in technology for solving environmental problems in the ocean caused by the warming climate. There are already some technological pilot schemes to help clean up the ocean's pollution.[cxxxvi]
- Paradigm innovation in technology to harvest minerals from the bottom of the ocean floor. Foresight is critically needed to develop a learning platform for how the independent Island Nations can participate in this major economic development initiative. The focus should be on education, research, and engagement at all levels. Exercise your property rights.
- Innovation in technology to optimize the potential for aquaculture industry in the Pacific Ocean. For example, local fish farms in lagoons can subsidize local populations suffering from overfishing in their oceans. Also, learning about the technology being developed and implemented by several countries in the Middle East to assist in the regrowth of reefs.
- Innovation in technology to efficiently accelerate cleanup efforts of the Pacific Ocean's disastrous pollution. There are already initiatives in this space, and it is critical for the independent Island Nations to be and stay engaged.
- Innovation in technology to implement effective project management of these technical initiatives is equally important.

The Independent Island Nations must be armed with this knowledge and competence to be aware of what is happening to their property rights.

- Implementation of sensor technology across the Pacific Ocean for monitoring initiatives. This technology is already established and available for development in the Pacific Ocean. Fishery inventories and tracking the depletion of various living species and vegetation are crucial to Pacific Ocean sustainability.

The greatest opportunity to foster innovation for entrepreneurs in Oceania is the Pacific Ocean. It is the last frontier for economic development in the world. From its surface to the deep-sea floor and below, it has not been explored to its full potential. In fact it's the most unknown area for potential exploration on earth. And yet the experts (the scientists) are in agreement, enormous mineral composites lie in the core of the ocean floor and are critical to energy production for the world. If effectively harvested, they could have a major impact on meeting the world's insatiable appetite for energy.

Economic development initiatives should follow the Marine Living Resources Act 18 of 1998 outlining of the rules of engagements:

- aquaculture farming initiatives include:
  - fisheries
  - crustaceans
  - vegetation
  - reef cultivation development
  - flooding seawall development and implementation
- agriculture initiatives include
  - native crops
  - the breadfruit initiative (see Example: The Breadfruit Initiative, page 346)
- energy initiatives: processes for harvesting energy from wind, sun (solar energy), and ocean waves have already been piloted and implemented on the ocean surface in Norway and other Scandinavian countries.

- Climate initiatives: there are financial assistance programs available for small developing countries to help deal with the climate's impact on their ocean shores. Taxation on the major contributors and countries with high consumption levels can cover the costs of erosion, due to high sea levels and pollution, on fishery populations and the costs of reef rehabilitation, due to reef depletion. These funds are made available, by these major contributors to ocean pollution and climate change, to help small countries such as the Independent Island Nations. Small, independent countries like Samoa, Toga, Fiji, and others contribute about 7% toward pollution and climate change, while the rest is produced by the major countries of the world. Thus the cost of solving climate change should not be equally shared by all nations. An equitable approach involves financing small nation's efforts to implement climate change solutions. Samoa should be seeking out these financial assistance programs.

Example: The Breadfruit Initiative

The potential of the *'Ulu* or breadfruit plant to become a breadbasket food-supplement to the human diet should not be underestimated. According to investigative efforts by the University of Hawaii's System-Pacific Business Center Program, Shidler College of Business, in Honolulu, Hawaii, directed by Papali'i Dr. Failautusi Avegalio, this indigenous plant or fruit-tree has the nutritional value and versatility equivalent to that of rice, wheat, potato, barley, and other foundational breadbasket food supplements, critical to offer the potential to subsidize the human diet.

Just 100g (about half a cup) of breadfruit provides 25% of the recommended daily allowance (RDA) for fiber, and 5-10% of the RDA for protein, magnesium, potassium, phosphorus, thiamine (vitamin B1), and niacin (B3). Breadfruit also provides some carotenoids, such as carotene and lutein, which are not present in white rice and white potatoes.

With roughly 450lbs (and up to 700lbs) of fruit produced per season, this makes breadfruit one of earth's most productive trees. This high-yield, low-maintenance, food-crop tree is robust enough to withstand the extreme weather conditions of the Pacific

Ocean, giving compelling prospects for production scalability. This is crucial to the region, and potentially to the whole world's population.

Early European explorers back in 1700s (Captain Cook, Captain Bligh, and others) discovered the breadfruit tree and its potential for food supplements, and they began exporting it to other countries in warmer climate regions, including Southern Asia, Southeast Asia, South America, and the Caribbean islands. While further development of the fruit into a potential main food supplement for global markets stayed minimal for centuries after those early explorers, it continued to be a mainstay for the Southeast Asia, Pacific Islands, and Caribbean Islands regions.

There are, of course, legends of the breadfruit tree's origin and migration path, but the consensus is that the tree and plant are indigenous to Southeast Asia and the wider Pacific regions. Today, there are several initiatives pursuing the potential value of adding the breadfruit tree and fruit to the regional breadbasket of food supplements. Micro farming and the economic development of planting, cultivation, and harvest of the breadfruit are being explored for the whole Pacific region. It will, however, take capital investment resources, to move this significant initiative to fulfillment, but the economic value-drivers are compelling.

Cooperation and Collaboration

Even competing companies cooperate and collaborate to forge new initiatives. Knowledge is not exclusive to the rich and powerful countries. "Seek and ask, and you shall find," to paraphrase the familiar Mathew 7:7 Scripture. Getting engaged and staying engaged must be a deliberate effort. We cannot wait to be invited. These are our property rights. These economic developments, in and on the surface of the Pacific Ocean, will forever change the environment and the future of the Pacific Ocean.

Conclusion

While my first book—*Navigators Quest for a Kingdom in Polynesia*—extends the definition and identity of the Polynesian Navigators of the Archipelago, not only to the Asian continent but all the way to Africa, we should recognize that the Polynesian Navigators are a thread of the whole world's human migration and evolution. A failure to do this would mean that Polynesians are just a mutation of some other ethnicity, altered in their long journey across Africa, the Levant, the Eurasian Steppe, the Chinese and Indian continents, and the Asiatic Archipelago. But Samoans have always believed that their ethnic identity is original and unique. I hope I have managed to illustrate this.

This second book's two volumes are undertaken to shed light on important and profound value propositions, which may not be so obvious. These are summarized as follows:

1. The longevity of a sustainable culture in evolutionary development leads to a robust, cohesive culture and a praxis that sustains the Samoans and Manu'ans for over 2500 years. The stability of the culture allows its roots to find that water well in the depths of the Pacific Ocean, which further leads to the stability of the society. This is a marked contrast from a volatile culture that often leads to unstable society. The Samoan and Manu'an cultural "blueprint" offers a historical heirloom to be shared with the world.

2. The unearthing and spotlighting of Samoa and Manu'a's ancient matriarchal society is evidence of a powerful invention from the past. It leads to respect for women, gives power to women, and reaffirms the fact that women in the world can be and have historically been great leaders, not servants, in the home and in society.

3. The old but simple, family-centric culture provides a model for developing leadership, making collective decisions, and understanding the freedom that comes with responsibility. It

not only previews democracy, but also emphasizes the importance of diversity and individual value and identity.

4. Deep-rooted traditions combined with a family-centric structure show the value of relationships, of respect induced by humility, and of the caring and love of family that propels the overall culture to become a peaceful and loving society. The cohesive cultural praxis and ceremonial practices provide in themselves evidence of verbal and nonverbal communication that reinforces the sustainability of the culture.

5. The rapid changes, brought about when Western culture arrived, hold a mirror up to rapid changes taking place in society today. The increase in diversity within a culture poses more challenges in how society will weave together these threads to ensure the culture stays cohesive and maintains a sustainable brand.

6. The misunderstandings between Samoan and Western culture highlight the importance of understanding a culture, not just understanding its words, in order to communicate effectively.

7. Samoa and Manu'a's easy acceptance of Christianity shows that the Christian faith has global truth and relevance, and is not just a branch of Western colonialism. This was a kingdom from heaven, prophesied and designated to reign over all Samoa by the Warrior "Queen" Nafanua.

8. The problems of global businesses, ecological disasters, super-power politics, and economic shortsightedness have a huge effect on these small countries, due to the importance of the Pacific Ocean. This gives these small countries the perfect voice to remind the rest of the world that what we fail to see will still hurt us. This is an appeal to the rich and powerful countries of the world, that in their quest to harvest the mineral wealth in the depths of the Pacific Ocean they should remember the indigenous people of the region who discovered and laid claims to the Pacific Ocean as their habitat. We must first solve the environmental disaster of pollution in the Pacific Ocean. We must legislate and provide governance to the process of

excavating the ocean floor. We must extend financial help to these island countries, to assist in solving their plight caused by rising ocean levels due to climate change. And ignoring these people, in the maze of geopolitics and pursuit of economic adventure, is an action of aggression and lack of caring for them and for the world.

Afterword

As I am concluding my efforts on the history and cultural development of the Polynesian Navigators of the Archipelago, I want to remind readers of my purpose, to quench the thirst for knowledge about the history and culture of Samoans and Manu'ans, and to provide an 'aerial survey'—a birds'-eye view—of that history in the context of the overall Polynesian race, of which we are a part. My hope is that this spatial approach to the information will offer a birds'-eye view of a very large, complicated subject, and will give a clearer image of who we are.

The Time Period

Stone Age Development

First I would like to remind readers of the time period and environment in which the Navigators endured their development in the Pacific Ocean, a very different environment vis-a-vis the one encountered by land-based migrations across the world's continents.

The Polynesian Navigators of the Archipelago made their intrepid migration journey to the East Pacific during the late Stone Age and early Bronze Age Neolithic periods. While indigenous ancestry in mainland Asia and the Southeast Asiatic had gone through the revolutions of hunter-gatherer and agricultural ways of life, followed by the flowering of the "metals" paradigm, the early Polynesians had not had the benefits of access to the arrival of the Bronze Age or the metals, such as copper or bronze and iron. This inhibited and handicapped their economic development in the isolated East Pacific Ocean throughout their history. Thus their dependence on the Stone Age technology of flint, obsidian, crustacean shells, and wood for construction of tools and weapons was due to the limited prevailing technology. For the early Polynesians were still living through the twilight of the Stone Age period.

The Search for Other Clues

The paucity of significant fossils in the islands means we must look for evidence in the cultural norms and ritual practices and, of course, the language to help reconstruct the physical environment that the Polynesian Navigators encountered during the Neolithic period in the East Pacific. There are a few fragmented clues in the language and cultural praxis that help define the anthropological environment of the Navigators' colonization period in Polynesia. For example, the emphasis on the Pacific Ocean as the origin of creation is their version of the Deluge story.

The Ocean

Paradigm Shifts

As we have seen, history, for the Navigators, does not follow the standard, linear, evolutionary metamorphosis (both human and cultural) of the hunter-gatherer period, followed by a paradigm shift when the invention of agriculture springs cultural and economic developments forward to helped build sophisticated cultures and societies. I kept looking out for these standard sequential changes, one footstep forward at a time, in culture and history departments within Samoan and Manu'an society, but I couldn't find them.

No. The dominant event in the life of the Polynesian Navigators is and was their seafaring movement. And their culture and philosophy, their perspective on the universe, are founded in the ocean.

Culture/Philosophy

The Navigators' view of the vast Pacific Ocean as a complete universe, in a perspective of time and space, became foundational to their psychology and understanding of sciences. Its vastness, in their belief system, was a phenomenon similar to that of the heavenly and celestials bodies. Hence it became part of the concept of time and space which they called home, for the travelers on a canoe were intuitively observing how the ocean moves and breathes, in waves, currents, swells. Thus they believed the ocean lives and breathes life, and that a god spoke to them in the ocean's waves, currents, swells. Viewing this through the lens of philosophy, we see how the universe of their cognitive development was based on the ocean's water rather than on unchanging land.

The Navigators' belief in the Ocean formed a continuous wave in their universe. They had intuitively understood their own mythology, giving them their respective purpose in life, such as to teach them their relationship with nature, natural events, and natural forces, and to provide a moral compass to know good from bad, and right from wrong; to avoid infringing or violating human, natural, and science-based boundaries; and to understand the human psyche—to understand human motivation, passion, greed, pain, love, empathy, and compassion. For every citizen was taught to seek two things in their life: wisdom and love. These, they saw, are the gifts from the God, before the dawn of Christian belief. And the path to receiving God's gifts is through the culture, even if not everyone achieves success in receiving both gifts.

Thus, they came to understand their Pacific Ocean and universe as a continuous wave of a single system, not as separate parts which make a whole. And thus, the Navigators' mythology taught emotional depth, gift-giving reciprocity, and love for the family at large, rather than good governance and leadership from a basis of cruelty and corruption.

Colonization/Migration

The Navigators managed to avoid infringing on the indigenous populations of islands where they sojourned (taking physical pauses as they undertook their migration journey). So they avoided physical conflicts such as wars. They didn't want to conquer a settled island, but rather continued with their quest to find a place they could settle for themselves.

In contrast, the seafaring people of the Mediterranean were not colonizers, but rather traders. So we have another reason why the Navigators' history and cultural development do not fit the evolutionary development patterns of hunter-gatherers and agriculture. So, while the Navigators' history and, to a lesser degree, their cultural development might be expected to fall into a pattern of colonization history, the pattern is only on the surface.

Once the typical colonial influences are peeled off from the way the story is told, the raw seafaring cultural patterns become evident again.

Thus it seems obvious, at this juncture, to present the hypothesis that the cognitive development of the Polynesian Navigators is dominated by the development of seafaring skills, rather than by the linear, overland migration routes of traditional processes in human evolutionary development. Their cognitive development was influenced by the tasks of understanding the movement and relationships of celestial bodies to each other, and applying this to their movement and behavior. Honing the skills to incorporate ocean environments and ecosystems with celestial movement, relationships, and patterns, and combining this recognition of behavior patterns of animals and fish, became the source and influence of the Navigators' cognitive development. As an ethnic group, Polynesians have successfully kept remnants of their culture and language pretty much intact, considering the enormous geographic distribution of their homestead islands. This gives a pattern of evolutionary development that is not at all the same as that of migrants on land-based migration paths.

Social Structures

Oral history speaks of seafaring inventions and development of skills as paradigm, cultural and economic developments with the Polynesian Navigators. But developments in Samoan and Manu'an culture and history, as I mentioned earlier, make no mention of any significant paradigm shift associated with hunter-gatherer or agricultural changes throughout their history. So we must see that the cultural developments associated with these innovations occurred here in spite of the absence of these significant phases of human evolutionary development. Instead, developments in organizational structures stemmed from the family structure. Authority and responsibility were born out of the bones and flesh of the organization. And collective identity and responsibility were derived from the circle of the family organization. The result is very different from the western, pyramidal structure.

Agriculture

For Samoans and Manu'ans, the agricultural "revolution" was limited to tropical crops and roots that the Navigators gathered and brought over with them on their journey. Island geography limited them to sustaining a small, tribal or clannish population. And scalable agricultural production was limited to the larger families. However, the Navigators took maximum advantage of the benefits afforded by the agriculture paradigm in organizational structures, division of labor, and the definition of responsibility, as is evidenced in the chieftain and family-centric culture. These factors, combined with the distance between populated islands, furthered that sense of isolation.

The Stories

Religions and Deities

The Navigators discovered early on the ideas of collective identity, collective function, cohesive cultural norms, and religious rituals and practices. Their religious rituals and ceremonial practices were dictated by the deity and the demigods, to be held at a designated sacred ground called Malae.

Social scientists have been pigeon-holing classifications and definitions of primitive, indigenous people's religions into patterns based on their observations and research. So the evolutionary development from polytheism to monotheism became a milestone paradigm that leads directly to the classification of modern religions—Christianity, Islam, Buddhism, etc. Other religions or forms of worshipping, such as animism (worship of nature and spirits—a word coined by British anthropologists[cxxxvii]) are fitted into an imagined timeline. Sir James G. Frazer and pioneering anthropologist Dr. Bronislaw Malinowski picked up on ethnographic, theological philosophy as "Art magic," describing the transition from worshipping nature's unexplainable phenomena to the magical phenomena choreographed by magicians.[cxxxviii] But the Samoan belief began with one god, *Tagaloalagi.*

Mythology

The Navigators' mythological storylines about discovery and the settlement of early human ancestors—e.g. *Saveasi'uleo* (the eel), *Fe'e* and *So'oialo* (the octopus), *Pilipa'ū* (Pili fall from Heaven), *Pilimoevai* (Pili who lived in the water-pool), *Pilia'au* (Pili the swimmer), and the Manu'an creation poem—are all based in the Pacific Ocean. The ocean, as a backdrop, is foundational to the environment of the Navigators' origins, cultural identity, and development, and perhaps even to their early-stage cognitive developmental abilities. Their skills, abilities, and mythology are sourced from the ocean and from seafaring experiences, reinforcing their ancient origins as descendants of the seafaring, indigenous, Austronesian-speaking peoples of the Asiatic Archipelago. Thus their affinity for ocean exploration as a way of life.

Conclusion

Many of my digressions in writing this book have been made to draw parallels with the footpaths of other world cultures in their respective cultural development, norms, and ritual practices. For cultural diffusion, and the infusion of cultural ideas, didn't happen in a linear fashion. Rather, these processes could happen in parallel, depending on when people left the African content. The starbursts of human migration wave out of Africa and other geographical areas, giving randomness to the migration directions of the human species. And, in the course of their quest for homesteading, each group went through their own processes of evolutionary development, with change and development happening in parallel along different timeframes and in different places.

I cannot find the ancestors' footsteps on the ground, on the sand, on the rocks, or on the Pacific Ocean floor. But I can feel them, when the gentle South Pacific Ocean breeze touches my skin, and that feeling of *'i'ike*, (described by Dr. Papali'i in the foreword to my first book: *Navigators Quest for a Kingdom in Polynesia*) overwhelms with messages from the ancient ancestors, that this is our *Fa'asinomaga*, these are our roots where our umbilical cords are buried—my identity, my freedom, my family, clan, village, district and country.

These may be simple words to the wind, but they also feed the unquenchable thirst of the earth in a flooding rain. And so the Polynesian Navigators' mosaic motif lies undisturbed, on bedrock of the mighty Pacific Ocean, impoverished of "footsteps," deficient in "scientific signs," but long in belief that this is the cradle of Polynesia.

NOTES

[i] This author. *Navigators Quest for a Kingdom in Polynesia*. 2020. pp.76-77

[ii] This author. *Navigators Quest for a Kingdom in Polynesia*. 2020. pp. 76-77.

[iii] This author. *Navigators Quest for a Kingdom in Polynesia.* 2020. pp.66-77.

[iv] This author. *Navigators Quest for a Kingdom in Polynesia.* 2020. pp.66-67

[v] This author. *Navigators Quest for a Kingdom in Polynesia.* 2020. pp. 76-77.

[vi] This author. *Navigators Forging a Matriarchal Culture in Polynesia*. 2021. pp.16-17.

[vii] Fraser in note #596: Krämer, Dr. Augustin. *The Samoa Islands: An Outline of a Monograph with Particular Consideration of German Samoa: Vol 1*. 1902. trans. Theodore Verhaaren. Auckland. Polynesian Press Samoa House. 1994 pp.528.

[viii] Fuimaono Na'oia, *O Le Suaga A Le Va'atele*. (The findings of the big canoe). The Samoa Observer Co Ltd. 1996, p.185.

[ix] Krämer, Dr. Augustin. *The Samoa Islands: An Outline of a Monograph with Particular Consideration of German Samoa*: Vol 1. 1902. trans. Theodore Verhaaren. Auckland. Polynesian Press Samoa House. 1994, p. 321-2, citing: v. Bülow #9, p. 10, Turner p. 238-240, Stuebel p.63, 150, Stair p.217, Pratt, Powell and Fraser pp.539-548.

[x] Pratt G. *Samoan Dictionary: English and Samoan, and Samoan and English, with a Short Grammar of the Samoan Dialect*, London Missionary Soc., 1862.

[xi] Krämer, Dr. Augustin. *The Samoa Islands: An Outline of a Monograph with Particular Consideration of German Samoa: Vol 1*. 1902. trans. Theodore Verhaaren. Auckland. Polynesian Press Samoa House. 1994 p.314.

[xii] Krämer, Dr. Augustin. *The Samoa Islands: An Outline of a Monograph with Particular Consideration of German Samoa: Vol 1*. 1902. trans. Theodore Verhaaren. Auckland. Polynesian Press Samoa House. 1994

[xiii] Krämer, Dr. Augustin. *The Samoa Islands: An Outline of a Monograph with Particular Consideration of German Samoa: Vol 1*. 1902. trans. Theodore Verhaaren. Auckland. Polynesian Press Samoa House. 1994, p.120.

[xiv] Krämer, Dr. Augustin. *The Samoa Islands: An Outline of a Monograph with Particular Consideration of German Samoa: Vol 1*. 1902. trans. Theodore Verhaaren. Auckland. Polynesian Press Samoa House. 1994. p.228-9.

[xv] Krämer, Dr. Augustin. *The Samoa Islands: An Outline of a Monograph with Particular Consideration of German Samoa: Vol 1*. 1902. trans. Theodore Verhaaren. Auckland. Polynesian Press Samoa House. 1994. P134

[xvi] Krämer, Lameko, Ape Tonumaipe'a, and Fuimaono Na'oia all give this information.

[xvii] Krämer, Lameko, Ape Tonumaipe'a, and Fuimaono Na'oia all give this information.

[xviii] Fuimaono Na'oia, *O Le Suaga A Le Va'atele*. (The findings of the big canoe). The Samoa Observer Co Ltd. 1996.

[xix] Fuimaono Na'oia, *O Le Suaga A Le Va'atele*. (The findings of the big canoe). The Samoa Observer Co Ltd. 1996 p.185.

[xx] Ali'i Felela Fred Henry, *Talafa'asolopito o Samoa*, Commercial Printers, Ltd. Apia, W. Samoa, 1945-1959, p.11-12.

[xxi] Lafai Sauoāiga F. S. Apemoemanatunatu, *O le mavaega i le tai*. The Malua Printing Press, Apia, Western Samoa, 1988, p.225.

[xxii] Schultz, Dr. E. *Samoan Proverbial Expressions Alagā'upu Fa'a-Samoa.* 1953. Translated into English by Brother Herman, Polynesian Press Samoa House, 1994 Edition.

[xxiii] Krämer, Dr. Augustin. *The Samoa Islands: An Outline of a Monograph with Particular Consideration of German Samoa: Vol 1*. 1902. trans. Theodore Verhaaren. Auckland. Polynesian Press Samoa House. 1994 referenced the works by Pratt, Powell, Fraser, Bulow and Baessler, expert of Society Island

[xxiv] Fraser, John (1896). "Some Folk Songs and Myths from Samoa". The Journal of the Polynesian Society (Vol. 5, No. 3(19) ed.). 3 (19): 171–183. JSTOR 20701427 *Manu'a Poem of Pili* (Powell and Pratt); also Krämer, Dr. Augustin. *The Samoa Islands: An Outline of a Monograph with Particular Consideration of German Samoa: Vol 1*. 1902. trans. Theodore Verhaaren. Auckland. Polynesian Press Samoa House. 1994.

[xxv] Krämer, Dr. Augustin. *The Samoa Islands: An Outline of a Monograph with Particular Consideration of German Samoa: Vol 1*. 1902. trans. Theodore Verhaaren. Auckland. Polynesian Press Samoa House. 1994.

[xxvi] Krämer, Dr. Augustin. *The Samoa Islands: An Outline of a Monograph with Particular Consideration of German Samoa: Vol 1*. 1902. trans. Theodore Verhaaren. Auckland. Polynesian Press Samoa House. 1994 p.528.

[xxvii] *Concise History of the World an Illustrated Timeline*. eds Neil Kagan, Jerry H. Bently, Director Board of Advisers. National Geographic. 2006.

[xxviii] Wallis, H.W. *The Cosmology of the Rigveda*; *An Essay*. London. Williams and Norgate 1887.

[xxix] Krämer, Dr. Augustin. *The Samoa Islands: An Outline of a Monograph with Particular Consideration of German Samoa: Vol 1*. 1902. trans. Theodore Verhaaren. Auckland. Polynesian Press Samoa House. 1994. p.399, 604.

[xxx] Krämer, Dr. Augustin. *The Samoa Islands: An Outline of a Monograph with Particular Consideration of German Samoa*: Vol 1; trans. Theodore Verhaaren. Auckland. Polynesian Press Samoa House. 1994. p20 & 29.

[xxxi] Krämer, Dr. Augustin. *The Samoa Islands: An Outline of a Monograph with Particular Consideration of German Samoa*: Vol 1; trans. Theodore Verhaaren. Auckland. Polynesian Press Samoa House. 1994, pp. 556-8, 562.

[xxxii] Schultz, Dr. E. *Samoan Proverbial Expressions Alagā'upu Fa'a-Samoa.* 1953. Translated into English by Brother Herman, Polynesian Press Samoa House, 1994 Edition. Aotearoa, New Zealand

[xxxiii] Krämer, Dr. Augustin. *The Samoa Islands: An Outline of a Monograph with Particular Consideration of German Samoa: Vol 1*. 1902. trans. Theodore Verhaaren. Auckland. Polynesian Press Samoa House. 1994. p.463, referencing Stuebel p.148.

[xxxiv] Krämer, Dr. Augustin. *The Samoa Islands: An Outline of a Monograph with Particular Consideration of German Samoa: Vol 1*. 1902. trans. Theodore Verhaaren. Auckland. Polynesian Press Samoa House. 1994. p.604-6.

[xxxv] Schultz, Dr. E. *Samoan Proverbial Expression Alagā'upu Fa'a-Samoa.* 1953. Translated into English by Brother Herman, Polynesian Press Samoa House, 1994 Edition. Aotearoa, New Zealand, p.136.

[xxxvi] Krämer, Dr. Augustin. *The Samoa Islands: An Outline of a Monograph with Particular Consideration of German Samoa: Vol 1*; trans. Theodore

---

Verhaaren. Auckland. Polynesian Press Samoa House. 1994; also Lafai Sauoāiga F. S. Apemoemanatunatu, *O le mavaega i le tai*. The Malua Printing Press, Apia, Western Samoa, 1988.

[xxxvii] Liumanu Fa'atonu. *Samoa Ne'i Galo*. Samoa Lest We Forget. Trans. Su'a Julia Wallwork. Prod. Hon Pule Lameko, Ministry for Youth, Sports and Cultural Affairs Government of Western Samoa. Pub. Dunelm Printing, St Heliers, Auckland, New Zealand, 1994.

[xxxviii] Liumanu Fa'atonu. *Samoa Ne'i Galo*. Samoa Lest We Forget. Trans. Su'a Julia Wallwork. Prod. Hon Pule Lameko, Ministry for Youth, Sports and Cultural Affairs Government of Western Samoa. Pub. Dunelm Printing, St Heliers, Auckland, New Zealand, 1994.

[xxxix] Schultz, Dr. E. *Samoan Proverbial Expression Alagā'upu Fa'a-Samoa.* 1953. Translated into English by Brother Herman, Polynesian Press Samoa House, 1994 Edition. Aotearoa, New Zealand #239.

[xl] Krämer, Dr. Augustin. *The Samoa Islands: An Outline of a Monograph with Particular Consideration of German Samoa: Vol 1*; trans. Theodore Verhaaren. Auckland. Polynesian Press Samoa House. 1994, p.529

[xli] Krämer, Dr. Augustin. *The Samoa Islands: An Outline of a Monograph with Particular Consideration of German Samoa: Vol 1*; trans. Theodore Verhaaren. Auckland. Polynesian Press Samoa House. 1994, p.520.

[xlii] Krämer, Dr. Augustin. *The Samoa Islands: An Outline of a Monograph with Particular Consideration of German Samoa: Vol 1*; trans. Theodore Verhaaren. Auckland. Polynesian Press Samoa House. 1994. Column B listed in p.529

[xliii] Schultz, Dr. E. *Samoan Proverbial Expression Alagā'upu Fa'a-Samoa.* 1953. Translated into English by Brother Herman, Polynesian Press Samoa House, 1994 Edition. Aotearoa, New Zealand, #267.

[xliv] Krämer, Dr. Augustin. *The Samoa Islands: An Outline of a Monograph with Particular Consideration of German Samoa*: Vol 1. 1902. trans. Theodore Verhaaren. Auckland. Polynesian Press Samoa House. 1994, pp.121-12

[xlv] Lafai Sauoāiga F. S. Apemoemanatunatu, *O le mavaega i le tai*. The Malua Printing Press, Apia, Western Samoa, 1988, pp.222-227.

[xlvi] Lafai Sauoāiga F. S. Apemoemanatunatu, *O le mavaega i le tai*. The Malua Printing Press, Apia, Western Samoa, 1988. pp.225-227.

[xlvii] Krämer, Dr. Augustin. *The Samoa Islands: An Outline of a Monograph with Particular Consideration of German Samoa*: Vol 1. 1902. trans. Theodore Verhaaren. Auckland. Polynesian Press Samoa House. 1994, pp.128-9.

[xlviii] Krämer, Dr. Augustin. *The Samoa Islands: An Outline of a Monograph with Particular Consideration of German Samoa*: Vol 1. 1902. trans. Theodore Verhaaren. Auckland. Polynesian Press Samoa House. 1994. pp.204, 224.

[xlix] Fuimaono Na'oia, *O Le Suaga A Le Va'atele*. (The findings of the big canoe). The Samoa Observer Co Ltd. 1996. p.211.

[l] Ali'i Felela Fred Henry, *Talafa'asolopito o Samoa*, Commercial Printers, Ltd. Apia, W. Samoa, 1945-1959, p.32.

[li] Krämer, Dr. Augustin. *The Samoa Islands: An Outline of a Monograph with Particular Consideration of German Samoa*: Vol 1. 1902. trans. Theodore Verhaaren. Auckland. Polynesian Press Samoa House. 1994. p.453.

[lii] Krämer, Dr. Augustin. *The Samoa Islands: An Outline of a Monograph with Particular Consideration of German Samoa*: Vol 1. 1902. trans. Theodore Verhaaren. Auckland. Polynesian Press Samoa House. 1994, p.136.

[liii] Krämer, Dr. Augustin. *The Samoa Islands: An Outline of a Monograph with Particular Consideration of German Samoa*: Vol 1. 1902. trans. Theodore Verhaaren. Auckland. Polynesian Press Samoa House. 1994, p.394.

[liv] This author, reference 2013 January Booklet p.10

[lv] This author, reference 2013 January Booklet p.10.

[lvi] Krämer, Dr. Augustin. *The Samoa Islands: An Outline of a Monograph with Particular Consideration of German Samoa*: Vol 1. 1902. trans. Theodore Verhaaren. Auckland. Polynesian Press Samoa House. 1994, p.313.

[lvii] Lafai Sauoāiga F. S. Apemoemanatunatu, *O le mavaega i le tai*. The Malua Printing Press, Apia, Western Samoa, 1988,, pp.75-77.

[lviii] Krämer, Dr. Augustin. *The Samoa Islands: An Outline of a Monograph with Particular Consideration of German Samoa: Vol 1*; trans. Theodore Verhaaren. Auckland. Polynesian Press Samoa House. 1994.

[lix] This author, reference: 2013 March Booklet pp.12–14.

[lx] Krämer, Dr. Augustin. *The Samoa Islands: An Outline of a Monograph with Particular Consideration of German Samoa: Vol 1*; trans. Theodore Verhaaren. Auckland. Polynesian Press Samoa House. 1994. pp.118-9.

[lxi] Pratt G. *Samoan Dictionary: English and Samoan, and Samoan and English, with a Short Grammar of the Samoan Dialect*, London Missionary Soc., 1862. p.279.

[lxii] This author, reference March 10, 2013 p.4.

[lxiii] Krämer, Dr. Augustin. *The Samoa Islands: An Outline of a Monograph with Particular Consideration of German Samoa: Vol 1*; trans. Theodore Verhaaren. Auckland. Polynesian Press Samoa House. 1994.

[lxiv] Liumanu Fa'atonu. *Samoa Ne'i Galo*. Samoa Lest We Forget. Trans. Su'a Julia Wallwork. Prod. Hon Pule Lameko, Ministry for Youth, Sports and Cultural Affairs Government of Western Samoa. Pub. Dunelm Printing, St Heliers, Auckland, New Zealand, 1994.

[lxv] This author, reference: 2013 March Booklet pp.14–19.

[lxvi] This author, reference: 2013 March Booklet p.19.

[lxvii] Krämer, Dr. Augustin. *The Samoa Islands: An Outline of a Monograph with Particular Consideration of German Samoa: Vol 1*; trans. Theodore Verhaaren. Auckland. Polynesian Press Samoa House. 1994. P.114.

[lxviii] Pratt G. *Samoan Dictionary: English and Samoan, and Samoan and English, with a Short Grammar of the Samoan Dialect*, London Missionary Soc., 1862. p.75

[lxix] Krämer, Dr. Augustin. *The Samoa Islands: An Outline of a Monograph with Particular Consideration of German Samoa: Vol 1*; trans. Theodore Verhaaren. Auckland. Polynesian Press Samoa House. 1994; Lafai Sauoāiga F. S. Apemoemanatunatu, *O le mavaega i le tai*. The Malua Printing Press, Apia, Western Samoa, 1988,; also Fuimaono Na'oia, *O Le Suaga A Le Va'atele*. (The findings of the big canoe). The Samoa Observer Co Ltd. 1996.

[lxx] Schultz, Dr. E. *Samoan Proverbial Expression Alagā'upu Fa'a-Samoa.* 1953. Translated into English by Brother Herman, Polynesian Press Samoa House, 1994 Edition. Aotearoa, New Zealand #402; also Krämer, Dr. Augustin. *The Samoa Islands: An Outline of a Monograph with Particular Consideration of*

German Samoa: Vol 1; trans. Theodore Verhaaren. Auckland. Polynesian Press Samoa House. 1994 (TuiAana Section).

[lxxi] This author, reference: 2013 April Booklet pp.6–8.

[lxxii] Krämer, Dr. Augustin. *The Samoa Islands: An Outline of a Monograph with Particular Consideration of German Samoa: Vol 1*; trans. Theodore Verhaaren. Auckland. Polynesian Press Samoa House. 1994, p.270.

[lxxiii] Krämer, Dr. Augustin. *The Samoa Islands: An Outline of a Monograph with Particular Consideration of German Samoa: Vol 1*; trans. Theodore Verhaaren. Auckland. Polynesian Press Samoa House. 1994, p.252-3.

[lxxiv] Krämer, Dr. Augustin. *The Samoa Islands: An Outline of a Monograph with Particular Consideration of German Samoa: Vol 1*; trans. Theodore Verhaaren. Auckland. Polynesian Press Samoa House. 1994.

[lxxv] This author, 2013 January Workbook pp.82-85.

[lxxvi] Reason, Joyce. *The Bricklayer and the King: Henry Nott of the South Seas*, London, Edinburgh House, 1938.

[lxxvii] Lovett, Richard, *The History of LMS 1797-1895*, London: London Missionary Society 1899; and Horne, C. Sylvester, *The Story of the L.M.S.* London: London Missionary Society, 1904. This material is held at School of Oriental and African Studies (SOAS) Archives, University of London Reference: GB 102 CWM/LMS/02 https://archiveshub.jisc.ac.uk/data/gb102-cwm/cwm/lms/02

[lxxviii] https//koloascenicbyway.org-history "Coming of the Missionaries".

[lxxix] This author. *Navigators Quest for a Kingdom in Polynesia*. 2020. p.32.

[lxxx] Christopher Columbus' letter to Ferdinand and Isabella, 1493. (The Gilder Lehrman Collection, GLC01427).

[lxxxi] Krämer, Dr. Augustin. *The Samoa Islands: An Outline of a Monograph with Particular Consideration of German Samoa: Vol 1*; trans. Theodore Verhaaren. Auckland. Polynesian Press Samoa House. 1994, p.3

[lxxxii] Krämer, Dr. Augustin. *The Samoa Islands: An Outline of a Monograph with Particular Consideration of German Samoa: Vol 1*; trans. Theodore Verhaaren. Auckland. Polynesian Press Samoa House. 1994, p.3

[lxxxiii] Krämer, Dr. Augustin. *The Samoa Islands: An Outline of a Monograph with Particular Consideration of German Samoa: Vol 1*; trans. Theodore Verhaaren. Auckland. Polynesian Press Samoa House. 1994, p.3

[lxxxiv] Fornander, Abraham. *An Account of The Polynesian Race. Its Origin and Migrations and the Ancient History of the Hawaiian People To the Times of Kamehameha I.* Volume I. London: Trűbner & Co., Ludgate Hill, 1878

[lxxxv] Fornander, Abraham. *An Account of The Polynesian Race. Its Origin and Migrations and the Ancient History of the Hawaiian People To the Times of Kamehameha I.* Volume I. London: Trűbner & Co., Ludgate Hill, 1878, pp. 191-201

[lxxxvi] Aiono Fanaafi Le Tagalo, "O le Fa'asinomaga", Lamepa Press, Alafua, Samoa, 1997, pp.184-5.

[lxxxvii] Krämer, Dr. Augustin. *The Samoa Islands: An Outline of a Monograph with Particular Consideration of German Samoa: Vol 1*; trans. Theodore Verhaaren. Auckland. Polynesian Press Samoa House. 1994, p.523.

[lxxxviii] Gilson, R.P. *Samoa 1830-1900 The Politics of a Multicultural Community*, Oxford University Press, 1970.

[lxxxix] *Concise History of the World an Illustrated Timeline*. eds Neil Kagan, Jerry H. Bently, Director Board of Advisers. National Geographic. 2006.

[xc] Gilson, R.P. *Samoa 1830-1900 The Politics of a Multicultural Community*, Oxford University Press, 1970.

[xci] Gilson, R.P. *Samoa 1830-1900 The Politics of a Multicultural Community*, Oxford University Press, 1970.

[xcii] Jensen, H.I. "The geology of Samoa, and the eruptions in Savai'i." Proc. Linnean Soc. New South Wales, 31: 641-672. 1906.

[xciii] "German Samoa 1900-1914" (PDF). p.121. Retrieved 02.09.2022.

[xciv] This author. *Navigators Quest for a Kingdom in Polynesia*. 2020. p.202

[xcv] Pratt G. *Samoan Dictionary: English and Samoan, and Samoan and English, with a Short Grammar of the Samoan Dialect*, London Missionary Soc., 1862, p.207; this author. *Navigators Quest for a Kingdom in Polynesia.* 2020. P.245.

[xcvi] This author. 2013 January Booklet p.10.

[xcvii] Gilson, R.P. *Samoa 1830-1900 The Politics of a Multicultural Community*, Oxford University Press, 1970.

[xcviii] Trood, Thomas *Island Reminiscences,* 1912, republished BiblioBazaar 2009.

[xcix] Gilson, R.P. *Samoa 1830-1900 The Politics of a Multicultural Community*, Oxford University Press, 1970. p.138.

[c] Gilson, R.P. *Samoa 1830-1900 The Politics of a Multicultural Community*, Oxford University Press, 1970. p.246.

[ci] Gilson, R.P. *Samoa 1830-1900 The Politics of a Multicultural Community*, Oxford University Press, 1970. pp.350-351.

[cii] Shaffer, J. Robert. *American Samoa: 100 Years Under The United States Flag.* Island Heritage, Honolulu, Hawaii, 2000.

[ciii] Gilson, R.P. *Samoa 1830-1900 The Politics of a Multicultural Community*, Oxford University Press, 1970. p.382-385.

[civ] Gilson, R.P. *Samoa 1830-1900 The Politics of a Multicultural Community*, Oxford University Press, 1970. p.432.

[cv] Shaffer, J. Robert. *American Samoa: 100 Years Under The United States Flag.* Island Heritage, Honolulu, Hawaii, 2000.

[cvi] Pratt G. *Samoan Dictionary: English and Samoan, and Samoan and English, with a Short Grammar of the Samoan Dialect*, London Missionary Soc., 1862. p.139.

[cvii] Fuimaono Na'oia, *O Le Suaga A Le Va'atele*. (The findings of the big canoe). The Samoa Observer Co Ltd. 1996, pp.138-147.

[cviii] Gilson, R.P. *Samoa 1830-1900 The Politics of a Multicultural Community*, Oxford University Press, 1970. p. 410-411.

[cix] Krämer, Dr. Augustin. *The Samoa Islands: An Outline of a Monograph with Particular Consideration of German Samoa: Vol 1*; trans. Theodore Verhaaren. Auckland. Polynesian Press Samoa House. 1994, and also Gilson, R.P. *Samoa 1830-1900 The Politics of a Multicultural Community*, Oxford University Press, 1970.

[cx]https://www.un.org/depts/los/convention_agreements/convention_historical_perspective.htm, United Nations Office of Legal Affairs

[cxi]https://www.un.org/depts/los/convention_agreements/convention_historical_perspective.htm United Nations Office of Legal Affairs

---

[cxii] Gudmundsson, Eyjolfur; Asche, Frank; & Nielsen, Max. "Revenue Distribution Through The SeaFood Value Chain", *FAO Fisheries Circular* No. 1019

[cxiii] World Bank 2017. *The Sunken Billions Revisited: Progress and Challengesin Global Marine Fisheries. Environmentand Development;. Washington, DC: World Bank. @ World Bank. https://www.openknowledge.worldbank.org/handle/10986/24056 License: CC BY 3.0 IGO*

[cxiv] Arnason, R; Kobayashi, M; & de Fontaubertm, C. *The Sunk Billions Revisited: Progress and Challenges in Global Marine Fisheries*, the World Bank, Washington D.C., 2017

[cxv] Seidel, Henrike; & Lal, Padma N. *IUCN Oceania 74pp: Economic Value of the Pacific Island Countries and Territories. PICT.* https://www.iucn.org, July 2010

[cxvi] Konar, Mansi and Sumaila, U. Rashid. "Illicit Trade in Marine Resources Keeps Billions out of Pacific Economies Every Year" published under the sponsorship of the High Level Panel for a Sustainable Ocean Economy, by (https://www.oceanpanel.org), 12/05/2019

[cxvii] the World Bank report: *The State of the World Fisheries and Aquaculture 2020*, Food and Agriculture Organization of the United Nations: www.fao.org

[cxviii] Heimbuch, Jaymi. "The Ocean Has Issues: 7 Biggest Problems Facing Our Seas, and How to Fix Them." Treehugger 2021: https://www.treehugger.com/the-ocean-has-issues-biggest-problems-facing-our-seas-and-how-to-fix-them-4858760

[cxix] "Coral reefs around the world," interactive page: https://www.theguardian.com/environment/interactive/2009/sep/02/coral-world-interactive.

[cxx] Wilkinson, Clive. "Status of Coral Reefs of the World." Global Coral Reef Monitoring Network and Australian Institute of Marine Science, Townsville. 1. 2004. Executive summary 2008.

[cxxi] Burke, Lauretta; Reytar, Kathleen; Spalding, Mark; Perry, Allison. "Reefs at Risk Revisited," World Resources Institute, February 2011

[cxxii] *Coral Reef condition status report for American Samoa.* NOAA Coral Reef Conservation Program, 2018, with J. Thomas, C. Donovan, A. Fries, and H. Kelsey from the University of Maryland Center for Environmental Science

[cxxiii] Ziegler, M; Quéré, G; Ghiglione, JF; Iwankow, G; Barbe, V; Boissin, E; Wincker, P; Planes, S; Voolstra, CR. "Status of coral reefs of Upolu (Independent State of Samoa) in the South West Pacific and recommendations to promote resilience and recovery of coastal ecosystems." 2018. Marine Pollution Bulletin. 129. 392-398. 10.1016/j.marpolbul.2018.02.044.

[cxxiv] National Geographic: "Great Pacific Garbage Patch." Nationalgeographic.org

[cxxv] Aguilera, Mario. "Scripps Study Finds Plastic In Nine Percent Of 'Garbage Patch' Fishes." https://scripps.ucsd.edu/news/scripps-study-finds-plastic-nine-percent-garbage-patch-fishes

[cxxvi] "Basic Information about Mercury." https://www.epa.gov/mercury/basic-information-about-mercury

[cxxvii] Chen, Tony. "The Ocean is a $100tln Market Opportunity." AgFunder Network Partners. 2021. https://agfundernews.com/the-ocean-is-a-100tln-market-opportunity.html; also Clarke, Rebecca. "The Environmental Impacts of

Deep-Sea Mining." Treehugger. 2021. https://www.treehugger.com/deep-sea-mining-impact-5181155

[cxxviii] National Geographic: https://www.nationalgeographic.com

[cxxix] This author. *Navigators Quest for a Kingdom in Polynesia*, 2020. pp.33-38.

[cxxx] Trivers, Robert L. Biological Laboratories, Harvard University, Cambridge, Mass.,03.15.1970), "The Evolution of Reciprocal Altruism," *The Quarterly Review of Biology, Vol. 46, No. 1* (Mar. 1971), The University of Chicago Press pp. 35-57. Stable URL: http://www.jstor.org/stable/2822435

[cxxxi] Lattorff, H. Michael G., & Moritz, Robin F.A. "Genetic Underpinnings of Division of Labor in the Honeybee (Apis mellifera)." *Trends in Genetics* 29.11(3013):64-48. Web; also Naeger, Nicholas L., et al. "Altruistic Behavior by Egg-Laying Worker Honeybees." *Current Biology* 23(2013): 1574-78 Print; Seeley, Thomas D. "Honeybee Ecology: A Study of Adaptation in Social Life" Princeton, N.J: Princeton UP, 1985. 20-38 Print; Taylor, Ken. "Psychological vs. Biological Altruism." *Philosophy Talk*-Web. 23 November 2015.

[cxxxii] Worm B. et al. "Rebuilding Global Fisheries." Science. 2009, 325:578-585. doi: 10.1126/science. 1173146 PubMed.

[cxxxiii] Galland, Grantley; Rogers, Anthony; & Nickson. *Netting billions: A global valuation of tuna.* The Pew Charitable Trusts, Washington, D.C., 2016.

[cxxxiv] Garland, G; Rogers, Anthony; Nickson, Amanda. *Netting billions: A global valuation of tuna.* the Pew Charitable Trusts, Washington, D.C., 2016.

[cxxxv] *FAO Fisheries and Aquaculture Department, National Aquaculture Sector Overview: Netherlands* https://www.fao.org/fishery/en/countrysector/naso_netherlands

[cxxxvi] https://theoceancleanup.com/

[cxxxvii] Burnett Tylor, Edward Burnett. *Primitive Culture*, 1871. Cambridge University Press, 2010.

[cxxxviii] Frazer, James George. *The Golden Bough.* 1890; and Malinowski, Bronisław. *Argonauts of the Western Pacific: An Account of Native Enterprise and Adventure in the Archipelagoes of Melanesian New Guinea* 1922.

Made in the USA
Las Vegas, NV
02 May 2022